FOUNDATIONS

OF THE

PUBLIC LIBRARY

The approach to history through the study of institutions marks such an advance over the old chronicles of kings that there is danger of overstressing this aspect of national development. Institutions are even more effects than they are causes of social movements. Like coral islands they are formed by the largely unconscious coöperative efforts of myriads of living organisms. Although we may describe and classify such islands as they appear above the surface, we cannot understand them unless we study first the silent forces working in the unseen depths below.—JAMES TRUSLOW ADAMS, *Revolutionary New England* (pp. 8–9).

FOUNDATIONS

OF THE

PUBLIC LIBRARY

*The Origins of
the Public Library Movement
in New England
1629–1855*

By

JESSE H. SHERA

THE SHOE STRING PRESS, INC.
1965

INTRODUCTION

THE history of the modern public library supports Émile
Durkheim's general principle that the origins of any social
agency must be sought in the internal constitution of the social
milieu. Therefore, the title of this volume is not intended to be
rhetorical. We are here concerned with those elements in American life which contributed directly or indirectly to the growth of
the public library as a social agency and the character of the
environment from which it emerged. Though attention is restricted to but one section of the United States, much of what
is said here with reference to New England is equally applicable
elsewhere as economic and social conditions began to approximate those of the northeastern Atlantic seaboard. But New England, because it is the cradle of American librarianship and because its cultural records have been so assiduously preserved,
was the logical, if indeed not inevitable, place to begin.

Throughout the following pages the public library has been
regarded as a social *agency* rather than, as Ballard would have it, a
social *institution*.[1] The distinction is fundamental to complete understanding of the relation between the library and its social
environment. Whereas the social institution is primary and basic,
the social agency is secondary and derived. The family and the
state are institutions; the school, the library, and the museum are
agencies. The one determines the pattern of society, and the
other is determined by that pattern. The agency is the instrument of the institution, and by means of it the institution exercises much of its social control. Thus the distinction is more than
a matter of degree; it involves a flow of power and authority. In
one way or another man determines the social goals that he will
seek and shapes the agencies of his group life to achieve those
ends. The history of the public library is a record of transition
from a narrowly conservational function to a broad program directed toward the advance of popular education. These changes

1. Lloyd V. Ballard, *Social Institutions* (New York: Appleton, 1936), chap. xii,
"The Public Library."

v

in the objectives of the public library were merely reflections of transformations in society itself. Libraries that were only storehouses of accumulated knowledge were not adequate to the needs of a society that was consciously seeking to encourage the participation of the individual in the life of the group. The modern public library in large measure represents the need of democracy for an enlightened electorate, and its history records its adaptation to changing social requirements.

To express adequately my debt to those who have assisted in the formulation and development of my ideas and point of view would demand an intensive autobiography, annotated with the incisive analysis and penetrating insight of the best of psychoanalysts and rivaling in magnitude the prefaces of Bernard Shaw. Personality is a variegated pattern the threads of which, contributed almost unwittingly by one's associates, have been inextricably interwoven by the ceaseless hand of time and so highly colored affectively by emotional residues that it is practically impossible to recognize clearly the basic forms. The danger, therefore, lies in acknowledging the immediate, and hence the more apparent, assistance while neglecting that which is fully as important though remote and obscure.

But even my obvious obligations are many and great. Louis Round Wilson, who was dean of the Graduate Library School of the University of Chicago during the greater part of the period when this study was first being prepared, not only contributed much to its planning and execution but by the generosity of his financial support revealed the depth and sincerity of his desire to participate in whatever success the undertaking might have. At the close of this long task it is pleasant to recall his great assistance in lightening the inevitable burden of drudgery that research involves. Throughout he has been a constant source of encouragement and sympathetic understanding. To me it is a matter of great personal regret that I was unable to complete the manuscript prior to his retirement; but historical research is scarcely immune to the inevitable changes that December 7, 1941, brought into our lives.

To Ralph A. Beals, now director of the New York Public Library but formerly director of the Library of the University of

Chicago and dean of the Graduate Library School, my obligations are especially difficult to express in words. With the hearty co-operation of his immediate successors in the school, Dean Clarence H. Faust and Dean Bernard Berelson, he is most responsible for the publication of this work. He has listened long and patiently to interminable elaborations of my subject, has contributed probably even more than I realize to the development of my thinking about the history of libraries, and during one particular crisis rendered a personal service that was greater than either of us then knew.

To my colleague on the faculty of the Graduate Library School, Miss Margaret Egan, I am deeply indebted for a particularly thorough reading of the revised manuscript, much constructive criticism, and many improvements in the text. To this task, which entailed a real sacrifice in time and effort, she brought an objectivity and freshness of viewpoint that the author himself could not have achieved.

Professor William T. Hutchinson of the Department of History of the University of Chicago read an earlier version of the manuscript and made many helpful suggestions. Professors Carleton B. Joeckel, Pierce Butler, and Leon Carnovsky, all of the faculty of the Graduate Library School, supervised the preparation of the study in its original form.

To the numbers of New England librarians who gave unsparingly of their time and resources I can here make only general acknowledgment. Throughout the six states I was greeted with the same eager co-operation. The limitations of space permit me to single out only a few for special recognition, but this does not imply that many others were not also helpful. To Lawrence C. Wroth of the John Carter Brown Library and to Clarence S. Brigham of the American Antiquarian Society my debt is especially great. Also I should mention Milton Lord and his able staff who made so freely available to me the records of the Boston Public Library; Elinor Gregory Metcalf of the Boston Athenaeum; Anne S. Pratt of the Yale University Library; Allyn B. Forbes of the Massachusetts Historical Society; Dennis A. Dooley, state librarian of Massachusetts; Keyes D. Metcalf, director of the Harvard University Libraries; Miss Harriet S.

Tapley, librarian of the Essex Institute of Salem; Miss E. Frances Abbott, librarian of the Wayland, Massachusetts, Public Library; Mrs. Howard Field of Durham, Connecticut; Miss Ethel Scofield, librarian of the New Haven Colony Historical Society; Miss Katharine A. Noyes of Pomfret, Connecticut; Miss Charlotte B. Norton, librarian of the Scoville Memorial Library, Salisbury, Connecticut; Miss Frances Hubbert, librarian, Redwood Library and Athenaeum, Newport, Rhode Island; Herbert C. Brigham, librarian, Newport Historical Society, Newport, Rhode Island; Miss Grace F. Leonard, librarian, Providence Athenaeum; Clarence E. Sherman, librarian, Providence Public Library; Henry B. Van Hoesen, librarian, Brown University Library; Miss Marie J. Tibbits, legislative reference librarian, Maine State Library; Miss Winifred Coombs, librarian, Witherle Memorial Library, Castine, Maine; Miss Mae Gillman, librarian, Maine Historical Society; Miss Marion F. Holt, librarian of the Public Library, Concord, New Hampshire; Miss Thelma Brackett, state librarian, Concord, New Hampshire; the reference staff of the New Hampshire Historical Society; Miss Martha E. Cutler, librarian, Peterborough Town Library, Peterborough, New Hampshire; Miss Hannah G. Fernald, librarian of the Public Library, Portsmouth, New Hampshire; Miss Agnes K. Lawson, librarian, Vermont State Historical Society; Mrs. Mary R. Allen, librarian, Maclure Library, Pittsford, Vermont; and many others who are, doubtless, as justly entitled to individual recognition.

To Luther H. Evans, now Librarian of Congress, I am grateful for the suspension of certain accepted library regulations so that I might more easily continue the investigation during my period of membership on the library staff. The library of the New York Historical Society made freely available to me the important manuscript materials assembled by Austin Baxter Keep, and Miss Eileen Thornton, librarian of Vassar College, placed the resources of her library at my complete disposal. In the work of Mary Frances Hedges, who in 1939–40 was my assistant at the University of Chicago, I recognize a long and tedious job competently done.

Philip D. Jordan of the Department of History of the University of Minnesota and Donald M. Dozer, formerly of the Department of History of the University of Maryland and now with the Department of State, have read the manuscript and offered many beneficial suggestions. Wilmarth S. Lewis of Washington, D.C., and Farmington, Connecticut, was of material aid in helping me to obtain certain records which I needed, and during the entire period that we worked together in the Office of Strategic Services he maintained a lively interest in the progress of the manuscript.

Finally, my wife, Helen B. Shera, not only aided with the investigation itself, especially with the assembly of the data and the revision of the final text, but, despite a ceaseless round of domestic responsibilities, gave unsparingly of her energy to the advancement of the work. The devotion of the pioneer women of New England was no greater.

JESSE H. SHERA

GRADUATE LIBRARY SCHOOL
UNIVERSITY OF CHICAGO
September 15, 1948

TABLE OF CONTENTS

xi

LIST OF ILLUSTRATIONS

LIST OF TABLES

CHAPTER I

NEW ENGLAND BACKGROUNDS

The Land

PLYMOUTH ROCK was no stepping-stone to a land of milk and honey. It was a hard land geologically, climatologically, agriculturally. Eroded by wind and rain, its ancient mountains ground by the continental ice sheets, its coastal lowlands frequently inundated by an ever encroaching sea, even its most fertile valleys yielding but stubbornly to the plow—it was a country that demanded much in toil and gave but sparingly in return. When the fitful winds drove the "Mayflower" from her course, the Pilgrims found no soft flat plain beside the sea. Along the rugged and deeply indented coast, waves pounded against the tops and sides of ancient hills.

Physiographically New England's outstanding characteristic is the effect of glaciation. As the continental ice sheets advanced and retreated, rock masses were wrenched from the mountains and strewn over the lowlands. Regions were thus made so rocky as to be impossible of cultivation. Elsewhere, soil was scoured from hillcrests, exposing the underlying granite. The debris carried by the ice was dropped in moraines, damming streams and impounding the waters in innumerable lakes and ponds. Bare rock ledges were left outcropping in many places. Rivers were diverted from original channels. Mountain freshets poured into the valleys, carrying away the finer earth and leaving only a residue of coarse sand. In such areas the percolation of rain was so rapid that even grass and trees found insufficient moisture to sustain life. However, on the floors of the numerous intervales, which range in size from small narrow valleys among the hills and along the stream beds to broader tracts of level land, the soil was found to be fine and light, easily workable, and of relatively high fertility.

Over most of the land lay a mantle of heavy forest. Its dense pines, spruces, and hemlocks, its deciduous oaks, maples, and hickories, spread up over the rugged highlands and down to meet the salt spray of the sea. The somber interior sheltered the wolf and the Indian, while thick intertwining underbrush closed about the explorer so that he might easily lose his way. Here was no invitation to an abundant husbandry. Even after the adventurer had driven the native farther into the interior and established the claims of a conqueror, years of labor were required to fell trees, grub out the bushes, pry up the stumps, and roll away the boulders to make a farm. As late as the beginning of the present century more than two-thirds of the land area of Maine was still forest-covered.

Over all whipped the sharp east wind, driving before it frequent storms and bearing snow that blanketed the earth for months at a time. In the northern upland severe winters shortened the growing season. Biting cold intensified the hardships of a life that at best was never easy. Small wonder that the Pilgrims found their first winters in the New World almost insufferable.

To the pioneer, New England was a natural geographic unit, and the physical barriers by which it was surrounded sharply circumscribed and molded the life that flourished there. To the west the Berkshire hills, to the west and north the mountain ranges of Vermont and New Hampshire, and to the north the densely wooded peaks of Maine—all were obstructions through which no easy river route facilitated travel. Eastward lay the Atlantic Ocean, and southward passage was hampered by the estuary of the Hudson. Within this area life was strikingly homogeneous. Its geographic unity rendered relatively negligible the artificial boundaries of the six states and allowed the generally similar economic, political, and religious institutions to follow a common historical development.

Population

The peopling of New England may be said to have begun in 1628 when the Council for New England, then suffering serious financial reverses, ceded its most desirable lands to the Massachusetts Bay Company. In the years immediately following began the period of the "great migration." The company experienced no difficulty in obtaining people in large numbers willing to venture to the New World, and a "rage of emigration" swept through the midland counties of England. Many sold their lands to take up residence abroad. By no means all were motivated by the desire for religious freedom; political unrest in the mother-country intensified the movement, and debtors were quite willing to escape beyond the sea. The volume of embarkations was so great as to cause concern among English authorities and to bring joy to the promoters on this side of the Atlantic. Under such conditions the restriction of immigration soon became advisable. Massachusetts officials began to exercise the utmost care that only those best fitted for colonization be permitted to stay. Similar restrictive measures were taken by the towns of Providence and Portsmouth in Rhode Island, and the New Haven Colony appointed a committee to sit in judgment upon the desirability of the new arrivals.

By 1640 this influx had ceased—almost as suddenly as it had begun. Hope of improved conditions in England, combined with increased restriction in America, virtually stopped the flow of migrants to New England's shores. Those in power did little to change the situation. The coastal line of Massachusetts was by that time entirely appropriated so that the future trend was necessarily directed toward the south, with the wilderness of the hinterland accessible only to the most experienced settlers.

In but one decade of intensive settlement, that of the 1630's, the nationality pattern of New England's population[1] was determined for generations to come. From this movement largely de-

1. Percentage distribution of the white population of each New England state as indicated by the names of heads of families for 1790 (adapted from William S. Rossiter, *A Century of Population Growth from the First Census of the United States to the Twelfth, 1790–1900*, U.S. Bureau of the Census [Washington: Government Printing Office, 1909], p. 116).

	Conn.	R.I.	Vt.	Mass.	N.H.	Me.
English.........	96.2	96.0	95.4	95.0	94.1	93.1
Scottish........	2.8	3.1	3.0	3.6	4.7	4.3
Irish...........	0.7	0.7	0.7	1.0	1.0	1.4
Dutch..........	0.1	....	0.5	0.1	0.1	0.3
French.........	0.2	0.1	0.2	0.2	0.1	0.1
German........	....	0.1	....	....	....	0.5
Other..........	....	....	0.2	0.1	....	0.3

rived the Colonial population of New England. The extent to which the English dominated the national stock of New England is apparent from the results of Rossiter's study of nationality as indicated by the names of heads of families enumerated at the first (1790) census. In no state did the English represent less than 93 per cent of the white population, and the British Isles as a whole contributed no less than 98 per cent. The English characterization of the Yankee as "our American cousin" was literally true. This common origin did not give rise to cultural isolation and stagnation as has been the case in many homogeneous ethnic populations. As Samuel Eliot Morison has said:

The seventeenth century stock completely absorbed its eighteenth century accretions, both English and non-English. To outsiders, as late as 1824, the population of seaboard Massachusetts seemed, and was, as racially homogeneous as that of Brittany. But the race was not Anglo-Saxon, or Irish. It was Yankee, a new Nordic Amalgam on an English Puritan base; already in 1750 as different in its character and its dialect from the English as the Australians are to-day. A tough but nervous, tenacious but restless race; materially ambitious, yet prone to introspection, and subject to waves of religious emotion. Conservative in its ideas of property and religion, yet (in the eighteenth century) radical in business and government. A people with few social graces, yet capable of deep friendships and abiding loyalties; law-abiding yet individualistic, and impatient of restraint by government or regulation in business; ever attempting to repress certain traits of human nature, but finding an outlet in broad, crude, humor and deep-sea voyages. A race whose typical member is eternally torn between a passion for righteousness and a desire to get on in the world. Religion and climate, soil and sea, here brewed of mixed stock a new people.[2]

The policies of exclusion based on such fundamental grounds as nationality and religion had their effect, and it is not surprising to discover an English merchant who, in 1689, found the New Englanders "a very home-like people, exceeding wedded to their own way."[3] This intense homogeneity is one of the most characteristic attributes of the New England population, for not until the beginning of the second quarter of the nineteenth century did a strong tide of immigration again turn toward New England's shores. During these two centuries when immigration was reduced to small accretions, quantitatively insufficient to affect the

2. Samuel Eliot Morison, *Maritime History of Massachusetts* (Boston: Houghton Mifflin, 1941), p. 22.

3. Quoted by Marcus Lee Hanson, *The Atlantic Migration* (Cambridge: Harvard University Press, 1940), pp. 31–32.

developing pattern of New England culture, the Yankee character was formed.

Whereas the diffusion of populations over unlimited space tends to weaken the hold on the land and retard the growth of a compact social pattern, this concentration of the English in such a limited area, restricted by the sea and the mountains, encouraged the growth of thickly settled, unified colonies within which communication was relatively easy and the emergence of community institutions was facilitated. It is, therefore, difficult to overemphasize the influence of a physically unified terrain, supported by the homogeneity of its population, in making of New England one of the most *sectional* of regions. It was no accident that the typical Yankee developed a strong self-conscious attachment for local forms and fought vigorously against threatened encroachment from without. Even today, despite the many social influences contributing to the breakdown of sectional differentiation throughout the country, the conservative New England type is still well defined.

A second characteristic of the New England population pattern is the steady trend toward urbanization. Early tendencies to cluster in small communities on the coastal lowlands and at strategic points along inland rivers increased, even as the population was spreading over the interior in search of adequate farm land. At the first census of 1790 New England was beginning to reveal the concentration of its population in the southern area, which is so apparent from Table 1 as to require no elaboration. The kinetic force of such a surge toward city life carried impor-

TABLE 1*

PERCENTAGE URBAN POPULATION, SIX NEW ENGLAND STATES, 1790–1860

State	1790	1800	1810	1820	1830	1840	1850	1860
R.I............	19.0	20.8	23.4	23.0	31.2	43.8	55.6	63.3
Mass..........	13.5	15.4	21.3	22.8	31.1	37.9	50.7	63.3
Conn..........	3.0	5.1	6.1	7.6	9.4	12.6	16.0	26.5
N.H...........	3.3	2.9	3.2	3.0	5.0	10.0	17.1	22.1
Me............	......	2.4	3.1	2.9	3.2	7.8	13.5	16.6
Vt............	......	......	......	......	......	......	1.9	2.0
New England...	7.5	8.2	10.1	10.5	14.0	19.4	28.8	36.6

* Data from U.S. Bureau of the Census, *Urban Population in the United States from the First Census (1790) to the Fifteenth Census (1930)* (Washington: Bureau of the Census, 1939), p. 7.

tant and far-reaching implications for the lives of the individuals concerned. It is at once evident that new forms of economic and social endeavor, new psychological adjustments, and new institutional patterns all resulted from the change.

A third demographic characteristic of New England is the importance of the area as a center of dispersion. Historical data on this subject are unfortunately scarce, since it was not until 1850 that the census began to record the birth states of the resident population. In every census for which this information is available there have been more people born in New England and living beyond the region than there were people born outside New England and living within that region. Doubtless this movement had begun quite some time before the middle of the nineteenth century, as is evident from the extent to which pioneer churches and schools on the western frontier were led by native New Englanders. But by 1850, as Irene Taeuber has written,

less than one-fourth of the non-resident natives of Massachusetts and Rhode Island were on the frontier, and even this proportion included survivors of the migrants of preceding decades in which migration to the frontier was probably relatively heavier. There were more non-resident natives in New York state in 1850 than in the eighteen frontier states taken together, and more in New York City alone than in any one of the fifteen frontier states. Industrial and urban occupations in their own and adjoining states appear to have been more desirable to the migrants from New England, than agricultural colonization on the frontier.[4]

The importance of New England as a center of population dispersion is significant not alone for the extent to which this was a medium of cultural dissemination. It bore a real relation to the economic ability of the region, for much of the capital that flowed into the area, especially that for philanthropic enterprise such as the establishment of libraries and museums, was obtained elsewhere by native sons who had gone to seek fame and fortune and, having found it, remembered to send at least part of their accumulated wealth back home.

Finally, one should mention the decline in human fertility that accompanied the trend toward urbanization and industrializa-

4. Irene Barnes Taeuber, "Some Demographic Aspects of the Second Colonization" (unpublished paper read before Section K of the American Association for the Advancement of Science, Durham, N.H., June 24, 1941).

tion that came to New England at the beginning of the nineteenth century. P. K. Whelpton has found that in 1800 there were fewer children under five years of age per thousand women aged sixteen to forty-four in industrial than in agricultural states.[5] Likewise Jaffe's analysis of census data for the years 1800, 1820, and 1830 reveals a higher birth rate in rural areas and an inverse relationship between size of city and human fertility.[6] The significance of this trend in relation to the cultural development of New England lies in the extent to which it portrays the steady maturing of the New England population from a primitive agrarian way of life, in which birth rates were high and the population "swarming," to a sophisticated urbanism characterized by low birth rates and a recession in rate of population growth. This decline in the size of the average family meant a resultant decrease in domestic responsibility and more leisure for cultural expression.

Agriculture

An early writing on Virginia, dated from London in 1649, says of the New England Colonies: "Except for fishing there is not much in that land, which in respect to frost and snow is as Scotland compared with England, and so barren withal that, except a herring be put into the hole that you set the corn or maize in, it will not come up."[7] But, for all the discouragements to farming, the early settlers were able to establish an agricultural economy. The New Englander took to farming naturally as a result of his English heritage. At the time of the great migration the mother-country was herself dominantly rural. Of the Pilgrims, William Bradford wrote that they "were not acquainted with trade nor traffique . . . but had only been used to a plaine countrie life & yᵉ inocente trade of husbandrey."[8] Hunting, fishing, and farming soon became the mainstays of New England

5. P. K. Whelpton, "Industrial Development and Population Growth," *Social Forces*, VI (1928), 458–67, 629–38.

6. A. J. Jaffe, "Differential Fertility in the White Population of Early America," *Journal of Heredity*, XXXI (September, 1940), 407–11.

7. Quoted in Albert Perry Brigham, *Geographic Influences in American History* (New York: Ginn, 1925), pp. 46–47.

8. William Bradford, *History of Plymouth Plantation* (Boston: Little, Brown, 1856), p. 11.

life. So much has been written of the growth of commerce and industry in the New England states that it is easy to forget that even the southern sections were dominantly rural until well into the nineteenth century. Cartoonists early began to personify American agriculture as a Yankee farmer, gaunt and horny-handed from unprofitable labor on his stony little farm.

During the first two centuries of New England life the rural economy of the region was centered about the family as a self-sufficient economic unit. The goal of production was consumption by the producer and his family; exchange in the form of barter was not uncommon, and such surplus as did accumulate was sold in the near-by towns. Except for those who were able to combine farming with some other occupation, such as smithing, preaching, or fishing, the modest cash return from the marketing of this limited excess provided the family with its sole purchasing power. Judged by any standard, the farms were small. Some larger holdings developed in the Narragansett country, but the more typical comprised only a few acres of plowland, meadow, and pasture, even though a considerable area of unbroken forest might be included. Within a society in which land tenure was relatively secure, tenancy negligible, and holdings small, democracy could operate effectively, while free and untrammeled movement within the social pattern was possible. That such freedom played a part in the encouragement of agricultural societies and other voluntary associations of individuals in group undertakings is readily apparent.

Between 1790 and 1830 New England agriculture enjoyed its greatest prosperity. In the valleys of the Green and White mountains a virgin soil was yielding abundant crops, the farmers were discovering a ready and expanding market for their products in eastern urban Massachusetts, and new facilities for transportation were giving promise of future wealth. During these years a young and vigorous population pushed northward into the hill country of Maine, New Hampshire, and Vermont. Lured by cheap land and the prospect of greater opportunities, these farmers from southern New England, especially Connecticut, carried with them their cultural heritage and social institutions much as the westward march of the frontiersmen carried the culture of the

Atlantic seaboard into the hinterland beyond the Alleghenies.

A second period of New England's agricultural development began in the 1820's and ended with the Civil War. During these forty years rural prosperity reached its zenith and began to decline. The early self-sufficiency of the New England farm home and its ability to survive despite the mediocrity of the soil was largely due to the indefatigable labor of the "womenfolk," who by unremitting toil produced for the family many of the commodities that later were purchased. The spread of factories throughout southern New England destroyed the self-sufficiency of the farms to the north. In the face of these changes a degree of agricultural specialization was necessary to produce the needed cash for the purchase of factory-made goods. An agriculture that had not been too rewarding under a self-sufficient economy could scarcely hope to survive commercialization. Wasteful practices in soil management had rendered the land decreasingly productive.[9] The railroad, which had seemed to promise so much for the expansion of the agricultural market, broke down the isolation of the New England region and flooded the urban centers with the cheaper farm staples of the expanding west. In addition, agriculture lacked the business enterprise and experience in marketing that commercial farming required. Self-sufficient husbandry had not provided the capital essential to commercialization. Nor was there an adequate farm leadership to crystallize into constructive action the sporadic efforts of a conservative individualism toward the solution of these new agricultural problems.

One of the most disastrous of all the influences that worked for the decadence of New England agriculture was the migration of farm youth into the agrarian west and the industrial cities to the south. Beyond a doubt this loss of youthful vigor accelerated the degeneration of New England farm life. The opening of the Erie Canal, the introduction of steam navigation on the Great Lakes, and, later, the building of the railroads not only introduced ruinous competition in agricultural products, it also facilitated

9. Percy W. Bidwell, "Rural Economy in New England at the Beginning of the Nineteenth Century," *Connecticut Academy of Arts and Sciences, Transactions,* XX (April, 1916), 241-399.

migration, and an expanding labor market beyond the New England hills supplied the incentive. This depopulation of the hill country through the dispersion of native youths, both men and women, to the industrial centers and the west, affected profoundly the future of New England and the social institutions that developed there.

Commerce

Denied a productive agriculture, Colonial capital was forced to seek other outlets for investment; indeed, commercial exploitation had been the primary concern of the builders of the Bay Colony. The Massachusetts Bay Company, which in 1628 took over the best lands of the Council for New England, never entertained any doubt as to what it wanted to do. Though Puritan divines might admonish their flocks to adhere strictly to the Christian life, "that otherwise they would contradict the main end of planting this wilderness," there were clear-sighted parishioners who knew well enough their real business—"Sir, you are mistaken . . . our *main end* was to *catch fish.*"[10] Likewise it was an accurate sense of economic values that prompted Captain John Smith to conclude his discourse on "The Present Estate of New Plimoth" with the prediction that the cod fisheries of New England would yield a rich harvest. "Let not the meannesse of the word Fish distaste you," he advised, "for it will afford as good gold as the mines of Guiana and Potassie with less hazard and charge, and more certaintie and facility."[11]

The great migration of the fourth decade of the seventeenth century could not have been possible without a steady and ample flow of capital from across the Atlantic, and in such enterprise the crown itself was vitally concerned. The founding of the colonies in America was predicated on hopes and plans envisaging the rise of economic satellites that would supply England with commodities she could not produce and, at the same time, open a market for English manufactures and stimulate English shipping.

It was natural that New England enterprise should first turn

10. Cotton Mather, *Magnalia Christi Americana* (Hartford: Silas Andrews, 1855), I, 66. Italics Mather's.

11. John Smith, "The Present Estate of New Plimoth," in his *Travels and Works*, ed. Edward Arber (Edinburgh: Grant, 1910), II, 784.

toward the sea. Fish were abundant, and the forests offered an inexhaustible supply of timber for the building of fishing vessels. The sunken coast, replete with bays, and the many rivers with wide estuaries were a ready invitation to the catching of fish and the sheltering of ships. Even the long, hard winters offered an abundant supply of ice for the preservation of the catch, and the cool summers permitted the drying of the fish for shipment before they spoiled.

Within the interior, the pine forest of Maine and New Hampshire provided the raw material for masts in quantity and size sufficient to command a ready market in timber-impoverished Old England. The first such shipment crossed the Atlantic in 1634, and for two centuries thereafter masts and other shipbuilding materials were major commodities in overseas trade. As the need for shipping vessels grew, the shipbuilding industry itself expanded until it became of prime importance. Some ships were sold to English merchants, but the greater number remained in the hands of New Englanders to meet the demands of an expanding commerce. So steadily had this expansion taken place that by 1660 Samuel Maverick reported that "I am confident there hath not in any place out of so small a number of people been raised so many able Seamen and Commanders."[12]

The decades of peace that followed the Treaty of Utrecht, in 1713, greatly accelerated the tempo of this rising maritime economy, brought about a broadening of all lines of marine activity, and generally stimulated commercial enterprise. This growth in trade between New England and the outside world facilitated the interchange of ideas and the borrowing of institutional forms. The cultural and intellectual bonds that had united Old and New England had always been strong, but this expanding transatlantic commerce brought a flood of books, pamphlets, and other mediums of intellectual communication that nourished an incipient New England culture and made it more than ever a beneficiary of its European heritage. As the succeeding chapters will attempt to show, the library as an institutional form was conspicuous among these cultural borrowings.

12. Samuel Maverick, *A Briefe Description of New England and the Severall Townes Therein Together with the Present Government Therein* (Boston: No pub., 1885), p. 27.

Within the country itself, constantly improving mediums of transportation and strengthening avenues of domestic commerce were playing an important part in the encouragement of cultural ferment. Kirkland attributes the "flowering" of New England directly to the coming of the railroad; and though he does not develop his thesis in detail, there can be no doubt that such improvements in communication promoted a cross-fertilization of local cultures.[13]

Manufacturing

Many factors contributed to the growth of manufacturing in the New England area. As previously indicated, of basic importance was the influence of topography which aided, positively, by providing an abundance of natural water-power and accessible harbors and, negatively, by denying the possibility of extensive agriculture. To these conditioning forces, arising from the physical environment, must be added certain immediate causes that emerged from the expanding economic pattern of the region. The rise of commerce and the profits derived therefrom resulted in the accumulation of surplus capital that sought investment. The last years of the seventeenth century and the early decades of the eighteenth were marked by a steady growth of accumulated wealth among Colonial capitalists. To this was added a steady flow of investment money from England and the Continent, and joint financing between the colonials and English capitalists was quite common.

Manufacturing was further encouraged by the development of markets for the goods produced. The domestic market emerged partially, but not exclusively, from the homespun industries that, except in very early times, produced a surplus above the actual needs of the family. As these early cottage industries outgrew the barter stage, they soon were absorbed into a true domestic trade that tended to become specialized and localized at points advantageous to production. Throughout the Colonial period the volume of the overseas market remained relatively stable, and, though it did increase during the seventeenth and eighteenth

13. Edward C. Kirkland, "Economic Ferment," in Caroline F. Ware (ed.), *The Cultural Approach to History* (New York: Columbia University Press, 1940), pp. 252–54.

centuries, it did not keep pace with increasing production or expand so rapidly as the domestic market.

The position of New England was particularly well adapted to the rise of industrial activity. Situated close to the urban centers of the colonies, and possessing excellent harbors, the region supplied a strategic site for the location of factories. Thus encouraged, in the space of less than two generations, manufacturing changed from household industry to the factory system—a transition which in England and Europe had been spread over centuries. Throughout this process there was constantly progressive differentiation. From the simple rural communities which comprehended the bulk of New England life at the beginning of the nineteenth century there unfolded a varied urban and industrial pattern. A primitive manufacturing that had begun in the farm home emerged as a diversified industry demanding a high degree of occupational specialization.

Because of the relative remoteness from the sources of raw materials and coal, "heavy" industry, with its large numbers of unskilled laborers, was necessarily precluded. To be profitable, the product of New England industry had to be one in which skilled labor played a major part, so that the bulk of the raw material used and the amount of fuel consumed would not be great in proportion to the value of the finished article. Shoes, textiles, silverware, watches, and other commodities, the fabrication of which demanded a relatively high proportion of trained workers, became the staples of New England manufacturing, and inevitably the development of skilled and semiskilled labor played its part in conditioning the cultural level of the region.

The advent of westward expansion, the opening of lands, and the tapping of resources beyond the Allegheny Mountains furnished competition to the inducements that New England offered to the growth of manufactures. But New England possessed the marked advantage of an early start. Industry once established may, with relative ease, be enlarged, but removal to a new location, even though it be more efficient, may be so expensive as to deny justification. Industry had come to southern New England seeking the power of its streams, the markets of its towns, the raw materials of its land and forests, its facilities for transportation;

and there, for better or worse, the industries remained. With this industrialization came a factory system that left its inevitable impression upon the culture of the area, a culture that could produce the journalistic yearnings of the mill girls of Lowell, the craving of young mechanics and apprentices for reading that would improve their occupational prospects, and the convictions of a capitalistic class which believed that it was the responsibility of every man of wealth to make a substantial contribution toward the preservation of the intellectual heritage of his community.

Conclusion

A formidable ring of natural barriers that sharply circumscribed the region and kept the early settlers within a compact area, a population that was nationally homogeneous but not isolated from cultural influences from without, a soil that discouraged agriculture, a coastline that stimulated a seaborne trade, natural resources that favored industrialization, an economy that progressed steadily from rural to commercial to industrial, a corresponding ecological succession in cultural pattern that began as primitive agrarianism and attained full maturity in its urban development, and, finally, the advantage of an early start—all these were necessary antecedents to the public library movement in New England. Benjamin Franklin recognized the importance of this sequence when he proposed the formation of the American Philosophical Society:

The first drudgery of settling new colonies, which confines the attention of people to mere necessities, is now pretty well over; and there are many in every province in circumstances that set them at ease, and afford leisure to cultivate the finer arts and improve the common stock of knowledge.[14]

Over a century later Henry Giles expressed, somewhat more rhetorically, the same opinion:

I see no more the groundling hut. The wilderness has sprung into bloom. A comely dwelling is embosomed amidst offices and orchards. A domain is conquered and possessed. Crops and cattle, rich fields and full barns, evince the patient loyalty of fortitude and toil. . . . The barren place is made a garden. Children sport where bison fed; herds of oxen fatten where deer had roamed;

14. Benjamin Franklin, "A Proposal for Promoting Useful Knowledge among the British Plantations in America. Philadelphia, May 14, 1743," in his *Representative Selections*, ed. Frank L. Mott and Chester E. Jorgenson (New York: American Book Co., 1936), p. 181.

and the house-dog bays where wolves howled. The man, come whence he may, who contributes to this work his share of thought and muscle, does much to make society his debtor. The fine action of genius is very pleasant to contemplate, but the hard effort of labor must come first. The pioneer and the settler must be in advance of the artist and the author; the sounds of music must come after the echoes of the axe; the painter must be in the wake of the hunter; the plowman must be before the poet; and the hut must be the herald of the temple.[15]

Probably none of the factors enumerated in the present chapter was directly responsible for the emergence of New England's public library movement. In and of themselves they did not guarantee a flourishing library development any more than the presence of a solid foundation assures the architectural success of the superstructure that is erected thereon. Furthermore, some of these elements may have been absent from areas evincing a comparable library development. But it is known that libraries are distinctly an urban phenomenon, that they flourish only when the economic ability of the region is sufficiently great to permit adequate support, and that they are the product of a mature culture. It follows, then, that any serious investigation of the library as a cultural phenomenon must be prefaced with at least a brief description of those elements which are most prominent in the general social pattern. It is impossible to measure the relative importance of each of these factors; all of them combined gave to New England its characteristic temper, and that temper inspired a genuine interest in library promotion. An awareness of what these influences were and what they meant in terms of their contribution to the cultural pattern of the region is essential to an understanding of library history in the six New England states.

15. Henry Giles, "Irish Emigration," in his *Lectures and Essays on Irish and Other Subjects* (New York: Sadlier, 1869), p. 156.

CHAPTER II

COLONIAL BEGINNINGS

The Salem Library of the Massachusetts Bay Company

IN MAY, 1629, a party of Puritans set off from the Isle of Wight, bound for John Endicott's settlement at Salem. Their ships, in addition to being "full of godly passengers," carried cattle, supplies, and a collection of books.[1] Of this last, eight titles had been on April 13 "freely bestowed upon this Company" by Mr. William Backhouse, "for wch thankes was given by the Governor and those present to the said Mr Backhouse in the Companies behalfe."[2] This gift was augmented by a collection of fifty-four doctrinal books and pamphlets and "2 dussen & ten Catechismes." All had been selected by the Rev. Samuel Skelton, one of the four ministers making the voyage and afterward pastor of the Salem church. For these he presented to the Massachusetts Bay Company a "Note of bookes" to the amount of £7/-/10.[3] What became of these volumes after the "Bonaventure," the "Lion's Whelp," and their companion ships were securely anchored on the New England coast is not known.[4] Littlefield's

1. Thomas Prince, *The Chronological History of New England* (Boston: Cummings & Hilliard, 1826), p. 259. See also J. T. Adams, *Founding of New England* (Boston: Little, Brown, 1927), pp. 124–28.

2. *Massachusetts Colony Records*, 2d ed., I, 37*f*, 37*g*, 37*h*. J. H. Tuttle, "The Libraries of the Mathers," *American Antiquarian Society, Proceedings*, new ser., XX (April, 1910), 271–72.

3. The titles contained in both the Backhouse gift and the Skelton purchase are given in the Massachusetts Colony Records, *op. cit.*, and in Tuttle, *op. cit.*

4. This was not the first library of a semipublic nature to be projected in British North America. Thomas Burgrave, onetime minister in Virginia, bequeathed to the proposed college at Henrico, Va., a library valued at one hundred marks. In 1620 the "college" received an anonymous gift from England of St. Augustine's *De civitate Dei*, "Master Perkins his works, and an exact map of America." A year later there came from the same unknown source "a small Bible with a cover richly

conjecture that the books were first placed in the Endicott house, later removed to Charlestown, and finally deposited in the Town House in Boston, where they were consumed in the fire of 1711, is no more than surmise.[5] Nor is there any reason for thinking that the Rev. Edmund Browne referred to this Massachusetts Bay Library when he wrote to Sir Simonds d'Ewes: "Wee have a Cambridge heere, a College erecting, youth lectured, a library, and I suppose there will be a presse this winter."[6] Since Harvard College was clearly the main subject of his remarks, one may logically assume that he was speaking of the college library. The contents of the Bay Library, especially the "2 dussen & ten Catechismes," indicates that the books were intended largely for use in the church. The conversion of the Indians was, at this stage of the enterprise, officially declared to be the main end of the plantation.[7] Doubtless, the books, though they may have been kept together for a time, were eventually scattered and lost.

wrought, a great church Bible, *The Booke of Common Prayer*, and other Bookes." The two gifts were valued at £10/–.

"November 15, 1620.—After the Acts of the former Courte were read a stranger stept in presentinge a Mapp of Sr Walter Rawlighes contayninge a Description of Guiana, and with the same fower great books as the Guifte of one unto the Company that Desyred his name might not be made knowne, whereof one booke was a treatise of St. Augustine of the Citty of God translated into English, the other three greate Volumes wer the werks of Mr. Perkins' newlie corrected and amended, wᶜʰ books the Donor desyred they might be sent to the Colledge in Virginia there to remayne in saftie to the use of the collegiates thereafter, and not suffered at any time to be sent abroade or used in the meane while. For wᶜʰ so worthy a guifte my Lord of Southampton desyred the p'tie that presented them to returne deserued thanks from himself and the rest of the Company to him that had so kindly bestowed them" (from MS records of the Virginia Company in the Library of Congress). The plan for the establishment of a college at Henrico was abandoned after the Indian massacre of March 22, 1622, when three hundred and forty-seven Virginia settlers were killed in one day, but Steiner brands as "a moral certainty" the belief that this was "the first public library in the British colonies" (Bernard C. Steiner, "Rev. Thomas Bray and His American Libraries," *American Historical Review*, II [1896], 60). See also Ainsworth Rand Spofford, "The Public Libraries of the United States," *Journal of Social Science*, II (1870), 92–114, esp. pp. 92–93.

5. George E. Littlefield, *Early Massachusetts Press, 1638–1711* (Boston: Club of Odd Volumes, 1907), I, 103–4.

6. Letter from Edmund Browne to Sir Simonds d'Ewes, Stowlancroft Hall, Suffolk, dated Boston, September 7, 1639 (see *Colonial Society of Massachusetts, Publications*, VII [1900–1902], 80).

7. See Charter of the Massachusetts Bay Company, *Massachusetts Colony Records*, I, 17.

September 14, 1638, less than ten years after Skelton and his companions brought their books to Salem, John Harvard died at Charlestown. By the terms of his will, dictated in the last hours of life, he left half of his property and all of his library of four hundred volumes to that "first flower of their wilderness," even then struggling bravely to rise above the cowyards of Cambridge. In gratitude the General Court on March 13, 1639, "ordered, that the college agreed upon formerly to bee built . . . shall bee called Harvard." Within the college "edifice," "very faire and comely," was placed "a large Library with some Bookes to it, the gifts of diverse of our friends."[8]

For all the antiquarian interest that attaches to the surviving fragments of information concerning these early libraries, neither had any organic relationship to the genesis of a public library movement. The Harvard library was not infrequently referred to as a public institution, and even President Dunster lamented, in 1645, that "the public library in the College is yet defective in all manner of books."[9] But the existence of the library was entirely contingent upon the establishment of the college, and while its modest resources may have been accessible to the divines and scholars of the region, there was no thought of its being available to the community at large.

The concept of community ownership was to a slight degree operative in the circumstances surrounding the formation of the Massachusetts Bay Library. Certainly it was looked upon as the property of the company, and it was to the officers of the corporation that Skelton presented the bill for his book purchases. Doubtless the books were, for a time at least, kept where they would be accessible to any who might wish to consult them. The purchase of the extra copies of the catechism indicates that circulation in some form was contemplated. But there is not enough evidence to justify any claim of a connection between the Bay Library and the future public library movement in New England. The first American public library did not come over on the "Mayflower"

8. Quoted in Samuel Eliot Morison, *Three Centuries of Harvard, 1636–1936* (Cambridge: Harvard University Press, 1937), pp. 9, 13. The Bay Library may have been given to Harvard College.

9. Quoted in Jeremiah Chaplin, *Life of Henry Dunster* (Boston: Osgood, 1872), p. 80.

or any of the ships that sailed westward in her wake. Public library beginnings were more closely related to the desire of a hard-fisted Boston merchant to gratify his ego and justify, in the eyes of his fellow-men, his manifest shortcomings.

Captain Keayne and the First Boston Public Library

Captain Robert Keayne, first commander of the Ancient and Honorable Artillery Company, merchant, military enthusiast, and extortioner, was scarcely the person one might expect to find in the role of pioneer library patron. But, even from its beginnings, philanthropy in America has frequently resulted in a curious blending of paradoxical and discordant interests, and the captain was among the first of a long line of public benefactors whose private business reputation might suffer from too close examination. That he was penurious and quarrelsome in his relations with his fellows the record makes abundantly clear. His will, of fifty-three closely printed pages, was begun in August, 1653, and not completed until December of that year and is a curious conglomeration of religious piety, philanthropy, and spleen, to all of which he added a verbose though not entirely unsuccessful attempt to justify his character and reputation.[10] Captain Keayne died on March 23, 1655/56, and his will was probated on the second of May following. By its terms three hundred pounds were appropriated for public purposes, especially the building of a "Market place & Cundit":

... the one a good helpe in danger of fyre ... the other usefull for the country people that come with theire provisions for the supply of the towne, that they may have a place to sitt dry in ... also, to have some convenient roome or too for the Courts to meete in ... also in the same building or the like there may be a convenient roome for a Library & a gallery or some other handsome roome for the Elders to meete in & conferr. .... Then in the same building there may be also a roome for an Armory to keepe the Arms of the Artillery Company & for the Soldiers to meete in when they have occasion.[11]

10. Robert Keayne, "The Last Will and Testament of me, Robert Keayne, all of it Written with my owne Hands & Began by me, Mo: 6: 1: 1653, Comonly Called August," in the *Tenth Report of the Record Commissioners of the City of Boston* (Boston: Rockwell & Churchill, 1886), Doc. 150—1886, pp. 1–53. See also Josiah Benton, *Story of the Old Boston Town House, 1658–1711* (Boston: Privately printed, 1908), pp. 61, 213. Michael J. Canavan, "The Old Boston Public Library, 1656–1747," *Proceedings of the Colonial Society of Massachusetts*, XII (March, 1908), 116–33.

11. Keayne, *op. cit.*, p. 4.

That the library room might not remain empty of books he made, with characteristic lack of modesty, provision for a nuclear collection:

I give and bequeath to the beginning of that Library my 3 great writing bookes wch are intended as an Exposition or Interpretation of the whole Bible, as also a 4th great writing booke in which is an exposition of the Prophecy of Daniel of the Revelations & the Prophecy of Hosea not long since began, all which Bookes are written with my owne hand so farr as they be writt & could desier that some able scholler or two that is active and dilligent & addicted to reading and writing were ordered to carry on the same worke by degrees as they have leasure and opportunitie & in the same methode and way as I have begun (if a better be not advised to).[12]

After granting permission to his son and executor, Benjamine Keayne, and his wife to select from his private library such books as they "shall desier & thinke needfull for [their] owne use and reading (not to sell)"[13] he further provided that

my brother Wilson & Mr Norton with my Executor & Overseers of the most of them may view over the rest of my Bookes and to choose from amongst them such of my Divinitie bookes & Commentaries, and of my written sermon bookes or any others of them as they shall thinke profitable & usefull for such a Library (not simply for show but properly for use) they being all English none Lattine or Greeke, then the rest which remaines may be sould for there due worth both the written and printed ones, and though my bookes be not many, nor very fitt for such a worke being English & smale bookes, yet after this beginning the Lord may stirr up some others that will add more to them & helpe to carry the worke on by bookes of more valew, antiquity use and esteeme & that an Inventory may be taken & kept of those bookes that they set apart for the Library.[14]

But the captain took no chance that his gift would be wasted upon an unappreciative citizenry, for if the town of Boston failed to build the structure for which he had provided, the money bequeathed for that purpose was to be given to Harvard College; and as to his books:

. . . if the towne of Boston should not within three years after my death build a handsome roome for a Library & anoth^r for the Eld^rs & Scholl^rs to walke & meete in, as before I have expressed, that then they may be delivered to the President or some of the Overseers of Herbert Collidge in Cambridge to be placed as my gift or addition to that Library that is already begun there.[15]

The building, with adequate space for the library, was erected

12. *Ibid.*, p. 5.   13. *Ibid.*   14. *Ibid.*, pp. 5–6.
15. *Ibid.*, p. 14. By "Herbert" College, Captain Keayne obviously meant Harvard.

and became known as the Town House (see Pl. I). The legacy, however, was insufficient to cover the costs of construction, and some three hundred pounds were obtained through private subscription to pay the deficit.

To what extent the library was consulted is not known, but the few fragments of surviving record do indicate that some use was made of it. At least the captain's hope that others might feel an urge to augment the collection was fulfilled. John Oxenbridge, erstwhile fellow of Eton College, friend of Andrew Marvell, self-styled "silly worme," so unkindly characterized by Thomas a Wood as "a strange hodg-podg of opinions not easily to be described," in 1674 left

the Public Library of Boston, or elsewhere as my executors or overseers shall judge best, Augustine's Works in six volumes; the Centurys in three vollummes; the Catalogue of Oxford Library; Trithemius' Catalogue of Ecclesiastick writers; Pauen's Works in two vollummes; Pineda on Job in two vollummes; Euclid's geometry; Willet on Leviticus; Davenant on Colossias and Pemile's Works.[16]

In 1711 the Town House was consumed by a fire from which most of the library was saved, though the "4th great writing Booke" on the prophecies of Daniel and Hosea is believed to have perished in the flames. Public interest was sufficient to permit restoration of the building and the re-establishment of the library. However, a second conflagration, more than three decades later (in 1747), resulted in such complete destruction of building and contents that from the ashes no successor ever arose.[17]

16. William D. Cooper, *The Oxenbridges of Brede Place, Sussex, and Boston, Mass.* (London: J. R. Smith, 1860), pp. 18–19 (reprints the complete will of John Oxenbridge). Also it is to be noted that Sir Thomas Temple, governor of Nova Scotia from 1656–70, in a will dated October 14, 1671, provided: ". . . all my Bookes which I estimate at £150/- &c in case of sd. Nelson's death before he receive them, then I doe give & bequeath . . . the Bookes above sd, as the selectmen of Boston dispose viz: such as are fit for the Towne Lybrary into that" (Canavan, *op. cit.*, p. 122). But a second will, dated at London, March 27, 1674, makes no mention of the Boston library, so either no books were received from him or Sir Thomas made provision for the library during his lifetime. Probably the former, since the library was only a contingent legatee in the first will.

17. The only book known to have survived was a copy of Samuel Mather's *A Testimony from the Scripture against Idolatry & Superstition*, probably printed at Cambridge in 1670 (see Evans, No. 151) inscribed "ffor the publike Library at Boston, 1674." The volume is now in the Boston Athenaeum, though there is no record to indicate how it got there.

For almost a century Boston's first public library "served" the town, but its significance for the development of public libraries as they are known today lies neither in the extent to which it was used nor in the circumstances surrounding the benefactions by which it was created and increased. It is not important that the collection was regularly called a "public library," for, as has already been indicated, that term was loosely applied to any collection of books not the exclusive property of a private individual. The essential fact derives from the relation of the library to the town government of Boston. There is ample evidence to prove conclusively that the town selectmen and other officials regarded the books as the common property of the town. The library was an integral part of the Town House, itself a focus of community life and government. The administration of the library was clearly a municipal concern, however much or little the books may have been consulted by the general reader. On August 31, 1702, the selectmen ordered that "Mr John Barnard, jun^r be desired to make a Cattalogue of all the bookes belonging to the Towns Liberary and to Lodge the Same in ye s^d Liberary."[18] Mr. Barnard having performed his appointed task to the satisfaction of those concerned, it was ordered by the selectmen, on February 28, 1704, that "Mr John Barnard jun^r having at the request of the Selectmen Set the Town Liberary in good order he is allowed for s^d service two of those bookes of wch there are in ye s^d Liberary two of a Sort."[19]

The following advertisement appearing in the *Boston News-Letter* for June 8, 1713, reflects the degree to which the contents of the library were considered public property:

ADVERTISEMENT

All Persons that have in their Keeping, or can give Notice of any of the Town Library; or other things belonging to the Town-House in Boston, before the late Fire; are desired to Inform the Treasurer of the said Town thereof in order to their being returned.

The first Volume of Pool's Annotations was carried away in the late Fire in Boston; any person that has it, or any other Books carry'd away at that time, or any other Goods, are desired to bring them to the Post Office, that the true Owners may have them again.

18. Boston Record Commissioner, "Reports," XI, 26.
19. *Ibid.*, p. 37. Unfortunately, Mr. Barnard's catalog has not survived.

The official position of the library is further evident from its use as a depository for public records. At a meeting of the council, held at Boston, December 8, 1686, it was voted: "The Colony records shall be put in the Library Chamber and kept there, and two lockes be put on the office, the keys to be kept by some one deputed to the service."[20] At the Boston town meeting, March 11, 1694/95, it was "voted that bookes of the Register of births and deathes in the Town of Boston shall be demanded by the Selectmen in whose hands soever they may be and that all Bookes and Other things belonging to the Library and all the goods or Estate belonging to the Town be demanded and Taken care of by the Selectmen."[21] Clearly, the library was regarded generally as public property and its adequate care as a public trust. In origin and support it was dependent upon private initiative and generosity; but, once accepted by the town, there was no question as to its unqualifiedly public character.

There is no real evidence of the extent to which the contents of the library influenced the cultural development of the community. But in a community that supported such a strict church system there may have been many laymen who were interested in the technicalities of theology. As an institution per se it was very real indeed. A public collection of books could scarcely exist for a period of ninety years without some influence upon the mind of the community. Its inception may have been fortuitous, its maintenance indifferent, its demise inglorious—but the books were there. From time to time they came to public attention, and by common agreement the possession of a library was a proper municipal right. One must be careful not to read too much into the significance of Captain Keayne's legacy; but tortuous though it may be, there is a thread of continuity that stretches over the two and a half centuries that separate the crude frame structure at "ye markett place" on King Street from McKim's architectural stepchild of "Sainte Genevieve" at Copley Square. In the annals of the American public library Captain Keayne has won his white plume. To be sure he wore it with not too much grace, and on occasion he used it rather inelegantly to dust off his own neg-

20. *Massachusetts Historical Society, Collections,* Ser. 3, VII (1838), 162; Canavan, *op. cit.,* p. 125.

21. Boston Record Commissioner, "Reports," VII, 220; Canavan, *op. cit.,* p. 125.

lected discourses on the Scriptures or to burnish a tarnished reputation—for all that, it is his plume and he deserves it.

Town Collections at New Haven and Concord

At the same time that Boston was involved with the Keayne legacy the Colony of New Haven received a comparable gift. By the will of Governor Theophilus Eaton, dated August, 1656, it appears that he had delivered to John Davenport "certain books lately belonging to my brother, Mr. Samuel Eaton, intended for the use of a college, and appraised, as I take it, to about, or near twenty pounds."[22] The collection, a catalog of which was inserted into the records of the meetings of the "Townes men," numbered some ninety-five titles, was heavily theological, but included Plutarch, Virgil, More's *Utopia*, Erasmus' *Proverbs*, all in Latin; Sandys' English translation of Ovid, Raleigh's *History*, Heylyn's *Cosmography*, Keckermann's *Mathematics*, Barrough's *Physic*, and an *Anatomy*, the author of which cannot be identified.[23] Two years later the collection was enhanced by the addition of a number of Latin school texts, delivered to the town by one "Mr. Gibbard" on behalf of a "friend in England."[24]

By 1668 Davenport had deserted the Colony of New Haven, mainly because of chagrin over its absorption into Connecticut, so that the college he had so strongly urged ten years before was never established, and the books thus held in trust for its realization naturally reverted to the town. Blake observes that the volumes probably were kept in the town schoolhouse, and he believes that they were little used, though Mr. Peck, the schoolmaster, did successfully petition the town for permission to consult them.[25] Whether the responsibility for the care of these books weighed heavily upon the city fathers is not recorded. In any event, in February, 1689, the townsmen voted to dispose of the

22. Quoted in Franklin B. Dexter, "The First Public Library in New Haven," in his *Selection from the Miscellaneous Historical Papers of Fifty Years* (New Haven: Tuttle, Morehouse & Taylor, 1918), p. 223.

23. *Ibid.*, pp. 230–34. Dexter reproduces the entire catalog.

24. Henry T. Blake, *Chronicles of New Haven Green, 1638–1862* (New Haven: Tuttle, Morehouse & Taylor, 1898), pp. 198–200.

25. Blake, *op. cit.*, p. 199. Also S. E. Morison, *The Puritan Pronaos* (New York: New York University Press, 1936), pp. 141–42.

lot to the Rev. James Pierpont, minister of the church of New Haven, for forty pounds of rye and thirty-two bushels of Indian corn, which, according to the town treasurer, were equivalent to twelve pounds and eighteen shillings. This official act was subsequently ratified at the town meeting, and therewith the record ends.

John Davenport's project for the establishment of a college in Connecticut had languished after he left New Haven in 1668, but the plan was revived by a group of clergymen of whom this same James Pierpont, who had married Davenport's granddaughter, was the leader. It was in Samuel Russell's parsonage at Branford, probably in October, 1701, that the ministers from the scattered settlements of Connecticut met on that eventful evening, as tradition has it, and so dramatically gave their books "for the founding of a college in this Colony."[26] Since Pierpont must have known that the books he had purchased from the town were originally intended for the use of a projected college, it is not unreasonable to suppose that these volumes played a part in that romantic meeting and eventually found their way into the library of the college, later named for Elihu Yale, that arose in John Davenport's commonwealth near the mouth of the Quinnipiac.

That Concord, Massachusetts, had a collection of books owned and administered by the town prior to 1672 is apparent, for in that year the selectmen were instructed "that ceare be taken of the bookes of marters & other bookes that belong to the Towne, that they may be kept from abeuceive vesage & not to be lent to any person more than one month at one time."[27] This is the only record, and though unfortunately meager it is of interest for the light it throws on the expanding concept of municipal ownership of books, the right of the town to regulate their use, and the extension of loan privileges for specified periods of time. Scattered as the evidence is, one can already begin to see, even in this early

26. Robert D. French, *The Memorial Quadrangle: A Book about Yale* (New Haven: Yale University Press, 1929), pp. 6–7.

27. Quoted in George B. Bartlett, *Concord Guide Book* (Boston: Lothrop, 1880), pp. 92–93. Charles H. Walcott, *Concord in the Colonial Period* (Boston: Estes, 1884), p. 128.

period, the slow emergence of certain principles basic to public library service today.[28]

The Rev. Thomas Bray and His Parish Libraries

The effective work of the Rev. Thomas Bray and his Society for Promoting Christian Knowledge did much to enrich the book resources of the clergy in the American Colonies at the beginning of the eighteenth century. Though the doctor's only official association with America was a brief service as commissary of the Anglican church for Maryland, and he visited the New World only once—a stay of less than six months—he was deeply concerned over the inability of the Colonial ministers to obtain the books they so badly needed. Through the influence of his untiring efforts, parish libraries were established along the Atlantic Coast from Charleston to Newport. His society is said to have been responsible for sending thirty-four thousand books to the thirty-nine parochial libraries established by him.[29] Most of his benefactions clustered in the colonies to the south, particularly Maryland; but even in New England, where the absence of the Anglican church discouraged gifts, he seems to have had some influence.

In a letter dated July 25, 1698, to Henry Crompton, bishop of London, a gift of books sent by King William III to King's Chapel in Boston, was acknowledged. The volumes, which numbered two hundred and twenty-one, were, according to Dr. Foote, "an admirable collection of the best books for the use of a scholarly theologian of the Church of England."[30] They were

28. The practice of bequeathing libraries, or money for the purchase of book collections, to towns was not peculiarly American. In England such institutions were fairly numerous in the seventeenth century. One such was founded at Norwich in 1608. Five years later provision was made by Dr. Toby Matthew, archbishop of York, and Robert Redwood to establish a city library at Bristol. The library was opened in 1615. In 1653 was founded the town library at Manchester, the bequest of Sir Humphrey Chetham (see John J. Ogle, *The Free Library, Its History and Present Condition* [London: George Allen, 1897], pp. 4–5).

29. Lawrence C. Wroth, "Dr. Bray's *Proposals*," *Massachusetts Historical Society, Proceedings*, LXV (February, 1936), 521. See also Steiner, *op. cit.*, pp. 59–75. William D. Houlette, "Parish Libraries and the Work of Rev. Thomas Bray," *Library Quarterly*, IV (October, 1934), 588–609.

30. Henry Foote, "Remarks on the King's Chapel Library, Boston, Mass.," *Massachusetts Historical Society, Proceedings*, 1st ser., XVIII (May, 1881), 423–30.

deposited in the rectory of the chapel and placed under the direct care of the minister, the Rev. Samuel Miles.[31] The prevailing assumption has been that in some way these books were given as a result of Bray's work, though just why this belief has gained currency is not clear. Steiner included the library in his study of the Bray parish collections, though he does not say that there was a direct relationship between the two.[32] Foote suggests that Dr. Bray's library plans were inspired by this gift of books from the king.[33] Until such time as more evidence is available, it must be assumed that there was no connection, though it is doubtless true that the idea of the parish library for the promotion of a more enlightened clergy was definitely in the air. Granting this, the simultaneous appearance of isolated but parallel examples is entirely possible.

It is generally assumed that the twenty-three folios, twelve quartos, and forty-two octavos that were sent on October 19, 1700, to Trinity Church at Newport, Rhode Island, came at the instigation of the Rev. Thomas Bray.[34] The books, of which all were theological except a geography, two dictionaries, a Greek grammar, and a book on gardening, were supplemented by a "layman's library" comprising forty-two theological books and one hundred pastoral letters. A number of other parish libraries were founded early in the eighteenth century in Massachusetts, Connecticut, Rhode Island, and New Hampshire, and most of

31. The records show that the Rev. Dr. Miles was reimbursed for the cost of making twelve chests in which the books were to be kept. The volumes were lettered on the back:

SVB	DE
AVSPICIIS	BIBLIOTHECA
WILHELMI	DE
III	BOSTON

Kept for years in the rectory of the King's Chapel, many of the books were lost during the Revolutionary War. In 1807 the surviving volumes were given to Boston's Fourth Social Library (the Theological Library), and in 1823 they were received by the Boston Athenaeum, where they have remained.

32. Steiner, *op. cit.*, p. 70.

33. Foote, *op. cit.*, p. 424. He also appends a catalog of the collection, pp. 426–30.

34. Steiner, *op. cit.*, p. 70. Edward Field, *State of Rhode Island and Providence Plantation . . . a History* (Boston: Mason, 1902), II, 615. Actually the present writer is not at all certain that even this library resulted from the work of Dr. Bray, but it is generally considered to have so originated, and the evidence against such a hypothesis is less strong than in the case of the King's Chapel collection.

these received books directly from England as a result of the work of Dr. Bray's Society for Propagating the Gospel in Foreign Parts, which was established in 1701.[35]

It is easy to overemphasize a hypothetical relationship between the Bray libraries and the origins of the public library movement. Especially is this true in New England, where these parochial collections were not particularly strong. There was no real continuity between these libraries and the public library development of later years.[36] It may be said that the libraries were more symptomatic than influential. Moreover, they did provide for a type of library service based on a political unit. Because the establishment of the Bray libraries was a Church of England move-

35. In Massachusetts these were "The Missionary Library" of Christ Church, Cambridge, and parish libraries at Marblehead, Newburg, Christ Church in Boston (Paul Revere's Old North Church), and at Quincy (the Braintree parish library). In Connecticut similar collections were founded at Stratford (1723), New London (1732), New Haven (1736), Litchfield (1769), Wallingford, Ripton (now Huntington), Norwich, Groton, Middletown, New Cambridge (Bristol), Fairfield (Southport), Reading, Newton, Woodbury, West Haven, Plymouth, and Wallingford. In Rhode Island there were S.P.G. benefactions at "Ye Library of Rhode Island" at Newport (1700), St. Paul's Church in Narragansett and Wickford, and at King's Chapel in Providence. In New Hampshire there was such a parochial library at Portsmouth.

Prior to his death Austin B. Keep began a thorough study of the Bray libraries in Colonial America, and his papers, including copies of the manuscript record books of the S.P.G., which are now in the New York Historical Society, are an important source for the further investigation of this subject.

36. One rather important exception to this statement must be pointed out, even though it did not take place in New England. Steiner shows that the gift of a Bray collection to South Carolina led directly to what is probably the first Colonial library law. This act, passed in 1700, provided that the books were to be placed in the direct care of the minister of Charleston (the librarian), whose duty it was to see to it that they were properly treated by the general public. But the affairs of the library were to be managed by nine commissioners (the library board) appointed by the General Assembly, whose places could be filled by gubernatorial appointment if vacancies occurred when the assembly was not in session. Use of the library was unrestricted, and the period of loan varied in duration from one to four months, depending upon the size of the book. Other provisions related to the preparation of a catalog, the annual inspection by the commissioners, and a system of penalties for delayed return or improper use. The parallel with the modern public library system is here startlingly close. Carelessness on the part of the public in the use of the books prompted the passage of an amendment in 1712 that authorized the minister to deny the right of use to any who he felt would not treat the books with proper respect. Certain other changes were also made in the details of organization of the commissioners (Steiner, op. cit., pp. 70–72).

ment, in New England, where there were few Anglican chuřches, the contribution of these libraries to the intellectual stream was slight, but they were an eddy in the main current of New England culture, and as such they merit some consideration.[37]

Other Early Town Book Collections

Three other town book collections were established in New England before library history entered a new phase. In 1719 the town of Oxford, Massachusetts, began to receive books from Judge Paul Dudley and others. The collection, which probably never numbered more than a few volumes, was primarily for the use of the ministers.[38] In 1731 the residents of Lancaster, Massachusetts, in town meeting assembled, voted that the town authorize the purchase of the Rev. Samuel Willard's *Complete Body of Divinity*, to be kept "in the meeting house for the town's use so that any person may come there and read therein, as often as they shall see cause, and said book is not to be carried out of the meeting house at any time by any person except by order of the selectmen."[39] One book may not make a library, especially if it be a modern book, but *A Compleat Body of Divinity in Two Hundred and Fifty Expository Lectures on the Assembly's Shorter Catechism wherein the Doctrines of the Christian Religion are Unfolded, their Truth Confirm'd, their Excellence Display'd, their Usefulness Improv'd; Contrary Errors & Vices Refuted & Expos'd, Objections Answered, Contraversies Settled, Cases of Conscience Resolv'd, and a Great Light thereby Reflected on the Present Age, by the Reverend & Learned Samuel Willard, M.A.*, late pastor of the South Church in Boston, and Vice President of Harvard College in Cambridge in New England, prefaced, by the Pastor of the

37. See Wroth, *op. cit.*, p. 522.
38. George F. Daniels, *History of the Town of Oxford* (Oxford: The author, 1892), p. 104. Mary Freeland, *The Records of Oxford* (Albany: Munsell, 1894), pp. 325–27. Massachusetts Free Public Library Commission, *Ninth Report; Free Public Libraries of Massachusetts, 1899* (Boston: Wright & Potter, 1899), Public Doc. No. 44. It should be mentioned that William Foster in his *Life of Stephen Hopkins* mentions a "circulating library" in the parental Hopkins home in the Louisquisset District of Rhode Island, about 1711. If such a library ever existed, it was probably no more than a private library the contents of which were generously loaned to others in the community (see William E. Foster, *Life of Stephen Hopkins* [Providence: Rider, 1884], I, 45–49).
39. Massachusetts Commission, *Report, op. cit.* D. H. Hurd, *History of Worcester County, Mass.* (Philadelphia: Lewis, 1889), I, 20.

same Church (Boston, 1726), could very nearly be accorded that distinction, especially since it was a folio of almost a thousand pages and is believed to have been the largest book published up to that time in the American Colonies.[40] It was purchased at public expense, owned and controlled by the town, and intrusted to the safekeeping of the selectmen. In the same year the Hon. Samuel Holden of London gave a collection of books, bound at the expense of Samuel Sewell, a Boston merchant, to the congregation of the church in East Sudbury, Massachusetts. Kept in the meeting house, the volumes were available to any who wished to consult them.

By the beginning of the fourth decade of the eighteenth century the public library movement in New England, if indeed it could as yet be so called, had ended its first phase. In accomplishment it was not conspicuously successful. The sporadic attempts to establish town book collections were not the result of organized municipal effort. Private gifts were almost the sole source of support, and there was no provision for future growth. Inadequate supervision resulted in loss, theft, or injury through careless handling. The appeal of their book collections was probably not sufficiently great to attract widespread popular support.

Though not organically linked with the public library of the present, the town collections were significant as foreshadowing what was to come. In a modest way they did contribute some fertility to that intellectual soil into which the public library of a later day deeply thrust its roots. Among the early town libraries that of the Boston Town House is most significant to the historian. Not only was it the first of its kind, but it was sufficiently important in the life of the community to justify at least a minimum of support for almost a century. One should not dwell too long over these first town libraries and the men who gave them, but neither should they be ignored.

The Beginnings of the Social Library

In 1723, at the age of seventeen, a precocious printer's apprentice who had quarreled with his brother thumbed his nose at the local authorities and stole secretly out of Boston. A journeyman

40. It was $8\frac{1}{4} \times 13\frac{1}{2}$ inches and contained 988 pages (see John Clyde Oswald, *Printing in the Americas* [New York: Gregg, 1937], pp. 78–79).

printer, first in Philadelphia and later in London, Benjamin Franklin was familiar with the principle of the social club. He knew that the intellectual life of a country—its politics, its drama, its journals, its scientific societies—could be fostered in the congenial, not to say convivial, atmosphere of the coffee-house and the tavern. Back in Philadelphia again, Franklin lost no time in bringing together, in the autumn of 1727, a group of intimate friends to form his Junto.

This organization, composed of young men who were with but one exception relatively poor, was a debating society concerned with both literary and scientific subjects. It had as its twofold objective intellectual improvement and social enjoyment.[41] In spite of Franklin's dislike of Puritanism, the Junto was modeled, in part, after the neighborhood benefit societies organized by Cotton Mather. It was Mather's plan that the discussion should be supported by a framework of ten leading questions that were to be read at each meeting. Franklin outlined the same procedure and even in certain instances suggested comparable questions.[42] It was his own peculiar genius, however, that provided for the drinking of a glass of wine between the reading of each proposition. This weekly ritual was supplemented by debates, general discussions, and the presentation of essays prepared by the several members. Such activities soon made necessary the accumulation of a library to support the work, and in 1730 Franklin arranged for the pooling of the private libraries of the members in a consolidated collection for the use of all:

About this time, our club meeting, not at a tavern, but in a little room ot Mr. Grace's, set apart for that purpose, a proposition was made by me, that, since our books were often referr'd to in our disquisitions upon the queries, it

41. Benjamin Franklin, *Autobiography* (New York: Random House, 1932), pp. 64–66, 75–76, 83–85. Carl Van Doren, *Benjamin Franklin* (New York: Viking, 1938), I, 30–33. Bernard Fay, *Franklin: The Apostle of Modern Times* (Boston: Little, Brown, 1929), pp. 119–23. Austin K. Gray, *Benjamin Franklin's Library: A Short Account of the Library Company of Philadelphia, 1731–1931* (New York: Macmillan, 1937), pp. 3–4.

42. Mather's plan was to "draw up certain Points of Consideration to be with due Pauses read in the Societies every time they met, for any to offer what Proposal he pleased upon any of the Points at the Reading of it" (Samuel Mather, *Life of the Very Reverend and Learned Cotton Mather* [Boston: Samuel Gerrish, 1729], p. 56). Van Doren, *op. cit.*, I, 75–77.

might be convenient to us to have them altogether where we met, that upon occasion they might be consulted; and by thus clubbing our books to a common library, we should, while we lik'd to keep them together, have each of us the advantage of using the books of all the other members, which would be nearly as beneficial as if each owned the whole. It was lik'd and agreed to, and we fill'd one end of the room with such books as we could best spare.[43]

But the scheme was not entirely successful, and though the books "had been of great use, yet some inconvenience occurr[ed] for want of due care of them, the collection, after about a year, was separated and each took his books home again."[44]

Undaunted by this initial lack of success, Franklin immediately "set on foot" his "first project of a public nature, that for a subscription library":

I drew up the proposals, got them put into form by our great scrivener, Brockden, and, by the help of my friends in the Junto, procured fifty subscribers of forty shillings each to begin with, and ten shillings a year for fifty years, the term our company was to continue. We afterwards obtained a charter, the company being increased to one hundred.[45]

In 1731 was founded the Library Company of Philadelphia, which, as Franklin says, "was the mother of all the North American subscription libraries, now [ca. 1772] so numerous." He continues:

These libraries have improved the general conversation of the Americans, made common tradesmen and farmers as intelligent as most gentlemen from other countries, and perhaps have contributed in some degree to the stand so generally made through the colonies in defense of their privileges.[46]

The first books for the library were ordered from Peter Collinson of London, on March 31, 1732. Toward the end of October, Captain Cornock brought his ship into the Philadelphia Harbor and with it "the Library Trunk," signalizing the initial success of the new venture.[47]

But Robert Grace's Pewter Platter Hall in Philadelphia was not the only scene of social library activity in the Colonies. Among the hills of the lower Connecticut Valley, eight citizens of Durham, Connecticut, united in 1733 to establish the Book-Company of Durham. Expressing the desire to enrich their "minds with useful and profitable knowledge by reading," but "unable

43. Franklin, *op. cit.*, p. 75.   44. *Ibid.*   45. *Ibid.*
46. *Ibid.*, pp. 75–76.   47. Gray, *op. cit.*, pp. 9–12.

to do so for the want of suitable and proper books," these men each contributed twenty shillings into a common fund for the purchase of books and drew up detailed regulations for the administration of the company. By the terms of the agreement a librarian was appointed to care for the material thus assembled and to regulate its use. The period of loan was specified as one month. Fines were imposed for mutilation, damage, or delinquency in return, and the lending of books to those not members of the company was forbidden. Likewise the sale of shares in the company was rigidly controlled.[48] The company gained in membership, prospered, and grew. Evidently the penalty for the loan of books to nonmembers was a regulation more honored in the breach than in the observance, for its books were used by President Clapp and the students of Yale. Not until 1856, more than a century after its founding, was the company dissolved.

Possibly the contagion of Durham's success spread to the nearby towns of Guilford, Saybrook, Killingworth, and Lyme, for in 1737 these four settlements had established a joint library which later received a gift of books from Isaac Watts[49] (see Pl. II). In 1787 the collection was valued at £167/7/–, it then having sixty folios, twenty-four quartos, and three hundred and seven volumes of other sizes.[50]

Less than two years after the founding of the collection at Guilford and adjacent towns, twelve citizens of Lebanon, Connecticut, and vicinity had (on January 4, 1739) signed their solemn compact with the Rev. Solomon Williams of that place, whereby each was to pay into a common treasury the sum of fifty pounds for the purchase of books to establish the Philogrammatican Li-

---

48. Manuscript records in the possession of Mrs. Howard Field, Durham, Conn. (see Appen. I). Also William Fowler, *History of Durham, Conn.* (Hartford: Wiley, Waterman & Eaton, 1866), pp. 103–6. C. G. Rockwood, Jr., "Presentation Address at Dedication of New Building for Durham Public Library, August 14, 1902" (MS in Durham Public Library). The eight founders were "Col. Elihu Chauncey, Capt. Nathaniel Sutlief, Mr. Hurt Strong, Mr. Samuel Seward, Capt. Ebenezer Carnsey, Lieutenant Nathaniel Seaward, Mr. Thomas Robinson, and Captain Robert Fairchild" (MS records).

49. Anne S. Pratt, *Isaac Watts and His Gift of Books to Yale College* (New Haven: Yale University Library, 1938), p. 3.

50. Trumbull MSS, Yale University Library. Bernard Steiner, *History of the Plantation of Menunkatuck . . .* (Baltimore: The author, 1897), pp. 410–11.

brary Company,[51] which also later received a gift of books from Isaac Watts.[52]

In September of 1739 thirty-four individuals from Pomfret, Connecticut, and surrounding towns formed there the United English Library for the Propagation of Christian and Useful Knowledge and expended four hundred and eighteen pounds for the initial purchase of books.[53] This new movement for the establishment of these joint-stock or *social* libraries that was spreading steadily along the eastern border of Connecticut was likewise taking root in near-by Rhode Island. Roger Williams' colony had long enjoyed an enviable reputation for freedom of thought and liberality of spirit. In religion it had been the most tolerant of any of the New England Colonies. At Newport, then its principal town, in 1747 the Rev. Ezra Stiles, later to become famous as president of Yale, and the Rev. Samuel West, established the Ecclesiastical Library. Its main purpose, as the name implies, was to supply books for the ministers of the region, and in this it is believed to have achieved some success. But the position of Newport in the record of American library history is secure not because of the Ecclesiastical Library; events much more significant for the growth of New England libraries had taken place in that focal point of Colonial cultural and social life long before Dr. Stiles and his friends had begun their modest collection.

The Redwood Library of Newport

At Narragansett Bay there arrived by accident on January 23, 1729, the distinguished Irish philosopher George Berkeley, dean of Derry and afterward bishop of Cloyne. Though still in his "early forties," he had won considerable recognition, and in England enjoyed the personal association of Steele, Addison, Pope, and Swift. Even Pope's customarily sharp pen had attributed "to Berkeley every virtue under Heaven." He had traveled extensively on the Continent and had spent considerable time in Italy. Five years before his arrival in America he had been named

---

51. Original contract among the Terry papers in the American Antiquarian Society (see Appen. II). Mrs. Martha Williams Hooker, "Booklovers of 1738," *Connecticut Magazine*, X (1906), 715–23.

52. Pratt, *op. cit.*

53. Early records of the society in the Public Library of Pomfret, Conn.

dean of Derry—"the best deanery in the Kingdom" and supposed to have been worth fifteen hundred pounds per annum. With his fortune thus secure he determined to take permanent residence in Bermuda and devote his labors to the establishment of a college there. Already he had prophesied the westward "course of empire." Many looked with favor upon his plan, and by them he had been promised considerable money for the advancement of the scheme. At that time the outlook for his philanthropic project was most encouraging. His residence at Newport, whence he went upon arrival at Narragansett Bay, convinced him that there was the ideal place for his college, but for almost three years he waged a discouraging and ultimately hopeless struggle for its founding.

His choice of Newport for his Colonial home was most appropriate. It was then the largest town in Rhode Island, and it evinced a cultural development and economic prosperity that made it one of the most interesting of all Colonial centers. At the beginning of the eighteenth century an expanding commerce in rum and molasses had laid the foundation for commercial enterprise that eventually enabled Newport to challenge the supremacy of even Boston and New York as commercial leaders in the New World. To this was added a prosperity deriving from a thriving slave trade and, during King George's War, much privateering. Few people had more to lose by a rupture with England than the merchants of Newport, for the economic bonds with the mother-country were strong. Not until the convulsions of the Revolutionary War destroyed the existing economic pattern did Newport lose its mercantile pre-eminence.

Not only did the rapidly accumulating wealth of Newport during the early years of the eighteenth century establish the economic basis for a cultural awakening, but the very fact of that commerce fostered contacts with Great Britain by which intellectual advance was readily transmitted. The private libraries of the wealthy were rich in the English classics. Tutors, brought from England, gave instruction to the children of the aristocracy. There was a landed gentry that owned slaves and followed the hounds in the chase as did the English gentleman. While Boston was wrestling with abstruse theological doctrine, Newport was experiencing a real intellectual awakening. The fourth town in New England and the seventh in Colonial America to establish a printing press was becoming increasingly aware of what was going on in the world of science, letters, and art.

Admittedly, Berkeley's primary objective failed, as the promise of financial aid did not materialize. Even his friends began to make sport of his college in Bermuda, and, discouraged, he returned to England in the autumn of 1731. But in its broader aspects his sojourn in America was far from a failure. He rendered important assistance to Colonial colleges that were already in operation, especially to Yale, which, he said, "breeds the best clergymen and the most learned of any in America" and which was probably most like the institution of his cherished ambitions. More significantly, he contributed much to the advancement of American culture. Though there is evidence of an intellectual awakening in Newport before Berkeley's arrival, his coming did a great deal to bring it to a focus and give it direction.

In 1730 there was established at Newport the Literary and Philosophical Society, and though it has not been proved that Berkeley was its actual founder, he certainly promoted its success by his active participation in its affairs. It afforded him excellent opportunities for contact with the intellectual leadership of Newport society, and its meetings were admirably adapted to the promotion of his idealistic doctrines. It has been suggested that his *Alciphron*, which was composed during Berkeley's Newport days, drew much from the deliberations of this association. In the congenial atmosphere of this group Berkeley came to know intimately the foremost minds of the town;[54] and in turn the success of the group and the influence it was able to exert in the encouragement of Newport's cultural growth may be largely attributed to Berkeley's stimulating leadership.

54. Among the original signers of the society's constitution and its most active members were Daniel Updike, attorney-general for Rhode Island for twenty-seven years; Edward Scott, grand-uncle of the great Sir Walter and master of the Newport grammar school; Henry Collins, educated in England, prosperous merchant, patron of the arts, and donor of the land for the Redwood Library building; William Ellery, ancestor of William Ellery Channing; Rev. John Callender, author of the first historical account of Rhode Island Colony; Stephen Hopkins, later governor of Rhode Island; and Rev. Samuel Johnson of Stamford, Conn., Berkeley's philosophical disciple and afterward president of King's College.

Details are lacking concerning the decision in 1747 whereby Abraham Redwood "generously engaged to bestow five hundred pounds sterling, to be laid out in a collection of useful books suitable for a public library proposed to be erected in Newport."[55] That it was an outgrowth of the work of the Philosophical Society and the influence of Bishop Berkeley seems certain, and Redwood saw, much as Franklin did, the need for such a group to promote an adequate supply of readily available books.[56]

Abraham Redwood, heir to his father's extensive sugar plantation in Antigua, was educated by private tutors in Philadelphia. He returned to Newport, where he divided his time between his country and town houses, managed his expanding commercial enterprises, and entered into the literary pursuits of the community. He became a shipowner and merchant as well as a planter, and the steadily accumulating profits derived from these several activities soon enabled him to assume an important place among the cosmopolitan group of merchant princes who dominated Newport's social life. At his one-hundred-and-forty-five-acre country estate in near-by Portsmouth he indulged his fancy for exotic horticulture, and there, according to a contemporary account, his "botanical garden . . . was stored with curious foreign as well as valuable indigenous plants, in either hot or greenhouses or in the open air."[57] The library benefaction was not the only one to the credit of this young philanthropist—he was less than forty years of age at the time the gift was made—but he contributed liberally to other projects for public improvement.

The company incorporated for the proper administering of Redwood's gift purchased books to the amount of the donation from London, through John Thomlinson, and the library became a reality.[58] The success of the enterprise was largely secured by the receipt of a tract of land from Henry Collins, so plans were

55. Act of incorporation of the Redwood Library, August 22, 1747, *Redwood Library, The Company of the Redwood Library and Athenaeum; Charter and Amendments, By-laws* (Newport: Franklin Printing House, 1937), p. 3).

56. George C. Mason, *Annals of the Redwood Library and Athenaeum* (Newport: Redwood Library, 1891), pp. 2–53; see also *Redwood Library and Athenaeum, Addresses Commemorating Its 200th Anniversary, 1747–1947* (Newport: Redwood Library, 1947), 31 pp.

57. Quoted in *ibid.*, p. 68. Also see biography of Redwood in the *Dictionary of American Biography*.

58. Mason lists the titles of the books purchased (*ibid.*, pp. 494–517).

immediately promoted for the construction of a library building. Collins, though not so wealthy as Redwood, was a product of Newport's rising prosperity. In England he was trained for a mercantile career. He returned to Newport, acquired a substantial fortune, and thereafter participated actively in philanthropic undertakings.[59] His gift of land stimulated a program for the solicitation of funds for an appropriate building, and a structure was erected in 1750. Designed by Peter Harrison, one of the two trained architects then in the Colonies and, according to tradition, a pupil of Sir John Vanburgh, the building, in its strict regard for classical proportions, is an excellent example of the Greek style. The roof extends forward to form a portico supported by four Doric columns seventeen feet high and curved in perfect entasis. The tympanum is severely plain. Though constructed of wood, the building, to which additions have been made from time to time, still stands—the oldest library structure in the United States to be used continuously as such since its erection (see Pl. III).

Perhaps no library was ever more truly a product of its social milieu than that founded by Abraham Redwood. A fruition of the cultural ferment that swept Newport in the eighteenth century, it was built upon the town's mercantile prosperity. The fortunes of the library ebbed and flowed with that of the community by which it was supported. Surviving British occupation, enduring neglect, the library is still a vigorous force in Newport's culture—significant for both the bibliographical value of its collections and the historical development that it reveals.

In the hundred years that separate the benefactions of Captain Robert Keayne and Abraham Redwood, American librarianship had taken significant strides. The early town collections were uncertain in the aims of their founders and largely unsatisfactory in execution. In general they were sporadic gifts by isolated individuals. With the application of the joint-stock principle to the library there came a new and vigorous spirit, a genuine expression of the collective need for books on the part of groups of individuals. Though the shelves might sag under the weight of many theological treatises, even in these earlier social libraries there

59. *Ibid.*, pp. 26–27.

was no insignificant proportion of secular writings. For these there must have been a real demand. The degree to which the Redwood Library was, even at that early date, the collection of a scholarly gentleman and cosmopolitan man of affairs is apparent from an analysis of the titles printed in the first catalog of the library, issued in 1764. At the time this catalog was published[60] the collection included some seven hundred titles, which were divided among the several subject fields as shown in the accompanying tabulation.

	PER CENT
Belles-lettres and the arts	33
Science	19
History (ancient and modern)	16
Theology (including philosophy)	13
Law	08
Biography	04
Travel	03
Agriculture	02
Military science	01
Miscellaneous	01
Total	100

Rooted as these first social libraries were in the voluntary associations of individuals for discussion and mutual enlightenment, they strove toward a twofold objective. Primarily, they were an attempt to satisfy a need of the colonist for group activity. The pioneer church had been serving that function and indeed still offered much as an instrument for the expression of community effort. But the literary circle and its library promised more latitude and greater possibility for variation, and the members were probably as much interested in conviviality as in the knowledge to be obtained from the discussions. Even of the Philosophical Society of Newport, Dr. Alexander Hamilton reported, "I was surprised to find that no matters of philosophy were brought upon the carpet. They talked of privateering and building of vessels."[61] The second objective was to meet the demand for books, which were, at best, not too plentiful.

60. *Catalog of the Books Belonging to the Company of the Redwood Library in Newport, R.I.* (Newport: Printed by S. Hall, 1764); reprinted in Mason, *op. cit.*, pp. 492–514.

61. Dr. Alexander Hamilton, *Itinerarium*, ed. A. B. Hart (St. Louis: Privately printed, 1907), p. 185.

But the emergence of the social library in mid-eighteenth century Colonial New England is to be attributed to something more than a psychological urge for the companionship of others and a desire to read an interesting book. Doubtless many a Yankee hunter stealthily making his way through the underbrush of the Maine woods yearned for an evening with congenial companions around a tavern fire. More than one New England farm lad, stopping to blow on numbed fingers as he carried in the frozen milk, would have preferred to spend the hour tracing the intricate script in Bickham's *Universal Penman*. But there were no libraries for such as these—no libraries because desire, however keenly felt, was not enough. A supporting economy and the beginnings of urban development, in addition to these social forces, were prerequisites to library formation.

The Economic Bases of the Emerging Colonial Culture

As was indicated in chapter i, the signing of the Treaty of Utrecht in 1713 brought to a close a long period of strife that had been both expensive and unproductive. New England then entered upon a thirty-year period of peace that was characterized by great commercial expansion, the secularization of thought, and increasing political self-consciousness. As in the case of Newport, the rise of a commercial economy in the older settlements along the coast brought an unprecedented prosperity and accumulation of wealth. Seaboard New England became merely Old England, writ small, and the rich West India merchant in his Boston counting-house had much more in common with his correspondent in London than with his pioneer "neighbor" but a few miles in the interior. Two aspects of this economic expansion were of direct cultural importance: the rise of a money economy as foreign trade developed and the growth of intercolonial communication with the increase of coastal shipping.

In the wake of this new commercial activity began the rise of the modern corporation. Men soon found that the risks of shipping could be appreciably minimized if groups of individuals took shares in several enterprises instead of each risking his all in a single venture. Concurrently, about the year 1720, the insurance corporation emerged in England, where its success soon prompted the formation in America of similar organizations for the mutual protection of maritime investment.

It was during this same period that manufacturing in contrast to home industry began to emerge. Rum was the chief product of early New England manufacture, but iron was also important. Though by 1720 Boston had lost her position of leadership in iron manufacture to the middle colonies, especially Pennsylvania, the industry was still important to the southern New England region. Capital, accumulated from the profits of commerce, sought investment in this expanding industrialization and returned additional profits. Obviously this new wealth resulted in important and far-reaching social change.

Changing Cultural Patterns

Under the impact of economic prosperity the life of the Colonies began to approach cultural maturity. The early culture of the settlements was entirely a transplanted growth, modified to some extent by the influences of the wilderness. The period of border warfare weakened this imported culture and brought on a brief time of extreme declination and hesitation. But the return of peace and the expansion of the economic system again promoted a cultural growth that, though still leaning heavily upon transatlantic influences, nevertheless began to evince unmistakably native characteristics.

In spite of the tendencies that were producing social cleavages there were important forces that had marked cohesive power. Better roads pierced the long stretches of wilderness that had separated many of the settlements and thereby weakened cultural isolation. This increased communication among the towns often followed the paths of the itinerant peddler and petty artificer and tradesman. Travel became popular and privately owned vehicles more abundant. The growth of population made a practically continuous line of settlement along the coast from southern Maine to Virginia, and people were brought into closer unity by the mere fact of physical propinquity. The extension of the postal service, for which a foundation had been laid several decades before, further served to destroy insulating barriers and facilitate the distribution of both private letters and print.

The new cultural growth was likewise reflected in a heightened standard of living among the wealthy class. New England merchants built for themselves homes of commodious proportion and genuine magnificence. That of Captain Godfrey Malbone, "a substantial trader," in Newport, was declared by Dr. Alexander Hamilton to be the "largest and most magnificent dwelling house" he had seen in all America.[62] The homes of Faneuil and Hancock in Boston were likewise famous. Country estates as well as town houses were popular with the merchant grandees, and elaborate furniture and "stamp paper in Rolls for to paper Rooms" were in demand. Stylish clothes and expensive jewelry were readily available from London merchants, who were quick to perceive that Boston was a ready market for such ware. So lavish did the life become that in 1721 the Massachusetts General Court found it necessary to pass laws against extravagant expenditure at funerals.

In the realm of the intellect developments were certainly less ostentatious, probably less spectacular, but more significant. With the expansion of urban life, education went forward, making the towns more than ever the educational centers of their respective provinces. Commercial maturity brought an increasing awareness of the need for education, and learning ceased to be the monopoly of the upper classes. Secular control and emphasis in the course of study began to supplant clerical domination, and there appeared an increasing tendency to emphasize useful and practicable vocational knowledge. Boston and Newport were the foremost New England towns to provide education for all classes. Five schools had been established in Boston before 1720, and these continued under competent town management. Private schools increased even more rapidly than the public institutions. Even the young ladies might receive instruction in reading, writing, ciphering, and the social graces of dancing and needle-work. Higher education was likewise prospering. One hundred years in the annals of Oxford, Cambridge, or the Spanish universities in Mexico and Peru were but a long summer afternoon; but in the American Colonies, Harvard's history of more than a century represented no mean educational accomplishment. During that

62. Hamilton, *op. cit.*, p. 125.

hundred years Harvard, the ancient stronghold of theocracy, had been profoundly affected by a new spirit of liberalism and change. When, in 1724, the death of President John Leverett terminated his administration, it was the moderate Benjamin Wadsworth, and not Cotton Mather, who was selected to fill the vacancy. Though throughout the period Harvard remained a denominational college dedicated to the tenets of Calvinism, the Overseers shared with the conservative group of the faculty a growing concern over the lessening of academic restraint. Following the plan of Harvard in its curriculum and organization, there came into being at New Haven a "Collegiate School" which, by the middle of the eighteenth century had for several decades been sending forth into the Colonial world divines and teachers prepared to spread the gospel of light and truth "for God, for Country, and for Yale."

However, church membership, during the period, was not keeping pace with population growth. The ministry, no longer the royal road to social and political influence, was losing ground as a career, and the fact that men like Stoughton, Gridley, and Stephen Sewall in Massachusetts, Gurdon Saltonstall, Jr., and Jonathan Trumbull in Connecticut, all of whom had been trained for the ministry, turned to secular life reveals the change. Men of proved business ability and marked commercial success took the place of theologians in public affairs. Not only was religion losing ground to competing social agencies, especially the club, but it was suffering schism and revolt within its own ranks. With the death of Increase Mather a great light went out in the New England church. Cotton struggled vainly to stem the rising tide, but his abilities were not equal to the task. The established doctrine of Calvinism was confronted by the new heresies of Arminianism and deism. Everywhere there was a secularizing of interests and an increased reaction against religious formalism that culminated in the sudden outburst of the Great Awakening. Despite its excesses, this movement gave to Colonial religion a new meaning, and in shaking the power of the established churches the people won the right to such religious life as seemed best for themselves. But the educational, social, and political consequences were even more important than the religious. There was a general challenge to the old order and a new spirit that was essentially humanitarian and democratic; the expansion of both these tendencies in Colonial society was directly related to contemporary religious movements.

A genuine interest in science was beginning to appear. Cotton Mather stubbornly fought the tide of religious and medical prejudice against smallpox inoculation, revealed himself to be an accurate and thorough observer of the New England fauna, and took real pride in his membership in the Royal Society. Isaac Greenwood, whose students listened eagerly to his lectures on "the incomparable Newton," was the first appointee to the new chair of mathematics and natural philosophy endowed at Harvard by Thomas Hollis; and in 1734 Professor Greenwood was giving public lectures on astronomy which the citizens of Boston were eagerly attending. Greenwood's successor as Hollis professor at Harvard was John Winthrop, who became a leader in establishing mineralogy as a science. Paul Dudley, of Roxbury, won distinction not only for his work in horticulture but also because of his authoritative reporting on the habits of the moose, deer, and other New England animals, his observations on earthquakes, and his *Essay upon the Natural History of Whales*, which was published by the Royal Society. Edward Bromfield, whose untimely death terminated a potentially brilliant scientific career, had as a lad of twenty-three been carrying out significant experiments in microscopy with lenses of his own grinding. The Rev. Jared Eliot of Connecticut had devoted many years to the intensive study of New England agriculture and the deterioration of the soil. His *Essay in Field Husbandry*, published first in 1747, represented the culmination of thirty years of experimentation. Also a member of the Royal Society, he kept in close touch with English mechanical developments, especially the wheat drill, and was among the first to foresee the future abandonment of New England farms.

Secular learning also began to concern itself with the writing of history. With the eighteenth century there appeared in American historical writing some evidence of the secular approach that represented a sharp break with the theologians; and, following King Philip's War, doctors, lawyers, merchants, and planters turned to the writing of history, with the result that a more critical temper and broader interests were reflected in their work. John Callender confessed that his account of Rhode Island was "very lame and imperfect," but for more than a century it remained the best survey of the colony's history. Thomas Prince strove to "cite vouchers to every passage" and to do his "utmost, first to find out the truth and then to relate it in the clearest order," though such as he were obviously hampered by inadequate resources, particularly in the scarcity of scholarly libraries. As provincial society approached maturity, it became more stable. Proud of the past, confident of the future, Colonial historians were eager to correct English misconceptions of America and zealous to portray the distinctive Colonial culture.

Art was largely the plaything of the rich. The wealthy of Boston and Newport had their favorite portrait painters, and the numbers of surviving canvasses testify to the productivity of the craft. Robert Feke of Newport is generally considered the best of those trained in America. John Smibert, who came to Newport on the same ship with Bishop Berkeley, not only achieved widespread renown as a painter but imported pictures for sale. In Boston, William Price did a thriving business in prints and maps at his "Picture Store." The youthful John Singleton Copley, whose "Boy with the Squirrel" was sent to England, where it received great praise, did his best work before he left American soil, and when, on the eve of the Revolution, he sailed for England, he carried with him a promise of future achievement that study abroad did not fulfil.

On February 18, 1729, Boston had its first public "Concert of Musick on Sundry Instruments," and similar performances became relatively common before the end of the Colonial period. Musical training in the harpsichord and spinet, especially for the children of the well-to-do, became entirely proper. Even in the Puritan churches, where the music had so long been dominated by metrical psalmody, the close of the period produced William Billing's *New England Psalm Singer*, which, though it added little to the charm of church music, did represent a break with tradition and point the way to the hymnology of such early nineteenth-century composers as Lowell Mason and Thomas Hastings. New England throughout the entire Colonial period was negligent in the development of drama and opera, probably because of Puritanic disapproval. But for all such restrictions the gentry of Boston were not wanting in means of entertainment. John Dyer's waxworks exhibited a "lively Representation of Margaret Countess of Harringburg, who had 365 Children at one Birth." Animal shows were allowed, and Benjamin Clements of New York was granted permission to exhibit his performing dog and horse; while a black moose from Cape Sable, a "peripatetic camel," a lion, and a tame bear were at various times on exhibition at Boston taverns.

Boston was the center of Colonial bookselling and indeed was surpassed, even in England, only by London itself. Worthington C. Ford's consideration of the surviving records of early Boston booksellers during the last quarter of the seventeenth century is ample evidence of the early pre-eminence of the Massachusetts capital in the Colonial book trade.[63] Such names as those of Benjamin and John Eliot, Samuel Gerrish, and the Phillips family loom large in the annals of book merchandising in Colonial Boston. The fire of 1711, which swept away Captain Keayne's Town House, took with it all Boston's bookshops save one.[64] But the trade survived the holocaust and emerged with renewed vigor. Book stocks were not composed chiefly of almanacs and religious tracts. Like their later associates, the rental libraries (of which more in chap. v), the booksellers' one objective was to make money. They harbored little zeal for the intellectual and spiritual improvement of society but gave the public what it demanded. Current literature from both England and the Continent came to American shores in a steady and voluminous stream; the wealthy were accumulating private libraries rich in both the classics and the contemporary English writings.[65] Willoughby has graphically portrayed the transition in cultural interests during the Colonial period and has shown that the plays of Shakespeare became popular during the early years of the eighteenth century:

63. Worthington C. Ford, *The Boston Book Market, 1679–1700* (Boston: Club of Odd Volumes, 1917), p. 197.

64. George E. Littlefield, *Early Boston Booksellers, 1642–1711* (Boston: Club of Odd Volumes, 1900), p. 256.

65. T. G. Wright, *Literary Culture in Early New England* (New Haven: Yale University Press, 1920), p. 322. Morison, *The Puritan Pronaos, op. cit., passim.*

The last decades of the seventeenth century saw even staid New England succumbing to the charm of worldly frivolity. By 1681 a dancing master had set himself up in Boston, and the invoices of books imported from 1682 to 1684 include not only Dekker's *The Gentle Craft*, and Marlowe's *Doctor Faustus*, such picaresque novels as Kirkman's *The English Rogue*, but even such ribald works as the Earl of Rochester's *Poems*, and Duprat's *Venus in a Cloister*. At the end of one of the book lists is even the ominous entry—"4 packs cards." Indeed among the books of New England some seem singularly unpuritanical, and no doubt some of the readers might be described by the same adjective.[66]

The works of the French philosophers Montesquieu, Voltaire, Rousseau, and the Encyclopedists, as well as the latest scientific and historical treatises from Great Britain, were purchased by the colonists with promptness at prices that were generally reasonable. Early printers heavily buttressed their own publications with stocks of importations. So prosperous had the enterprise become that in 1724 the Boston booksellers formed an early trade association to establish prices and formulate regulations for the conduct of their business. In the year 1720 Daniel Neal testified to the leadership of Boston among the book marts of the Western Hemisphere, when he said:

> Exchange is surrounded by Booksellers' Shops, which have a good trade; there are five Printing Presses in *Boston*, which are generally full of Work, by which it appears that Humanity and the Knowledge of Letters flourish more here than in all the other *English* Plantations put together; for in the City of *New York* there is but one little Bookseller's Shop, and in the Plantations of *Virginia, Maryland, Carolina, Barbadoes*, and the Islands, none at all.[67]

Over a century had elapsed since Stephen Daye allegedly first pulled the *Freeman's Oath* and William Pierce's *Almanack* from his press at Cambridge, and during the succeeding years Massachusetts had become a publishing as well as a bookselling center. Samuel Green and his descendants made printing their family craft and established presses in Massachusetts and Connecticut and, in the South, Maryland and Virginia. In 1704 came the first issue of the Boston *News-Letter*, a small four-page, two-column

66. E. E. Willoughby, "The Reading of Shakespeare in Colonial America," *Bibliographical Society of America, Papers*, XXXI (1937), 49–50.

67. Daniel Neal, *History of New England* (London: Clark, Ford & Cruttenden, 1720), II, 587. Cf. Benjamin Franklin, *Works*, ed. John Bigelow (New York: Putnam, 1904), I, 167–68. Austin B. Keep, *History of the New York Society Library, with an Introductory Chapter on Libraries in Colonial New York, 1698–1778* (New York: DeVinne, 1908), p. 101.

sheet, the first long-lived newspaper published in the Colonies. At the beginning of the eighteenth century Governor Saltonstall advocated the appointment of a resident printer for Connecticut, and Thomas Short began printing in New London in 1709. Short's death in 1712 brought to the establishment Timothy Green, and thus began in Connecticut the family tradition that included the establishment of presses in New London, New Haven, Hartford, and other Connecticut towns. There appeared in the same colony its first newspaper when in 1755 James Parker began at New Haven the *Connecticut Gazette*. During these years the atmosphere in Boston had grown somewhat less congenial to the untrammeled press, and the authorities were attempting to regulate the press in the same way it was being done in England at that time. In 1727 James Franklin, who had fled from Boston even as his brother had done before him, opened a printshop in Newport, Rhode Island, and in 1756 Daniel Fowle turned his back on the Boston courts and set up New Hampshire's first press at Portsmouth.

Although journalism, in the modern sense, was still in its infancy, its cultural significance for Colonial America is not to be minimized. If its range was narrow, at least it was broader and freer than either the pulpit or the classroom. Its vitality could not be suppressed by Colonial authorities. James Franklin's *New England Courant*, established in 1721 and supported by the "Hell-Fire Club," poured ridicule in the manner of Addison and Steele upon the great and the good of Boston. Only a few years later the first contest in America over the freedom of the press opened in New York with the arrest of Peter Zenger.

The leadership of the New England region in Colonial publishing has been graphically presented by Arthur Berthold in an unpublished investigation into the influence of contemporary cultural forces upon printing in the American Colonies. Though this study, from which Table 2 has been taken, was completed before the work of the *American Imprints Inventory* brought to light many previously unlisted items, it is believed that the findings of that survey have not invalidated Berthold's conclusions as to the relative importance of the three regions as regards publishing activity.

The importance of New England in Colonial bookselling and publishing activities arose from a number of related factors: The homogeneity of the population, the growth of important urban centers, a carrying trade that made Boston a Colonial maritime center, and a cash economy that brought money which could be spent in local stores all encouraged the publishing and sale of books. There is no direct information on the extent of literacy in the Colonies, but there is abundant correlative evidence to indicate that the proportion of the public able to read and write was

TABLE 2*

AVERAGE NUMBER OF YEARLY IMPRINTS FOR NEW ENGLAND,
MIDDLE COLONIES, AND SOUTHERN COLONIES, 1639–1763

Section of Country	Years of Printing	Total Output	Imprints per Year	Per Cent
New England.....	125	5,360	42.88	61.2
Middle colonies....	79	3,149	39.86	35.9
Southern colonies..	38	251	6.07	2.9
Total........	....	8,760	....	100.0

* Arthur Berthold, "American Colonial Printing as Determined by Contemporary Cultural Forces, 1639–1763" (unpublished M.A. thesis, Graduate Library School, University of Chicago, 1934), chap. ii, "Factors Determining the Spread and Activity of the Press." (Percentages mine.)

very large. The school had become intrenched in the Colonial folkways, and in countless homes patient mothers and fathers pored with their children over crude primers and spelling-books.

An interesting, but little investigated, development in the new culture was the rise of the tavern as a rendezvous for public discussion and the emergence of the intellectual importance of the social club, both directly imported from England, where they had gained even greater prominence. In the urban centers men were uniting in a variety of voluntary associations for all manner of purposes: to discuss the progress of science, to argue theology or politics, to write essays, to publish pamphlets or periodicals, even to fight fires or merely, as Franklin said, to gain "rest from their wives." The Philosophical Society of Newport has already been considered in these pages. Boston had a Physical Club and the "Club at Withereds." Freemasonry was likewise being transplanted from England, for it was in 1733 that Henry Price of

London founded at Boston the first Masonic lodge in the Colonies. The club as a tangible expression of man's gregariousness contributed much to the cultural development of early America, and not a few library collections were formed by just such voluntary associations. The Redwood Library of Newport was directly related to the Philosophical Society of that same place. The emergence of the Philadelphia Library Company from Franklin's Junto is a familiar historic fact. At Salem, Massachusetts, the Social Library, established in 1760, grew directly from the Social Evening Club, established ten years before, which met at Mrs. Pratt's "Ship Tavern."[68] Such early gatherings of townsfolk seeking social intercourse and mutual enlightenment profoundly contributed to the establishment of association libraries.

To picture the cultural life of the eighteenth century from the gaiety of the social gatherings, the dignified homes of the wealthy merchants, the graceful beauty of their furniture, the books found in their personal libraries, may lead one to forget that many of these cultural influences were absorbed at the "top" of the social order and percolated downward but slowly. Though inventories of estates have been found to be filled with book titles, it must be remembered that such cultural remains are not a valid sample of the entirety of provincial life but are heavily weighted on the side of wealth and aristocracy. Though social libraries were becoming increasingly prominent, their presence does not mean that book starvation was keenly felt by the mass of the people. To say that illiteracy was surprisingly low is not to prove that book reading was therefore unusually high.

But slowly and resolutely New England was laying the foundation for a later cultural development that would give to American life a new richness and depth. Parrington has warned against hasty dismissal of the Colonial period as unworthy of serious examination:

The colonial period is meager and lean only to those whose "disedged appetites" find no savor in old-fashioned beef and puddings. The seventeenth century in America as well as in England was a *saeculum theologicum*, and the eighteenth century a *saeculum politicum*. No other path leads so directly and intimately into the heart of those old days as the thorny path of their theological and politi-

68. Harriet S. Tapley, *Salem Imprints, 1768–1825: A History of the First Fifty Years of Printing in Salem, Massachusetts* . . . (Salem: Essex Institute, 1927), p. 220.

cal controversies. . . . The foundations of a later America were laid in vigorous polemics, and the rough stone was plentifully mortared with idealism . . . to learn that the promise of the future has lain always in the keeping of liberal minds that were never discouraged from their dreams, is scarcely a profitless undertaking, nor without meaning to those who like Merlin pursue the light of their hopes where it flickers above the treacherous marshlands.[69]

The colonists themselves had no illusions, they knew very well what they were about: "No thing new and extraordinary in literature from this part of the world is to be expected," wrote Cadwallader Colden, "but as we are improving this wilderness and have in some measure in some places given it the appearance of cultivated grounds in Europe, so we make some small attempts for improvement in learning."[70]

The Growing Importance of the Social Library

In the increasingly complex cultural pattern the formation of the quasi-public social libraries was a distinct and important thread. Like the culture that supported it, the library was contingent upon the prosperity of the prevailing economic system, the means by which a livelihood was secured, the development of patronage, the amount of leisure, and the concentration of population. But the relationship between the prevailing culture and the spread of the library was reciprocal. If libraries derived their sustenance from the cultural milieu, so also they contributed to the widening and deepening of the stream of life upon which they were borne.

Between the founding of the Book-Company of Durham in 1733 and that of the Redwood Library in 1747, no less than seven such institutions were formed,[71] and an equal number appeared in the decade of the 1750's. In the year that the Redwood Library was being erected on the land given by Henry Collins, a lottery was set up in Portsmouth, New Hampshire, to raise funds for the

69. Vernon L. Parrington, *Main Currents in American Thought* (New York: Harcourt, Brace, 1927), I, "The Colonial Mind," vi–vii.

70. Quoted in Michael Kraus, *Intercolonial Aspects of American Culture* (New York: Columbia University Press, 1928), p. 126.

71. In 1737, Library of Guilford, Saybrook, Killingly, and Lyme, Conn.; 1739, Philogrammatican Library Company of Lebanon, Conn.; 1739, United English Library of Pomfret, Conn.; 1743, Ecclesiastical Library of Newport, R.I.; 1745, United English Library of Woodstock and Killingly, Conn.; 1745, First Society Library of Milford, Conn.; and 1747, Church Library of Yarmouth, Me.

establishment of a social library there, and the citizens of that town authorized the Portsmouth selectmen to purchase one hundred and twenty-five lottery tickets at public expense to encourage the project.[72] In 1751 the towns of Kittery and York, Maine, united to form their "Revolving Library," which altered between the towns and was customarily kept at the homes of the ministers.[73] These were followed by the Newington (Connecticut) Book Company in 1752;[74] the Providence (Rhode Island) Library Company in 1753, which united with the Providence Athenaeum in 1836;[75] the West Hartford (Connecticut) Book Society in the same year;[76] and in 1758 two libraries in Boston, the Prince Library and the New England Library, both arising from bequests of Thomas Prince.[77] The decade of the sixties was even more productive of social libraries; eleven such institutions were established during that decennial period.[78] Clearly, the social library was becoming firmly established in provincial culture. The colonists were discovering that, as an organizational form, it could be made to proceed with an efficiency and directness that was not inherent in the nature of the earliest town collections. The members of the library societies were not content placidly to await the post-mortem gift of a fellow-citizen. They knew that

72. Nathaniel Adams, *Annals of Portsmouth* (Portsmouth: The author, 1825), pp. 189–90, 286.

73. Horace E. Scudder, "Public Libraries a Hundred Years Ago," in U.S. Office of Education, *Public Libraries in the U.S.* (Washington: Government Printing Office, 1876), p. 20.

74. Connecticut Writer's Program, "Inventory of Town Archives in Newington, 1940," p. 18 (mimeographed).

75. Grace F. Leonard and W. Chesley Worthington, *The Providence Athenaeum: A Brief History, 1753–1939* (Providence: Printed for the Athenaeum, 1940), p. 60.

76. Florence Crofut, *Guide to the History of Connecticut* (New Haven: Yale University Press, 1938), I, 340.

77. Justin Winsor, *Memorial History of Boston* . . . (Boston: J. R. Osgood, 1880–81), IV, 280–81. Carl L. Cannon, *American Book Collectors and Collecting* (New York: Wilson, 1941), chap. i, "Thomas Prince."

78. In 1760, Social Library of Salem, Mass.; *ca.* 1760, Social Library of North Guilford, Conn.; 1761, Associate Library, Milford, Conn.; 1761, North Preston Parish Library, Griswold, Conn.; 1763, Social Library, Leominster, Mass.; 1765, Library Company, Middletown, Conn.; 1765, Library Society, Portland, Me.; *ca.* 1765, Association Library, Plainville, Conn.; 1766, Social Library, Canton, Mass.; 1768, Social Library, Norwich, Conn.; and 1768, United Lyon Library, Woodstock, Conn.

they wanted books, and they proceeded to get them. Compro-
mises among the membership there undoubtedly were, and probably a certain amount of submission to the dictates of contemporary mores as to what the well-informed young gentleman
should read; but by and large it may be assumed that the collections represented a relatively high degree of freedom of choice.
Writes Douglas Waples:

> Many libraries were established by groups of townsfolk to economize the
> expense and trouble of obtaining what they all wanted to read. Libraries of this
> sort were highly efficient. They approximated the most efficient sort of library
> there is, namely, the personal library of a scholar who adds only the books he
> needs in his special field.[79]

So important is the social library in the history of the American
public library that its genesis as an organizational form, its development during the century that followed, the nature of the interests that promoted its growth, the reasons for its general success,
the character of its book collections, and its relation to a true
public library movement all merit detailed consideration.

79. Douglas Waples, "People and Libraries," in C. B. Joeckel (ed.), *Current Issues
in Library Administration* (Chicago: University of Chicago Press, 1939), p. 357.

CHAPTER III

THE SOCIAL LIBRARY. I: ORIGINS, FORM, AND ECONOMIC BACKGROUNDS

THE movement for the formation of social libraries, begun in the fourth decade of the eighteenth century, gathered increasing momentum to the eve of the Revolutionary War. By 1775 each of the present New England states[1] had at least one such institution (see Table 3), while in Connecticut these libraries evinced a particularly vigorous growth. Clearly, by the end of the Colonial period the social library had exhibited a vitality that promised survival where earlier "public" library forms had either failed or met with indifferent success. For more than a century after Elihu Chauncey and his companions first met together as the Book-Company of Durham, Connecticut, the social library, structurally modified from time to time to meet new conditions, by the superiority of numbers alone dominated American librarianship. Accordingly, any treatment of the early New England libraries must consider in some detail the origins of the social library, the institutional form which it assumed, its growth and decline, and the economic influences upon it.

Origins of the Social Library

Unfortunately, no record has survived to tell of the first social library or even of the earliest examples. But it was not the invention of Benjamin Franklin, nor was it even an American innovation. Probably the idea of the social library came from a number of different sources, and among these the influence of England was undoubtedly strong.

1. For the sake of clarity the present boundaries of the six New England states have been retained throughout the study. Vermont was not admitted to the Union until 1791, and Maine not until 1820.

England was familiar with the social library before any were established in Colonial America, for there were book clubs in England as early as the third decade of the eightᵥenth century, if not before. On August 5, 1725, Philip Doddridge, nonconformist minister and author of hymns, wrote from Burton-on-Tyne to his brother-in-law, the Rev. John Nettleton:

> I have besides a watch, bought twenty pounds worth of books within these two years, most of them cheap enough; and it is my happiness to be a member of a society in which, for little more than a crown a year, I have the reading of all that are purchased by the common stock, amounting to sixteen pounds yearly. They are generally some of the most entertaining and useful works that are published.[2]

TABLE 3

SOCIAL LIBRARIES IN NEW ENGLAND BY DATE OF
ESTABLISHMENT, 1731-80

	1731–40	1741–50	1751–60	1761–70	1771–80	Total
Conn.	4	2	3	8	9	26
Mass.			1	4	11	16
R.I.		2	1		1	4
Me.		1	1	1		3
N.H.		1				1
Vt.					1	1
Total	4	6	6	13	22	51

The casual tone of this statement is significant. Doddridge was revealing to his brother-in-law no great piece of news concerning the invention of the book club; in fact his letters make no further reference to the organization. He was merely submitting as evidence of his thrift the relative cheapness of the books he had purchased and his savings through membership in a book society. It is also known that a Gentlemen's Society was founded in Spalding in 1710, the rules of which required that members on their admission "present some valuable book to the Society"[3] and that they pay twelve shillings a year besides one shilling at each meeting. "By this means they formed a valuable library,"[4] which

2. Philip Doddridge, *Correspondence and Diary*, ed. John Doddridge Humphreys (London: Colburn & Bentley, 1829), II, 57.

3. John Nichols, *Literary Anecdotes of the Eighteenth Century* . . . (London: Nichols, Son & Bentley, 1812), VI, 9.

4. *Ibid.*

in 1743 was distributed to other, and more permanent, institutions.[5] From these examples it would seem reasonable to assume that such book clubs, which were, of course, a variant form of the social library, were not uncommon in England in 1725.

It was just at this time that Benjamin Franklin was in London, where, as a journeyman printer and something of a leader among the men employed at the establishment of James Watts in Wild's Court, he likely learned of the social club as an instrument of book distribution.[6] While apprenticed to his brother James, he was familiar with a small collection of reference books which was maintained at the office of the *New England Courant* for the benefit of its contributors and, presumably, for any others who might wish to consult it, since the titles were made known to the reading public in the pages of the *Courant*.[7] Thus, at an early age, Franklin became familiar with the need for extending the meager book resources of the community—there being "not a good bookseller's shop in any of the colonies southward of Boston."[8] But Franklin, who was as free as anyone from illusions of inferiority, never claimed to have invented the social library form; he boasted only that the library of the Junto was "the mother of all North American subscription libraries,"[9] and even this is excessive. That the Philadelphia Library Company antedates all other such institutions in what is now the United States may be accepted as a proved historic fact, but to say that this library was in any way responsible for those Connecticut associations that followed it so closely is to stretch credibility beyond reasonable limits. Even when one admits that news, because of the steadily improving mediums of inter-Colonial communication, spread more rapidly than is now frequently supposed, it must be remembered that in 1730 there was little magic in the name Franklin and that Benjamin was at that time only an obscure printer—a youth less than

5. See also Frank Beckwith, "The Eighteenth-Century Proprietary Library in England," *Journal of Documentation*, III, No. 2 (September, 1947), 83.

6. His statement that "circulating libraries were not then in use" in England is obviously incorrect and understandably so since the observation was made fifty years later (see Benjamin Franklin, *Autobiography* [New York: Random House, 1932], p. 47).

7. *New England Courant*, June 25–July 2, 1722.

8. *Op. cit.*, p. 83.　　　　　9. *Ibid.*, p. 75.

twenty-five years of age who had become "a little obnoxious" to the governing party of Boston and had taken to his heels that he might practice his chosen trade unmolested. It is improbable that this young man was the only one in the Colonies to think of adapting the joint-stock principle to the formation of a book club.[10]

In October, 1739, Isaac Watts dispatched from London a gift of fourteen books intended for the newly formed Philogrammatican Library of Lebanon, Connecticut.[11] In a letter announcing the dispatch of the gift Watts wrote:

> There is a library set up at Salisbury or Sarum by Mr. Fancourt, a Dissenting minister there, which has been now maintained several years and is of great advantage to the country ministers and the gentlemen around about, and happening to have the rules of that library by me I take the freedom to send them to you, to see if there be anything in them that may assist the gentlemen in Connecticut towards such a useful design.[12]

The extent to which the library at Salisbury, England, influenced the Philogrammatican at Lebanon, Connecticut, is not known, but at least the incident reveals the ease with which news of library developments in England was received by those interested in library formation in the Colonies.

The Institutional Form

Generically and reduced to its simplest constituent elements, the social library was nothing more than a voluntary association of individuals who had contributed money toward a common fund to be used for the purchase of books. Though every member had the right to use the books of the organization, title to all was retained by the group. Book acquisition might proceed by large purchases or through gradual accumulation and could therefore be financed either by a considerable investment or by moderate

10. Perhaps Franklin never even heard of the social libraries that were formed in Connecticut in the 1730's; but in after years, when such associations became common and the name of Franklin was given to many of them, he really did come to believe that the Junto had served as a model for them all.

11. Anne S. Pratt, *Isaac Watts' Gift of Books to Yale College* (New Haven: Yale University Library, 1938), pp. 3–4.

12. Letter published in *Massachusetts Historical Society, Proceedings*, 2d ser., IX (1894–95), 368. The letter was found among the papers of Dr. Colman and bears the notation that the recipient transmitted the contents of the letter to Solomon Williams at Lebanon, Conn., in January, 1740 (see Thomas Milner, *Life, Times, and Correspondence of the Rev. Dr. Watts* [London: Richardson, 1834], p. 653).

annual fees received from the members. Social libraries could be either informal or legal. Legalization was usually achieved by an act of incorporation, but in at least one instance, that of the Philogrammatican Library of Lebanon, Connecticut, it was by contract. In actual practice this basic pattern was subject to adaptation and variation which resulted in the development of several types. These have been reduced to a simple classification that is as satisfactory as any likely to be devised.[13] Two principal groups have been distinguished: (a) proprietary and (b) subscription (or association) libraries.[14] The proprietary libraries were common-law partnerships; based on the joint-stock principle, they involved ownership of shares in the property of the group. Such shares were transferable by sale, gift, or bequest. Only by a valid charter could the proprietary library change its legal nature. The subscription library, on the other hand, was from the first a common-law corporation. Its annual fees bought its services, not title to the property. But even in this simple division the lines of demarcation were not always clear and there was much blending of types. It early became the practice of proprietary libraries to permit nonproprietor use of books by those annually paying a stipulated fee,[15] while the proprietors were themselves frequently subject to annual assessments or "taxes" on their shares of stock which, if not paid, resulted in forfeiture of library privileges.

13. Carleton B. Joeckel, *Government of the American Public Library* (Chicago: University of Chicago Press, 1935), pp. 2–8. Cf. Charles K. Bolton, *Proprietary and Subscription Libraries* (Chicago: American Library Association, 1917), 10 pp.; reprinted from *Manual of Library Economy* (Chicago: American Library Association, n.d.), chap. v. Horace E. Scudder, "Public Libraries . . . 1876 Report," in U.S. Bureau of Education, *Public Libraries in the United States* . . . (Washington: Government Printing Office, 1876), pp. 1–37.

14. The terminology has never been standardized. In the beginning the terms were used with little discrimination, and the few contemporary writers on the subject have made no particular effort to define them. Joeckel is followed closely here because he is the only one who, in print, has seriously considered the matter and because it is time that there be definitions that are generally accepted. It is interesting to note that the *Oxford English Dictionary* does not include the term "social library" though other compounds with "social" are listed.

15. This is the practice today at the Boston Athenaeum, the Redwood Library, and many other such associations. It is, of course, a device for broadening the economic base of the organization while at the same time extending the benefits of the library to a larger portion of the community.

Though subscription libraries were organized to appeal to a general clientele, there was a strong tendency for them to break down into subordinate groups according to a particular kind of user or a special reading interest. In this manner there originated in the nineteenth century the mercantile and apprentices' libraries, the collections belonging to such special organizations as the Y.M.C.A. and the numerous young men's institutes, and the book clubs for "ladies." The subscription libraries, both by virtue of their organization and the general youth of their membership, were consciously democratic.

The proprietary library, in general, appealed to a somewhat wealthier patron than did the subscription library. Shares sold at prices usually well above the costs of subscription memberships. It might have been less democratic, too, since the voting strength of the proprietor was not infrequently proportionate to the number of shares held. Of the Social Library of Salem, Massachusetts, formed in 1760, it has been said that the list of members was a "veritable Social Register of Salem during the fifty years of the library's existence."[16]

If the members of these social libraries wished to co-operate to the fullest extent, it became necessary to secure an act of incorporation. By the terms of this instrument the joint enterprise of individuals ceased to be a personal partnership and became itself a fictitious legal person, "able to sue and be sued." The Colonial and, later, the state governments were quite ready to recognize the social libraries, give them legal status, and grant them the power to control and regulate their affairs. As far as is known to the writer, the Redwood Library Company of Newport was the first New England group to receive such rights from a Colonial governing body.[17] On August 24, 1747, the governor of the English Colony of Rhode Island and Providence Plantation, at the direction of the Colonial Assembly, affixed his signature to the charter that made of the Redwood Library Company "a body

16. Harriet S. Tapley, *Salem Imprints, 1768–1825: A History of the First Fifty Years of Printing in Salem, Massachusetts* . . . (Salem: Essex Institute, 1927), p. 245.

17. It was not the first in the country, however; Franklin's Library Company of Philadelphia was incorporated March 24, 1742 (see Austin K. Gray, *Benjamin Franklin's Library: A Short Account of the Library Company of Philadelphia, 1731–1931* [New York: Macmillan, 1937], p. 17).

politic and corporate to subsist at all times for ever hereafter in deed and name."[18] As a legal instrument the charter may be said to consist of four parts: First, the recognition of Redwood's social vision in encouraging the formation of a "Public Library" by the generosity of his gift and the desire of the new company to propagate "virtue, knowledge, and useful learning"; second, the concurrence of the Assembly in this laudable design and its wish to "give all assistance and encouragement which it justly merits"; third, the decree proper, making of the company a true corporation; fourth, the delineation of the corporate powers. These were presented with a high degree of specificity. To the new corporation was granted the right to

1. Have the privilege of perpetual succession
2. Purchase, hold, and dispose of real and personal property
3. Receive gifts, bequests, and donations of real or personal property, to be held in fee simple or for specified periods of time
4. Sue or be sued, plead or be impleaded
5. Hold a common seal, that may be changed or altered at the discretion of the company
6. Hold meetings at designated intervals
7. Elect officers and a board of control
8. Formulate and enforce bylaws and regulations that would be binding upon the membership.

Because of the common-law concept of corporations, the provisions of the Redwood charter were typical of the hundreds of others that were to follow. First granted by the Colonial governors and assemblies, they were, after the establishment of the Republic, conferred by the legislatures of the several states. The form and phrasing became stereotyped, but not because of any slavish following of library precedent. The form itself was not an indigenous outgrowth of the library function; rather it was a direct borrowing from the corporation charter in general, with only such verbal changes as were necessary to the needs of a book-collecting enterprise. The proprietary library was first of all a corporation—a corporation established not to make money for the proprietors but to assemble books for their use.

That these acts of incorporation were much more than gestures

18. *Rhode Island Colony Records, 1746–1757* (Providence: A. C. Green, 1856–65), p. 79.

of legal recognition is apparent from the importance attached to them. Fundamentally, the limited liability resulting from the process of incorporation enabled the membership to work together as individuals without surrendering any of their personal liberties. Those persons who had united for the purpose of assembling book collections were all aware of the value of corporate power in controlling the conduct of the membership and in preserving the inviolability of their property. In such terms the Social Library of Lunenburg petitioned the Massachusetts General Court:

To the Honorable Senate and House of Representatives
of the Commonwealth of Massachusetts.

HUMBLY SHEW:

Your Petitioners, the Proprietors of the Lunenburg Social Library, that in January 1792 they formed themselves into a society, established a code of by-laws suitable for their due regulation, raised money, and purchased a reputable library; that for several years the laws were respected, the Library increased, & the Society flourished; But that of late certain Members have proved refractory; & disregarding their regulations, they have witheld or detained both money & Books belonging to the Society, whereby the Society has been greatly discommoded and are in danger of crumbling to pieces.

And as the great utility of social libraries, in diffusing useful knowledge among the People, is generally acknowledged; and your Petitioners, from a full conviction that the most effectual Way to render them permanent would be to put them under the protection of Law, beg leave to solicit the Aid of your fostering Hand, & Pray for an Act of Incorporation, with Powers and Privileges calculated to embrace the benevolent objects of such associations for general improvement in Knowledge and the Public Good.

By order & in behalf of the Society

LUNENBURG, January 8, 1798   JOSIAH STEARNS
WM. CUNNINGHAM }*Committee*[19]
ABRAHAM HASKELL

Similarly, the Providence Library Company, formed in 1753, discovered that over a period of years many books disappeared from their collections. Consequently, the state legislative assembly was petitioned for an act of incorporation, giving the company authority to make and enforce regulations governing the use of the books. The act was granted in October, 1798.[20]

When the social libraries became increasingly numerous, these

19. From original petition in the Massachusetts State Archives.
20. Records of the company, now in the Providence Athenaeum.

individual acts of incorporation for specific institutions were supplemented by general permissive legislation empowering the officers of such libraries to formulate and enforce appropriate regulations for the management of their collections. The first such legislation was passed by the New York State legislature on April 1, 1796,[21] but less than two years later, on March 3, 1798, the Massachusetts General Court enacted its law "to Enable the Proprietors of Social Libraries to Manage the Same."[22] Vermont followed with similar legislation in 1800, Connecticut in 1818, Maine in 1821, New Hampshire in 1831, and Rhode Island in 1839.[23]

Examined chronologically, these seven statutes reveal a decided trend from the specific to the general. The New York law is long, precise, and exacting in its requirements. By its terms an incorporated social library could be composed of no fewer than twenty persons who had signified their desires in writing and had subscribed "on the whole" not less than forty pounds. The time of meeting, the number of trustees, and the manner of elections were definitely fixed. To the trustees was given entire authority over the library, the management of its affairs, the designation of officers, and the formulation of bylaws. To the membership remained only the privilege of electing this governing board, and in such elections the franchise was directly proportionate to the number of shares of stock held. Further, the social libraries were forbidden to hold real or personal property in excess of "the

21. An Act To Incorporate Such Persons as May Officiate for the Purpose of Procuring and Erecting Public Libraries in This State (19th sess. [1796], chap. 43).

22. *Acts and Laws*, 1798, chap. 45, pp. 200–201. Revised March 8, 1806. The petition of the Lunenburg Social Library quoted above was instrumental in advancing this general act.

23. Vermont, *Acts and Laws*, October, 1800, pp. 12–15. Connecticut, *Public Statute Laws*, October sess., 1818, Book II, pp. 328–29. Maine, *Laws*, Vol. II (1821), chap. 141, pp. 617–20. New Hampshire, *Laws*, June sess., 1831, chap. 36, p. 30. Rhode Island, *Acts and Resolves*, January, 1839, "An Act To Revise and Amend the Several Acts Relating to the Public Schools." Sec. 25, p. 59, relates to the formation of social libraries.

The chronological order in which the states passed these acts bears slight relation to their relative library development. Though Connecticut had an early and rich social library growth, it was the third New England state to pass general permissive legislation encouraging such libraries.

annual value of $500," at any one time, "exclusive of the books and the annual payments directed to be made by the members of the corporation." Finally, the act summarized in detail the rights and privileges of corporate status.

The Massachusetts law followed a similar pattern, though it revealed greater leniency in permitting the individual association to formulate its own administrative design. Corporate status was granted to those organizations having not fewer than seven members, though holdings of property were still limited to $500,[24] and franchise was still based upon the number of shares held. The Vermont law broke sharply with precedent, was relatively brief, free from detail, and general in its requirements. It limited membership to no minimum number and placed no upper limit upon property holdings. The Connecticut law was even more general, specifying only that a copy of the bylaws of each social library must be filed with the secretary of state.

The Maine law was a direct descendant of that of Massachusetts and indeed incorporated certain portions of the older legislation. It did add, however, provisions for the formation of law and military libraries.[25] In the case of New Hampshire the trend toward generality was resumed, and in the laws of Rhode Island the social library received only brief treatment in but one section of a larger act codifying the general legislation for the public school system.

The enactment of these seven statutes spanned a period of almost half a century—fifty years in which the corporate form as an instrument of enterprise and the social library as one segment of the larger corporate pattern were becoming more prevalent in American society. As public familiarity with both steadily increased, there was a corresponding decrease in the need for spe-

24. When the act of 1798 was revised by the passage of a new act on March 8, 1806, this was raised to $5,000, and the treasurer of the society was required to "give bond with sufficient surety or sureties faithfully to account for all monies he may receive by virtue of this Act" (Massachusetts, *Acts and Laws*, March 8, 1806).

25. The Massachusetts law of 1806 was amended February 24, 1807, to provide for military library societies permissible of establishment by "seven or more persons who are Officers in any Division of the Militia of the Commonwealth" (Massachusetts, *Acts and Laws*, February 24, 1807).

cific details in the regulatory legislation. The text of these laws reveals the simultaneous evolution that characterized the development of both the corporation and the social library during the closing years of the eighteenth century and the first decades of the century that followed. The crystallization of the social library pattern is important, but even more significant is the factual relationship between the emerging library and the expanding corporation.

Genesis of the Form

In the beginning, corporate existence was not a matter of precise definition; it arose in response to immediate circumstances and was molded and modified according to economic, geographic, and social environment. The corporation was an instrument for the accomplishment of a specific purpose; and since that purpose was paramount in the minds of the colonists, they set up a corporate mechanism which their experience, and intelligence, indicated as most likely to give effect to their efforts and aspirations. Until 1684 Massachusetts was itself a corporation deriving authority from a crown charter, and the New England town a corporation which, from the earliest period, "carried on the major powers that are associated with corporate capacity."[26] In law, the charters were little more than medieval grants had been; in fact, they were free constitutions regulating the lives of increasing thousands of British subjects.

Though the corporation as an institutional form gave evidence of a ready adaptability to the needs of Colonial enterprise, it was by no means an American invention. As W. R. Scott has shown, by the time this continent was discovered, the corporation had attained a definite status in the social constitution of England.[27] The first century of contact between Europe and the New World was a period of steady growth in the number of uses made of the corporate form. A variety of commercial and industrial undertakings—fishing, whaling, land speculation, trade with the Indians, banking, insurance, and manufacturing—were established as corporations. Of the whaling industry at Martha's Vineyard,

26. John F. Sly, *Town Government in Massachusetts, 1620–1930* (Cambridge: Harvard University Press, 1930), p. 70.

27. William Robert Scott, *The Constitution and Finance of English, Scottish, and Irish Joint Stock Companies* (3 vols.; Cambridge: University Press, 1910–12).

Crèvecœur wrote: "They have no wages; each draws a certain established share in partnership with the proprietor of the vessel; by which economy they are all proportionately concerned in the success of the enterprise, and all equally alert and vigilant."[28]

Not only the library but many other early private corporations were created to perform public functions that later became the proper province of governmental agencies. As the public library of the nineteenth century was preceded by, and to an important degree actually emerged from, the corporate social library, so many municipal functions and responsibilities were in the beginning executed by associations of private individuals operating under special charters. The maintenance of an adequate water supply, the construction of municipal piers, the erecting of bridges, the building and repairing of roads, the improving of the navigability of streams and small rivers, the construction of locks and canals, and the fighting of fires all were at one time or another the objectives of voluntary associations organized as corporations by groups of individuals. In this general tendency for local government to assume certain responsibilities previously accepted by private organizations, the library was one specific example.

The corporate form was not limited to economic endeavor and the provision of public utilities. Among the oldest uses of the corporation were those for religious, charitable, and educational undertakings. In Connecticut religious "societies" were definitely authorized by act of the Assembly, and to them were granted certain privileges of unified action. In Rhode Island charters were awarded to the ministers, churchwardens, vestry, and congregations of specified churches in Providence and Newport. Massachusetts, by act of the General Court passed in 1755, provided that the deacons and other governing bodies of Protestant churches should be "deemed so far bodies corporate as to take in succession all grants and donations, whether real or personal, made either to their several churches, the poor of their churches, or to them and their successors."[29]

28. J. Hector St. John Crèvecœur, *Letters from an American Farmer* (New York: Fox Duffield, 1904), I, 169, Letter 6.
29. Massachusetts, *Provisional Acts*, III, 778, 818.

Corporations for the promotion of religious ends were likewise represented by the missionary societies and church charity associations. Similarly, there were corporations partly or completely independent of church control formed for charitable and educational purposes, and not always were the lines of demarcation among the three areas sharp or well defined. The church was frequently charged with the administration of charity. Likewise, being vitally concerned in the education of its ministry, it actively participated in the encouragement of schools. Quite naturally there resulted a frequent blending of function in the promotion of schools for the poor under the direct supervision of the church. Other eleemosynary associations existed as autonomous units, and the great Colonial colleges such as Harvard and Yale held charters in their own right. An adequate historical interpretation of the rise of the social library must avoid a point of view that might separate the library as an institutional form from the totality of contemporary agencies of which it was a part. The social library was a corporation, not because of any inherent virtue in the corporate form as an instrument of book distribution, but because the other social agencies coexistent with the social library were organized in a similar manner.

Not only did the colonists bind themselves in mutual agreement to accomplish certain activities necessary to daily life, but they conceived of government itself as based on and derived from a perpetual civil contract. Burke had rested his interpretation of the English constitution on the legal ground of the common law of contract and had argued that the English people through their legal representatives had entered into a solemn contract, binding "themselves, their heirs, and posterities forever," to certain express terms.

The Puritan not only entered into contracts with his neighbor for economic, social, and political ends but also made covenants with his God. To the Calvinist all life was governed and controlled by these legal concepts. Cotton Mather saw every "Citie . . . united by some Covenant among themselves, the Citizens . . . received into *jus Civitatis*, or right of Citie privileges, by some Covenant or Oath."[30] Likewise, to John Cotton it was "evident by the light of nature, that all civill Relations are founded in Covenant."[31]

The social library, then, in all its forms involved no legal innovations; both the corporation and the contract had long been used for many and widely varying purposes. The Philogrammatican Library of Lebanon was founded by a covenant between Solomon Williams and his associates, and so occupied were the signatories with the legal precision of their contract that their main objective, to establish a library, became almost incidental.[32] This does not mean, of course, that the outward form was being mistaken for the substance; though it does show that the social library was growing, as social agencies generally grow, by drawing upon available methods of procedure and by the slow, unsteady, but seemingly necessary, process of trial and error. When the colonists felt the urge to combine their efforts for the building of a library that would be available to the entire group, they did not stop to speculate about the opportunity to create a new and radically different medium for the promotion of this end. Rather they did the easy, the natural thing and turned, with justifiable confidence, to forms that were common in the communities about them, measures that had been tested in the mother-country and had grown familiar to all. To these patterns they merely added such modifications as seemed desirable and concerned themselves with principles only to the extent that the main object was thereby advanced.

The very fact of structural diversity in the earlier social libraries testifies to the absence of any slavish following of a single example. The Book-Company of Durham, Connecticut, was based upon the principle of stockownership with specific rights accruing thereto.[33] The Philogrammatican of Lebanon, as has been indicated, was a covenant between one man and the remaining members of the association. The charter of the Redwood Library of Newport displayed the characteristics of the true cor-

---

30. Quoted by Perry Miller, *The New England Mind* (New York: Macmillan, 1939), p. 448.

31. *Ibid.*   32. See Appen. II.   33. Appen. I.

porate form.[34] The social library of Portsmouth, New Hampshire, was based upon the principle of a tontine,[35] supplemented with income derived from a lottery.[36] These early variations soon disappeared as the pattern of the social library became set, and by the end of the Colonial period it had become reasonably standardized. Experience and the evolution of the corporation in other areas of endeavor had contributed to a growing uniformity.

The Expansion of the Social Library

The Revolutionary War and its aftermath of political uncertainty and economic depression were only pauses in the advance of the social library. No new libraries were established in any New England state during the years 1776 and 1777, and only three or four such institutions appeared during the remainder of the decade,[37] but the 1780's produced more new social libraries than the entire previous half-century.[38] The new nation, having successfully survived its initial vicissitudes, was again prepared to focus attention upon cultural undertakings and to resume the establishment of social libraries at the level attained before the interruption by the war.

The year 1790 may be considered a mid-point in the history of the social library in New England. During the preceding half-century the institution passed through an age of experimentation, adaptation, incipient growth, and final recognition as a wholly

34. George C. Mason, *Annals of the Redwood Library, and Athenaeum, Newport, Rhode Island* (Newport: Redwood Library, 1891), pp. 31–33.

35. The tontine is an arrangement whereby the rights and benefits accruing to any individual member of the group revert to the surviving members of the group at his death until at last the whole descends to the final survivor. Because of abuses the tontine was later outlawed.

36. Nathaniel Adams, *Annals of Portsmouth* (Portsmouth: The author, 1825), p. 189.

37. In January, 1778, was formed the Library Company of Royalston, Mass., and on November 5, 1779, a social library at Farmingbury, Wolcott, Conn., was established. At about this same time there was founded the United Library Association at Templeton, Mass., and a social library at Green Farms, Conn., though the exact dates of these last are not known (from Trumbull MSS in Yale University Library; also see L. B. Caswell, *History of the Town of Royalston, Massachusetts* [Royalston: Published by the town, 1917], pp. 106–8; D. Hamilton Hurd, *History of Worcester County, Massachusetts* [Philadelphia: Lewis, 1889], I, 146).

38. Fifty-one libraries between 1731–80; fifty-nine libraries between 1781–90. See Tables 3–4 and Pls. XIV–XV.

satisfactory library form. The fifty years that followed brought to the social library a period of expansion that might be characterized as its "golden age." During the twenty-five years between 1790 and 1815 the social library experienced unprecedented

TABLE 4

DISTRIBUTION OF LIBRARIES, SIX NEW ENGLAND STATES
BY DATE OF ESTABLISHMENT, 1776–1850*

	1776–80	1781–85	1786–90	1791–95	1796–1800	1801–5	1806–10	1811–15
Conn...........	3	9	24	61	29	21	19	14
Mass...........	5	6	15	35	34	20	33	24
R.I.............	......	......	......	3	6	2	6	1
Me.............	......	......	2	4	8	6	4	5
N.H............	......	......	1	18	54	51	23	24
Vt.............	......	......	2	4	10	5	5	3
New England	8	15	44	125	141	105	90	71

	1816–20	1821–25	1826–30	1831–35	1836–40	1841–45	1846–50	Total
Conn...........	14	18	15	9	11	2	4	253
Mass...........	31	30	35	24	23	15	25	355
R.I.............	4	8	6	4	2	2	21	65
Me.............	17	4	5	8	2	8	6	79
N.H............	9	23	27	15	5	8	8	266
Vt.............	2	3	5	3	3	1	......	46
New England	77	86	93	63	46	36	64	1,064

* The term "library" as here applied may be interpreted to mean social library in all its forms. A very few truly public libraries, such as those of Peterborough, N.H., Wayland, Mass., and Boston, Mass., have been included, but their number is so small as to make no real difference. Academic, circulating, private, and school libraries have been excluded.

The data for this and the following tables of this chapter have been taken wherever possible from the surviving records of the individual libraries. In many cases, however, these records have not been preserved, and it has been necessary to rely upon such secondary sources as are available. Reference should also be made to the general statement concerning sources in the Introduction and to the Selected Bibliography.

growth; literally scores of New England towns, especially in Connecticut, Massachusetts, and New Hampshire, organized such book clubs. The editors of the *Massachusetts Register* for 1802 estimated that "though it would . . . require much time and pains to obtain a complete enumeration" of these libraries, "at a random conjecture they now probably amount to one hundred in Massachusetts."[39] Many, as later tabulation will show, were small

39. *Massachusetts Register and United States Calendar* (Boston, 1802), p. 60. This estimate approximates to a surprising degree the totals for the Massachusetts area given in Table 4.

and short lived, but at this time there were also laid the foundations of some of the most important future collections. The Boston
Athenaeum, the American Antiquarian Society, the Massachusetts Historical Society, and the Social Law Library all were begun during these years.

Evidence of the vitality of the social library movement at the
turn of the nineteenth century is to be found not only in the
enactment of general permissive legislation providing for the establishment of such libraries but also in the eagerness with which
local booksellers competed for social library patronage. Such
merchants openly boasted that the titles they stocked were particularly appropriate for the shelves of library societies and vied
with each other in offering substantial discounts for quantity
purchase.[40] "Purchasers for Public, Social, and Private Libraries
are respectfully solicited for their favors; and all orders for Books
to be had in Boston will be promptly answered at the most liberal
discount."[41] Henry Knox, proprietor of the London Book Store in
Boston, added a not too subtle flattery to his offer of special discounts to "Those Gentlemen in the Country who are actuated
with the most genuine Principles of Benevolence in their Exer-
tions to Exterminate Ignorance and Darkness, by the noble
medium of SOCIAL LIBRARIES."[42] But Charles Pierce, bookseller of
Portsmouth, New Hampshire, wasted no idle words of flattery
when he offered a discount policy that would seem to have presented almost unlimited possibilities to ingenious patrons:

G. Pierce is determined to sell all his articles at such prices as that purchasers
cannot better themselves elsewhere. The regular discount to Libraries is 10

40. In 1796 Joseph Nancrede, Boston bookseller, announced: "To country-
Booksellers and shop-keepers, purchasers for Social Libraries, and others who buy
in quantities a considerable abatement will be made from the usual retail prices"
(from title-page of Joseph Nancrede's catalog of books [Boston: Joseph Nancrede,
1796], also carried on the 1798 ed.). E. and S. Larkin, in 1802, and Lincoln and
Edmonds, in 1814, pressed similar offers: ". . . purchasers of Social and Private
Libraries are respectfully requested to favor the publishers of this Catalogue with
their orders, who will engage to furnish them on the most liberal terms; and such
scarce books as are not to be had in town, will be immediately procured, if to be had
in England" (E. & S. Larkin, *Catalogue of Books for Sale* [Boston: Larkin, 1802], p. 2).

41. *Catalogue of Books in the Branches of Divinity, History, Biography, Classics, Poetry,
Miscellanies, &c., for Sale at Lincoln and Edmonds' Theological and Miscellaneous Book-
Store* (53 Cornhill, Boston: Lincoln & Edmonds, 1814), p. 1.

42. *Massachusetts Gazette*, March 31, 1774.

percent, but if any other person in Boston, Newburyport, or Portsmouth, will make 12, he will make 15. And if they make 15 he will make 20 percent, even should he lose by the articles he is determined not to be undersold.

His Books and other articles are nearly all marked by a Boston catalogue, but if higher in any instance than can be purchased elsewhere, he will deduct from said prices. Every favor gratefully acknowledged.

PORTSMOUTH, Aug. 5, 1806.[43]

Quite evidently the increasing popularity of the social library offered to the book-dealers a promising field for exploitation, and the more enterprising were by no means reluctant to encourage the movement by emphatic price reduction.

During the years immediately following 1815 the social library entered another phase. Whereas the twenty-five years between 1790 and 1815 were for the most part a period of vigorous and general expansion, those between 1815 and 1850 were character-ized by less striking growth, a pronounced tendency toward ex-perimental adaptation of the social library form to special pur-poses, and during the closing decade a marked decline. During the early years of the nineteenth century the social library was overwhelmingly a "general" collection, evincing no dominant single interest or purpose on the part of its membership. Indeed, it has largely remained thus throughout its history. But with the appearance of the short-lived lyceum movement, and the growing concern of the workers with vocational subjects, there emerged a strong tendency to develop social libraries, the collections of which were pointed toward some specific reading end. The ex-tent of this diversity is apparent from Table 5.

In a sense these were "special" libraries in the restriction of their collections to some precise area of print or in the limitation of membership to a homogeneous group based on sex, age, or occupational interest. The importance of these special associa-tions is much greater then their numbers would indicate. They were of consequence by virtue of their novelty and the degree to which they revealed a desire to adapt the social library form to differences in reader interest. But, most important of all, these specialized types reveal the great diversity of interests that con-

43. *Catalogue of Books for Sale and Circulation by Charles Pierce at His Brick Book Store, in Daniel-Street, Portsmouth, New Hampshire* . . . (Portsmouth: Printed for Charles Pierce, 1806), p. 105.

tributed to the development of the concept of the public library. Each was within itself the crystallization of a desire, or cluster of desires, that when added to its fellows composed a totality of forces that converged to bring tax support for a truly public library service.

In addition to being a period of experimentation, the twenty years before 1850 were an era of consolidation and replacement. The average expectation of life of the social library was not

TABLE 5

DISTRIBUTION OF SOCIAL LIBRARIES BY TYPE
OF INTEREST, 1733–1850

Type	No.	Type	No.
General	906	Science (including natural history)	4
Mechanics and mechanics' apprentices	30*	Law	3
Juvenile and youth	21*	Masonic lodges	3†
Ladies' libraries	20†	Medical	3
Lyceum libraries	20‡	Military	3
Young men's libraries	16	Periodical clubs	3
Theological	16	Mercantile	2
Historical	14*	Antislavery	1
Agricultural	12*	Fire company	1
Manufacturers and factory workers	6	Music	1
		Total	1,085

* One example before 1800.
† Two examples before 1800; includes sewing-circle libraries.
‡ No examples before 1820.

great. Relatively few survived their founders.[44] Many lapsed into inactivity long before their lives were actually terminated by official decree. As Table 6 shows, a number were absorbed by later institutions, but most slipped quietly into oblivion, leaving only a meager record to tell of their ephemeral existence. Specific data on the duration of life are available for only four hundred and thirteen of almost eleven hundred, but from Table 7 it

44. The social Library Society of Belfast, Me., is an excellent example of an organization built around a single individual, a Mr. Price, who kept the society active as long as he lived in the community. After his departure, however, the library steadily declined and finally became extinct (see Joseph Williamson, *History of Belfast* (Portland: Loring, Short & Harmon, 1877), pp. 319–20. Likewise, the Proprietors' Library Association of Dover, Mass., was largely motivated by the efforts of the Rev. Ralph Sanger, and his departure brought decline and extinction to the organization (see Frank Smith, *A Narrative History of Dover, Massachusetts* [Dover: Published by the town, 1897], pp. 343–45).

is apparent that about half of these existed less than thirty-five years. Further, it is safe to assume that those libraries for which there is no record probably existed for only a very brief period.

TABLE 6

DISTRIBUTION OF SOCIAL LIBRARIES ACCORDING TO
THEIR ULTIMATE DISPOSITION

Disposition	No. of Libraries
Libraries still extant...........................	32
Absorbed by other libraries still extant...........	76
Taken over by town as free public library........	53
Subtotal.....................................	161
Absorbed by libraries later themselves defunct....	73
Sold at auction................................	65
Dissolved and books divided among the membership	75
Destroyed by fire but not revived...............	12
No surviving record of disposition..............	699
Total...................................	1,085

TABLE 7

DISTRIBUTION OF SOCIAL LIBRARIES ACCORDING
TO LENGTH OF LIFE

Duration of Life	No. of Libraries
Still extant or lasted over 100 years.............	60
75–99 years...................................	11
50–74 years...................................	53
40–49 years...................................	53
30–39 years...................................	70
(35 years and up.................... approximately 212)	
20–29 years...................................	62
10–19 years...................................	63
5– 9 years...................................	28
2– 4 years...................................	13
Total...................................	413

In consequence, many towns that could boast of a social library during the decade of the 1790's found themselves in 1830 either without any or with one that was but a ghost. Under the influence of the cultural ferment that swept through New England after the termination of the War of 1812 many new libraries were established, old ones reorganized, or existing institutions merged and the life-cycle begun anew. By 1850 two hundred and fifty-nine New England towns had established more than one library, and though every case did not represent the substitution of a new library for one that was defunct, the proportion is sufficiently great to indicate that such replacement was common. Distribution by states of towns having more than one library is as follows: Massachusetts, eighty-six; Connecticut, seventy-eight; New Hampshire, fifty-six; Maine, eighteen; Rhode Island, sixteen; and Vermont, five; totaling two hundred and fifty-nine.

Above all, the period of 1825–50 was significant for the beginning of a movement that eventually replaced most of the social libraries with municipally owned institutions that were actually public both in support and in patronage. During the years immediately preceding the middle of the century the social library had reached a stationary though not decadent stage. Numerically the number of libraries was great. In 1840 Horace Mann, surveying the library resources of Massachusetts, reported that the returns of his census indicated no less than two hundred and ninety-nine such institutions, with an aggregate of 180,028 volumes having an estimated value of $191,538 and available to 25,705 proprietors or other persons having access to the books "in their own right."[45]

Considered collectively, such numbers are impressive. It may be said that the agglomeration of social libraries that covered New England was in itself a great public library system. Every town then had its social library, as it was later to have its public library. As organizations they were not essentially democratic in control or patronage, but practice strongly modified their theoretical limitations so that their collections were in reality rather widely available to the community at large. Fees were generally low, and it is quite doubtful whether any serious reader was denied access to the books because of poverty. The variety of types of the social library likewise represented a genuine attempt on the

45. Massachusetts Board of Education, "Third Annual Report of the Secretary of the Board," *Common School Journal*, II (1840), 122–28. To obtain this information, Horace Mann sent out a questionnaire to all Massachusetts towns, asking the number, size, value, and patronage of libraries, either social or school district. Information was also obtained on lyceums, mechanics institutes, literary societies, and other mediums of "adult education." Mann's results probably exaggerate the true state of affairs because of the part played by local pride in encouraging the reporting as active of many institutions that were probably quite defunct.

part of incorporators to meet diverse wants. Though many classes of society were not adequately represented, neither were they entirely ignored. It is, then, not an exaggeration to say that this network of social libraries was more than a forerunner of the public library pattern—it *was* a public library system based on the ability of the patron to pay for the services he received. The failure of the social libraries to attain the later results of a public library system arose not from any inadequacy of the whole to achieve a sufficiently comprehensive distribution but from the

TABLE 8

DISTRIBUTION OF SOCIAL LIBRARIES BY SIZE
OF BOOK COLLECTIONS, PRIOR TO 1800

No. of Vols. in Library	No. of Libraries
10,000 or more....................	6
5,000–9,999.....................	13
3,000–4,999.....................	12
1,000–2,999.....................	50
800– 999.....................	16
500– 799.....................	34
300– 499.....................	46
100– 299*.....................	141
Less than 100.....................	68
Total........................	386

* A total of 137 libraries estimated their collections at 100 volumes, the other 4 gave more precise figures.

weakness inherent in voluntary societies. Viewed collectively, the large numbers of social libraries do constitute an impressive picture; examined independently, the component libraries are revealed as being far from strong.

Factors in the Decline of the Social Library

Expressed in terms of absolute numbers of titles and contrasted with libraries of the present day, the size of the book collections of the social libraries was small. Even when considered in relation to contemporary university libraries or the private libraries of scholars and wealthy patrons, except in a few instances, they were not impressive in size. From Table 8 it appears that data are available for only three hundred and eighty-six institutions, of which over half had no more than one hundred volumes. Though there is a tendency for the data to cluster about the round numbers of one hundred or one thousand, such inaccuracies scarcely invalidate the major conclusion that the book stocks were small, an inference that is further substantiated by the absence of information concerning the size of book collections in the remainder of the libraries.

Data relative to the size of the original membership are even less abundant, being available for but sixty-six associations (Table 9) of which over half fall within the group of from twenty-five to forty-nine members. Obviously, such information does not indicate the eventual size of the membership, but statistics on that point are so meager as to be practically worthless. The surviving

TABLE 9

DISTRIBUTION OF SOCIAL LIBRARIES ESTABLISHED
1790–1850 BY SIZE OF MEMBERSHIP
AT TIME OF ORGANIZATION

No. of Members	No. of Libraries
100 or more......................	1
75–99...........................	4
50–74...........................	21
25–49...........................	39
Fewer than 25....................	1
Total.........................	66

record reveals that in many instances the membership of the societies grew very little beyond the numerical limit of the founding group. Local historians may boast in vague terms about the "prosperity" and thriftiness of these little groups, but much too frequently enthusiasm for sporadic manifestations of indigenous culture has obscured strict historical accuracy.

There is no precise gauge by which one may measure the financial stability of these social libraries, though some insight may be gained from the scattered statements revealing the limitations imposed upon their financial structures. The general permissive legislation of the several states usually placed a limit on the amount of property, exclusive of book stocks, these libraries might hold—$500.00 in Massachusetts; $5,000.00 in Maine; $1,000.00 in New Hampshire; $2,000.00 in Rhode Island. In general it may be said that the proprietary libraries represented the larger capital outlay, but even the stock of these sold at prices that, with only a few exceptions, were quite low. In two-thirds of the institutions for which data are available, shares ranged from $1.00 to $4.00 per unit, and in only a few instances was the cost in excess of $25.00. Entrance fees were even less, the majority being but a dollar or two. In more than half of the examples annual dues were only $1.00.

TABLE 10

DISTRIBUTION OF SOCIAL LIBRARIES ESTABLISHED
BETWEEN 1790 AND 1850 BY SOURCES
AND EXTENT OF INCOME

Prices of Shares (Proprietary Libraries)*	No. of Libraries
$300.00	1
100.00	2
50.00	2
25.00	2
15.00–$24.00	2
10.00– 14.00	4
5.00– 9.00	18
1.00– 4.00	54
0.50	1
Total	86

Entrance Fees	
$25.00	1
5.00–$9.00	6
1.00– 4.00	16
0.50	2
Total	25

Annual Dues†	
$10.00	5
5.00	4
2.00–$4.00	10
1.00– 1.99	22
Less than $1.00	49
Total	90

* Omitted are certain early institutions that recorded their stock prices in English currency: 20s. for the Book-Company of Durham, Conn.; £50, Philogrammatican Society, Lebanon, Conn.; £10, United English Library, Pomfret, Conn.; £50, Redwood Library, Newport, R.I.; £50, bond required of subscribers to library at Milford, Conn.; and £10, bond required of subscribers to library at Warren, Conn. It is a curious fact that the prices of shares were uniformly higher for those institutions known as Athenaeums.

† Certain institutions scaled their dues: The Young Men's Library Association of New London, Conn. (established 1840), charged men over twenty-one years of age $3.00; boys under twenty-one were required to pay but $2.00. Library Association, North Woburn, Mass. (established 1840), charged men $1.00 per year but women only $0.50 for the same period. The Social Library of Royalston, Mass. (established 1778), accepted grain, butter, flax, or flax seed in lieu of money for membership assessments.

Though this information is available for a limited number of all the social libraries known to have existed, yet when the composite results of the sample are examined—revealing limited book stock, small numerical membership, and circumscribed financial structure—the conclusion cannot be other than that most of the libraries were very weak indeed. Even the Boston Athenaeum, despite its relative financial strength, more than once hung precariously between survival and extinction. To those who, in the middle decades of the nineteenth century, became interested in the encouragement of public libraries, especially the proponents of the school-district libraries, it was clear that the shifting sands of voluntary support were not a sufficiently solid foundation upon which to build a universal library service.[46] As Rev. John B. Wight told the Massachusetts General Court in 1854:

> While they have contributed much to a more general diffusion of knowledge and mental culture among their associated proprietors, experience has fully shown that their *permanence* is not to be depended on. With the exception of a few in the large towns which have been well maintained, their fate has been very much as follows. For a few years after the formation of the library everything goes on well. Its books are read with avidity. New books are occasionally added. Those who have shares find it pleasant and improving to participate in its advantages. But before many years its prosperity begins to decline. Some of the proprietors have deceased. Others have removed from the town. Others have been unfortunate in business. The annual assessments cease to be paid. New publications are no longer purchased. The library gradually falls into disuse. For a long time there are no books in circulation and then perhaps when the attention of some influential person happens to be drawn to the subject the old library is reorganized or a new one formed, to pass through a similar course of growth, decline and neglect.[47]

Economic Influences and the Social Library

A discussion of the economic influences upon social library development between the years 1790 and 1850 should be prefaced with a review of the chronology of the social library movement. As was pointed out earlier in this chapter, the history of the social library resolves itself into a series of distinct and clearly defined

46. See Sidney Ditzion, "The District-School Library, 1835–1855," *Library Quarterly*, X, No. 4 (October, 1940), 545–77.

47. John B. Wight, "A Lecture on Public Libraries Delivered in Boston in the Hall of the House of Representatives, 1854, and in Several Other Places" (unpublished MS in the possession of Mrs. John B. Wight of Wayland, Mass.).

periods which are summarized in Table 11. Such an outline illuminates social library development during the years between 1790 and the middle of the nineteenth century and provides a frame of reference within which may be surveyed the cyclical character of social library progress (see Pls. IV–VI). This pattern

TABLE 11

THE CHRONOLOGICAL PERIODS OF SOCIAL
LIBRARY DEVELOPMENT

I. 1733–90
    The first half-century of the social library
    From the foundation of the Book-Company of Durham,
    Conn., to the general acceptance of the social library as
    a satisfactory form
    A period of beginnings and early growth

II. 1790–1840
    The second half-century of the social library
    The social library's "golden age"
    A period characterized by two subordinate phases:
    1790–1815: A period of lush growth and great numerical
    increase during the first decade but with a marked decline in the rate of increase just prior to and during the
    War of 1812
    1815–40: Revival of interest during the cultural ferment
    that followed the Peace of Ghent
    A period of experimentation and replacement
    Vanguard of a free public library system

III. 1840–90
    The decline of the social library
    The birth of the public library movement as a real force
    in American library development
    Increasingly important competition from the public library brought declining influence to the social library
    Relatively few social libraries established in New England after 1890

of library growth reveals certain definite relationships of the social library to the economic and social forces that contributed to its expansion and decline.

Perhaps the most striking of all is the similarity among the several New England states. In all but Maine, which did not become a state until 1820, the ten years between 1795 and 1805 were the most prolific period of library establishment. A second crest was reached between 1825 and 1835, this time with Maine more nearly conforming to the trend in the other states. The intervening years evince alternating crests and troughs of lesser magnitude, but all, save Maine, exhibiting a relatively high degree of coincidence. The obvious inference that may be made is that, in all the states, essentially similar forces were operating to encourage the formation of libraries. Furthermore, Maine is an exception only in the extent to which it represents a time lag; its profile is approximately the same as that of its sister-states.

The second fact indicated by Plates IV–VI is that library establishment was not a continuously increasing process but was cyclical. Periods of rapid expansion were followed by years of less vigorous activity in the creation of new institutions. The growth that characterized the decades before 1790 may be described as rising sharply. But after the peak at the turn of the century fluctuations became pronounced and well defined. Three major factors are responsible for this cyclical quality. As has been previously stated, the replacement of neglected institutions by new and, at least temporarily, more vigorous successors accounts in large measure for the crests.

Recurrent periods of saturation prevented the establishment of new institutions. Finally, there was a tendency for the formation of libraries to follow in general the trend of the business cycle. If one were to superimpose upon the graph of library growth in New England (Pl. IV) a chart of wholesale price fluctuations in that region during the same period, the coincidence would not be perfect but the configurations would be strikingly similar. Over the second half of the eighteenth century, when the social library movement was gaining momentum in Massachusetts and other New England states, Boston was steadily improving its economic relations with the outside world. The trend of prices for its major export commodities—rum and codfish—moved upward in contrast to its imported goods—tea, cotton, and flour.

Likewise the period of prosperity that followed the sharp depression of the Revolutionary War and postwar reconstruction years is coincident with the peak in library establishment at the end of the century. Thereafter the parallel is somewhat less accentuated, but crests in business activity as indicated by wholesale price fluctuations are evident just prior to the 1820's and during the 1830's, and in both instances the prosperity they produced must have helped to cement the economic foundations of the library development that followed. It is not wise to press too far a strictly economic interpretation of the library movement, particularly if such a point of view excludes the social and cultural factors which so profoundly influenced library growth. But neither should this expansion of library agencies be dissociated from general economic conditions. Library formation during the Colonial period necessarily waited upon adequate economic ability for its fullest expression, and library history following the establishment of the Republic displays the same economic dependence.

The cyclical character of social library formation emphasizes anew the uncertainty of voluntary support as a motivating force in library promotion. Clearly, the trend of library establishment, far from being the ever upward progress of an urge that pressed constantly forward in its demand for expanding library resources, reveals an inconstant and shifting desire—an uncertain groping toward cultural values that waxed and waned as the social and economic forces about it surged forward or ebbed. Libraries were promoted because a few people felt the need for books and had adequate, or at least partially adequate, resources for a beginning. But with the removal of the founders or a faltering of the initial enthusiasm the real instability of the institution was revealed, decadence being an almost inevitable result. Constant vigilance was indeed the price of culture, and there were but few in most communities who were both willing and able to give to the social libraries the care and attention that they demanded of their members.

The urge toward library formation that followed the creation of the new nation was, in its social milieu, much like that which came after the Peace of Utrecht and the resultant rise of a prosperous Colonial economy. A sharp period of depression succeeded the Revolutionary War. The problem of bringing the Colonies under one unified government was no easy task. But even more disturbing was the serious dislocation of the Colonial economic balance. In spite of American dissatisfaction with England's colonial policy, the confederation found itself, after the close of the Revolution, without any direction. Public debt, instability of the currency, unpaid soldiers, and, above all, disrupted trade seriously undermined the earlier Colonial economic structure. Prosperity had not immediately followed the signing of the peace;

and by the impact of subsequent economic maladjustments the whole institution of property, the foundation stone upon which the social order rested, was assailed.

The adoption of the Constitution and the formation of the Union marked the beginning of a new commercial era for all New England. Compelled by adverse circumstances, the Yankee merchants had, in the Far East, tapped a new source of wealth. From this thriving trade with China developed fortunes that brought renewed prosperity to New England ports. From this revival of commercial activity there arose a new wealthy class. Elias Haskett Derby, Israel Thorndike, Simon Forrester, and William Gray left estates that were appraised in the millions. Few represented old families, some began as laborers or sailors, and many were but one generation removed from a "shirt-sleeve" origin.

As in the days when a thriving foreign trade brought wealth to New England ports and gave impetus to the social library, so a half-century later the revival of commerce helped materially to finance a widely spreading social library movement. The fortunes of the library had gone full circle and once again a period of striking development was coincident with a prosperous maritime trade.

The prosperity that was characteristic of the 1790's came to an abrupt termination during the first two decades of the nineteenth century. The grievances that brought the United States into a second major conflict with Great Britain are not the concern of the present study. It is important, however, that, in an attempt to avoid the ruinous consequences of another war with England, Thomas Jefferson signed an act forbidding American vessels destined for foreign countries to sail from any American port. By this legislation it was hoped that, through economic pressure, England could be brought to terms without resort to arms. But this embargo brought New England's economy to the very brink of catastrophe. Farmers and mechanics as well as those directly concerned with foreign commerce felt keenly the loss of oversea trade. A Rhode Island citizen complained: "There is but little market for the productions of our labor. . . . Our crop of hay will but little more than pay for the making. What last year brought twenty will this year bring but ten dollars. Pork at the last market of it was worth ten cents, now it will command but little more than five."[48] On the other hand, the cost of imported necessities and luxuries advanced sharply. George Cabot prophesied aright when he wrote from Boston soon after the embargo was proclaimed that unemployment would be an immediate consequence.[49]

Concerning the economic maladjustments that preceded the War of 1812 it is important to point out that once again the trend of social library formation is seen to follow closely that of general economic conditions. The depression in the early years of the nineteenth century was reflected in a decline in the rate of library growth. Many smaller social libraries, later replaced by a second generation, died of an economic starvation that was a direct consequence of the ruin confronting New England enterprise.

The Peace of Ghent that terminated the second war with England came with a suddenness that astonished the entire nation. In spite of Clay's condemnation of it as a "damned bad treaty," his skill had been much more successful in dictating its terms than one would have expected from the blundering that characterized the prosecution of the struggle. Though the nation had been brought to the verge of ruin and dissolution, the recovery was rapid. For a brief period after the return of peace Massachusetts enjoyed a revival of maritime prosperity. But this foreign trade concentrated to an increasing extent in Boston while such smaller towns as Newburyport, Salem, and Marblehead failed to convalesce from the effects of the war until they began to participate extensively in the new trend toward manufacturing.

If the embargo and the war had brought serious consequences to the shipper, they had acted almost as a protective tariff to industry; and Yankee ingenuity, frustrated by increasing restriction on the seas, turned its attention to the latent power of the New England rivers and streams.

In the wake of industrialization came a complete transformation in New England life. The problems of the industrial worker assumed greater proportions in contemporary social and political

48. An address to the citizens of Rhode Island, November, 1808, quoted by James Truslow Adams, *New England in the Republic* (Boston: Little, Brown, 1927), p. 252.

49. Henry C. Lodge, *Life and Letters of George Cabot* (Boston: Little, Brown, 1877), chap. xii, "New England Federalism and the Hartford Convention."

thought. Social cleavages appeared that tended to stratify community relationships along entirely new and different lines. For the first time in its history New England began to struggle with the influx of a large group of non-English immigrants, especially the Irish.

Notwithstanding the restlessness and turmoil released by these new forces, southern urban New England in general and Boston in particular was growing wealthy as never before. The city on the banks of the Charles was rapidly becoming a regional capital, and it was with justification that its citizens were assuming an obvious self-esteem. With the statesmen of Virginia it had shared leadership in the formation of the new nation, and it had played an important part in both the wars in which England had been defeated.

No one could guess what happy fortunes lay before the valiant young republic, and Boston hoped for a special dispensation [writes Van Wyck Brooks]. The old dream of a Puritan commonwealth, a true city of God, lingered in the New England mind, and it seemed as if the appointed hour had come. Cotton Mather had foretold this hour. Jonathan Edwards, on his lonely rides over the forest hills of leafy Stockbridge, had seen the millennium approaching. Bishop Berkeley, on his farm at Newport, had prophesied the golden age. The hard conditions of life in earlier days had yielded to more propitious circumstances. The time was surely ripe; and what wealth was unable to compass might be left to piety and reason.[50]

Boston was not the only place in New England where a new urge was manifest. Along the coast and through the hinterland, during that period when the social library was enjoying a second growth, the spindles were weaving a new pattern for New England life.

In every corner of this New England country, where the ways of the eighteenth century lingered on, a fresh and more vigorous spirit was plainly astir. On the granite ledges of New Hampshire, along the Merrimac River, in Essex and Middlesex counties . . . or westward, on the lovely Housatonic, life was filled with a kind of electric excitement. The air resounded with the saw and the hammer, the blows of the forge, the bells in the factory-towers. In all directions the people were building turnpikes, hundreds of miles of straight lines that cut athwart the old winding roads. The Green Mountain boys had erected

50. Van Wyck Brooks, *The Flowering of New England* (New York: Dutton, 1937), p. 5.

their State House. Dwellings were going up in clearings and meadows. . . .
Villages, towns sprang from the fields. A current of ambition had galvanized
New England.[51]

Clearly, the fortunes of the social library movement were reflections of the undulations in economic activity from the middle
of the eighteenth century to the middle of the nineteenth. As
money became relatively abundant and enterprise prosperous,
libraries flourished; when business activity receded, the libraries
were much more likely to fail. Save in the very few instances
where endowment was sufficient to provide a buffer to depression, these institutions were so directly dependent upon the day-
to-day incomes of their members that they reacted as delicate
barometers of economic activity.

51. *Ibid.*, p. 46.

CHAPTER IV

THE SOCIAL LIBRARY II: CULTURAL RELATIONSHIPS

THE economic influences were but a fraction of the forces that contributed to the growth of the social library. To consider in detail the cultural relationships that gave to the social libraries their intellectual content does not minimize the importance of an adequate supporting economy. Wealth made the social library possible; the intellectual interests of its members gave the institution its fundamental drive.

In chapter ii the origins of the social library were described in terms of the expanding Colonial culture. The same relationship persisted as the Republic approached intellectual maturity. The kinship that existed between the social library and its coeval culture is fully appreciated only when the pattern of social library growth is examined in relation to contemporary intellectual currents.

Culturally the period from 1790 to 1850 divides into two major parts, with 1815 the approximate date of transition. Of the earlier years Emerson has written:

To write a history of Massachusetts, I confess, is not inviting to an expansive thinker. . . . From 1790 to 1820 there was not a book, a speech, a conversation, or a thought in the State. About 1820 the Channing, Webster, and Everett era began, and we have been bookish and poetical and cogitative ever since.[1]

Emerson's criticism of the sterility of the parochial world of Fisher Ames, which looked with such suspicion on the new century already crowding in upon its comfortable preserves, was too severe. The historian of American culture cannot dismiss so easily a period that brought with it the great expansion in social library

1. Ralph Waldo Emerson, *Journals, with Annotations* (Boston: Houghton Mifflin, 1912), VIII, 339.

development; the formation of the Boston Athenaeum, the American Antiquarian Society, and other important collections; and the first advances toward municipal library support. In contrast to the golden age of New England culture that followed the conclusion of the War of 1812, these earlier years do seem relatively insignificant. But it was during this very time that the foundations of New England's greatest cultural achievements were laid. From Europe a new spirit of liberalism was reaching New England shores. From German idealism and French utopianism the New England liberals drew freely.[2]

The Church

This movement toward liberalism was first apparent within the established church. For over a century and a half the New England mind had been oppressed by excessive dogmatism, and, though revolutions in speculative thought had taken place in both English and Continental theology, New England orthodoxy had kept rather closely within the confines of a narrow creed. With the romantic revolution in France had come new theories of human nature and society, and by 1800 it was indeed time that the old Congregationalism of Jonathan Edwards undergo a searching self-criticism. Against these new forces the established church fought stubbornly, but, despite such opposition, liberalism slowly gained control. The victory came in the name of Unitarianism, which accomplished for the church what Jeffersonianism achieved for government—a wide acceptance of the principles embodied in European liberal trends.

The quarter-century between 1790 and 1815 was the formative period of Unitarianism, and during this time the old dogmas were being re-examined and weighed against new conceptions of man and God. Fundamentally the Unitarian revolt was a reassertion of the original principle of New England Separatism: a belief in religious democracy. The importance of Unitarianism as a liberalizing force is not easily overemphasized. Like its parallel in government, it was more than a creed or doctrine; its motives were based on the conscious assumption that (a) man is by nature good and intelligent, (b) every truth can be rationalized, (c) no

2. Vernon L. Parrington, *Main Currents in American Thought* (New York: Harcourt, Brace, 1930), II, 317–20.

institution is sacred, and (d) the living generation has a right to make whatever changes it pleases. Its influence was revealed in social ideas because it developed a new philosophy of the relation of man to his fellows. The same ferment was to produce transcendentalism, utopian experiments, and social reforms. Whether Unitarianism was the cause or merely a manifestation of this new cultural spirit may be a matter of opinion; but certainly at this time the social library, particularly as it related to the urge for improvement and enlightenment of the "masses," was a direct beneficiary of this larger conception of human freedom. From these broadened horizons derived a clearer vision that was to give to New England leaders a conspicuous position in the social developments of the next half-century.

Political Thought

The new liberalism was by no means confined to theology. A wave of enthusiasm for the French Revolution swept across the land. In these popular demonstrations in support of what was then called "democracy" New England was most active. The Boston populace was aflame with excitement, and the Civic Feast of January 24, 1793, in honor of the events in France, was long remembered. Public feeling was expressed in the organization of numerous Democratic Clubs in all the New England states. Quite obviously, such enthusiasm was not shared by all New Englanders. George Cabot, Fisher Ames, Theophilus Parsons, and their colleagues in the Essex Junto regarded this rising spirit of democracy with contempt and fear. "Ought we not to consider democracy as the worst of all governments, or if there be a worse, as the certain forerunner of that? What other form of civil rule among men so irresistibly tends to free vice from restraint, and to subject virtue to persecution?"[3] With no less rancor George Cabot condemned the growing spirit of "turbulent mobocracy" and questioned the necessity for "popular meetings."

Support of the French Revolution was not merely a polite acknowledgment of the interest that France had displayed in American political freedom; it went much deeper than that. The social cleavages between the wealthy Federalists and their less opulent

3. Fisher Ames, *Works, with Selections from His Speeches*, ed. Seth Ames (Boston: Little, Brown, 1854), II, 364.

contemporaries, the Democrats, were being carved with greater and greater sharpness. The French Revolution served to force into high relief the emerging spirit of militant democracy. There was much popular resentment against those who had fattened on the results of the American Revolution. The established churches joined with financial leaders in a vain effort to suppress the rising tide, and for a while this coalition of Fisher Ames's "wise, rich, and good" was successful. The later excesses of the French Revolution alienated American sympathies, thereby temporarily weakening the Democratic cause in New England. There the election of 1800 was a Federalist victory, but the Democratic party was gaining; the movement against the old order was acquiring momentum.

Literary Expression

The literature that was created between the time of the Revolutionary War and the year 1815 was more notable for intensity of feeling than for artistic merit or permanence of appeal. Unblushingly imitative of English and classical models and lacking skill in execution, it partially justified Emerson's condemnation and Sydney Smith's reproachful words:

In the four quarters of the globe, who reads an American book? or who goes to an American play? or who looks at an American picture or statue? . . . Literature the Americans have none. . . . It is all imported. . . . Why should the Americans write books when a six weeks' passage brings them, in their own tongue, our sense, science, and genius, in bales and hogsheads?[4]

Literature survived more because of what it tried to be than for what it was. Its poetry especially represented the enthusiasm of a new nation eager to win a place of distinction in the world of letters. Americans had suffered under the lash of an uncompromising criticism from a flood of English travelers who came between 1785 and 1815 to view the new country, give it "sound advice," and accept its money. Americans had been told that their manners were uncouth, their literature sterile, and their libraries empty. In 1794 Thomas Cooper of Manchester had complained that in America literature was an amusement only and that Americans were inferior to the English in "opportunities

4. Sydney Smith, "Review of *Statistical Annals of the United States* by Adam Seybert," *Edinburgh Review*, XXXIII (January, 1820), 79–80.

of knowledge." "Their libraries are scanty, their collections are almost entirely of *modern* books; they do not contain the means of tracing the history of questions; this is a want which the literary people feel very much, and which it will take some years to remedy."[5] The problem of how to be cultured though a Yankee was acute; and if an indigenous literary productivity would help to avert stigma, there were many who were willing to champion the new culture.

Poetry was represented by John Trumbull, Timothy Dwight, Joel Barlow, and their fellow Connecticut Wits who with Hudibrastic imitations or heroic couplets strove to picture in glowing colors the achievements of the new Republic.

The novels of the period were even more vapid and devoid of literary merit than its poems. It was the age of sensibility, and most of the writing drew both inspiration and incident from the work of Richardson and Sterne. As a literary form the novel came relatively late to America, for it was not until 1789 that the first appeared.[6] The temper of the American reading public of the period was revealed when in 1794 Mathew Carey republished Susanna Rowson's *Charlotte Temple*, which within a few years sold twenty-five thousand copies, was acclaimed the most popular book of its generation, appeared in more than one hundred editions, and became America's first fiction best-seller, unsurpassed in popularity until the arrival of *Uncle Tom's Cabin*. *The Coquette; or the History of Eliza Wharton* (1797), written by "a lady of Massachusetts," Hannah Foster, reached its thirteenth edition in Boston in 1833, and it was not long before the popular novel, in either book or periodical form, became almost the only kind of reading indulged in by women. The pulpit and the press suddenly awoke in a storm of indignation and protest; but such remonstrances, while they revealed accurately the mounting popularity of the sentimental novel, had little influence in deflecting the trend. The current periodical press, which was one of the most

5. Thomas Cooper, *Some Information Respecting America* (London: J. Johnson, 1794), p. 64.

6. The book was *The Power of Sympathy; or the Triumph of Nature Founded in Truth*, by William Hill Brown, and was issued from the Boston press of Isaiah Thomas. New England took the lead in introducing native fiction to the American reading public.

active sources of opposition to novel reading, was at the same time a major medium for the publication of that very fiction it most deplored. Editors and publishers alike were quite willing to join in the chorus of condemnation and thus insure their intellectual self-respect, but they had no intention of forsaking the rewards to be derived from a growing market for fiction.

Through their popularity these novels clearly reveal the reading tastes of the public. As Herbert R. Brown has shown, they were welcomed along the entire length of the Atlantic seaboard, a fact that destroys much prevalent misapprehension concerning any regional character of reading habits.[7] The enthusiasm with which they were received and the persistence of their popularity explain why villages have been known to tax themselves willingly to provide public libraries filled with fourth-rate novels. Many of these tales were written by women. Up to this time American culture in general and literary effort in particular had been the exclusive province of men. With the emergence of the women writers during the 1790's a new influence came into American letters—the feminization of American culture. Not until after 1850 were women important in American librarianship; but their future role in American culture may be said to have been forecast by the scratching pens of Susanna Rowson, Hannah Foster, and, a few decades later, the mill girls of Lowell.

During the first fifteen years of the nineteenth century American literature reached its nadir. Notwithstanding the talk about a native culture, it was still largely derivative. English models at the moment were not particularly helpful, and the editors of the *Monthly Anthology* perceived this: "The age of good English poetry ended with the reign of Queen Anne; the British muse has from that period been declining in a gradual nervous decay; her young offspring, the American muse, inherited from her parent the same disorder; and both are now in the last stage of an incurable hectic."[8] The pessimism was scarcely justified—the "hectic" was curable. But the relationship which the editors saw between the English and American muses did exist, and what they said of

7. Herbert Ross Brown, *The Sentimental Novel in America, 1789–1860* (Durham: Duke University Press, 1940), *passim*.

8. *Monthly Anthology* (1805); quoted by F. L. Pattee, *The First Century of American Literature, 1770–1870* (New York: Appleton, 1935), p. 168.

poetry was equally true of the other forms of literary expression. "Native literature" was neither native nor literary.

Yet this stagnant period cannot be dismissed as lacking in significance. The spirit of the eighteenth century died hard, but it did die. If American culture could not stand on its own feet, at least there was an intense conviction that it should. Every college commencement had its oration on the deplorable state of American letters. The era was dominantly one of transition, with the confusion, uncertainty, and apparent absence of substantial achievement that seem often to accompany such periods of change. Beneath the surface there were forces at work inevitably leading to a new cultural pattern.

Of all the forms of literary expression the newspaper was the first to discard European influences and assume a truly native quality. The period of the Revolution marks a clear break between the old journalism and the new. Originally newspapers were conventional in the selection of news items and lacking in interpretation and "editorial policy." The political controversies that accompanied the Revolution revealed the importance of the press in political argument, and the editor began to emerge as a new force in American journalism. In short, the press was gathering its newly discovered strength for the coming struggle between Federalist and Democrat. "Newspapers," wrote Noah Webster in his paper, the *American Minerva*, "in a great degree supersede the use of Magazines and Pamphlets. The Public mind in America, roused by the magnitude of political events, and impatient of delay, cannot wait for monthly intelligence."[9]

Though the newspaper had taken the place of the political pamphlet, the magazine was far from suffering popular neglect. The Postoffice Act of 1794 gave tacit acknowledgment of the magazine as a proper commodity for transportation in the mails "when the mode of conveyance and the size of the mails will permit."[10] But during the period of nationalism the magazine remained almost entirely regional both in circulation and point of view. As late as 1821 Jared Sparks complained to Edward Everett

9. Quoted by Pattee, *op. cit.*, p. 173.

10. *U.S. Statutes at Large* (3d Cong., 1st sess.), chap. xxiii, sec. 22, passed May 8, 1794.

of the lack of national vision in the *North American Review*, and Everett, then the editor, acknowledged the fault.[11] Among the geographical centers of magazine production Boston was tremendously important. There flourished the *Monthly Anthology*, *General Repository*, *North American Review*, and *Atlantic Magazine*. The faculty of Harvard College participated extensively in current periodical publication, and the town was the home of many other important magazine contributors.

In content the periodical was an index of the popular taste of the day. Fiction, especially in the weekly miscellanies and women's magazines, occupied a steadily increasing proportion of the whole. The essay was important from the beginning, and both history and biography were well represented. Much of this last was borrowed from English magazines, but there was also a substantial quantity of original work. Travel was scarcely less popular than history, though a good portion of it was abstracted from current books. Finally, there were periodicals devoted to the interests of women, children, science (including both medicine and agriculture), and even the theater.

The parallelism between the development of the social library and the use of newspapers and magazines is marked. This increase in general interest in current journals was a strong motivating factor in social library formation. The periodical club was an important adaptation of the social library, and the periodical reading-room was a frequent adjunct of the social library book collection.[12] The Boston Athenaeum began as a reading-room affiliated with the *Monthly Anthology* known as the Anthology Reading Room and was "furnished with . . . the Boston papers, and all other celebrated gazettes published in any part of the United States . . . with magazines, reviews, and scientific journals; London and Paris newspapers."[13] This Reading Room, as distinct from the library proper, was a definite concept in the

11. Herbert B. Adams, *Life and Writings of Jared Sparks* (Boston: Houghton Mifflin, 1893), I, 242–43.

12. See, e.g., the Periodical Library of Pawlet, Vt., the leading function of which was to subscribe to the most important reviews (Abby Maria Hemenway, *Vermont Historical Gazetteer* [Claremont, N.H.: Claremont Manufacturing Co., 1877], III, 887).

13. From the prospectus of the Reading Room quoted by Josiah Quincy in *The History of the Boston Athenaeum . . .* (Cambridge: Metcalf, 1851), p. 7.

minds of the Athenaeum founders. "We must, at least for some time, think of popularity," wrote Joseph Buckminster to William Smith Shaw, when the former was purchasing materials for the Athenaeum while in London. "I know of no method so likely to procure it as to keep our rooms furnished with abundance of magazines, pamphlets, and *new books* [italics his]. This, I am satisfied, should be our primary object."[14]

The content of the social libraries was similar to that of the current periodical press. In both the emphasis was on history, biography, travel, and belles-lettres. The interest in scientific journals was reflected in the formation of scientific libraries. The many juvenile magazines may be compared with the numerous juvenile libraries and the ladies' magazines with those associations of women for the purchase of popular fiction. This relationship is not surprising; the magazines were forced to recognize and follow the prevailing interests reflected in popular demand, and the social libraries were definitely pointed in the direction of current reading.

Interest in Science

Throughout the whole land, in colleges, libraries, and amateur laboratories, there was a constant searching for the secrets of nature. From England had come Joseph Priestley and Thomas Cooper, both ardent apostles of scientific investigation, whose labors did much to encourage research here. In 1802 Nathaniel Bowditch, who had studied with the passion of genius the scientific works in the Philosophical Library of Salem, Massachusetts, published *The American Practical Navigator* and a few years later translated Laplace's *Mécanique céleste* into English.[15] The expedi-

14. Quoted by Quincy, *op. cit.*, p. 52 (Appen.).

15. Bowditch was the only member of the Philosophical Library whose name appears on the "charge book" as a borrower of Newton's *Principia*, which he was so eager to read in the original that he taught himself Latin. That he found in this library the scientific treatises so much to his liking was a happy accident itself linked with the vagaries of the sea. The books that comprised the Philosophical Library had been the property of Richard Kirwan, LL.D., of Dublin, but during the Revolutionary War they had been seized, along with other goods, in the Irish Channel by Captain Joseph Robinson, one of Cabot's privateersmen, and brought to Beverly Harbor, where they were purchased by an association of gentlemen of Salem and vicinity. When the origin of the books became known, the purchasers offered to compensate Dr. Kirwan for the loss, but he graciously refused, expressing gratifica-

tion of Lewis and Clark was of real scientific importance, and it added greatly to existing knowledge. While America had produced no distinguished generalizer in the realm of pure science, in the applied sciences the prestige of Yankee ingenuity spread rapidly to Europe. To the early Republic may be credited two major inventions, the cotton gin and the steamboat, of which the latter prompted De Tocqueville to observe that if America had made no important contribution to the laws of mechanics, it had introduced into navigation an engine that had revolutionized the maritime world.

Co-operation was also playing its part in the advance of scientific investigation by stimulating and supplementing the efforts of isolated individuals. Leadership among such organizations was assumed by the American Philosophical Society of Philadelphia, which was revived after the Revolutionary War, and New England had, at Boston, her own American Academy of Arts and Sciences, modeled upon the pattern of the French Academy. The industrial arts were encouraged by the spread of associations of manufacturers and mechanics, by the institutes these organizations promoted, by the libraries they assembled, and by the constant search for new ideas and designs that they fostered. Between 1815 and the Civil War there developed the tendency for such voluntary groups to organize along lines of specialization, and national societies of geologists, geographers, ethnologists, and statisticians were formed in a movement which was climaxed by the formation in Boston in 1847 of the American Association for the Advancement of Science. The labors of these individual associations, national, state, and local, were supplemented by the various surveys and other activities directed toward the accumulation of scientific data sponsored by and executed under government auspices.

Finally, there was the influence of the colleges and universities, which not only provided instruction in the sciences and facilities for research but in the case of Agassiz at Harvard and Silliman at Yale furnished financial aid for important investigations.

---

tion that the books had been put to such a good use (see Harriet S. Tapley, *Salem Imprints, 1768–1825: A History of the First Fifty Years of Printing in Salem, Massachusetts* ... [Salem: Essex Institute, 1927], pp. 248–60).

Education

Education was beginning to feel the impact of new forces. During the Colonial period the course of study in the colleges had been uniform. The influence of English universities, especially Cambridge and Oxford, was strong because many who were helping to determine the curriculum of the Colonial college had been trained abroad. General interest in theological subjects was responsible for the importance of divinity in the arts college; and the needs of future ministers, for the inclusion of Hebrew along with Latin and Greek as a major language. The teaching of philosophy was dominated by logic because logic was still regarded in Europe as the basic philosophical subject.

After the Revolution the college program was expanded. Latin and Greek retained their positions of importance, the scope and popularity of mathematics was greatly extended, and astronomy received increasing attention. From natural philosophy, which, during the Colonial period, had been the foundation of scientific instruction, the several branches of science tended to separate. Chemistry, largely because of its relation to medical training, was one of the first to emerge. Mineralogy, with the ubiquitous cabinet of specimens, was likewise popular. In 1805 a group of Boston citizens subscribed to a fund to establish a professorship of natural history at Harvard, and in the same year the Harvard Botanic Garden was established, though it was not actually opened until two years later. The modern languages of French and Spanish were beginning to be studied, and history, which hitherto had come into the curriculum as a by-product of classical studies, began to be recognized in courses in "chronology," though not until 1838, with the establishment of the McLean professorship in ancient and modern history at Harvard, was there a chair in an American college or university devoted exclusively to history. During the first quarter of the nineteenth century American higher education was still dominated by tradition, but unmistakable forces were at work that eventually led to a broader curriculum.

During this period, however, it was in secondary education that the most thoroughgoing innovations were made. Popular education for children had been seriously neglected in the period of the Revolution and its immediate aftermath. The influence of European educational doctrines, especially those of Rousseau's *Émile* and the experiments of Basedow and Pestalozzi, resulted in a flood of proposals for educational reform. A general liberalization of the curriculum was advocated; education in the manual arts, modern languages, geography, history, and science were henceforth to play an important part in the education of the child.

Though practice lagged behind theory, there were evidences that the new forces were beginning to be absorbed into existing situations, particularly in the academies which were less hampered by tradition. Since communities generally were as yet unready to tax themselves for the support of public schools, many of these academies received indirect grants toward their support from the states. With the development of settled conditions and general prosperity the middle classes were able to establish academies and thus open to a great segment of the population, particularly farmers and mechanics, advantages hitherto available only to the wealthy.

The poorer classes were still a serious problem confronting the sponsors of public education. The urge for free schools was little more than an expression of hope on the part of state legislators. The Sunday school movement, imported from England at the end of the eighteenth century, was much more than sectarian indoctrination. Within its limits it was a real contribution toward the elimination of illiteracy among the children of the poor. The city school societies, formed by philanthropic interests in an effort to provide the rudiments of education to those too poor to obtain it in other ways, were an interesting example of voluntary associations established to perform a service that was later recognized as a proper public function. Even the widespread adoption of the Lancastrian monitorial schools, with all their faults, focused popular attention on the need for universal education, conditioned the public mind to the idea of tax support for schools, and materially hastened the advent of a free school system. The educational scene at the beginning of the nineteenth century may not have been one to inspire pride in the minds of those eager for

popular education, but there were developments that unmistakably foreshadowed the work of Henry Barnard and Horace
Mann.

The Idea of Progress

The idea of progress was deeply embedded in the spirit of the
time. This concept, particularly as it was expressed in the philosophical speculation of Chastellux and Condorcet, had especial
significance for the American people. Conditions in the United
States were particularly adapted to its favorable application. In
this nation there was no monopoly of learning, social classes were
fluid, and there was an abundance of natural wealth. Here at
last was an opportunity to lift the dream of progress from the
realm of speculation and give it effect in the life of the common
people. The formation of the social libraries was one manifestation of this general urge for the improvement of the individual.

The years between 1790 and 1815, when the social library was
making its most abundant growth, cannot easily be characterized
in sweeping generalizations that would at once describe the period realistically and at the same time do justice to its latent
potentialities. Emerson's wholesale condemnation of the sterility
of thought in Massachusetts was something less than fair. Likewise, Henry Beers's witticism at the expense of Moses Coit
Tyler's history of American Colonial and revolutionary literature as being "for the most part a much ado about nothing" fails
to recognize the struggle of a new nation toward cultural self-
sufficiency. Overshadowed by the brilliance of the years that followed, this period has suffered a neglect which it does not de-
serve. It was an era of transition when the new Republic had
shaken off nominal dependence but had not learned to think of
itself as purely American. The actual conflict of the Revolution
had temporarily united discordant elements which split into a
multitude of conflicting interests and suspicions when the tension
of war was removed. The debtor class, fired by the doctrines of
the French Revolution, was in constant opposition to the reaction
of the property-owners. In New England the "codfish aristocracy" made no effort to conceal an Anglomania that looked forward to possible reunion with the mother-country. This spirit

was manifest both in studied imitation of English customs and manners and in open political agitation.

In the face of such conditions an indigenous culture was much more than a luxury; it was an essential element that would help to bind the nation together. Two powerful forces had converged to promote the emergence of that culture—the westward expansion of the frontier and the conclusion of the War of 1812. Out into the West was pouring a steadily growing stream of American youth—young men who were filled with the urge for adventure, eager for increased economic opportunity, and largely indifferent to British culture. Not only was the "cutting edge" of the frontier striking forward to level the great trees of the forest; ultimately it was to swing backward, severing the bonds that had so securely held America to her Anglican past.

The sudden and successful termination of the War of 1812 cut the ground from under the New England secessionists and established the national government upon a new level of authority. United and free, America faced a promising future. The native culture of earlier decades was nourished by economic expansion until it gradually developed the maturity of the middle years of the nineteenth century. The taunts of Sydney Smith were answered by the pages of Emerson, Hawthorne, Thoreau, and a host of others. If Emerson had been ruthless in his condemnation of the cultural sterility of a former time, he greeted the new era with a shout of expectation:

Our day of dependence, our long apprenticeship to the learning of other lands draws to a close. The millions, that around us are rushing into life, cannot always be fed on the sere remains of foreign harvests. . . . I read with joy some of the auspicious signs of the coming days, as they glimmer already through poetry and art, through philosophy and science, through church and state.[16]

That culture which flourished in New England from the Peace of Ghent to the beginnings of the war between the states justified Emerson's enthusiasm. These decades were certainly the most dramatic, and perhaps the most important, for the development of the library—years in which the social libraries were being adapted to new uses and the incipient movement for public li-

16. Ralph Waldo Emerson, "The American Scholar, an Oration Delivered before the Phi Beta Kappa Society, at Cambridge, August 31, 1837," in his *Works* (Philadelphia: Morris, 1906), III, 77, 105.

brary support was making progress. Some evidence has already
been presented to show the interrelationships between the library
movement and other cultural phenomena. The importance of
this connection may also be seen from an examination of the book
collections placed in these social libraries, the use that was made
of them, and the extent to which both reflected contemporary
cultural interests.

The Book Collections of the Social Libraries

The book collections of these early social libraries were conditioned by two major influences: the "universe" of books available
to the members of the societies and the desires and interests of
those who decided what books were to be purchased. If the first
influence were always constant, then the book collections could
be assumed to be a very accurate index of cultural shifts during
the period. But the universe of print is never constant; it is always
fluctuating in response to many cultural movements. What was
printed depended upon the interests of the author, on the one
hand, and upon the demand anticipated by the publisher, on the
other. But these stimuli were themselves in part an effect of the
books that were published. The entire relationship becomes a
complex of interacting forces that cannot be arrested to permit
examination, though it is possible to make certain assumptions
concerning the validity of these social library book collections as
indices of contemporary reading interests.

Existing studies of library history, analyses of European and
American book markets during the Colonial and early national
periods, and the present knowledge of the American book trade
at that time make it abundantly clear that reading materials were
being published in great variety—even during the eighteenth
century—and that a surprisingly large amount of such reading
matter was available at reasonable prices on this side of the
Atlantic. Not only was a steady stream of print coming from
American presses, but many titles were arriving from European
book-sellers in a thriving import trade. Almost from the beginning, books, both in variety and quantity, had been a substantial
commodity on the American market. Those who selected the

books for the social libraries, then, had a wide latitude of choice, and the contents of these libraries should reveal a great deal concerning the reading interests and habits of the period.

An overwhelming concern with theology has long been associated with New England, and there is a tendency to assume that because religious convictions were influential in Puritan life, the New England forefathers turned only to solid theological treatises when they wished something to read. There is just enough evidence in support of this belief to account for its general adoption.[17] No óne should deny that theology was tremendously important in the cultural life of New England from the time when the Pilgrims first landed on Plymouth Rock. But after the death of Increase Mather its power steadily declined and other influences took its place; the private and "public" libraries of New England became just as general and secular in content as those of the tidewater South and the middle colonies. The early South was as zealous in the intensity of its religious feeling as was New England during the same period. The striking fact about the cultural pattern of the Atlantic coast during the age under consideration was not its regional diversity but its relatively high degree of homogeneity. The landholding class was important in southern economy, but it should not be forgotten that seaboard New England was dominated by wealthy merchants and their dependents. The New England Puritan saw the library as an instrument for promoting religion, but for similar reasons the Rev. Thomas Bray urged the establishment of parish libraries in

17. Thomas Keys's essay on the supposed relation of the Colonial library to the development of sectional differences in the American Colonies shows how badly one can go astray in following this extreme regional point of view. The purpose of his study is "to discuss the development of sectional differences as represented in the private and semi-private colonial libraries. Each group had its own personality, and the striking differences revealed in the libraries of the North and South, for example, show the beginnings of the disastrous sectional cleavage which continued for the next hundred years." From these sectional differences developed "the New England Puritan's feeling of religious superiority which conflicted harshly with that of the southern aristocracy and probably was the basis for differences that were to submerge the American states several years later in bitter conflict" (Thomas Keys, "The Colonial Library and the Development of Sectional Differences in American Colonies," *Library Quarterly*, VIII [1938], 373–90).

Maryland, Virginia, and·other southern colonies.[18] If church membership were a prerequisite to franchise in Colonial Massachusetts, the Anglicans, once they had gained undisputed control of Maryland, lost no time in establishing there the Church of England, authorized the collection of taxes for its support, and forbade the admittance of Catholic immigrants. Against the historian who is "wont to speak of Puritan New England, the Cavalier South, and the commercial Middle Colonies as representing distinct schemes of culture," Charles A. Beard has directed justified criticism. Such oversimplification he finds "responsible for many an error."

If we look at the statute books, which pretend to universality, it appears that delights of the flesh and skepticism in religion, even the faintest, were condemned with equal severity in Virginia and Massachusetts. Puritan Boston gave to mankind one of the greatest freethinkers of the Colonial era, Benjamin Franklin. . . . On the other hand, under genial Southern skies were reared the families that brought forth in America two outstanding pietists of the nineteenth century, Robert E. Lee, whose lips were never profaned by an oath, whiskey, or tobacco, and Stonewall Jackson, who opened every battle with a prayer. . . . Rum as hot and wines as rich as any that graced the planter's table were found on the boards of the noblest divines and the strictest merchants in Boston.[19]

The records of the southern colonies may not be so liberally sprinkled with biblical quotations or allusions to the wonder-working providence of God, but their statutes, orders, and decrees (witness the Maryland Toleration Act of 1699) reveal their authors to have been as greatly moved by religious emotion as were their contemporaries in Salem and Plymouth.

In the light of existing knowledge of Colonial and early national culture it is to be expected, then, that the book collections of these social libraries should reveal a wide variety of interests, a general catholicity of taste, and, above all, a reflection of the issues and controversies, both political and economic, that were dominant in the minds of the respective memberships. Such conjecture finds ample substantiation (see Table 12). It has already

18. In his doctoral dissertation Joseph T. Wheeler has shown the regional thesis to be as wrong for Maryland and the South generally as it is for New England (see Joseph T. Wheeler, "Literary Culture in Colonial Maryland, 1700–1776" [Ph.D. thesis, Brown University, 1938], chaps. ii, viii). See also *Maryland Historical Magazine*, Vols. XXXIV–XXXVIII (1939–43), *passim*.

19. Charles and Mary Beard, *The Rise of American Civilization* (New York: Macmillan, 1927), I, 139.

TABLE 12

SUBJECT ANALYSIS OF SOCIAL LIBRARY BOOK COLLECTIONS, 1760–1841, BY PER CENT

SUBJECT	SAYBROOK, LYME, AND GUILFORD, CONN., ca. 1760* (1)	FARMINGTON, CONN., 1785† (2)	BROOKFIELD, VT., 1791‡ (3)	MECHANIC LIBRARY, NEW HAVEN, CONN., 1793§ (4)	FRANKLIN LIBRARY, NORWICH, CONN., 1794‖ (5)	PITTSFORD, VT., 1796¶ (6)	NORTHINGTON, CONN., 1798** (7)	LIBRARY COMPANY, HARTFORD, CONN. (8) 1818	(8) 1818/22††	ATHENAEUM, PORTLAND, ME., 1828‡‡ (9)	ROXBURY, MASS., 1832§§ (10)	MECHANICS' LIBRARY, NEWPORT, R.I (11) 1835	(11) 1841‖‖	YOUNG MEN'S INSTITUTE, HARTFORD, CONN., 1839¶¶ (12)	YOUNG MEN'S LIBRARY ASSOCIATION, NEW LONDON, CONN., 1841*** (13)
No. of titles	232	107	248	204	104	93	118	1,170	158	844	699	307	450	2,222	810
Theology, religion	69	22	28	9	32	18	38	22	11	24	8	18	15	16	11
History, biography	14	27	29	25	16	31	13	36	44	25	25	28	27	24	36
Literature (incl. drama)	4	28	9	20	24	17	18	23	27	30	30	20	21	22	18
Travel (incl. geography)	2	10	11	17	9	16	13			13	13	8	7	12	6
Science (incl. agriculture)	3			1	7	3		6	4				14	5	12
Fiction		5	12	22	10	5	15	10	8	8		17	10	11	10
Miscellaneous (incl. periodicals, law, politics, and unidentified)	8	8	11	6	2	17	3	3	6		24	9	6	10	7
Total	100	100	100	100	100	100	100	100	100	100	100	100	100	100	100

* Broadside in Yale University Library. See Pl. IV.

† Manuscript record book in Farmington Village Library.

‡ Manuscript records of the library in the Vermont Historical Society.

§ *The Constitution and By-laws of the Mechanic Library Society of New Haven, with a Catalogue of Books and List of Proprietors* (New Haven: Abel Morse, 1793), in Yale University Library.

‖ *The Constitution of the Franklin Library Company, also Subscribers' Names and Catalogue of Books* (Norwich, Conn.: John Trumbull, 1794), in Yale University Library.

¶ Manuscript records of the society in the McClure Library, Pittsford, Vt.

** Note that fiction outranks history. *Catalogue* (broadside) *of Books Belonging to the Northington Public Library, November 4, 1798*, in Yale University Library.

†† The second column represents additions to the first and is not cumulative (*Catalogue of the Books Belonging to the Hartford Library Company, April 1, 1818, and Extracts from the By-laws of Said Company* [Hartford: Hamlen & Newton, 1818], in Connecticut Historical Society; *Catalogue Number 2, of Books Added to the Hartford Library from April 1, 1818 to April 1, 1822* [Hartford: Peter B. Gleason, 1822], in Connecticut Historical Society).

‡‡ *Catalogue of Books in the Library of the Portland Athenaeum; with the By-laws and Regulations of the Institution* (Portland: Shirly & Hyde, 1828), in Maine Historical Society.

§§ *Catalogue of Books in the Social Library of Roxbury, January 1, 1832* (Boston: Munroe & Francis, 1832), in Essex Institute.

‖‖ In this instance the second column does cumulate the first since it represents a second edition of the original catalog (*Catalogue of the Newport Mechanics' and Apprentices' Library, Established by the Newport Association of Mechanics and Manufacturers* [Newport: James Atkins, 1835], in Newport Historical Society; also 1841 ed. in Newport Historical Society).

¶¶ *Catalogue of Books in the Library of the Young Men's Institute, Hartford, 1839* (Hartford: Case, Tiffany & Burnham, 1839), in Connecticut Historical Society.

*** *Catalogue of the Books Belonging to the Young Men's Library Association, New London, 1841* (New London: Benjamin Bissell, 1841), in Connecticut State Library.

been shown that more than two-thirds of the early collection in the Redwood Library at Newport was composed of literature, science, and history.[20] Similarly, history, fiction, and literature account for two-thirds of the total collection of two hundred titles in the Mechanic Library of New Haven, Connecticut, in 1793[21] (Pl. XIII), and practically the same proportion characterized the original book purchase of one hundred and ninety-seven titles made in 1785 for the Farmington, Connecticut, library.[22] In the Librarian Society of Pittsford, Vermont (1796), history, religion, literature, and travel accounted for over 80 per cent of the total collection, which numbered a modest ninety-three titles.[23] Significantly, the first book chosen for inclusion in the new library was Williams' *History of Vermont,* which in itself testifies to the rise of popular concern with the origins of the region and the genesis of local institutions. Though the preamble to the constitution states that the purpose of the society was to assemble books "of a moral, historical, philosophical and theological kind . . . calculated to promote useful literature," with a view to "improvement" of the membership "in knowledge, virtue, and piety," it soon seemed wise to pass a regulation stipulating that "all religious and sectarian books are forever excluded."[24] At Brookfield, Vermont, the holdings of the "Publick Library" (1791) show history and biography again to have been most prevalent, though fiction represented more than one-tenth of the collection.[25]

20. The surviving records of the Book-Company of Durham, Conn., are not sufficiently complete to permit an analysis of the books in its collection, but the absence of any member of the clergy among the founders of the organization would suggest that the theological influence in the book collection may have been no stronger than at Newport.

21. *The Constitution and By-laws of the Mechanic Library Society of New Haven, with a Catalogue of Books and List of Proprietors* (New Haven: Abel Morse, 1793), 17 pp.; copy in Yale University Library. See Table 12, col. 4.

22. Manuscript record book of the library in the Farmington Village Library, Farmington, Conn. See Table 12, col. 2.

23. Manuscript records of the society in the McClure Library, Pittsford, Vt. See Table 12, col. 6.

24. From the records of the society in the McClure Library. The language of the preamble has little significance; it is thoroughly stereotyped. The same phrasing occurs repeatedly in the records of early library societies.

25. From the early records of the society in the Vermont Historical Society. The original collection contained 248 titles. See Table 12, col. 3. It is interesting to note

Evidence in support of Waples' belief that these social libraries resembled the private collections of individual scholars becomes abundant when comparisons are drawn between the two. Actually the social libraries, in the character of their collections, were nothing more than private libraries of a group of like-minded individuals. In content they were precisely analogous to the secular collections of laymen. The private library of Matthew Robinson of Hopewell, Narragansett, was said to be the largest such collection of mid-eighteenth-century Rhode Island. Strong in history, literature, poetry, current periodicals, and pamphlets, its emphasis was clearly upon the cultural and social movements of the time. Likewise the collection belonging to Colonel Daniel Updyke, one of the founders of the Philosophical Society of Newport, reflected his interest in literature, history, and the political controversies of the day.[26]

Though theology and religion were not always subordinate to other interests,[27] the generalization is true that as the Puritan theocracy receded, the importance of religion in determining the character of these libraries steadily declined. After the beginning of the nineteenth century theology became a secondary influence. The Lancaster, Massachusetts, Library, established in 1790, was from the beginning dominantly historical and belletristic with relatively little theological material.[28] Among the founders of the Boston Athenaeum the ministry was only slightly represented, and the work of those charged with the selection of the books

that this library is still operating and that until relatively recent years it retained the practice of auctioning the use of books to the highest bidder, the auctions being held at the quarterly meetings on the first Monday of March, June, September, and December. According to letters from members, the auctions were important social events in the little community, and the bidding was lively. From such auctions revenues were derived for the promotion of the association.

26. Daniel Goodwin, "Some Early Rhode Island Libraries, Address before the Rhode Island Historical Society, January 26, 1909" (unpublished MS in Rhode Island Historical Society), pp. 5, 11–12.

27. In the catalog of the library of Saybrook, Lyme, and Guilford (Conn.) (ca. 1760), religion outnumbered all other titles by a ratio of over two to one. Of a total of 232 titles, 160 were clearly religious in content. This preponderance of religion may be partly explained by the gift of books from Isaac Watts. See Pl. II and Table 12, col. 1.

28. A. P. Marvin, *History of the Town of Lancaster, Massachusetts* (Lancaster: Published by the town, 1879), pp. 540–45.

clearly revealed the secular approach. The contents of these social libraries supplies unmistakable evidence that as a generic institutional type the agency represented a wide cultural interest in which the concern of the membership was directed toward the accumulation of a balanced book supply. The steady trend away from a culture dominated by theology is evident from an examination of successive catalogs of the same library; these show a progressive liberalization of book selection policy.[29]

Specialization in book acquisition appears to be the exception rather than the rule; those associations formed in response to a specific reading interest—law, children's literature, periodicals— being relatively few in number. The manuscript catalog of the Peterborough, New Hampshire, Juvenile Library shows the collection to have been largely current books for young readers, though there were some adult books on travel, history, and general literature.[30] The Concord, Massachusetts, Agricultural Library, which was formed prior to 1821, contained mainly books on agriculture, geology, chemistry, and botany.[31] From the beginning the library of the Middlesex Mechanics' Association (1827) was largely history, travel, literature, and science, with very little theology. Though prepared for a specialized clientele, membership being limited to mechanics and manufacturers, the collection approximated that of the average social library.

The importance of the social library book collections is emphasized by the seriousness with which the membership regarded the task of book selection. At Abington, Connecticut, the Social Library (1793) was subject to so much criticism because of its excessive emphasis on theological works that in 1804 the Junior Library of Abington was organized in protest. The tone of the new collection was much "lighter" with considerable fiction and other books of more general appeal.[32] At Poultney, Vermont, two

29. See Table 12, cols. 8 and 11, Hartford Library Company and Newport Mechanics' Library.

30. Manuscript catalog of the library, dated November 1, 1827, in the Peterborough Public Library.

31. Catalog in the Concord Public Library.

32. In 1815, however, the differences were subordinated to the interests of harmony, and the two were merged to form the United Library (see Ellen D. Larned, *History of Windham County* [Worcester: C. Hamilton, 1880], II, 285–86).

ministers who had joined the local social library, established in
1790, became so exercised over the quantity of "infidel" books in
the collection that they were successful in promoting the sale of
the entire stock so that more orthodox volumes could be purchased. The ministers themselves bought the "infidel" titles and
righteously consigned them to the flames.[33] The book collection
was the focal point at which converged the collective effort of the
entire group. What books were to be purchased with the always
limited financial resources of the organization was a moot and
ever urgent question. Seldom was it intrusted to the "librarian";
often it was the function of a special committee; and frequently
book purchases required the approval of a membership vote for
authorization. Indeed, this is still the practice at Arlington, Vermont, where the Board of Directors must approve all titles before
they can be added to the town library.[34]

The history of the social library in general, and especially this
early concern of the membership with the choice of books, reveals
the steadily increasing flow of authority from the supporting
group as a whole to the librarian. While the collections were
small, the librarian was only a member of the group who was
delegated as custodian. His duties involved little expenditure of
time or attention. As the collection grew, the responsibilities became greater, and finally someone was *hired* to do the work, but
authority and responsibility were retained by the group which
generally acted through a governing board. Even in this stage of
development the librarian was little more than a glorified janitor,
a "keeper" in the most elementary sense. He saw to it that the
books were distributed and returned; he collected fines and otherwise enforced the rules. But he did nothing "professional" and
exercised only the limited authority granted him; he was a
servant rather than an administrator. One of the most comprehensive early statements of the duties of the librarian is contained
in the records of the Providence Library Company, under the
date of August 7, 1754:

33. Joseph Joslin, Barnes Frisbie, and Frederick Ruggles, *History of the Town of
Poultney* (Poultney: Journal Printing Office, 1875), pp. 46–49.
34. Dorothy Canfield Fisher, "The Library in Our Town," *Atlantic Monthly*,
CLXXVIII, No. 4 (October, 1946), 127–30.

When the library is so far furnished with books as to make it fit to be opened for use, some proper person be appointed Librarian, whose business and duty it shall be to see that all things be wrote in the Register agreeable to the foregoing rules, take care that the books be kept clean, and in their proper places, to deliver out books and replace them, and discharge the receipts, to call for all books kept longer than they ought to be, to take care that the rooms, where the books are, be kept clean and neat, to attend one afternoon in each week the opening of the Library, deliver out and receive in Books, to attend to shew the Library to all Strangers who are Gentlemen and who desire to visit it.[35]

At the library of the United Society at Union, Rhode Island (1820), it was the duty of the librarian to "keep account of the title, size, number of pages, and the prints or maps, if there be any, of each book drawn from the library."[36] Even in the early days of the Boston Public Library the librarian had surprisingly little authority. But as the tasks of administration increased in complexity, professionalization became necessary, and the membership at large and the governing boards were compelled to relinquish authority to the librarians.

In some instances principles governing the selection of books were written into the bylaws. On March 7, 1787, the members of the social library at Royalston, Massachusetts, voted that the book fund be allocated according to the following schedule: 30 per cent for divinity; 30 per cent for history and biography; 20 per cent for arts and science; 10 per cent for law and "physic"; and 10 per cent for poetry, fiction, and miscellany.[37] At Laconia, New Hampshire, the regulations for the Meredith Bridge Social Library stipulated that "no professional books in law, physic, or divinity could be purchased at the expense of the proprietors."[38] The Arlington, Vermont, Library Society intrusted book selection to a Committee on Purchase and Inspection, which chose the books, "Having regard to the wishes of the Society and always excluding Law and Physic and never allowing books on Divinity to exceed one-thirtieth part of the value of the Library."[39] "Nov-

35. Records of the company in the Providence Athenaeum.

36. Rhode Island Board of Education, *Report*, 1901, pp. 42–43.

37. L. B. Caswell, *History of Royalston* (Royalston: Published by the town, 1917), pp. 106–8.

38. D. H. Hurd, *History of Merrimac and Belknap Counties, New Hampshire* (Philadelphia: Lewis, 1885), pp. 815–16.

39. Correspondence with Walter Hard, Jr., quoted by him from the records of the society.

els, romances, tales or plays," were denied inclusion in the Social Library of New Haven, Connecticut (1808), unless approved "by a vote of two-thirds of the members present at any single meeting."[40] The library of the United Society at Union, Rhode Island (1820), allowed "only such books as relate to history, biography, philosophy, theology, chemistry, and poetry. Religious and political dissertations favoring any one party or sect more than another" were excluded from the society "unless donated."[41] The Young Men's Library of Woburn, Massachusetts (1835), was confined to "such books as treat of facts," books of fiction and theology being forbidden.[42] The recorded purpose of the Young Men's Library of Deep River, Connecticut (1831), was to form a collection that "shall consist of Books of History, Biography, Voyages, Travels, and such other works as are calculated to improve the morals, strengthen the mind, and promote virtue."[43] At the Boston Mercantile Library Association the committee in charge of book purchase took particular pains to meet the needs of the membership, and it was one of the few early institutions to make extensive purchases of duplicate copies of those titles most in demand.

The committee to whom this important feature [i.e., the library] in our institution has been entrusted, we have endeavored to study the wishes of the members by using all possible care and judgement in their selection. To meet the more immediate demand for books we have procured duplicate volumes of works already in the catalogue, for which there is a continual demand. We have also, with a view to the permanent interests of the Association, aimed to purchase standard works that will enrich our library, as we conceive that much of its future usefulness depends upon the judicious selection of books which are not for a day but for all time.[44]

During the years 1806 and 1807 Joseph Stevens Buckminster, honors graduate of Harvard and afterward professor of biblical criticism there, was traveling in England and on the Continent.

40. Article IX of the Constitution of the society, in the New Haven Colony Historical Society.

41. Rhode Island Board of Education, *Report*, 1901, pp. 42–43. E. Field, *History of Rhode Island* (Boston: Mason, 1902), II, 637.

42. Massachusetts Free Public Library Commission, *Ninth Report, 1899* (Boston: Wright & Potter, 1899), p. 421.

43. Manuscript record book in Connecticut Historical Society.

44. Mercantile Library Association, *Thirty-first Annual Report* (Boston: Dutton & Wentworth, 1851), p. 4.

He had been authorized by the Boston Athenaeum to act incidentally as its purchasing agent. His correspondence with William Shaw reveals clearly the opinions of both regarding the
character of the Athenaeum's book collections. Though Buckminster had been trained in the ministry and had even for a brief
period been in charge of the church in Brattle Street, Boston, he
showed no theological bias in his conception of the function of the
Athenaeum. His approach to the problem of book selection was
entirely pragmatic. He recognized that the future of the Athenaeum depended upon continuing voluntary support, i.e., upon
the degree to which its book stock corresponded to popular demands. Writing to Shaw on the third of April, 1807, he said:

> I sent out about a dozen works because they are new; it should be an im-
> portant object in our establishment to take almost all the new publications. . . .
> Society papers are extremely valuable, but I think our funds are not sufficient
> to procure them. We must, at least for some time, think of popularity; and I
> know of no method so likely to procure it as to keep our rooms furnished with
> abundance of magazines, pamphlets, and *new books* [italics his]. This, I am
> satisfied, should be our primary object; and our second, to lay slowly and
> secretly the foundation of a permanent library of works difficult to be procured
> in America.[45]

So important was the wise choice of books to the promoters of
social libraries that the librarian of Harvard College had published, a decade earlier, a pamphlet which long remained the
fullest statement of the subject.

Thaddeus Mason Harris and His Treatise on Book
Selection for Social Libraries

In the year 1793 Thaddeus Mason Harris, who at the age of
twenty-five was just completing his term as librarian of Harvard
College, published his *Selected Catalogue of Some of the Most Esteemed Publications in the English Language Proper To Form a Social
Library*—the earliest attempt to formulate a general policy of book
selection for "public" libraries (see Pl. VIII and IX).

Harris' entire life was a personification of the spirit of the
antiquarian. Timid and sensitive by nature, harassed by long
periods of serious illness, and in later years "indescribably
bent"; he so typified the popular conception of the academician

45. Reproduced by Quincy, *op. cit.*, Appen., p. 52.

and bibliophile that Leonard Withington, writing under the pseudonym of John Oldbug, satirized him in *The Puritan* as Doctor Snivelwell; and Nathaniel Hawthorne testified to having often seen his ghost in the reading-rooms of the Boston Athenaeum.[46]

Harris was born in 1768, at Charlestown, Massachusetts, the son of a schoolmaster who died when the boy was but two years old. Thus from early experience he knew the handicap of poverty and misfortune. In 1787 he graduated from Harvard, where he had financed his education by serving as a waiter in the commons hall. After a brief period of schoolteaching at Worcester, he returned to Harvard to prepare for the ministry, was licensed to preach in 1789, and received his A.M. in 1790. In 1791 he became librarian of Harvard College, a position which he held for only two years.[47] From 1793 to 1836 he was pastor of the First Church of Dorchester, Massachusetts, but in addition to his career as a minister he was, in 1795 and 1796, editor of the *Massachusetts Magazine*, assistant to Jared Sparks on his edition of Washington's writings, and from 1837 until his death in 1842, librarian of the Massachusetts Historical Society. Extensive travel, usually prompted by an effort to regain physical vigor, punctuated his life and frequently was the stimulus for writing. A four months' western sojourn resulted in his *Journal of a Tour into the Territory Northwest of the Allegheny Mountains* (1805), and temporary residence in Georgia furnished an opportunity to collect material for his most considerable literary labor, the *Biographical Memorials of James Oglethorpe* (1841). His other published writings form a list of considerable length of which the more important are *The Natural History of the Bible* (1793, reissued in greatly enlarged form in 1820), and the *Minor Encyclopedia*, in four small volumes (1803).[48]

Harris' *Selected Catalogue* was a logical outgrowth of the contemporary interest in social libraries and the bibliographical en-

46. Nathaniel Hawthorne, "The Ghost of Doctor Harris," *Living Age*, CCXXIV, (February 10, 1900), 345–49.

47. His son, Thaddeus William Harris, held that position for twenty-five years.

48. N. L. Frothingham, "Memoir of Thaddeus Mason Harris," *Massachusetts Historical Society, Collections*, 4th ser., II (1854), 130–55.

thusiasms of its compiler.[49] By the year 1793 social libraries had become sufficiently prevalent to justify this attempt to generalize about their policies of book selection. That Harris, who had known the pinch of poverty and the need for judicious spending, should turn his hand to the task is not surprising. Even though young when the pamphlet appeared, Harris was an antiquarian and bibliophile with some library experience. Favored by his position as librarian of Harvard, he was aware of the right this office gave him to speak with authority. "Surrounded by the largest collection of books in America, and having made it a practice to read *all* the English reviews,"[50] he was convinced of the propriety in his pronunciation of ex cathedra judgments upon book-selection practices. He was doubtless familiar with the struggles of the social libraries to make limited budgets encompass balanced selection from the ever increasing volume of print that came from busy American presses. "Books, of course, are in great demand, and eagerly read," he wrote in the Preface to his catalog, "but they have become so exceedingly numerous as to require uninterrupted attention, through more than the longevity of an antediluvian to peruse them all. Indeed it would be a vain attempt to read all of those only that are really valuable."[51] The limitations of prevailing circumstance required that Harris restrict his collection both as to quantity and price. Data in the previous chapter indicate that most of the social libraries possessed collections well under three hundred titles in size, and Harris' catalog lists two hundred and seventy-seven.

> It has been my endeavor to form a catalogue for a *small* and *cheap* library, intended to suit the tastes and circumstances of common readers; many valuable works, in the higher departments of science, have been intentionally omitted. And imperfect as the list may be found, in other respects, yet I trust it will appear that there are *sufficient under each head* to give a *satisfactory* and *comprehensive* (though in some instances *very short*) view of that particular department of knowledge.[52]

Harris explains the principles by which he classified his catalog:

49. Thaddeus Mason Harris, *A Selected Catalogue of Some of the Most Esteemed Publications in the English Language Proper To Form a Social Library, with an Introduction upon the Choice of Books* (Boston: I. Thomas & E. T. Andrews, 1793); copies held by the American Antiquarian Society and the Massachusetts Historical Society (see Pl. XI).

50. *Ibid.*, p. iii.   51. *Ibid.*   52. *Ibid.*, p. v. Italics his.

I have deemed it convenient to arrange the books according to the subject of which they treat. This renders a catalogue perspicuous; and will be found of essential advantage to the reader, who will be pleased with seeing, at one view, the different authors upon the branch of knowledge he is prosecuting. The general delineation of human science, suggested by the immortal Bacon and since illustrated and enlarged by the learned D'Alembert, of dividing and sorting books into three classes, corresponding with the three great divisions of the mental faculties, *memory*, *reason*, and *imagination*, has been adopted as the most rational and clear.[53]

The following data indicate the classes used by Harris, with the number of titles in each: (1) memory: sacred history, 8; ecclesiastical history, 2; civil history and biography, 40; natural history, 6; voyages and travel, 23; and geography and topography, 8; *totaling 87;* (2) reason: theology, 34; mythology, 3; ethics, 8; grammar and dictionaries, 7; logic, rhetoric, and criticism, 5; general and local politics, 10; law, 6; metaphysics, 3; arithmetic, 5; natural and experimental philosophy (including astronomy), 4; chemistry, 3; agriculture, 3; and arts and manufactures, 18; *totaling 109;* (3) imagination: poetry and drama, 30; fiction, 11; fine arts, 5; and miscellanies, 35; *totaling 81.*[54]

How widely Harris' slender pamphlet was circulated and how much influence it had in molding the character of the subsequent social library book collections is not known. Only two copies of the treatise seem to have survived.[55] So far as the writer is aware, there are extant no contemporary references to it,[56] though Harris is known to have given personal aid during the summer of 1804

53. *Ibid.*

54. Reclassified according to the broad groups used in the analysis of the social library catalogs, Harris' list reveals the following percentages: literature, 28; religion, 21; science, 17; history and biography, 14; travel, 8; government and law, 6; fiction, 4; and fine arts, 2; totaling 100 per cent.

55. These are in the American Antiquarian Society at Worcester and in the Massachusetts Historical Society in Boston. This fact of limited survival means little regarding the distribution of the book. It might mean that only a few copies were printed and distributed; on the other hand, it might mean that the book was widely distributed and used but, because it was the kind of pamphlet which would soon be out of date, was generally destroyed when its first usefulness was past.

56. It seems first to have come to light in 1916 when Earl Bradsher discovered it in the collections of the American Antiquarian Society, and since that time no one seems to have paid any attention to it (see Earl L. Bradsher, "A Model American Library in 1793," *Sewanee Review*, XXIV [1916], 458–75). Bradsher reprints the book list and extracts from the Introduction. His treatment of the pamphlet suffers, however, from the misunderstanding of the term "social library."

in selecting the books for the Western Library Association of Ames, Ohio.[57] Furthermore, the pamphlet did come from one of the presses of Isaiah Thomas, which would indicate some opportunity for general public notice.[58] Perhaps its significance rests more upon the fact of its existence than upon any especial influence. That by 1793 it should have been considered desirable to attempt the formulation of policies of book selection for social libraries in general in itself reveals the growing importance of the social library as an institutional form. That the breadth of interest encompassed by the suggested list of titles roughly parallels that found in actual collections emphasizes once more the variety of interests that entered into the early development of the library as a popular institution. As a product of those expanding cultural forces that surrounded him, Harris' desire to formulate social library policy is significant. His part in influencing library development may not have been a large one, but as a reflection of the extent to which librarianship was progressing his work is of value for the historian.

Social Library Use and Contemporary Reading Interests

The surviving records are adequate to justify some generalization about the extent and character of the use of social libraries. The prevailing practice was to record circulation in blank books comparable to those used by the eighteenth-century bookkeeper. In fact, the procedure had much in common with accounting methods. To each user was assigned a page in the library ledger, and thereon were recorded the successive loans and discharges. In general, books were recorded not by author and title but by

57. This was the so-called "Coonskin Library." In August, 1804, Samuel Brown of Ames was visiting in Boston, where he was commissioned to purchase books for the Western Library Association then being formed. At that time he appealed to Thaddeus Mason Harris for aid in selecting the proper titles, and as a result Harris' judgment is largely responsible for the titles in the Coonskin Library (see Sarah J. Cutler, "The Coonskin Library," in *Ohio Archaeological and Historical Society, Publications*, XXVI [1917], 58–77).

58. This point of view is strengthened by the notice on the title-page: "CATA-LOGUES GIVEN GRATIS BY THE PUBLISHERS." This statement seems to signify that the pamphlet was used by Thomas as something of an advertising medium; and, if so, it would have been widely circulated.

their serial (accession) numbers.[59] A considerable number of these ledgers have been preserved, and they are a rich source for investigation of contemporary reading. By and large the members of the social libraries had much the same reading habits as those who frequent the public library of the present. History, biography, travel, natural science, literature, and fiction all were interesting to the eighteenth-century library patron, and the readers, then, turned to books on those subjects just as public library patrons turn to them today.

Theology was read, but not in the quantity generally supposed. Moreover, and this fact has been too frequently forgotten, the scholar and the academician studied books on theology and religion not because they necessarily planned to enter the ministry as a career or even because of any particular sense of piety or devotion. They read sermons and religious tracts for the simple reason that such were the main source of knowledge concerning man in his relation to other men. Theology stood to the eighteenth century much as sociology stands today. The dictates and admonitions of Puritanism were in themselves pragmatic and utilitarian to a striking degree, fostered, as Marcus Hansen has so clearly shown, by the hard necessity of pioneer life.[60] As pioneer society yielded to Colonial provincialism and this in turn gave way before the increased self-sufficiency of independent national life, man clung to religion for the insight it gave him into his relations to the social environment. Not until there emerged the new science of society by which man learned to use the processes of rational analysis in examining his social conduct did the old religion begin to lose its great appeal. Whatever the inner compulsions that prompted the eighteenth-century reader to select religious tracts, the essential fact that emerges from the available evidence is that the reading of theological treatises was then scarcely more prevalent than twentieth-century popular concern in sociological theory and research.

59. Records of fines were entered in the same way. Rules and regulations for many libraries imposed penalties not only for late return of books but also for physical damage. In certain institutions an elaborate system of fines for ink spots, candle drippings, torn pages, and other forms of injury was set forth in the bylaws.

60. Marcus L. Hansen, *The Immigrant in American History* (Cambridge: Harvard University Press, 1940), pp. 101–5.

In their reading, people, then as now, were motivated by the same demands that today may be identified with corresponding social groups—"prestige, income, security, power, relief from anxiety, vicarious adventure, and the gratification of the variety of emotions produced by the psychological mechanism in a given social environment."[61] It has been shown that the Junior Library of Abington, Connecticut, was formed in protest against the excess of theology in the older social library there. Of the Manufacturers' and Village Library (1841) of Great Falls, New Hampshire, it was reported that, though the collection was well rounded in scope, fiction "was most read"; and the famous Revolving Library of Kittery and York, Maine (1751), was so filled with theological treatises that for years its books lay strewn upon an attic floor neglected and forgotten.[62] The experience of the youthful Leonard Withington is probably not unlike that of many users of the early social libraries. At home he had access to only the library of his grandfather, which was "very small and confined to a few books of theological cast," but later in life he recalled "with gratitude, that in the town . . . there was a social library selected by the worthies of the place." This collection, which was "well selected, containing some of the most approved books of European authors, supplied the deficiencies of the domestic one and indeed contained some books which I have often wondered how my grandfather, strict as he was in his own theological principles, could admit among his intimates."[63]

This quotation suggests the possibility that the private libraries may have contained a somewhat larger proportion of religious books than the public collections, a fact which, if it be true, may have contributed to the prevalent belief in the dominance of theology in New England reading matter. It is likely, however, that this opinion has arisen from the tendency to assess book collections from their remnants. In the struggle for survival the books

61. Douglas Waples, Bernard Berelson, and Franklyn Bradshaw, *What Reading Does to People* (Chicago: University of Chicago Press, 1940), p. 21.

62. U.S. Bureau of Education, *Public Libraries in the United States of America, Their History, Condition, and Management* (Washington: Government Printing Office, 1876), p. 20.

63. Leonard Withington, *The Puritan* (Boston: Perkins & Marvin, 1836), I, 17, 24–25. The sequence of this quotation has been altered somewhat to fit the present context, but the meaning remains unchanged.

on theology were favored by the very fact of their austerity, while the books that enjoyed the greatest popularity were worn out by constant use.

The most significant bit of evidence relative to social library use has been preserved in the records of the Library Company of Providence, Rhode Island, which was the institutional ancestor of the present Providence Athenaeum.

In the early spring of 1753 eighty-six residents of Providence, recognizing that a "Collection or Library of useful and Edifying Books will most certainly tend to the Benefit and Instruction of the Inhabitants of this Town and County of Providence, and the Rising Generation thereto belonging,"[64] subscribed £1,500 old tenor, no insignificant sum for a town of three thousand population, for the promotion of such an institution. Within a year or so the books were assembled (they had been purchased mostly from England), Mr. Nicholas Brown was appointed librarian, and the collection was appropriately housed by permission of the General Assembly in the council chamber of the State House.

After the five hundred and eighty-three books were suitably arranged upon the shelves, and their three hundred and forty-five titles entered in the Register Book, the collection was opened for use. All went well until Christmas eve of 1758 when the State House and all its contents were entirely consumed by fire. From this destruction of the library there survived only the Register Book and those volumes actually in the hands of borrowers at the time of the conflagration. Though it was a misfortune for that little band of library subscribers, the fire was responsible for preserving the very information that the historian most desires. Here was saved for future inspection a complete catalog of the parent-library and a similarly complete listing of the titles "as were saved in the Proprietors' Hands when the late Library was burnt."[65] A comparison of these two lists is singularly revealing as

64. Preamble to the Providence subscription list, dated March 22, 1753 (see Grace F. Leonard and W. C. Worthington, *The Providence Athenaeum, a Brief History, 1753–1939* [Providence: The Athenaeum, 1940], 61 pp.; Joseph L. Harrison, "The Providence Athenaeum," *Seventh Annual Report of the Athenaeum, September 25, 1911,* pp. 19–55; also published in *New England Magazine,* September and October, 1911).

65. From the records of the library now in the Providence Athenaeum. The Register Book is still preserved in the Athenaeum. In February, 1760, the General

to the complexion of library use in a prosperous community in Colonial New England on that bleak December day in the middle of the eighteenth century. Obviously, history, biography, and travel were prevailing interests, the classics of English literature were a library staple, concern with scientific inquiry was on the

TABLE 13

COMPARISON OF TYPES OF BOOKS IN THE ORIGINAL COLLEC-
TION OF THE PROVIDENCE LIBRARY COMPANY WITH THOSE
HELD BY THE SUBSCRIBERS AT THE TIME OF THE FIRE

Subjects	No. of Titles in Old Library	No. of Titles Surviving
History and biography............	70	21
Literature*......................	68	8
Theology*.......................	51	4
Geography and travel............	17	7
Science (including medicine and current reference books)*...........	136	12
Unidentified....................	3	3
Total......................	345	55

* Among the surviving titles were (1) literature: Dryden, Pope, Milton, Voltaire, Shakespeare, and the *Spectator;* (2) theology: one volume on ecclesiastical law and one on the lives of the saints; (3) sciences: two chemistries and one volume on natural science; and (4) miscellaneous: the ubiquitous, and seemingly always popular, Bickham's *Universal Penman.*

march, and theology was more revered on the library shelf than in the reader's hand. This is corroborated by contemporary accounts and later studies of general reading interests throughout the period.

Our knowledge of reading behavior during the Colonial years is scanty, but it may be sufficient to suggest certain characteristics. John Dunton, writing from Boston, on March 25, 1686, to Mr. George Larkin, a London printer, thus describes one of his customers and her reading tastes:

The next is Mrs. ———, who takes as much state upon her as wou'd have serv'd Six of Queen Elizabeth's Countesses . . . she looks high, and speaks in a Majestick Tone like one acting the Queen's Part in a Play. . . . For to hide her Age, she paints; and to hide her painting, dares hardly laugh. . . . She was a

Assembly of Rhode Island authorized, in response to petition, a lottery from which was deducted $1,000, to be appropriated for the purchase of new books for the library. In 1768 a catalog of the library was printed, and in this list the surviving titles of the old library appear as starred entries.

good Customer to me, and whilst I took her Money, I humour'd her Pride. . . .
The chief Books she bought were Plays and Romance; which to set off the
better, she wou'd ask for Books of Gallantry.[66]

Doctor Alexander Hamilton, while visiting Boston in 1744,
found that *Pamela* and Ovid's *Art of Love* sold equally well with
Modern Divinity at a book auction in that town:

Tuesday, July 24th., [1744]. . . . After dinner I went with Mr. Vane to an
auction of books in King Street [Boston] where the auctioneer, a young fellow,
was very witty in his way. . . . The books that sold best at this auction, while I
was there were *Pamela, Antipamela, The Fortunate Maid,* Ovid's *Art of Love,* and
The Marrow of Modern Divinity.[67]

A century later Alfred Bunn wrote of the Bostonians:

They are a reading public: from the daily literature on a newsvender's coun-
ter, to the thoughtful volumes of the scholar's study, nothing escapes their
attention; and to such a pitch is this determination to acquire knowledge carried, that the coachman who drives you to hear a lecture will pay his money to
go in and attend its delivery. . . . In [New England] there is scarcely a village
that has not some institute for the delivery of lectures, the formation of a
library, and the study of various acquirements, while in all their cities and large
towns there are at least two and sometimes three. (We have been told that there
are upwards of three hundred in the six States.)[68]

The English publisher, William Chambers, who was deeply
impressed by the Yankee enthusiasm for books, reports a Boston
publisher as saying:

Everybody reads and everybody buys books. Every mechanic worth anything
at all, in Massachusetts, must have a small library which he calls his own;
besides, the taste for high-class books is perceptibly improving. A few years ago,
we sold great quantities of trashy Annuals; now, our opulent classes prefer works
of a superior quality.[69]

Royall Tyler has given what is perhaps the most complete account of the transition in reading interests that took place during
the closing years of the eighteenth century. In this pseudo-
biographical tale, Tyler's picaresque hero, Dr. Updike Under-

66. John Dunton, *John Dunton's Letters from New England* (Boston: Prince Society,
1867), p. 16.
67. Dr. Alexander Hamilton, *Itinerarium,* ed. A. B. Hart (St. Louis: Privately
printed, 1907), pp. 136–37.
68. Alfred Bunn, *Old England and New England* (Philadelphia: Hart, 1853),
pp. 22, 29.
69. William Chambers, *Things as They Are in America* (London: William & Robert
Chambers, 1854), p. 219.

hill, returning to Boston in 1795, after an absence of seven years, is represented as seeing a marked change in reading habits among the rural population of New England during the period of his captivity in Algeria. Fiction, which had previously been popular only in the seacoast towns, had now spread into the rural areas, largely through the influence of the social libraries. Underhill writes in the Preface:

One of the first observations the author of the following sheets made upon his return to his native country, after an absence of seven years, was the extreme avidity with which books of mere amusement were purchased and perused by all ranks of his countrymen. When he left New England, books of biography, travels, novels, and modern romances, were confined to our seaports, or if known in the country were read only in the families of clergymen, physicians, and lawyers; while certain funereal discourses, the last words and dying speeches of Bryan Shaheen, and Levi Ames, and some dreary somebody's Day of Doom, formed the most diverting part of the farmer's library. On his return from captivity, he found a surprising alteration in the public taste. In our inland towns of consequence, social libraries had been instituted, composed of books designed to amuse rather than to instruct; and country booksellers, fostering the newborne taste of the people, had filled the whole land with modern travels, and novels almost as incredible. . . . In no other country are there so many people, who, in proportion to its numbers, can read and write; and, therefore, no sooner was a taste for literature diffused than all orders of country life, with one accord, forsook the sober sermons and practical pieties of their fathers, for the gay stories and splendid impieties of the traveller and the novelist. The worthy farmer no longer fatigued himself with Bunyan's Pilgrim up the "hill of difficulty" or through the "slough of despond"; but quaffed wine with Brydone in the hermitage of Vesuvius, or sported with Bruce on the fairyland of Abyssinia; while Dolly the dairy-maid, and Jonathan the hired man, threw aside the ballad of the cruel step-mother, over which they had often wept in concert and now amused themselves into so agreeable a terror with the haunted houses and hobgoblins of Mrs. Radcliffe, that they were both afraid to sleep alone.[70]

Recent research is revealing with increasing precision the true nature of popular reading preferences between the years 1780 and 1850. The initial chapter of Herbert Brown's study of the sentimental novel in America gives a particularly comprehensive picture of reading interests during the closing decades of the eighteenth and the first half of the nineteenth century.[71] Brown's presentation is well supported by the statistical findings of Lyle

70. Royall Tyler, *The Algerian Captive* . . . (Hartford: Peter B. Gleason, 1810), pp. v–vi.

71. Brown, *op. cit.*, pp. 3–27.

H. Wright, whose analysis of the publication of fiction to the year 1850 reveals its steadily rising popularity.[72] Based on his own bibliography of novels published in book form,[73] Wright's data indicate that American publishers were issuing fiction in increasing quantities until it became the most important staple of the book market. The statistics in Table 14, taken from this study, do not include fiction published in the periodical press and are restricted to works by American authors. These data are supplemented by Brown's statement that "from 1789 to the turn of the century American presses struck off upwards of three hundred and fifty titles of popular foreign novels."[74]

TABLE 14*

FICTION TITLES PUBLISHED 1770-1850

Decade	No. of Titles	Decade	No. of Titles
1770–79	1	1830–39	290
1780–89	3	1840–49	765
1790–99	33	1850	90
1800–1809	25	No date	14
1810–19	28		
1820–29	128	Total	1,377

* Lyle H. Wright, "A Statistical Survey of American Fiction, 1774–1850," *Huntington Library Quarterly*, II (1939), 309.

Wright defends this flood of mediocrity as having value for the cultural historian even though it lacks literary merit: "The writings of many of the forgotten authors, true enough, may not be literary masterpieces, but the point so often overlooked is the contemporary taste for such literature. Publishers do not bring out second, third, fourth, and fifth editions of any author's titles unless the demand justifies it."[75] Parenthetically, it may be added that Wright might have further indicated the didacticism of such writing, particularly as it related to propaganda in support of current social reform; for, as he himself has shown in a subsequent study,[76] the novel was frequently employed as an instrument for

72. Lyle H. Wright, "A Statistical Survey of American Fiction, 1774–1850," *Huntington Library Quarterly*, II (1939), 309–18.

73. Lyle H. Wright, *American Fiction, 1774–1850, a Contribution toward a Bibliography* (San Marino: Huntington Library, 1939).

74. Brown, *op. cit.*, p. 15.

75. Wright, "Statistical Survey," *op. cit.*, p. 312.

76. Lyle H. Wright, "Propaganda in Early American Fiction," *Bibliographical Society of America, Papers*, XXXIII (1939), 98–106.

advancing opposition to lotteries, debtors' imprisonment, slavery, bad working conditions for women, and intemperance. The presence of a "moral" did not appear to diminish the appeal of the narrative; the frequency of successive editions is one of the most convincing evidences of continuing popularity. To his statistical survey Wright has appended a bibliography of over fifty titles that before the year 1850 had been issued in more than three editions.[77]

TABLE 15*

DISTRIBUTION OF LOANS BY TYPE OF LITERATURE
FROM NEW YORK SOCIETY LIBRARY, 1789–90

Class	Titles	Circulation
Biography and letters...........	76	712
Classics......................	20	74
Essays.......................	99	615
Fiction.......................	138	3,133
History.......................	151	1,550
Poetry and drama.............	66	351
Reference and periodicals.......	51	872
Religion and philosophy........	69	282
Science......................	66	264
Travel and discovery...........	82	1,172
Total....................	818	9,025

* From Frank Monaghan and Marvin Lowenthal, *This Was New York, the Nation's Capital in 1789* (Garden City: Doubleday, Doran, 1943), p. 151.

The study made by Monaghan and Lowenthal of the charge-out ledger belonging to the New York Society Library shows fiction to have been the most popular class of literature borrowed during 1789–90. The authors contrast this table with a similar analysis of books published in America in 1789–90 as listed in Evans' *American Bibliography* and explain that the reason for the high proportion of theology may be found in the fact that ministers were willing to subsidize the publication of their own sermons and religious tracts (see tabulation on p. 123).

The conclusion seems inescapable that, over the three centuries that span American library history, the reading habits of the populace were striking not for their divergencies in time and place but for their similarity among the several regions of the

77. Wright, "Statistical Survey," *op. cit.*, pp. 316–18. He points out that, because of the absence of complete statistical data on publication, the number of editions is the most accurate available guide to popularity.

country and throughout the passing years. It is evident, too, that the social library and the book interests it represented were very real to those groups of individuals who united in formal associations to pool their resources. There may have been some who joined for the prestige value of appearing to be well read, and local pride was doubtless a factor in the urge to library formation, but, most of all, the proprietors were motivated by the hard fact of necessity that compelled them to work together in order that they might obtain the books that each most wished to use.

Class	Imprints	Per Cent of Total Imprints
Theology........................	370	25
History.........................	82	6
Travel and geography.............	62	4
Fiction.........................	55	4
Total imprints issued during period..	1,493	....

From Frank Monaghan and Marvin Lowenthal, *This Was New York, the Nation's Capital in 1789* (Garden City: Doubleday, Doran, 1943), p. 152.

The Decline of the Social Library

The advent of the public library in the middle of the nineteenth century was only partially responsible for the general decline of the social library that began about the same time. Obviously, competition from the new agency accelerated this movement, but the structural weaknesses that handicapped the social library were apparent some time before the public library had made material progress. The social library carried within itself the seeds of its own deterioration, and its general inability to survive the initial enthusiasm of its founders contributed directly to the demand for a library form that would evince some promise of permanence and stability.

This growing awareness of the inadequacy of the social library to meet the needs of a changing age was frankly expressed in George Ticknor's crusade for the union of the Boston Athenaeum with the proposed public library. Surely the Athenaeum had been one of the most prosperous of its kind, and "while, on the one hand, it is a monument to the liberality of its proprietors and benefactors, on the other hand, it has rarely ceased to struggle with difficulties, and has never satisfied the reasonable wants of those who most frequent it."[78] In its weaknesses the Athenaeum was representative of the social library as a type, a form which must eventually give way before the efficiency of the public library:

> Indeed, if we do not mistake the signs of the times, such efficient Public Libraries are soon to be generally substituted for the private corporations which have heretofore imperfectly satisfied the demands of the communities where they have existed, and, unless we are further mistaken, these private corporations will, by the generous and judicious action of their own members, be made the foundations of the Public Libraries, that are so fast springing up on all sides.[79]

The social library was becoming obsolete—no longer able adequately to meet the expanding demand for greater library resources. It belonged to another age:

> We should bear in mind, that the Athenaeum belongs to a class of establishments for instruction, beginning with the Lycée in Paris, and the Royal Institution in London, which were created by a state of society, that existed from fifty to eighty years ago in Paris, London, and this country, and that are now changing their character, or else are passing or have passed away, with the circumstances that gave them birth.[80]

Ticknor's prognostications were less accurate for the Athenaeum than for the social library in general. But there were others, too, who were charging that the restricted services of this agency were not compatible with contemporary enthusiasm for popular education. Edward Everett, in the first report of the Trustees of the Boston Public Library, held the system of social libraries to be inadequate to the task of supplying the book needs of Boston, just as the private schools were not equal to the demand for universal common-school education.[81] John B. Wight, in urging general permissive legislation for public library establishment in Massachusetts, charged that "where there are social libraries" they had "but partially supplied to a select number" the books needed by the entire community.[82]

78. George Ticknor, *Union of the Boston Athenaeum and the Public Library* (Boston: Dutton & Wentworth, 1853), p. 3.

79. *Ibid.*, p. 12.   80. *Ibid.*, p. 11.

81. Boston Public Library, Trustees, *Report, July 1852* (Boston: J. H. Eastburn, 1852), pp. 7–9 and *passim*.

82. John B. Wight, "Public Libraries," *Common School Journal*, XIII (1851), 260. For a further consideration of this legislation see chap. vi, pp. 189 ff., chap. vii, pp. 202 ff.

Though the tax-supported free public library eventually overshadowed the social library, the corporate library form was far from obsolete. As late as 1906 Harry Lyman Koopman foresaw a new age of expansion for the social library. Speaking before a conference of the American Library Association, he said, in part:

It is striking testimony to the permanence of American institutions that the three public libraries established by the people of Rhode Island before the Revolution are all entering upon the twentieth century in vigor and usefulness. At this point I will venture the prophecy that the proprietary library, to which type two of these belong, is destined not to disappear in competition with the free public library, but to come again into favor in our cities and larger towns during the century before us. For instance, in the last two years, the number of shareholders of the Providence Athenaeum has increased ten percent, and its circulation thirty-three percent.[83]

In the same year Willis K. Stetson, writing in the *Connecticut Magazine*, saw no essential conflict but a basis for division of function between the social library and its tax-supported contemporary. "It may well be contended that in a city the size of New Haven there is a place for a subscription library. It offers advantages which a public library can with difficulty, if at all, provide."[84] In Stetson's dichotomy of purpose it is the province of the public library to supply the ephemeral and popular reading material, while the subscription library should concentrate on books of a more permanent value and restricted demand.

The renaissance of the social library movement which Koopman envisaged did not occur; few such institutions were established after the nineteenth century,[85] but the form is today far from extinct. Specific data on the exact number of these libraries now operating are not available, but Joeckel has estimated that of the sixty-five hundred public libraries in the United States in 1939, more than one-tenth were of the association or corporation

83. Harry L. Koopman, "Library Progress in Rhode Island," A.L.A. Conference, Narragansett Pier, 1906, "Proceedings," *Library Journal*, XXXI (1906), c. 11.

84. Willis K. Stetson, "Development of the Free Public Library in New Haven," *Connecticut Magazine*, X (1906), 130.

85. The Bridgewater (Conn.) Library Association was established in 1905. The East Norwalk (Conn.) Improvement Association founded its social library in 1915. The Kent (Conn.) Library Association was formed in 1916 (from a survey of the public libraries in Connecticut prepared by the state Public Library Committee, Connecticut, Public Library Committee, *Report to the Governor for the Years 1915, 1916, 1917, and 1918* [Hartford: Published by the state, 1919], pp. 40, 56, 58).

type.[86] These he finds mainly concentrated along the Atlantic coast from New England to the South. Particularly in Connecticut is the form prevalent; there it has been estimated that "more than one half" of the libraries in the state are of this type.[87] In many instances the constant struggle of the social library to maintain adequate support in the face of declining revenue from memberships has been alleviated by direct grants from the town treasury, in which instances the services of the library have been made available to the residents of the town or city. Though in such cases the body politic may lack representation in the government and administration of the library, as the agency retains full autonomy in operation, the library does become a municipal service so far as the patrons are concerned.[88]

It is important here to record that with the passing of time there appears to be a definite trend toward both increased public support and increased responsibility on the part of the social library. Many are aware of the obligations involved in the possession of rare materials, such as the extensive collections of the Boston Athenaeum, and make them freely available to scholars whose work justifies their use. Almost from the beginning the social library movement assumed the essential attributes of a public library system. Those characteristics have increased rather than diminished. By virtue of the implications for the future, as well as of the character of its past, the social library is an important factor in the evolution of the modern public library.

86. Actually these figures underestimate the number of social libraries still operating, for Joeckel has considered only public libraries which give general service to the entire population of their respective communities. His data do not include the various kinds of association and subscription libraries which still exist for the benefit of only their own membership, i.e., his data exclude the Boston Athenaeum, the Social Law Library of Boston, and similar special collections (see Carleton B. Joeckel, *The Government of the American Public Library* [Chicago: University of Chicago Press, 1935], p. 344; also unpublished data, 1939).

87. Unpublished estimate from Miss Katharine H. Wead, secretary, Connecticut Public Library Commission.

88. There are many examples of this kind of arrangement between the town government and private association libraries. The McClure Library of Pittsford, Vt., and the Scoville Memorial Library of Salisbury, Conn., are examples.

CHAPTER V

THE CIRCULATING LIBRARY

WHEREAS the social libraries in general represented the more sophisticated book requirements of the community and their collections were formed by men with real enthusiasm for good literature, the coexistent circulating libraries reflected much more popular reading tastes, and their shelves were filled with fiction—those "greasy combustible duodecimos" denounced by the moralists. Because the social libraries and the circulating libraries operated simultaneously and to a great extent supplemented each other, the neglect of either leads to an unbalanced presentation of American public library history.

What would today be called a "rental library" was, during the eighteenth and nineteenth centuries, known as a "circulating library," though the basic idea, the loan of books in exchange for a stipulated fee, has remained unchanged. Generically the name clearly reveals the antiquity of the form—a survival from a time when conservation was held to be a primary function of the library and books could not be removed from the building in which they were housed. "Circulating" libraries, by contrast, were established to permit extra-mural use, provided that a fee was paid for the privilege. The books in the social libraries "circulated" also, but the name "circulating library" has so long been associated with the rental function that it was retained in spite of ambiguity.

The circulating library was, first of all, a commercial enterprise inaugurated to make money for the owner. Promoters of these libraries entertained no illusions of martyrdom in the cause of culture, nor had they any enthusiasm for improving the intellects of their patrons or for advancing the educational level of their communities; their one objective was to show a profitable return on their investments. This desire for gain encouraged the selection of popular and ephemeral titles and the rejection of more substantial works for which there was less demand. By adherence to the current demands of its borrowers, the circulating library retained its vitality as a partial substitute for the public library and perhaps delayed the appearance of the latter.

The structure of the circulating library was, from the beginning, both simple and surprisingly uniform. Books were available for loan either by the payment of a rental fee or by "memberships" which entitled the patron to withdraw at one time a predetermined number of volumes in exchange for quarterly, semiannual, or annual "dues," in which case their structure approximated that of the social library. Such subscription rates were generally $7.00 per year, $4.50 per half-year, or $2.00 per quarter, for which the patron was entitled to from two to four "books"[1] at a time for a period of one month. Nonsubscribers were charged a weekly rental, the rate varying according to the size of the volume.[2] Rentals generally were $0.20 to $0.25 for a quarto or larger volume, $0.10 to $0.15 for an octavo, $0.05 to $0.10 for duodecimos, and $0.03 to $0.05 for pamphlets or single issues of magazines.[3] On occasion slightly higher charges were in effect, permitting the retention of loans for a fortnight.

The penalty for loss or injury was usually the imposition of damages equal to the cost of the book or set of books if the title comprised more than one volume. In the eyes of the proprietor the cardinal sin of the subscriber was the relending of books to

1. The prefatory notices in the catalogs listed in Appen. IV are the sources for these data. It is not clear whether "books" meant titles or volumes, though it would seem that the former was intended. Books could be exchanged as frequently as the subscriber desired.

Charles Whipple of Newburyport also loaned books upon payment of $1.00 per month. Cushing and Appleton of Salem permitted the taking-out of six books at a time upon payment of $10.00 annually.

Even in 1765 John Mein's rates were much the same as those of his successors since he charged £1/8s./–per year or 18s. for six months. He also charged 1s. for his catalog, a practice that was later abolished as paper and printing facilities became more abundant.

2. Charges were assessed by the week or fraction thereof.

3. Contrary to present-day policies rates frequently increased after the third or fourth week. William Martin of Boston, 1786, charged on the basis of "a week or ten days."

others. Such a practice, as the management quickly foresaw, would result in a serious reduction in revenue. "Subscribers lending their books will be charged for them as non-subscribers, separate from their privilege as subscribers" announced Cushing and Appleton of Salem.[4] William Pelham of Boston, by contrast, rationalized his disfavor of this practice in quite altruistic terms of the greatest benefit to the greatest number: "Subscribers lending their books to forfeit their subscriptions," he cautioned in the Preface to his catalog of 1804, "as this practice causes not only injury to the library, but disappointment to other readers."[5] But such admonitions, though they may have epitomized the need of the proprietor to safeguard his income, probably exercised little influence in restraining the subscriber who felt impelled to share the latest book with his neighbor. The rule was certainly difficult, if not impossible, of enforcement.[6]

Origin of the Circulating Library

Information concerning the early circulating libraries is scattered and fragmentary; surviving printed catalogs and newspaper advertisements are the best sources available. Evidence of their importance is their commercial success as indicated by length of activity; their survival after the original owner's death; statements of contemporaries; and records of sale, transfer, or other business transactions. Doubtless many have left no trace of their existence, yet enough information is available to indicate a great deal about the nature of these collections, their prevalence, and the kinds of books they contained.

In the middle of the eighteenth century, when the social library began to be important in the American Colonies, the circulating library was an old and familiar institution to the readers of England and the Continent. As early as the fourteenth century,

4. Cushing and Appleton, *Essex Circulating Library Catalogue* (Salem: Thomas C. Cushing, 1818), p. 2.

5. William Pelham, *Catalogue of Pelham's Circulating Library* (Boston: Munroe & Francis, 1804), p. 4.

6. Howe and Deforest, *A Catalogue of Books in Howe and Deforest's Circulating Library* (New Haven: Sidney's Press, 1814). A second practice which similarly encroached upon the profits of the management was the extensive reading of library books at the library room. This was strictly forbidden by Howe and Deforest of New Haven.

when books were scarce and their prices correspondingly high, French booksellers kept books to be borrowed at a stipulated charge. A Paris statute of 1342 required that such booksellers rent a portion of their stocks to the students of the universities, the rate to be established by the universities; and fines were imposed upon those found guilty of renting defective copies or of failing to post a public catalog of all titles with a clear indication of the rental fee for each.[7] Similar early forms of the circulating library appeared at Toulouse, Vienna, and Bologna, as well as at Paris.

No one knows precisely who was the first to establish a circulating library in England, but certainly among the earliest was Francis Kirkman, a London bookseller who flourished in 1674 and combined with his business a circulating library specializing in plays, poetry, and romances.[8] Other such collections are reported to have been in operation at the turn of the eighteenth century, one at Dunfermline, Scotland, in 1711; and seven years later a reading-room in London was renting newspapers and current periodicals. Perhaps the best-known early circulating library in the British Isles was that started about 1725, or shortly thereafter, by Allan Ramsay when he began the practice of renting books from his bookstore at a charge of a penny a night.[9] This

7. F. Somner Merryweather, *Bibliomania in the Middle Ages* (London: Woodstock Press, 1933), p. 60. André Chevillier (*Qrigines de l'imprimerie de Paris* [Paris: G. de Laulane, 1694], p. 319) gives a long list of books with the charges established for their use. Among them are: Gregory, *Commentaries upon Job*, 100 pp., 8 sous; Gregory, *Book of Homilies*, 28 pp., 12 deniers; Isidore, *De summa bona*, 24 pp., 12 deniers; Anselm, *De veritate de libertate arbitrii*, 40 pp., 2 sous; Peter Lombard, *Book of Sentences*, 3 sous; *Scholastic History*, 3 sous; Augustine, *Confessions*, 21 pp., 4 deniers; Thomas Aquinas, *Gloss on Matthew*, 57 pp., 3 sous; *Bible Concordance*, 9 sous; and Bible, 10 sous.

8. The *Dictionary of National Biography* attributes the introduction of the circulating library to both Kirkman and Samuel Fancourt (1678–1768) though Kirkman's venture was probably in operation before Fancourt was born. Fancourt's collection was an important one, and his library became well known (*Dictionary of National Biography*, VI, 1036–37; XI, 219–20). Charles Evans (*American Bibliography* . . . [Chicago: Blakely Press, 1907], IV, x) likewise attributes to Fancourt the invention of the circulating library.

9. Burns Martin, *Allan Ramsay, a Study of His Life and Works* (Cambridge: Harvard University Press, 1931), pp. 33–34. Martin dates Ramsay's library about 1728, denying the validity of evidence for any earlier date. However, he makes the error of assuming that Ramsay was responsible for the introduction of the form. It is to

collection, which incurred the righteous indignation of many good Scottish ministers, grew rapidly in size and influence, came eventually to be known as the Edinburgh Circulating Library, and prospered for more than a century. The unqualified success of these ventures in the renting of books, coupled with the popularity of the English literary club and the rise of the novel as a literary form, soon resulted in the spread of the institution throughout Great Britain.[10]

Beginnings in Colonial America

The circulating library came relatively late to Colonial America, and if existing knowledge of its beginnings on this side of the Atlantic is complete, the earliest attempts to establish such institutions did not appear in New England. If one were to define the circulating library in its broadest sense, the first example would probably be the attempt in 1745 of James Parker, partner of Benjamin Franklin, to revive the fortunes of the New York Corporation Library by hiring the books to patrons. The city fathers, who had the library in custody, acquiesced in the plan, but sufficient patronage was not forthcoming to justify maintenance, so the scheme was abandoned.[11]

What is believed to have been the first real circulating library in the Colonies was an abortive venture promoted by William Rind of Annapolis, Maryland, in the autumn of 1762. His was a

---

be noted that in 1720 the booksellers Robert Willoughby and A. Jackson were each advertising books for rent at their respective bookstores in London. See also the chapter on circulating libraries in Pearl G. Carlson, "Libraries for the People, a Study of English Library History" (unpublished MS in possession of its author). See also Taylor Brown, "A First Circulating Library—a Venture of Allan Ramsay," *Publishers' Circular*, CLIII (1940), 173–74.

10. One of the most influential English circulating libraries was that of the Minerva Press, which flourished at the turn of the nineteenth century. Not only were its books widely circulated in "branch" provincial libraries throughout the British Isles, but there were American agents on this side of the Atlantic. One of these was H. Caritat, who operated a circulating library in New York City (see Dorothy Blakey, *The Minerva Press, 1790–1820* [London: Printed for the Bibliographical Society by the Oxford University Press, 1939], chap. xi, "The Circulating Library," pp. 111–26).

11. Austin B. Keep, *History of the New York Society Library* (New York: Printed for the Society by the DeVinne Press, 1908), pp. 72–76.

grandiose scheme designed to supply books at a moderate rental to the entire colony:

TO THE PUBLIC

The great Utility of diffusing a Spirit of Science thro' the Country, is too obvious to need any Proof, and if the Author of the following Plan has been so fortunate as to adapt it to this important Object, he presumes to hope that his Endeavors will be well received and supported by the Public. Nature (it is generally acknowledged) has been sufficiently bountiful to the Natives of this Country, in bestowing upon them the happiest Talents; but as the richest Soil, without due Cultivation, runs into rank and unprofitable Weeds, so little Fruit can be expected from the best natural Endowments, where the Mind is not under the Direction of proper intellectual Aids. Among the many Obstacles to literary Acquirements, which the Youth of this Country are liable to, the Want of Books proper for their instruction, is justly esteemed one of the greatest. The furnishing of a competent Library, for any tolerable advancement in Letters, requires a Fortune which few People in this part of the World are Masters of, whence it comes to pass, that many a fine Genius languishes and dies in Obscurity. The Purpose, therefore, of this Plan, which is to open and extend the Fountains of Knowledge, which are at present Shut against all but Men of sufficient Fortunes, it is hoped, will meet with the Countenance and Patronage of every Friend of his Country. If the Author of this Scheme finds sufficient encouragement from this Essay, he proposes to enlarge his Plan by the addition of many more Books to his Catalogue, so that the Means of Knowledge will thereby become accessible to Men of middling Fortunes, and every Man will be furnished at a very easy Rate with Books which best suit his Taste, or correspond with the natural Propensity of his Genius. As a Scheme of this Nature is quite new in this Part of the World, the Author has not the Vanity to think, but that what he has proposed is capable of many improvements, and therefore will be much obliged to any ingenious Gentleman, who will point out its Defects, and furnish him with any Amendments or Additions, which may more effectually conduce to the perfection of his Plan.

WILLIAM RIND[12]

12. *Maryland Gazette*, September 2, 1762. In 1758 Rind had become a partner of James Green, publisher of the second *Maryland Gazette*, and the two operated a printing and bookselling establishment at Annapolis. The original plan was to permit the use of two books at a time for an annual fee of 27s. Annapolis subscribers were permitted the use of a folio for one month, a quarto for three weeks, and an octavo for one week. Patrons living more than thirty miles from Annapolis were granted an additional two weeks. In January, 1763, Rind restricted loans to a district within thirty miles of Annapolis and the limit was reduced to one book per subscriber at one time, though the loan period for folios was extended to two months. What actually became of the collection is unknown. Attempts to sell the books at auction and later to dispose of them by lottery both failed. See also Lawrence C. Wroth, *History of Printing in Colonial Maryland* (Baltimore: Typothetae of Baltimore, 1922), p. 85; Joseph Towne Wheeler, "Literary Culture in Colonial

Success was not so great as its promoter had anticipated, and the collection was abandoned in the summer of 1764.

Six months after the inauguration of Rind's venture George Wood, a bookbinder and stationer in Charleston, South Carolina, advertized his intent "to set on foot A CIRCULATING LIBRARY" for "Gentlemen and Ladies that approve this plan."[13] But it was scarcely more profitable than its Maryland contemporary. On August 29 of the same year the *New York Gazette* announced:

> To those who delight in Reading, And would spend their Leisure Hours and Winter Evenings, with Profit and Entertainment THIS IS TO GIVE NOTICE, that this Day is opened by GARRAT NOEL, Bookseller next door to the Merchants Coffee-House, A CIRCULATING LIBRARY; Consisting of several Thousand Volumes of Choice Books, in History, Divinity, Travels, Voyages, Novels, &c.[14]

The library met with indifferent success and was abandoned as profitless in the autumn of 1765.[15] Thus, by the year 1765, when John Mein founded in Boston the first circulating library in New England, a number of similar attempts had already been made in the other Colonies, but none was so profitable as its English contemporaries. The historic importance of these early collections is their obvious English derivation and the rapidity of their establishment in the New World when and where the Colonial environment had come to approximate that of Britain.

Circulating Libraries in Boston

If the Colonies of New England were somewhat slower than their neighbors to the south in experimenting with circulating libraries, an abundant later development was characteristic of the region; for, once the agency had been established, it spread

---

Maryland, 1700–1776" (Ph.D. thesis, Brown University, 1938), pp. 256–62; Joseph Towne Wheeler, "Literary Culture in Eighteenth Century Maryland: Booksellers and Circulating Libraries," *Maryland Historical Magazine*, XXXIV (1939), 111–37.

13. *South Carolina Gazette*, March 5–12, 1763.

14. *New York Gazette*, August 29, 1763. In addition to operating a bookstore, Noel advertised that he had "likewise to sell, the very best of Durham Flour of Mustard and a fresh Parcel of very fine Snuff, commonly called Black Guard" (*loc. cit.*). See also Keep, *op. cit.*, pp. 102–4.

15. The rental terms offered by Noel were much like those of Rind. The annual fee was placed at $5.00, and loans were restricted to one book at a time.

rapidly throughout the New England area and became a profitable form of enterprise.

There may have been a real connection between the success of Allan Ramsay's circulating library and the first such undertaking in Colonial Boston. From the Scottish city of Edinburgh there came to Boston in October, 1764, one John Mein, who in his homeland had been a bookseller. Mein brought with him a quantity of books, linens, and other goods; and upon arriving at the Massachusetts port he immediately entered into partnership with Robert Sandeman. Together they advertised for sale divers wares including "English and Scotch Prayer-Books" and "Edinburgh Beer and Porter by the Cask or Doz."[16] The partnership soon dissolved, and by the summer of 1765 Mein alone was occupying the shop.[17] By October of that year he had opened a bookselling business and circulating library at the London Book-Store, "Second Door above the British Coffee-House," in King (now State) Street.[18] Specific evidence concerning the success of Mein's circulating library is lacking; by inference from the size of the collection and the nature of the advertisements it seems reasonable to assume that its fortunes were somewhat better than those enterprises in the southern Colonies. In 1767 the proprietor increased his business by publishing a number of books and the *Boston Chronicle*, the latter being an organ in support of British colonial policy. Mein was so outspoken in his approval of the British government and so openly opposed to the boycott of goods subject to stamp duties that in October, 1769, he was

16. *Massachusetts Gazette*, October 10, 1765. Sandeman was a nephew of the Rev. Robert Sandeman, Scottish minister. The three had sailed from Scotland in the same ship, their arrival in Boston having been noted in the *Gazette* for October 22, 1764, p. 3. The *Boston Gazette* for November 19, 1764, carried the first advertisement of the new firm of Mein and Sandeman:

> Mein & Sandeman
> Have imported from Great-Britain
> the following Articles, which are to be
> Sold very cheap for CASH, at their
> Shop nearly opposite to Bromfield's
> Lane, Marlboro'-Street, Boston

17. The name of Mein and Sandeman last appears in the *Boston Gazette* for February 18, 1765 (p. 2). In the same publication, for June 17, 1765 (p. 3), Mein's name alone appears as operator of the business.

18. *Boston Gazette*, October 7, 1765, p. 3.

mobbed. In the scuffle that ensued he shot a grenadier and fled to England, where he communicated to Lord Dartmouth his opinions on the state of affairs in the American Colonies.

But his troubles were not all political. With more persistence than the mob of irate citizens, his debts pursued him across the sea. He returned to Boston and was convicted in the courts of Suffolk County for failure to meet his financial obligations—no one seems to have been concerned about the grenadier—and during this second sojourn attempted to re-establish his bookselling and library business, though still continuing his opposition to a boycott of English goods.[19] So, confronted by defeat in the Superior Court of Judicature and by inability to revive his business, Mein, who had spent some time in Boston's prison, again fled to England, where he remained, and New England's first circulating library came to an inglorious close.[20]

In 1765 when Mein's plans for a circulating library were most ambitious, he published a catalog of his collection listing over six hundred and fifty titles in more than twelve hundred volumes,[21] "in most Branches of Polite Literature, Arts, and Sciences" (see Pl. X). Books were available to prospective patrons upon payment of "One Pound, Eight Shillings, lawful Money, per Year; Eighteen Shillings per Half-Year; or Ten and Eight Pence per Quarter." The catalog itself sold for one shilling. Fines were, of course, imposed for loss of or damage to volumes or for lending books to nonsubscribers; but delinquency in return was penalized only when it extended beyond the period for which the subscription fee had been paid. Loans were restricted to one book at a time, except for those living "in the Country" who might take

19. March 19, 1770, the town of Boston voted that, the merchants having engaged to suspend importation from Great Britain, John Mein's name be entered on the records as one of twelve persons "so thoroughly and infamously selfish as to obstruct *this very* measure by continuing their importation (Boston Record Commissioner, "Reports," XVIII, 16).

20. Charles K. Bolton, "Circulating Libraries in Boston, 1765–1865," *Colonial Society of Massachusetts, Publications*, XI (1906–7), 197–98; Isaiah Thomas, *The History of Printing in America* . . . (Worcester: Press of Isaiah Thomas, Jr., 1810), I, 362–65, and II, 247; John E. Alden, "John Mein, Publisher," *Bibliographical Society of America, Papers*, XXXVI (1942), 199–214.

21. Alden shows, on the basis of typographical similarities, that the catalog was printed by M'Alpine of Boston, who also printed certain books issued by Mein (Alden, *op. cit.*, pp. 201–2).

two books at once, provided double the fee was paid, and the expense of carriage was borne by the patrons. The library was open from "Ten o'Clock to One in the Forenoon, and from Three to Six Afternoon." Subscribers, to avoid disappointment, were urged to submit several choices, though this may have been no more than an advertising device to create the impression of great popularity.[22]

The unhappy outcome of Boston's first attempt to establish a circulating library may have immediately discouraged any further effort in that direction. It is more probable, however, that political distractions, difficulty of obtaining book stock, and the general economic disturbances accompanying the Revolution delayed the initiation of any subsequent venture until after the formation of the Republic and the stabilization of the economic and social structure. Almost two decades passed before Boston again had a circulating library.

On May 27, 1784, William Martin, a Boston shopkeeper, announced in the *Independent Chronicle* that to his general stocks of books for sale he had added "a Library of Bibles and other Books." A scant year thereafter, on April 28, 1785, he advertised in the same journal apropos of his book department that "a part of said Collection [had been] appropriated to let out by week or quarter." That the library prospered may be assumed, for Martin moved from Seven Star Lane to a more desirable location and expanded quarters at 45 Main Street. At this new place of business the collections of the library were increased and it became known as the Boston Circulating Library. A catalog of the books was announced in the *Independent Chronicle* for December 29, 1785, and actually made its appearance early in the following year.[23] Though constantly annoyed by the negligence of subscribers in the return of books, Martin continued his library until the autumn of 1787. In the spring of the preceding year he had complained in the pages of the *Independent Chronicle* of the delinquency of his patrons:

22. See "Conditions To Be Observed by Every Subscriber," John Mein, *Catalogue of Mein's Circulating Library* (Boston: John Mein, 1765), p. 2.
23. Martin's *Catalogue*, 1786; see entry in Appen. IV.

MR. MARTIN

Begs leave to remind those Ladies
and Gentlemen who have kept BOOKS
of his beyond the limited time,
and still do so, that such delay is
a great injury to his business, both as
to the accommodation of his *good*
customers, and the profit to himself;
it tends to frustrate the very
establishment, and, instead of a
Circulating, to render it a *Stagnated*
Library.[24]

In the summer Martin repeated his protest, insisting that a number of the titles, among them *Clarissa Harlowe*, *Peregrine Pickle*, *Gil Blas*, and the *Adventures of a Valet*, had been absent more than two months, to the "great disappointment of the Subscribers and disgrace of the establishment."[25] Whether this laxity of his patrons weighed heavily in Martin's decision to abandon his book business is not apparent, but in the autumn of 1787 he did dispose of all his book stock either by sale or exchange for West India goods and continued in business as a merchant.

While Martin was endeavoring to persuade his subscribers to return their books, another circulating library was operating in Boston. Of the names associated with the development of the circulating library in Boston perhaps the most prominent is that of Guild. Benjamin Guild, Harvard graduate, college tutor, sometime minister, and member of the American Academy of Arts and Sciences, in March, 1785, purchased the Boston Book-Store from Ebenezer Battelle of Marlborough Street, and later operated a circulating library in conjunction with it.[26] Of the library, located at No. 59 Cornhill Street, three catalogs (1788,

24. *Independent Chronicle*, May 25, 1786, p. 2.
25. *Ibid.*, August 31, 1786, p. 3. Note that all titles are fiction.
26. The name Guild is important in New England history. Benjamin was baptized on April 30, 1749. Graduating from Harvard College just twenty years later, he was tutor there from 1776 to 1780. Subsequently he entered the ministry. One year before he purchased the Boston Book-Store, in 1784, he married Elizabeth, the daughter of Colonel Josiah Quincy (*ibid.*, March 10, 1785). Guild died in 1792. His death, as given by Bolton (p. 201), occurred on October 15; Burleigh gives the date as September of the same year (Charles Burleigh, *The Genealogy and History of the Guild, Guile, and Gile Family* [Portland, Me.: Brown Thurston, 1887], p. 85).

1789, and 1790) with one supplement (1791) were published.[27] The steady growth of the book stock listed in these annual catalogs indicates that the enterprise was profitable.[28] After the death of Benjamin Guild in the autumn of 1792, the Boston Book-Store and its circulating library was taken over by William P. Blake, who, with the widow and John Guild, was an administrator of Benjamin's estate.[29] In May of the following year Blake issued his first catalog of books "for sale or circulation" which represented an inventory even larger than that of his predecessor.[30] In 1798 Blake took his brother Lemuel into partnership, and the bookstore and circulating library prospered on into the new century.[31] Removal to better quarters in 1796 and the appearance of a new catalog in 1798 indicate a prosperous business.[32] Financial reverses, about 1805, necessitated the sale of the enterprise, and in 1806 creditors disposed of the business to the firm of Andrews and Cummings, who may have retained the library service.[33]

The life of the collection begun by Guild bridges an era when the circulating library, like the social library, was subject to rapid growth. No sooner had William Blake vacated, in 1796, the familiar stand at 59 Cornhill, than William Pelham continued the tradition of the location by establishing there a bookselling business and circulating library.[34] The institution was one of the

27. See entries under corresponding dates in Appen. IV.

28. *Independent Chronicle*, May 10, 1787.

29. *Ibid.*, October 25, 1792; Suffolk probate files quoted by Bolton, *op. cit.*, p. 202.

30. See entry in Appen. IV.

31. William Pinson Blake was born in Boston, January 9, 1769. He died, June 5, 1820, unmarried, in New York City, where he had been for some years operating as a bookseller. Lemuel Blake, bookseller, publisher, and proprietor of a paper warehouse, was born at Dorchester, Mass., August 9, 1775. He died, also unmarried, in Boston, March 4, 1861. The two brothers were associated in publishing as well as in bookselling and together issued, among other books, the *Junius Letters* (1804) about the authorship of which there was so much speculation (see Bolton, *op. cit.*, p. 202).

32. Appen. IV.

33. *Independent Chronicle*, March 28, 1805. Cummings retired in 1809, leaving the business to the bookbinder, William Andrews, who died in 1812 (see Bolton, *op. cit.*, p. 203).

34. Pelham, born at Williamsburgh, Va., August 10, 1759, was the grandson of Peter Pelham of Boston, who had married Mrs. Mary Copley, the mother of John Singleton Copley. William Pelham moved to Zanesville, Ohio, in 1810, and died at New Harmony, Ind., February 3, 1827 (see Bolton, *op. cit.*, p. 204).

most profitable of its generation. It was transferred to Pelham's nephew, William Blagrove, in 1804, at which time an elaborate catalog was issued.[35] Blagrove renamed the collection the Union Circulating Library and provided boxes with lock and key for the convenience of those subscribers who lived at a distance. The Union Circulating Library prospered, passed into the hands of Samuel H. Parker in 1810, and for a decade thereafter was considered one of the foremost collections of its kind.[36]

The early affinity between the bookstore and the circulating library was a natural relationship; but other forms of enterprise supplemented revenues with income from book rentals. In 1802 Miss Mary Sprague added a circulating library to her millinery shop in No. 9 Milk Street, and her announced plan evinces a variety and scope in book selection that was designed to attract a diversity of readers:

Having been careful in selecting Books, she hopes to meet encouragement. She has spared no pains to make her collection deserving circulation, by mingling the useful with the amusing. In selecting volumes she has not confined her choice to Romances and Magazines,—Philosophy, History, Biography, valuable Travels, useful Miscellany, Moral Essays, the various productions of the Muses, and whatever instructs while it pleases, have portions of her shelves allotted to them.[37]

Miss Sprague was not alone in her eagerness to mingle millinery with culture. Two years later Kezia Butler added a similar undertaking to her millinery shop in the south part of town. That she achieved at least a measure of success must be assumed from the fact that her library and shop are mentioned in the *Boston Directory* as late as 1828.[38] The millinery shop, stocked as it was with ribbons, lace, and other finery, in addition to hats and

35. "The following catalogue comprises the Whole Circulating Library that has been gradually increased during eight years past, under the direction of Mr. Pelham, at No. 59 Cornhill; who has transferred its future management to the subscriber, the constant endeavor of whom shall be to merit, by his attention to the wishes of his customers, a continuance of the liberal encouragement bestowed on the establishment. Boston, November 26, 1804.—William Blagrove" (Pelham, *op. cit.*, p. 3). See Appen. IV. Pelham, however, retained in his own hands the bookselling business.

36. An extensive reading-room was operated in connection with the library. The books were dispersed in 1833, when Parker began the operation of a music store (Bolton, *op. cit.*, p. 204).

37. *Independent Chronicle*, May 17, 1802.

38. Quoted by Bolton, *op. cit.*, p. 206.

bonnets, was in reality a "woman's store," and the success with which the circulating library was added to this enterprise is largely to be interpreted in terms of sex of readers.

The circulating library was not always an economic superstructure built upon some other enterprise. As an institutional form it was quite capable of self-support, and circulating libraries existed in their own right as independent enterprises. As early as 1783 the Circulating Library was operating at No. 1 Cambridge Street, with seven or eight hundred titles. In 1817 there flourished the Shakespeare Library at 25 School Street, operated by Charles Callender. The collection remained in his family until the middle of the century. The Franklin Library at 67 Court Street and the Boylston Library in Newbury Street exemplified the prosperous independent type.[39] while a particularly "aristocratic" patronage frequented the circulating library of A. K. Loring, who counted among his clientele George Ticknor, Wendell Phillips, and Edward Everett. Loring, whose library was established in June, 1859, experimented in a house-to-house delivery and collection of books, first carried out by boys and later by men on horseback. This proved most profitable in the less fashionable sections of Boston, such as East Boston and Chelsea. Though Loring's library may be considered one of the most successful, its owner, in later life, expressed the opinion that the circulating library as a form of enterprise was not profitable except when appended to another business.

Several factors favored the success of the circulating library. Economically it was an efficient and flexible method of print distribution. Little capital was required to place it in operation, and returns on investment were immediate and large in proportion to the original expenditure. Though primarily associated with publishing and bookselling, it might be, and frequently was,

39. About 1830 Thomas Burnham opened a small bookstore, circulating library, and museum at 58 Cornhill. This blending of forms in one enterprise shows the difficulties inherent in attempting to differentiate and classify the types of circulating libraries. This particular undertaking, about five years later, was operated by the son, Thomas Oliver Hazard Perry Burnham. As the bookselling enterprise developed and expanded, the circulating library and museum were abandoned. Burnham's eventually became an important Boston rare book shop and the rendezvous of Emerson, Holmes, and Longfellow (*ibid.*, pp. 206–7).

attached to a variety of business undertakings. John Mein, in addition to his book stocks, offered his Boston patrons linens and liquors. William Blake, in his catalog for 1793, announced a full line of "Fancy Articles," including "Ladies Paste Shoe Buckles and Rosettes . . . Gold and Gilt Earings . . . Silver Tooth Pick and Pencil Cases . . . Thimbles, Hat Pins, Ivory Bodkins . . . and Perfumes of all kinds." William Pelham sold playing cards, and Charles Whipple of Newburyport kept a complete line of family and patent medicines. The cultural atmosphere of the eighteenth and nineteenth centuries, with widespread public interest in contemporary authorship, furnished an admirable environment for the encouragement of the circulating library; such advantages during a period of literary sophistication were no greater than the potentialities of the form in a simpler society, poor in both money and books. As an economical method of book distribution the circulating library has never been rivaled.

The circulating library did not adapt itself to special reading interests to the same extent as the social library. Nevertheless, scattered examples of "special" circulating libraries in Boston have survived. T. O. Walker, whose circulating library was located at 68 Cornhill, prospered in the 1840's largely because his collection was built around a nucleus of French novels. In sharp contrast to this was the Juvenile Circulating Library, operated by Mayhew and Baker at 208 Washington Street, who warned their "young applicants for books" that they were "*liable* to be refused, unless introduced by their parents."

The Spread of the Institution throughout Massachusetts

At about the time Benjamin Guild was promoting his Boston venture similar enterprises were being initiated in near-by Salem, where the first circulating library was established in 1789 by John Dabney, bookseller, binder, and postmaster.[40] His library existed for nearly thirty years, and when he retired from active business in 1818, the collection numbered about eight thousand volumes, of which the majority were either science or fiction.[41] A catalog of this circulating library, considered by

40. *Salem Gazette*, October 14, 1789.
41. See Harriet S. Tapley, *Salem Imprints, 1768–1825: A History of the First Fifty Years of Printing in Salem Massachusetts* . . . (Salem: Essex Institute, 1927), pp. 172–76.

Harriet Tapley to be the first book catalog published in Salem, appeared in 1791, with a revised edition almost double in size ten years later.[42] John Dabney, whose book stocks were augmented by "a considerable supply from Europe and various parts of the Universe of all the New, Curious, and Interesting Publications in every branch of Polite Literature,"[43] was in the vanguard of Salem's cultural development. After his death in 1819 the *Register* spoke of him as "the first person who ever opened a Bookstore with a regard to the literary character of Salem." His bookshop and library consisted of, as fine a

collection of the best authors as was then to be found in this part of the country. . . . Our best libraries will continue to tell of the benefits we have derived from the bold project of our departed friend, who could while living have no other pleasure from his purpose than the hope of its ultimate success. We begin to feel the importance of collecting among ourselves all the means for the best choice of books, and of rewarding those who do much to preserve the best resources of our literature.[44]

Of Dabney's attempts to awaken Salem to public enthusiasm for better literature, the Rev. William Bentley, pastor of the East Church, wrote in his diary on October 22, 1819:

Mr. John Dabney has not been recalled in his true character. When he first opened a bookstore in Salem, anything deserving the name was unknown. . . . Dabney began as if we were readers of a higher class, as if we read from our enquiries & not in books long used & by the wise forgotten. His display was in considerable amount & when he found that he had outstripped the wishes of the hour I well remember I purchased many books he could not sell to relieve him. Others were as willing but not to indemnify him for an experiment in which the whole town was profited.[45]

Such praise was not usually the reward of circulating library proprietors, customarily more concerned with profit to themselves than with public enlightenment. The cultural influence of the circulating library in public library advancement was certainly not great, but John Dabney, who attempted to make his circulating library responsive to those intellectual and cultural

42. William Bentley, *Diary* (Salem: Essex Institute, 1905–14), I, 152, IV, 621, 624; Joseph B. Felt, *Annals of Salem* (Salem: W. & S. B. Ives, 1849), II, 33.

43. Quoted by Tapley, *op. cit.*, p. 172.

44. *Register*, October 23, 1819; quoted by Tapley, *op. cit.*, p. 176.

45. Bentley, *op. cit.*, IV, 624.

demands that later found expression in the movement for public libraries, was an interesting and important figure.[46]

While Dabney was endeavoring to encourage the reading of good books in Salem, other circulating libraries were operating in the town. In 1804 Lyman Homiston opened a bookshop in Essex Street, where he established an "infant library" to which he promised to make important and continuous additions.[47] In 1812 Thomas Porter, bookseller and Salem pioneer in the soda-fountain business,[48] also rented books, though of his success little is known. About 1814 a collection was opened to the public by Cushing and Appleton's Book Store and Lottery Office,[49] which in 1818 came to be known as the Essex Circulating Library and which contained some four thousand volumes, of which a considerable number related to navigation. In 1821 the collection, then numbering some three thousand titles, passed into the hands of John M. Ives, who operated a bookstore at the Sign of the Globe and Harp.[50] Ives continued the operation of the library until 1835, when it was dispersed at public auction. Other Salem institutions included the Central Circulating Library, operated by Mrs. Hannah Harris in the early years of the 1820's. Mrs. Harris boasted of a stock of four thousand volumes.[51] A small collection was owned by John D. Wilson, Jr., between 1819 and 1821,[52] and one was kept by Benjamin Coleman from 1832 to

46. Of the sale of Dabney's book collection, the Rev. William Bentley wrote in his diary under date of September 8, 1818: "8. Began the sale of Dabney's Circulating Library. As this was the first circulating library known to me in Salem. The Books were chiefly novels & few books of science were in the Collection. The whole number of works in 57 pages is 2,281, the whole reckoned between 6 and 7,000. We advanced as far as 900 in the first day, but I could purchase but a few books of those sold while I was present, from any choice I had of them. The sales of the afternoon were better than of the morning, & it was a vendue day by being stormy" (ibid., pp. 546, 621).

47. Tapley, op. cit., p. 204; Felt, loc. cit.

48. Concerning the latter he said, "a fountain of soda water which cools the blood, restores appetite and exhilarates the system without intoxication" (see Tapley, op. cit., p. 207).

49. Felt, loc. cit.; Tapley, op. cit., pp. 177–81, 185–86.

50. Felt, loc. cit.; Tapley, op. cit., p. 213.

51. Bookplate of conditions of the Central Circulating Library kept by Hannah Harris: "Salem. [1823?] Broadside. (Essex Institute)" (Felt, loc. cit.).

52. Ibid.

1837.[53] Doubtless none of these compared in literary importance and merit to that owned by Dabney, but the very fact that so many such enterprises were active in Salem at the same time in itself reveals the degree to which this medium for the distribution of print was being accepted.

From the Boston basin the circulating library spread along the Massachusetts coast and into the interior of the state. At Newburyport at least seven such institutions were in operation during the period of the greatest development.[54] At Fitchburg the local *Gazette* and the *Worcester County Courier* contained numerous advertisements of recent additions to the stocks of the circulating libraries in that town.[55] Other Massachusetts communities where

53. *Ibid.*

54. Prior to 1794 George Osburne, a Newburyport bookseller, established a circulating library in his store. In 1797 Edmund Blunt had in his bookshop on State Street a circulating library which in 1798 contained fifteen hundred volumes, eighteen hundred volumes in 1800, and three thousand volumes in 1802. The library, which was open to patrons from five o'clock in the morning to nine at night, was purchased in 1803 by the bookseller Ebenezer Stedman, who considerably augmented the size of the collection. In 1807 the library was again sold, this time to William Sawyer and Edward Little, who operated it under the firm name of William Sawyer and Company. In 1809 Little organized the firm of Edward Little and Company, at the same time assuming responsibility for the library, which he operated until it was discontinued a few years later. In 1803 the Essex Circulating Library was established by Angier March, printer and bookseller. In 1807 the Merrimac Circulating Library was founded by Timothy Webb and Thomas Kettell under the name of Webb and Kettell. In 1815 it was removed to the offices of W. and J. Gilman, printers, at No. 2 Middle Street, where it remained until February 26, 1839, when it was sold at auction. In 1815 Charles Whipple announced a "new circulating library" at No. 4 State Street. In 1837 John Gray, Jr., had a circulating library at No. 3 South Row, Market Square, which was subsequently known as the Phoenix Circulating Library. On January 4, 1842, it was sold to the bookseller, A. A. Call. In 1840 the Washington Circulating Library was established by John G. Tilton; though closed in 1846 for a five-year period, it was reopened in 1851 and did a profitable business until the establishment of the Newburyport public library in 1855 (see John J. Currier, *History of Newburyport, Mass., 1764–1905* [Newburyport: The author, 1906], I, 518–22).

55. The Fitchburg Circulating Library appears to have been operated successively by Wilson Baxter; Whitcomb and Cook; and W. S. Wilder. In addition, Isaac Cushing owned a small circulating collection during the same period (*Fitchburg Historical Society, Proceedings*, I, 197–200). "Notice.—Clark Adams will much oblige the Librarian of the Fitchburg Circulating Library, by returning a book entitled the *Naval Temple*, and paying the charges from the 21st., of July 1830.—Wilson Baxter" (*Fitchburg Gazette*, October 19, 1830).

"Circulating Library.—The subscriber offers for the entertainment of the

the institution was prevalent were scattered throughout the Commonwealth. Records have survived from Fairhaven,[56] Charleston,[57] Lynn,[58] Hingham,[59] North Adams,[60] and Danvers.[61]

Circulating Libraries Elsewhere in New England

Though the New England circulating library originated in eastern maritime Massachusetts, it spread into other New England urban centers until the entire region was well supplied. A thorough search through the New England newspapers during the early years of the Republic and the beginnings of the nineteenth century would doubtless reveal that few communities

---

reading portion of the community some hundred or two hundred volumes of the latest published works of the best authors. . . .

"He has also made arrangements to be supplied with all the most popular new books, as soon as they are issued from the press.

"Terms of letting: 6 cents a volume per week.—WHITCOMB & COOK" (ibid., September 20, 1831).

In the Gazette for December 13, 1831, Whitcomb and Cook boasted that their library was "daily receiving additions of the most popular Standard and Fashionable publications." See also the Gazette for May 2 and August 14, 1832, April 17 and November 16, 1833; the Worcester County Courier, June 28, 1836, July 21, 1837; and the Fitchburg Directory for 1835.

56. As early as 1800 a circulating library in Fairhaven was supposedly "well patronized" (A Brief History of the Town of Fairhaven, Mass. [Fairhaven: Published by the town, 1903], p. 99).

57. In 1819 there was published a catalog of T. M. Baker's Circulating Library, 24 Main Street, Charleston. It listed some twenty-five hundred volumes in history, biography, voyages, travels, novels, tales, and romances. In 1821 the collection was augmented by a large addition of titles, including "a liberal sprinkling of sensational titles" (James F. Hunnewell, A Century of Town Life: A History of Charleston, Mass., 1775–1887 [Boston: Little, Brown, 1888], p. 99).

58. Lynn opened its first circulating library in 1822. It was a very small collection. In 1827 a second library was promoted by Charles F. Lummus, who continued the enterprise until 1832. The collection may well have been an enlargement of the original library begun in 1822 (Alonzo Lewis and James Newhall, History of Lynn, Mass. [Boston: Shorey, 1865], p. 387).

59. In 1827 a circulating library was owned by Caleb Gill, Jr., of Hingham. It contained upward of five hundred volumes (Solomon Lincoln, History of the Town of Hingham, Mass. [Hingham: Gill, Farmer & Brown, 1827], p. 13).

60. In 1830 Ezra D. Whitaker kept a circulating library in his store in North Adams. It was continued for many years. In 1844 Edwin Rogers had a circulating library of some eight hundred volumes in his store at Main and Eagle streets (W. F. Spear, History of North Adams, Massachusetts, 1749–1885 [North Adams: Hoosac Valley News, 1885], p. 114).

61. About the year 1836 the Holton Circulating Library was established in Danvers. It existed for five years.

of importance were without at least one such institution. Advertising was essential to the promotion of these libraries, and their respective owners were not tardy in making public the arrival of additions to their stocks. Further evidence of the prevalence of the circulating library at this time is to be found in the quantity of printed catalogs that have survived; and there is no reason for assuming that even a majority of these libraries issued such ambitious listings of their wares.

If the names of Mein, Guild, and Dabney were prominent in the annals of the circulating library in Massachusetts, that of James Hammond was no less conspicuous in Rhode Island. In 1811 he was operating a dry-goods business when he learned that Wanton and Rathburn of Providence and Newport had placed their circulating library on sale. Having purchased the collection and brought it to Newport, the new proprietor announced that it was particularly rich in novels and romances, in addition to some three hundred bound volumes of current periodicals and a complete file of the *Gentlemen's and Ladies' Magazine*. A dealer in dry goods, Hammond apparently knew how he might best appeal to the taste of his feminine patrons, so that this innovation in his business prospered to an unusual degree. Soon he was boasting that it was the largest circulating collection in all New England, enumerating his stock at over eight thousand volumes (see Pl. XI), and reaping from the venture a very substantial profit.[62] In 1848, when Henry Barnard made an inventory of the library resources of the state, Hammond's collection was awarded a distinction usually denied others of its kind. Though it was usual for educators to decry the influence of the circulating library, Barnard wrote of Hammond that his collection numbered some forty-two hundred volumes, was "one of the oldest in the country and contains many rare books"[63] (see Pl. XI).

In Providence, Perrin's Circulating Library was founded in

62. There can be little doubt that this library really made money for its owner. In his will Hammond left to a woman who had been his chief assistant in the management of the business an option on an outright bequest of $3,000, or entire ownership of the circulating library. She chose the latter and managed it for a time, though apparently with considerably less success. Its remaining seven thousand volumes were eventually sold under the hammer for $2,500 (see George C. Mason, *Reminiscences of Newport* [Newport: C. E. Hammett, Jr., 1884], pp. 275-79).

63. Henry Barnard, *Report and Documents Relating to the Public Schools of Rhode Island, for 1848* (Providence, 1849), p. 426.

1820 by George Dana, and by 1855 it had acquired over five thousand volumes. Twenty thousand volumes, of which seven-eighths were fiction, were circulated annually to twenty-five hundred persons. In the same city Winsor's Circulating Library, established in May, 1848, showed a parallel growth and equal patronage.[64]

In the other New England states circulating libraries were flourishing, though perhaps somewhat less conspicuously than in Massachusetts and Rhode Island. At least it may be said that the surviving evidence is more scanty, if such remains are to be considered as indicative of comparative prosperity. Circulating libraries are known to have existed in New London[65] and New Haven,[66] Connecticut; Keene,[67] New Hampshire; Woodstock,[68] Vermont; and Hallowell,[69] Belfast,[70] and Waterville,[71] Maine.

64. William J. Rhees, *Manual of Public Libraries . . . in the United States . . .* (Philadelphia: Lippincott, 1859).

65. The New London (Conn.) Circulating Library flourished about 1793 (MS materials in the Terry collection in the American Antiquarian Society).

66. In New Haven, Conn., the Crosswell Circulating Library was in operation during the 1840's (Terry collection, *ibid.*).

67. In 1805 a circulating library was established in the bookstore and printing office of John Prentiss, publisher of the *New Hampshire Sentinel*, founded in 1799 (S. G. Griffin, *History of the Town of Keene . . .* [Keene: Sentinel Publishing Co., 1904], p. 342).

68. July 23, 1821, Haskell's Circulating Library was established in Woodstock by Charles Henry and Isaac N. Cushman. Some years later it was purchased by Nahum Haskell, who operated it until his death in 1867. The library was still effectively serving patrons as late as 1889. R. Colton and Company established the Franklin Circulating Library on August 6, 1828, which, after a few years, was absorbed by the Haskell enterprise. About 1835 O. C. King opened a circulating library at the home of Eben King near the foot of Pleasant Street, though the library did not continue many years (Henry S. Dana, *History of Woodstock, Vt.* [Boston: Houghton Mifflin, 1889], p. 510).

69. A catalog of the circulating library of Ezekiel Goodale of Hallowell, Me., was published in 1820, indicating that the collection was in operation at that time. The collection was relatively large, as Goodale was a printer and bookseller of importance, who imported much of his book stock from England (Emma H. Nason, *Old Hallowell on the Kennebec* [Augusta: Burleigh & Flynt, 1909], pp. 235–36).

70. In 1824 a circulating library of two hundred volumes was opened at the bookstore of Fellows and Simpson, publishers of the *Belfast* (Me.) *Gazette*. In 1829 it was taken over by Noyes P. Hawes, who increased the collection to over six hundred volumes. In 1844 H. G. O. Washburn of Belfast began a circulating library that was maintained for several years (Joseph Williamson, *History of the City of Belfast* [Portland: Loring, Short & Harmon, 1877], I, 321).

71. In 1826 William Hastings, bookseller, printer, and publisher of Waterville, Me., established a small circulating library which he operated for two years.

The real focus of New England circulating library development was in the urban maritime region of Rhode Island and eastern Massachusetts, but it is equally certain that the institution did spread out into the smaller towns and less populous districts; and in some instances the collections—witness those of Nahum Haskell of Woodstock, Vermont, and Ezekiel Goodale of Hallowell, Maine—were quite comparable in size and influence to those of Boston, Salem, and Newport.

There is no reason for assuming that existing knowledge of these libraries even approximates completeness, for the circulating library was mainly an ephemeral venture. Momentarily coming to public attention, individual undertakings profited for a few brief years, changed management at frequent intervals, and then passed into an almost if not quite complete oblivion, leaving but a fragmentary record of their existence.

The Book Collections of Circulating Libraries

The evidence presented by the surviving catalogs shows that the book collections of the circulating libraries differed sharply from those of the contemporary library societies. Like the proprietors of the social libraries, the enterprising owners of circulating collections at first endeavored to appeal to a wide variety of reading interests in the expectation of attracting a substantial patronage. But experience soon revealed that profits followed the fiction market, with the result that, whereas the social libraries frequently developed in response to varying cultural demands, the circulating libraries, after 1785, followed with surprising fidelity an accepted pattern in which the same kinds of reading material were almost invariably dominant.

An analysis of eleven typical collections appears in Table 16. From this array of data two major generalizations emerge. First, the circulating library collections encompassed a rather surprisingly wide variety of subjects; second, the bulk of the holdings was restricted to no more than four dominant classes. Fiction,

---

Hastings' main occupation was the publication of the *Waterville Intelligencer* (E. C. Whittemore, *Centennial History of Waterville, Maine, 1802–1902* [Waterville: Centennial Association, 1902], p. 387; see also N. Orwin Rush, "Maine's First Circulating Library," *Maine Library Association, Bulletin,* III [1942], 13–14).

literature, history, and theology, following almost invariably that sequence, accounted for over 70 per cent of all titles. The proportion of each of these categories—save for the decline in theology and a corresponding increase in fiction—remained relatively constant throughout the entire period. In the im-

TABLE 16*

SUBJECT ANALYSIS OF CIRCULATING LIBRARY BOOK COLLECTIONS, BOSTON AREA, 1765–1816, BY PER CENT

Subject	Mein, Boston, 1765	Martin, Boston, 1786	Guild, Boston, 1788	Guild, Boston, 1789	Guild, Boston, 1791 (additions)	Dabney, Salem, 1791	Blake, Boston, 1793	Dabney, Salem, 1794	Blake, Boston, 1798 (Incomplete)	Pelham, Boston, 1804	Whipple, Newburyport, 1816
	(1)	(2)	(3)	(4)	(5)	(6)	(7)	(8)	(9)	(10)	(11)
No. of titles.........	655	500	515	1,085	324	531	1,319	750	1,175	1,602	2,239
Fiction..............	12	34	33	30	29	36	37	36	43	45	20
Belles-lettres (incl. drama)...............	11	27	20	16	15	18	13	13	11	27	19
History and biography	17	6	19	14	13	15	13	14	12	14	16
Theology and religion.	30	11	7	10	10	4	8	8	10	1	22
Description and travel (incl. geography)...	4	3	9	6	7	6	7	8	6	7	9
Science..............	8	6	3	9	8	5	7	5	7	†	5
Medicine............	6	3	0	5	1	1	4	3	4	0	2
Law.................	5	3	0	2	2	1	3	1	†	0	†
Education (incl. textbooks).............	†	3	4	3	3	7	3	3	2	†	4
Social and political science.............	2	†	1	2	2	2	2	3	2	2	2
Military and naval science.............	†	†	0	1	1	1	†	†	0	0	†
Juvenile............	0	0	1	0	†	0	†	†	0	0	0
Dictionaries and encyclopedias..........	3	3	1	1	3	1	1	2	2	†	†
Miscellaneous (incl. periodicals).........	1	†	2	1	5	3	1	3	†	3	†
Total..........	99	99	100	100	99	100	99	99	99	99	99

* For references see corresponding entries in Appen. III.

† Represented, but less than 1 per cent.

portance of history and belles-lettres the circulating libraries were following the traditional interests reflected in the selection policies of the social libraries. It was the emergence of fiction as the dominant concern of the circulating library that gave to these collections their most striking quality. In this they were at once following a significant and marked trend in popular taste while, consciously or unconsciously, imitating their predecessors across the Atlantic where the circulating libraries were even more heavily loaded with novels.

As early as 1838 a statistical survey of the book collections of certain circulating libraries in England appeared in the *Journal of the Statistical Society of London*, the organ of the group later known as the Royal Statistical Society. Table 17, taken from this article, reveals the dominance of fiction, even though the qualitative judgments of the compiler may be viewed with a certain skepticism.

If fiction, literature, history, and theology accounted for three-fourths of the collection, the remaining quarter was significant

TABLE 17*

THE NUMBER OF BOOKS FOUND IN 10 SMALL CIRCULATING LIBRARIES IN
THE PARISHES OF ST. GEORGE, ST. JAMES AND ST. ANNE

	Number	Per Centage Proportion
Novels by Walter Scott, and Novels in imitation of him, &c.	166	7.57
Novels by Theodore Hook, Lytton Bulwer, &c............	41	1.87
Novels by Captain Marryat, Cooper, Washington Irving, &c.	115	5.24
Voyages, travels, history, & biography..................	136	6.21
Novels by Miss Edgeworth, and moral and religious novels..	49	2.27
Works of good character, Dr. Johnson, Goldsmith, &c......	27	1.23
Romances, Castle of Otranto, &c.......................	76	3.46
Fashionable novels, well known........................	439	20.
Novels of the lowest character, being chiefly imitations of fashionable Novels, containing no good, although probably nothing decidedly bad...............................	1008	46.
Miscellaneous Old Books, Newgate Calendar, &c..........	86	3.92
Lord Byron's Works, Smollett's do., Fielding's do., Gil Blas, &c...	39	1.78
Books decidedly bad..................................	10	.45
Total...	2192	100.

* Rev. Edgell Wyatt Edgell, "Moral Statistics of the Parishes of St. James, St. George, and St. Anne Soho in the City of Westminster," *Statistical Society of London, Journal*, I (1838), 485.

only for the wide variety of the titles it contained. In no instance did any of these categories include so much as a tenth of the total. Many were represented by only a few titles. But it is noteworthy that those who sought to encourage public patronage thought it desirable to balance their stocks with titles selected from some dozen different fields. Of this remaining group, travel and science were numerically most important—a reflection, doubtless, of the contemporary spirit of inquiry. Social and political science, which was composed largely of materials pertinent to the formation of the new government, maintained a steady and consistent trend. Military and naval treatises, never very important numerically, were somewhat more conspicuous between the years 1789 and 1791, but dwindled to less importance as the Revolution receded in time. None of these minor subjects was of sufficient size in relation to the whole to justify any striking deduction. Many reasons suggest themselves as possible explanations for the inclusion of such a variety of titles. It may have been that certain books were regarded as basic to any library and their proportion in relation to the whole varied according to the size of the total collection. Also there was the personal equation of the proprietor, his own preferences in reading, and his a priori ideas of what his public wanted.

Although the circulating library may have had a substantial backbone of solid treatises in history, religion, and learning in general, it was as purveyors of entertainment that these collections were generally recognized. The proportion of fiction in the collections leaves no doubt of that. James Hammond of Newport, who boasted that he had the largest circulating library in New England, was proud to announce that five thousand of his eight thousand volumes were "Novels, tales, and romances"; similar reading material was conspicuously advertised on the title-pages of many of the printed catalogs.

The wares of the circulating library may have been eagerly sought, but there were few who would publicly come to its defense. John Dabney, who was more solicitous than his contemporaries in the selection of desirable titles, was surprisingly moderate in his praise of circulating libraries, tempering his eloquence with a rather frank admission that they did not always stock the best books. He wrote in the Preface to his catalog of 1791:

A Circulating Library, like the volume of Nature, is found to be an interesting Miscellany, but composed of an assemblage of productions extremely opposite in their nature and tendency. Many of these productions are known to be highly beneficial, others very agreeable and engaging; and some, it will be added, are injurious to Society. If as many of the latter are excluded as possible, and an arrangement be formed of the most eligible, it may be considered not only as a Repository of Rational Amusement, but as a Museum, from whence may be derived materials capable of forming the minds of individuals to solid virtue, true politeness, the noblest actions, and the purest benevolence.[72]

Condemnation of the circulating libraries, like clerical contempt for fiction, began in the British Isles, where these libraries

72. John Dabney, *Catalogue of Books for Sale or Circulation* (Salem: Printed for J. Dabney, 1791), p. 2.

were completely subservient to popular taste. Those collections that were established at the public watering places were especially notorious for the inferior quality of their book stocks. In Bath the libraries of Leake and Meyler were an integral part of the recreational life of the resort; their subscribers' lists were a veritable social register, and their books were important mainly because they kept the patrons abreast of the latest fiction of the day. Criticism from the moralists was to be anticipated, but opposition to the circulating libraries and their stores of fiction became a fixed convention in the popular mind. The Society for the Suppression of Vice advocated the regulation of circulating libraries. Parents were concerned over the use of such institutions by their children, and the patronage of these libraries by women brought to the surface serious discussion as to the propriety of teaching the feminine sex to read. "A circulating library in a town is an ever-green tree of diabolical knowledge!" complained Sheridan's Sir Anthony Absolute; "It blossoms through the year!—And depend on it, Mrs. Malaprop, that they who are so fond of handling the leaves, will long for the fruit at last."[73]

Antagonism toward the circulating library followed it across the Atlantic. As early as 1784 Boston's *Independent Chronicle* quoted as a warning to the local gentry an article, depicting the degeneracy of Edinburgh, which spoke with ironical contempt of the Miss who "improves" her mind from the "precious stores" of the circulating library.[74] Doubtless T. O. Walker, who, in the early decades of the nineteenth century, drew about his library a thriving if not a very discriminating clientele by the circulation of French novels, more than once suffered the condemnation of the moralists.

The widespread criticism that arose in response to the circulating library was identical, both in origin and motive, with that brought to bear against the popularity of the novel. As one of the

73. Richard Brinsley Sheridan, *The Rivals*, Act I, scene ii. An interesting consideration of the novels satirized by Sheridan in *The Rivals* is to be found in George H. Nettleton, "The Books of Lydia Languish's Circulating Library," *Journal of English and Germanic Philology*, V (1905), 492–500. For other attacks against the circulating library see Blakey, *op. cit.*, pp. 111–24, chap. vi, "The Circulating Library."
74. *Independent Chronicle*, August 19, 1784.

most effective mediums for the dissemination of fiction, it was caught in the storm of indignation and protest that greeted this discredited literary form. By their own admission the proprietors of circulating libraries were ever on the defensive against charges of corrupting the youth of the town. Surrounded by her books and millinery, Miss Mary Sprague protested: "She has spared no pains to make her collection deserving circulation by mingling the useful with the amusing."[75] John Dabney evinced a similar solicitude for the "Patrons of Literature—the Lovers of Intellectual Entertainment,"[76] was careful to remind the public of his industry in promoting "in the town of Salem and its vicinity, the interests of POLITE LITERATURE, and the LIBERAL SCIENCES,"[77] and spoke with true feeling of his "most sedulous endeavors, directed to please the mental taste with a rich variety," thereby to "ensure the future favours of his friends and the publick."[78]

The early circulating libraries cannot properly be compared with the modern drug-store "rentals," owned by an impersonal corporation operating a great number of deposit collections distributed over a wide geographic area. By contrast, the clientele of the former was personally acquainted with the proprietor, who was seeking the patronage of his friends and neighbors. If the enterprise was to show a satisfactory profit, it was necessary that the intellectual self-respect of the community be preserved without sacrificing the rewards to be derived from the rental of fiction.[79] Diversity of the collection offered the easiest escape from the dilemma. The financial return from following popular taste

75. *Ibid.*, May 17, 1802. See quotation in full on p. 139.
76. John Dabney, *Additional Catalogue of Books . . .* (Salem: John Dabney, 1794), p. 2.
77. *Ibid.*, The title-page of this catalog carried the quatrain:
    "Here you may range the world from pole to pole,
    Increase your knowledge, and delight your soul;
    Travel all nations, and inform your sense,
    With sale and safety, at a small expense.—ANON."
78. *Ibid.*
79. In many respects the position of the proprietor of the circulating library was analogous to that of the magazine publishers, a business which, during this same period, was also highly personal (cf. Herbert Ross Brown, *The Sentimental Novel in America, 1789–1860* [Durham: Duke University Press, 1940], chap. i).

should be sufficient to support a stock of more "respectable" books.

The circulating library manager might attempt to explain away a latent sense of cultural inferiority and social guilt and show an eagerness to justify existence in terms of intellectual values, but the fact still remained that the growth and prosperity of the circulating library was concurrent with and in large measure dependent upon the rising popularity of the novel as a literary form. If the ridicule of the moralists on this side of the Atlantic was somewhat less sharp than that directed against the circulating libraries in England, it may have been because the collections here were less degenerate than those in the resort towns of the mother-country.[80] The prevalence of the social library may have been a cultural check against the complete deterioration of its sister-institution. More likely, the costs and difficulties of importation might have had a selective effect. Certainly it does not mean that Americans necessarily read "better" books than did their English cousins; and there is still ample evidence that these libraries fared rather badly at the hands of the reformers.[81]

Any attempt to evaluate the contribution of the circulating library toward the emergence of a public library system must recognize that there was little relationship of motive and no historical connection between the circulating library and the later public library. Because they were competitors for popular support, the former probably encouraged the latter to respond more quickly to current demands for ephemeral books. Few public librarians, eager to show a constantly increasing circulation, have been willing to surrender entirely to the "drug-store rentals" the substantial patronage for "western," mystery, and detective stories. Eventually the public library did make use of the circulating library principal in its "pay duplicate" collections. But throughout the last two centuries the circulating library has remained a thing apart from the public library and was not sub-

80. The surviving evidence indicates this. Judged on the basis of an analysis of collections, the stocks of American circulating libraries generally were of a higher literary quality than those of England.

81. See Brown, *op. cit.*, chap. i; also George G. Raddin, *An Early New York Library of Fiction* (New York: H. W. Wilson, 1940), pp. 5–9.

merged, as was the social library, in the wave of popular enthusiasm for public library promotion that swept the country after the Civil War. There is no evidence that any circulating library became the nucleus of a later public library, though this was the fortune of many social library collections. Probably because the circulating library was a private enterprise, municipal authorities did not assume responsibility for its operation, and the element of profit may have served somewhat to insulate it from collectivization. The social library, as a voluntary association, contributed much to the collective principle characteristic of the public library: the same groups within the population who, for their own benefit, had fostered social libraries later pressed for the creation of public libraries.

The relation of the circulating library to our cultural pattern is especially important. Because it was dependent upon profit derived from the ability of its owners accurately to estimate popular reading interests, it was one of the most sensitive barometers of popular reading tastes. Were we able to examine the loan records of these early libraries, we would doubtless know much more about contemporary reading. But imperfect as our knowledge is, it does shed much light on that culture from which the public library emerged.

CHAPTER VI

THE BEGINNINGS OF THE
PUBLIC LIBRARY

THERE have been many claimants to the distinction of having created the first truly public library in the United States, but this antiquarian controversy is rooted not in ignorance of historical fact but in uncertainty as to the precise definition of terms. Joeckel, in the introduction to his *Government of the American Public Library*, has called attention to the difficulties inherent in any attempt to express accurately the exact meaning of the term "public library."[1] Yet, without first defining the terms, one cannot dogmatically assert that the public library movement began at any specific time.

If the custodianship of a common collection of books by public authorities be the criterion, then the institution may truthfully be said to have begun in 1629 when the Massachusetts Bay Company authorized the shipment to Salem of those books assembled by the Rev. Samuel Skelton. But mere possession, while it may have legal implications, fails to denote the functional purpose of the public library. Joeckel, therefore, has focused attention upon availability and use:

> The only really essential requirement in the definition of a public library is that its use should be free to all residents of the community on equal terms. . . . any library which has been officially charged with the responsibility, or has voluntarily assumed the responsibility, for providing free library service of a general nature to a particular community, or more or less definite portion of it, [is] considered to be a public library.[2]

Such a definition, like the criterion of ownership, would not deny to the Skelton collection its primacy. Conceived in general terms,

1. Carleton B. Joeckel, *The Government of the American Public Library* (Chicago: University of Chicago Press, 1935), p. x.
2. *Ibid.*, p. x.

Joeckel's standard is probably as satisfactory as any yet devised, but for the purpose of the present discussion the writer prefers the statement prepared for the *1876 Report* of the United States Bureau of Education by William F. Poole: "The 'public library' which we are to consider is established by state laws, is supported by local taxation or voluntary gifts, is managed as a public trust, and every citizen of the city or town which maintains it has an equal share in its privileges of reference and circulation."[3] At one and the same time, Poole has acknowledged the necessity for universal service, has revealed the essential link with governmental authority, and, above all, has portrayed the complexity of the public library as an institutional form. Any attempt to define with precision the term "public library" results in confusion because the institution itself is a blending of interests, objectives, and forms. The meaning of "public library" varied as the institution evolved under the impact of social and economic changes and acquired quite different implications and connotations over successive periods of time.

But the question of *when* the public library first came into being is much less significant than the broader problem of *how* it attained its present stage of development. The opening, on March 20, 1854, of the reading-room of the Boston Public Library at the Adams schoolhouse in Mason Street was not a signal that a new agency had suddenly been born into American urban life. Behind the act were more than two centuries of experimentation, uncertainty, and change. The erection of the Boston Town House, established by Captain Keayne, and the occupation of the two dingy rooms in the Adams school were in themselves occasions of significance in the history of public library development in New England; of even greater importance was the fact that during the period which separated these events countless citizens in Salisbury, Peterborough, Wayland, and elsewhere had been exploring various methods of municipal support for public book collections. Attention in the present chapter will be directed toward the evolutionary process that these events reveal.

3. U.S. Bureau of Education, *Public Libraries in the United States: 1876 Report* (Washington, D.C.: Government Printing Office, 1876), p. 477.

First Steps toward Municipal Control

In January, 1803, Caleb Bingham, Boston bookseller and publisher, wrote to his brother Daniel in Salisbury, Connecticut:

> I well remember, when I was a boy, how ardently I longed for the opportunity for reading, but had no access to a library. It is more than probable that there are, at the present time, in my native town, many children who possess the same desire, and who are in the like unhappy predicament. This desire, I think I have it in my power, in a small degree to gratify; and however whimsical the project may appear to those who have not considered the subject, I cannot deny myself the pleasure of making the attempt. . . . Should it so happen that the books should be rejected, or there should be any disagreement, so that the object in view is like to be defeated, please retain the books until you hear further from me.[4]

A collection of one hundred and fifty titles accompanied the letter.[5] The books were to be placed under the control of a self-perpetuating board of trustees and were to be made freely available to the children of the community between the ages of nine and sixteen years. Subsequent events did not justify Bingham's apprehensions that the "whimsical" donation might be rejected by the town, for the gift was warmly received by the residents of Salisbury, became known as the Bingham Library for Youth, and survived until its absorption into the present Scoville Memorial Library.[6] For seven years after its establishment there was

4. Quoted by William B. Fowle, "Memoir of Caleb Bingham," *American Journal of Education*, V (1858), 343.

5. Of the original collection forty-six titles yet remain and are now preserved in the Scoville Memorial Library at Salisbury, Conn. By subject they are distributed: history and biography, 22; theology, 11; travel, 8; literature, education, and miscellaneous, 4 each; and science, 3. This is, of course, no guide to the proportions in the original collections since it may have been that the most popular titles were the ones which were worn out with use or lost through repeated lending.

6. Surviving records of the library in the Scoville Memorial Library at Salisbury (Fowle, *loc. cit.*; Samuel Church, *Historical Address Delivered at the Commemoration of the 100th Anniversary of the First Annual Meeting of the Town of Salisbury, October 20, 1841* [New Haven: Hitchcock & Stafford, 1842], pp. 39–41).

Bingham's personal life is closely linked with the gift and its subsequent fortunes. Educator, publisher, and pioneer writer of textbooks, Caleb Bingham was born at Salisbury, Conn., April 15, 1757. Educated at Dartmouth, he received his Bachelor's degree there in 1782, presenting the class valedictory in Latin. Immediately thereafter he became master of Moore's Indian Charity School, founded by President Wheelock of Dartmouth in 1754. Having moved to Boston in 1784, Bingham was appointed by the selectmen to manage a school for young ladies. It was for the use

nothing remarkable about the structure of the Bingham Library. Except for its emphasis on the needs of youthful readers it was like many other institutions bestowed upon small New England communities by loyal native sons. But Salisbury, Connecticut, did not accept its gift with a mere polite indifference. Caleb Bingham's vision of a public library for the young people of the town seems to have been shared by the inhabitants of Salisbury, for on April 9, 1810, the citizens in town meeting assembled "voted that the selectmen of the town be authorized and directed to draw upon the town treasurer for the sum of one hundred dollars payable in favor of the Trustees of the Bingham Library for Youth to be laid out and expended in purchasing suitable Books for said Library, provided said Town can procure the loan of said sum for the Term of One Year"[7] (see Pl. XII). The library received further aid from the town from time to time[8] but eventually fell into neglect. Its books, together with volumes from other collections, were absorbed in the late decades of the nineteenth century by the Salisbury Library Association. This organization became

of this institution that he published his first textbook, *The Young Lady's Accidence, or a Short and Easy Introduction to English Grammar; Designed Principally for the Use of Young Learners, More Especially of the Fair Sex, though Proper for Either* (1785), which was the second English grammar to appear in the United States, that of Noah Webster having preceded it by one year. In 1789 he assisted in the reorganization of the Boston elementary-school system and was appointed master of one of the three new Reading Schools. Because of ill-health he resigned his position in 1796, opening a bookstore and printing establishment at 44 Cornhill, which he operated until his death in 1817. The author of many successful textbooks, probably he is known best for *The American Preceptor: A Selection of Lessons for Reading and Speaking* (1794) and its companion volume, *The Columbian Orator* (1797), which for more than a quarter of a century out-distanced all competition, particularly in the district schools.

His gift to Salisbury was not his only activity in behalf of library support. The establishment of small local libraries to supply reading matter especially for the young was a favorite design of Caleb Bingham. His bookstore was well stocked with such titles; and, when agents for social libraries went in search of suitable collections, his advice was frequently sought. In addition, he was one of the principal agents for the establishment in 1792 of the Boston Society Library (Fowle, *op. cit.*, pp. 325–49; and *Dictionary of American Biography*).

7. Town records, Salisbury, Conn. Also records in Scoville Memorial Library. See also Charlotte B. Norton (comp.), *History of the Scoville Memorial Library* (Salisbury: Lakeview Journal Press, 1941), pp. 10–11, which reprints some material from the town records but in general draws its facts largely from the Church address.

8. Salisbury town records show that appropriations were voted on November 5, 1821 ($20), April 3, 1826 ($50), and October 3, 1836 ($50).

the Scoville Memorial Library Association, which today oper-
ates a social library receiving annual appropriations from the
town.[9]

That the Bingham Library for Youth represents the first instance in which a municipal governing body contributed active
financial assistance to public library service seems certain.[10]
Here was the earliest real recognition by a municipality that aid
to library development was a proper function of the town. Unfortunately, little is known of the manner in which this action was
taken, the argument advanced in support of the appropriation,
and the nature of the opposition, if any existed. The record reveals only the final action. But for the purposes of the historian
the net result may in itself be sufficient. Stimulated by philanthropy and encouraged by popular use, public support for library
service had at last begun. The contribution was modest, but the
precedent had been established; it would be the task of later generations to enlarge upon and refine the initial plan.

For seventeen years Salisbury remained the single example of
municipal library support.[11] The second step in public library
development occurred at Lexington, Massachusetts, when, in
1827, the town meeting voted to establish a juvenile library and
to raise sixty dollars with which to purchase books and employ a
librarian. The collection, which was kept in the town church, was
supplemented through municipal appropriations at irregular intervals, but so inadequate were these contributions that it passed
out of existence in 1839. Viewed even in the most favorable light,

9. Norton, *op. cit.*, pp. 14–15.

10. On February 23, 1807, at a town meeting in Meriden, Conn., it was voted
"that the Books belonging to the town be left with the town Clerk," "that the Books
be loaned out for the term of four weeks," and "that if the Books are kept over one
month the forfeiture shall be twenty-five cents with an increasing forfeiture of one
cent per day until returned" (quoted from the town records in G. M. Curtis and C. B.
Gillespie, *A Century of Meriden* [Meriden: Journal Publishing Co., 1906], p. 46). Just
how the town acquired the books is not known, but there is no reason for believing
that the collection represented a public library in the Salisbury pattern.

11. Jonas Reed, in his *History of Rutland, Massachusetts* (Worcester: Mirick &
Bartlett, 1836), pp. 190–91, says that about 1820 there was formed in Rutland a
library that was "owned and controlled by the town . . . free to all that conform to
the rules and regulations," and that in 1836 had 1,065 volumes. There is no evidence that this institution was really supported from municipal funds, and, indeed,
the absence of the word "supported" in this account may be significant.

the results were not impressive, yet here was the first Massachusetts town to do what had already been done in Connecticut— provide from the public treasury support for a library.[12]

It is significant that Salisbury and Lexington represent two distinct approaches to public library promotion which are a recapitulation of earlier methods of library initiation and maintenance. At Salisbury municipal support was prompted by the philanthropy of a single individual; in Lexington it was a response to the pressure of a group. Each was typical of a major method of library encouragement; in these two ways had "public" libraries originated—either as the direct result of an outright gift to the community or as the creations of voluntary association. Quite logically, municipal assistance began as a superstructure upon existing, and generally familiar, library forms and was tending toward the initiation of a public library by municipal action. There remained the proving of municipal support as a source of institutional permanence and stability for the public library; in neither Salisbury nor Lexington had this been assured. Thus by 1830 the future pattern of the modern public library had begun to emerge, though it was not yet clearly defined.

The public library is in every sense an institutional descendant of the social library, but in its governmental relationships it represents an innovation. At Salisbury and Lexington municipal support was introduced to strengthen existing social libraries, but at Peterborough, New Hampshire, in 1833, a library was established which from the beginning was truly a public institution and in all its relationships to the community was remarkably like the public library of today. The significance of the Peterborough Town Library, then, lies less in its primacy than in its modernity.

The Peterborough Town Library: Its Founding and Significance

The town library at Peterborough was an indirect result of the Dartmouth College case. In 1819 the Supreme Court of the

12. Arthur E. Bostwick, *The American Public Library* (New York: Appleton, 1929), p. 11. E. Louise Jones, "Horace Mann and the Early Libraries of Massachusetts" (unpublished MS, Massachusetts Department of Education, Division of Public Libraries).

United States handed down its important decision that the charters of private corporations must be regarded as contracts between the legislature and the corporations, having for their consideration the liabilities and duties which the corporations assume by their acceptance, and that such grants of franchise can no more be revoked by the legislature or the benefits of such franchise be impaired without the consent of the grantees than any other grant of property or object of value unless the right to do so be reserved in the charter itself.[13] Denied the power to control the college and indignant over the frustration, the state of New Hampshire embarked on the promotion of an ill-conceived and abortive plan to establish a state university.

To this end there was enacted on June 29, 1821, legislation imposing a tax on the capital stock of banks operating within the state, the revenue thus derived to be used for the establishment of a "literary fund" "appropriated to the endowment or support of a college for instruction in the higher branches of science and literature." It was not to be "disposed of or applied to any other use or purpose whatever."[14] After seven years it became apparent that the vision of a state university was no more than an illusion, so on December 31, 1828, an act was passed ordering the liquidation of the accumulating Literary Fund, the money thus received to be distributed and paid over "to the several towns in this state their equal share or proportion of the whole of said fund to be divided among them severally according to the apportionment of the public taxes existing at the time of such distribution." It was further enacted that "the said share or proportion of said fund, so paid over, shall be applied by the respective towns to the support and maintenance of common free schools, *or to other*

13. *Trustees of Dartmouth College* v. *Woodward,* Henry Wheaton (ed.), *Reports of Cases Argued and Adjudged in the Supreme Court of the United States,* IV (February term, 1819), 518–715. The case grew out of a controversy between President John Wheelock and the College Board of Trustees, which, after it had become a political issue, culminated in 1815 with the removal of the president. In 1816 the state legislature changed the name of the college to Dartmouth University, appointing the deposed president as its leader. Daniel Webster's plea in behalf of the college was supported by Chief Justice John Marshall's famous decision of February 2, 1819 (Leon B. Richardson, *History of Dartmouth College* [Hanover: Dartmouth College, 1932], I, chap. vii, "Storm and Stress").

14. *Laws of the State of New Hampshire* [compiled in 1830], Title 73, chap. 1.

purposes of education, in addition to the sums which may be required by law to be raised and expended for these purposes, in such manner and at such time as said towns may order."[15] Provision for the continuation of the fund was afforded by section 3 of the same act: "The whole amount of the sums which may hereafter be received by the treasurer of the state under the act of June 29, 1821 . . . shall be by him distributed among the several towns in this state, annually in the month of June, according to the then existing apportionment of the publick taxes."[16]

New Hampshire towns in general accepted without further question the stipulation that the proceeds from the fund should be used for the improvement of the public schools. At Peterborough, on the contrary, committees considered the problem from 1828 until 1832. Then, at the town meeting on April 9, 1833, the proposal was presented that the Literary Fund be used, among other things, for the purchase of books for a town library that would be publicly owned and free to all the inhabitants of the community. The town records have preserved only the final action:

On motion, voted that out of the money to be raised the present year from the State Treasury on account of the Literary Fund, so much be added to the literary fund of the town as to make the principal thereof amount to seven hundred and fifty dollars, to remain a permanent fund.

On motion, voted that the remainder of said money to be raised from the State Treasury, together with the interest of said fund, be appropriated the present year.

On motion, voted that the portion of the Literary Fund and the interest thereof to be appropriated the present year be divided among the small school districts and applied to the purchase of books for a town library.

On motion, voted that a committee of one from each school district be raised to make the division and appropriation mentioned in the foregoing vote.[17]

15. *Ibid.,* chap. 3, secs. 1 and 2. Italics mine. The phrase "or to other purposes of education" was struck from the law in 1891, the fund thereafter being available only for schools.

16. *Ibid.,* sec. 3.

17. Even as early as 1876 Albert Smith, author of the standard history of Peterborough, was complaining that, much to his surprise, almost nothing was known of the details which resulted in the action, all participants were by that time dead, and the town records gave but slight assistance. "The town records have been carefully examined, but they furnish poor and scanty materials for history; they faithfully record votes and the results of various transactions, but of those who made the mo-

The legal basis for such a disposition of the Literary Fund was the construction of the clause "or to other purposes of education," as written into the law of 1828. Whether anyone raised a question as to the propriety of the action is not known, but at the next annual meeting of the town, April 8, 1834, the committee of ten members reported that the library was an accomplished fact:

REPORT

The committee chosen in April last have received the sum of 118 dollars and distributed it according to the vote of the Town, 51 dollars to 5 of the smaller districts, and the residue, amounting to 67 dollars has been appropriated to a Library for the use of the town. With so small a sum your Committee was obliged to purchase small Books to the neglect of the larger and more expensive works, altho they have endeavored to make the selection as useful and profitable as possible to the Town. The Book Case, printing and other incidental expenses have been paid out of the Bible Fund. The Bible Society having 130 dollars, appointed a committee to lay out this sum in books relating to Moral and Religious subjects for the benefit of the Town.

The money has been nearly expended by the Committee and the Books placed in the Case with the Books purchased with the Money from the Literary Fund. The number of volumes from both amounts to 370, the committee avoided purchasing expensive volumes in order that every family in Town might have access to the Library.

In the short time the Library has been in operation it is pleased to observe that the books have been called for in no inconsiderable numbers, and read with satisfaction, as we believe.

Your Committee would take liberty to recommend to the Town to authorize the Selectmen to appoint 3 suitable persons as directors to manage the concerns of the Library, who shall be required to report to the town annually the state of the Library and their doings relating to it. They further recommend the appropriation of a part of the avails of the Literary Fund for the improvement of the Library by the purchase of useful publications and the increase of the number of Books.

Your Committee has agreed with Smith and Thompson to take care of the Books and to distribute and receive them to the inhabitants of the Town, agreeable to the following rules. [Rules omitted.]

It will be seen by above rules that there is not a book for each family and person entitled to the use of the books. But your Committee could not well restrict the distribution to a narrower compass.

---

tions, or advocated the measures they are entirely reticent" (Albert Smith, *History of the Town of Peterborough, Hillsborough County, New Hampshire* [Boston: Ellis, 1876], p. 117).

The Juvenile Library, consisting of about two hundred books procured by subscription, has been placed with the Town Library. Most of these Books having been in use for several years, are considerably worn, and the number is not sufficient to accommodate the young persons in Town, as is very desirable.

JONATHAN SMITH
For the Committee

PETERBOROUGH, April 8, 1834[18]

The modest collection was placed in charge of three trustees chosen in accordance with the recommendations of the committee[19] and was housed in a privately owned store together with the town post office.[20] Appropriations, which averaged in excess of one hundred dollars annually for the maintenance of the new library, were made from the proceeds of the Literary Fund until 1849, when New Hampshire state legislation permitted towns to appropriate directly for library promotion.[21]

The book collection of this first public library was similar to those of its social library contemporaries. The original purchase, as listed in the manuscript catalog of 1834, included an even 300 titles, 499 volumes, of which a good proportion had been purchased with money given by the Peterborough Bible Society.[22]

18. The occupational distribution of the membership of this original committee is interesting: farmers, 5: John Scott, James Cunningham, Hugh Miller, W. M. White, and Silas Barber, Jr.; industrialists, 5: H. F. Cogswell, millowner; Moses Dodge, cotton-millowner; John Steele, civil engineer, schoolteacher, farmer, and millowner; Jonathan Smith, businessman, judge, and author of the report; and John H. Steele, millowner and later governor of New Hampshire.

19. The members of the original board were John H. Steele, Timothy Fox, and Abiel Abbot, chairman. This form of trusteeship has been retained to the present day, except for the change from appointment to election of the board membership.

20. The library remained with the post office until 1861, and the successive postmasters, Riley Goodridge, Samuel Gates, and Henry Steele, acted also as librarians. The later peregrinations of the library are carefully set forth in J. F. Brennan, "Peterborough Town Library, the Pioneer Public Library," *Granite Monthly,* XXVIII (1900), 281–91. This article leans heavily upon Smith's history of the town. See also George Abbot Morison, "Address before the Forty-fourth Annual Meeting of the New Hampshire Library Association, Peterborough, August 23, 1933," published in the *Proceedings* of the meeting, pp. 5–28.

21. Records and other manuscript materials in the Peterborough Town Library.

22. The early records are very precise on this point. The Peterborough Bible Society was established in 1814, and in 1815 it received a gift of money from William Phillips, lieutenant-governor of Massachusetts. In January, 1834, the society voted to give the Phillips Fund, then amounting to $130.00 to the town library for the purchase of books. Accordingly, $126.75 was spent for books, $2.75 for a bookcase, and the remaining $0.50 for "paper." When it is recalled that the original grant from the town amounted to only $67.00, it is obvious that the Bible Society dominated

This latter donation may have increased somewhat the usual proportion of theological works. A printed catalog, published in 1837, shows a total of 465 titles, or an increase of more than 50 per cent over the original collection.[23] A comparison of these two lists shows no marked changes, the additions being mainly in fiction, travel, science, and education. But the relative importance of the several types remains the same.

TABLE 18

CHARACTER OF THE BOOK COLLECTION, PETERBOROUGH
TOWN LIBRARY, 1834 AND 1837

Subject	MS Catalog, 1834 (Per Cent)	Printed Catalog, 1837 (Per Cent)
History and biography.........	40	37
Theology....................	33	28
Belles-lettres*...............	12	10
Travel......................	7	9
Science.....................	4	6
Fiction†....................	2	7
Education...................	2	3
Total..................	100	100

* The relatively small proportion of belles-lettres may be accounted for by the fact that there were social libraries also operating in the town.

† In the original collection the fiction section was composed mainly of Maria Edgeworth, Irving, Defoe, and Cervantes.

The original proposal for the formation of the Peterborough Library was advanced by the Rev. Abiel Abbot, who, in 1827, at the age of sixty-one, went to Peterborough as pastor of the Unitarian Church. Born December 14, 1765, graduate of Harvard, teacher at Andover, tutor of Greek at his alma mater, minister, and later principal at Dummer Academy, he had for fifteen years held a pastorate at Coventry, Connecticut, until his liberal theological views brought him into conflict with the conservative

the original purchase since it stipulated that its fund be used for the purchase of books on "Moral and Religious subjects for the benefit of the Town." The collection was also probably augmented by the transfer of "about two hundred books" that had belonged to the Juvenile Library. The manuscript catalog of the Juvenile Library, dated November 1, 1827, in the Peterborough Town Library, reveals a collection comprising mainly juvenile books of the day with a scattering of titles in travel, history, and literature.

23. *Catalogue of Books of the Town Library at Peterborough, 1837* (Keene, N.H.: John Prentiss, 1837).

church authorities of Tolland County. In spite of advancing years, he was in the forefront of library promotion in Peterborough. Finding the town with no book collection other than the remnants of a social library formed in 1799, he set about the organization of the Juvenile Library. His report of December 27, 1828, as chairman of the committee on that library, shows that he had begun to think of universal library service in terms of voluntary co-operation:

The desire of knowledge is ardent in the youthful mind, curiosity is awake & there are leisure hours which may be profitably improved. Books suitable to the young will afford them a rich entertainment, keep them from idleness & vicious companions, & improve their minds & manners. There are none who are insensible to the value of books to the rising generation. One family cannot well furnish the number & variety of books desirable. But many families at a small expense each, can be well supplied. Children receiving books from the same library in which they have a common interest, will be likely to cherish a friendly intercourse, & whenever they meet, will have subjects of conversation suggested, improving & useful.

Where Juvenile Libraries have been formed, they have been thought very useful to the children & youth, & have assisted parents in instructing & managing their families, & have served very much in forwarding their education. As to the expediency of procuring a Juvenile Library for the use of the children & youth in Peterboro', there is probably no doubt; as to the best method of procuring it, there may be some doubt. But the method which seemed liable to fewest objections & most feasible is the following:

Let an agent be appointed in the several school districts, who may give every family an opportunity of voluntarily contributing towards procuring the library. Immediately after the collection has been made, let the contributors have a meeting & appoint three or five directors to select & purchase the books, & make such regulations as may be necessary for managing the library, & act as general agents.

A proportion of the books when procured, shall be deposited in the several school districts, under the care of some suitable responsible person, for the use of the children & youth according to the regulations of the directors. As often as expedient, the books in the several districts shall be exchanged & once at least in every year, the books shall be carefully inspected by the directors. An agent shall be appointed annually in every district, whose duty it shall be to give every family an opportunity of contributing for the benefit of the library, & to transfer the contributions to the directors.

The following Resolutions are recommended to be adopted relative to procuring a Juvenile Library for the use of the children & youth in this Town. Resolved: 1. That it is expedient that a Juvenile Library for the use of children & youth be established in Peterboro'. 2. That a committee be appointed to draw up a subscription paper, expressive of the design & plan of the Library, & to be circulated in the several school districts; & at a proper time give notice to the contributors to assemble to choose directors of the Library &c. 3. That an agent in each school district be appointed to procure contributions for the Library & make return as soon as may be, to the above named Committee.[24]

Dr. Abbot's official connection with the town library was his position as chairman of the first Board of Trustees. Evidence that he actually originated the plan for a free public library rests entirely upon the statements of two contemporaries. Dr. N. H. Morison wrote from Baltimore in 1884:

I am anxious to give the credit of this enterprise to the person to whom it properly belongs, the beloved and revered pastor of my youth, Rev. Abiel Abbot, D.D. I was there and well remember the ernest efforts of Dr. Abbot to carry his design into execution. He was the head and front of the whole movement, without him nothing would have been done.[25]

Perhaps even more dependable is the testimony of Jonathan Smith, author of the first report on the organization of the library.

In this movement he [Dr. Abbot] was far in advance of his time. With prophetic vision, he saw the possibilities of the library as a factor in public education and in the spread of knowledge and virtue among his people. It remained for him to give practical expression to an idea hardly second in importance to the public school itself, and to lead in a plan hitherto untried which to many must have seemed wild and chimerical in the extreme. The wonder is that he could have persuaded the conservative, hard-headed men of his parish, John H. Steele, James Walker, Timothy K. Ames, William Scott, Henry F. Cogswell and others, to follow him.[26]

While Dr. Abbot was leading Peterborough in the direction of free public library support, he was also engaged in the formation of a social library, the Peterborough Library Company, which was organized, as a result of his efforts, on January 21, 1833. Obviously, he did not see the new public library as a competitor of the social library, but such competition began almost immediately. As early as 1834 dues in the social library began to lapse, and in 1853 the minutes of that institution record: "Since the establishment of the Town Library very few books have been taken

24. Submitted by A. Abbot, of the Committee on the Library, December 27, 1828 (quoted by Morison, *op. cit.*, p. 17).

25. *Ibid.*, p. 22.

26. *Ibid.*, pp. 22–23.

from the Peterborough Library."[27] It was accordingly voted to transfer the collection to the Ministerial Library, which was another of Abiel Abbot's enterprises.[28]

The formation of the Peterborough Town Library possesses all the elements that make for popular fable—romantic beauty of natural setting, uncertainty as to precise detail, nostalgic longing for a vanishing small-town life, and popular conviction that American leadership finds its greatest expression when it is nurtured by the homespun simplicity of a rustic environment. But such emotional adornments of the Peterborough tradition must not obscure the true importance of what took place there. The fundamental significance of Peterborough's contribution stands clearly revealed. There for the first time an institution was founded by a town with the deliberate purpose of creating a free library that would be open without restriction to all classes of the community—a library supported from the beginning by public funds. There for the first time were united all the elements that today distinguish the modern public library. The fundamental concept of the public library has advanced but little beyond this basic pattern devised over a century ago.[29]

27. Records in Peterborough Town Library. Abiel Abbot was librarian and clerk of the Peterborough Library Company.

28. Dr. Abbot was instrumental in the promotion of a number of civic undertakings. The Ministerial Library was organized by him in 1836 and incorporated in 1838. The Peterborough Lyceum was begun by him in 1827 just after his removal to the town. He assisted in the organization of the Peterborough Academy, incorporated in 1836. In 1840 he organized the Tree Society to encourage the cultivation of useful and ornamental trees and shrubs. As a member of the local school committee he became involved in a long but eventually successful campaign to improve the salaries of teachers and the physical conditions of the schoolhouses. A fairly complete biography of Dr. Abbot is given in Morison, *op. cit.*

29. In a paper presented before the South African Association for the Advancement of Science, meeting at Cape Town in 1903, Bertram L. Dyer, librarian of Kimberley, claimed the honor of the first public library for South Africa. According to his report, as early as 1818 Cape Colony established a public library with funds derived from a tax on wine. In the words of the proclamation establishing the library the design of the government of the Cape was "to lay the foundation of a system which shall place the means of knowledge within the reach of the youth of this remote corner of the globe, and bring within their reach what the most eloquent of ancient writers has considered to be one of the first blessings of life—Home Education." In 1825 the wine tax was diverted to the general funds of the colony, and in 1827 the tax was repealed. Between the years 1825 and 1827 £300 per year was paid out for library support, but with the complete elimination of the wine tax the library

The Historical Significance of the
Boston Public Library

The greatest single contribution to the development of the public library movement made by the founders of the Boston Public Library is to be understood largely in terms of the size and importance of the Bay State capital. After all, Salisbury, Lexington, and Peterborough were only small, isolated New England towns, and though they had established a pattern that later generations were to follow, what the public library movement most needed in the fifth decade of the nineteenth century was the stimulus to be derived from the acceptance of its principles by a major metropolitan community. Such recognition and prestige were exactly what Boston could, and did, give. Whereas Peterborough had, in 1840, a population of barely two thousand,[30] Boston ranked as the fourth largest city in the United States;[31] and though it had lost its earlier maritime and commercial priority to rapidly growing centers farther south, it was still a major force in American social and economic life.

By 1840 Boston had achieved complete municipal maturity and was conscious of the new currents that were sweeping over the country. For almost two decades the former town had been a city, its charter having been granted in 1822; and for six years, 1823 to 1829, it had enjoyed the leadership of its "Great Mayor," Josiah Quincy the elder (1772–1864). The transition from the pure democracy of the town meeting to the representative government of the incorporated city was no easy or simple step; and

---

was given over to a committee, thus ceasing to be a public library under statute control (Bertram L. Dyer, "The Public Library Systems of Great Britain, America, and South Africa," *South African Association for the Advancement of Science, Report: First Meeting, Cape Town, 1903* [Cape Town: Cape Times [Printing Office], 1903], pp. 415–16). This could scarcely be called the first publicly supported library—Mr. Dyer seems never to have heard of Salisbury and Lexington. The significant point about the Cape Colony event is that in newly settled communities the impulse to establish libraries at public expense may be spontaneous. Furthermore, the Cape Colony library was the first example of such an agency supported from funds derived from a political unit larger than the municipality.

30. Peterborough, 2,163; Salisbury, 2,562; and Lexington, 1,642 (*Sixth Census of the United States, 1840*).

31. New York City, 312,710; Baltimore, 102,313; Philadelphia, 93,665; and Boston, 93,383 (*ibid.*).

even Quincy himself, at an earlier date, had opposed the change. Mayor Quincy's great task, and his major contribution to Boston's municipal development, was to give to the new city a vigorous and effective leadership during a period of initial uncertainty. His object was to bring the responsibilities of the chief executive into distinct relief before the citizens. To exercise this power and to inject vitality into the new system, he did not hesitate to appoint himself chairman of all committees of the Board of Mayor and Aldermen. A less skilful person might have failed at this crucial point, but his effective reorganization of municipal boards and committees gave to the city government a community leadership that was then badly needed.

This dominant role of the city administration in directing the life of the people was continued under Harrison Gray Otis and was revived with renewed vigor in the 1840's by Josiah Quincy, Jr. The importance for the encouragement of the Boston Public Library of this trend toward centralization of municipal power was very great. By the fifth decade of the nineteenth century the Boston citizens had seen their local government freely exercise authority over many functions related to community welfare. A long succession of official acts had encouraged and improved municipal services promoting public health, fire protection, education, care of the poor, water supply, and many similar activities. The promotion of a public library for the common use was accepted without question as a proper function of the city government. If the existing record is complete, any doubt as to the propriety of municipal participation in library promotion went unexpressed.

Socially, Boston of the 1840's was ripe for a public library. The community had survived the vicissitudes of political controversy and a second war with England. It had regained its economic stability and once again could look upon the future with confidence. A new wealth was being created by men of such commercial eminence as Joshua Bates and George Peabody, who maintained offices in London and were important in the life of the Massachusetts capital. Though Emerson might suffer fears that the swiftly increasing power of wealth would "upset the balance of man, and establish a new universal monarchy more tyrannical than Babylon or Rome," class cleavages were not yet sharply drawn. Boston, like other cities of the period, had its slums, but freedom of movement within the economic structure was not inhibited by social stratification. The opportunities afforded by an expanding economy preserved the ideals of Jacksonian democracy.

Boston had shaken itself free of an obsolete theology. In an age when men seemed able to realize their fullest possibilities a reaction against a religion built upon a concept of human depravity was inevitable. William Ellery Channing was the spokesman for the inner life of Boston—the Channing who before his days of passionate social reform taught the freedom of the spirit in the same way that Webster had defended political liberty. Under the influence of Emerson and Channing the implications of these old religious dogmas were tempered and given a new social meaning. Fish writes:

> Self improvement . . . under the impulse of national elation . . . became not merely a solemn duty, with fear of failure always present and with escape from damnation as its most insistent motive; it was a thrilling, almost gay, opportunity; a sure key to treasures of earth and heaven. Seldom have people thronged so merrily to school.[32]

Such was the community life that surrounded the emerging Boston Public Library. When Edward Capen placed on the shelves of the Adams schoolhouse the first volumes of the new library, he was laying the foundation stones of an institution which was in every respect a physical embodiment of the culture from which it had grown. Observed from every point of view, the Boston Public Library emerges as the product of its social environment. That it appeared in Boston during the middle years of the nineteenth century should not be attributed to a simple coincidence of fortunate circumstances. It was the product of forces that for years had been slowly developing in New England life.

On the evening of April 24, 1841, a public meeting was held in the rooms of the Mercantile Library Association of Boston for the purpose of considering the plans of M. Nicholas Marie Alex-

32. Carl Russell Fish, *The Rise of the Common Man* (New York: Macmillan, 1927), p. 10.

andre Vattemare to encourage the international exchange of cultural materials. For almost fifteen years M. Vattemare, French actor and ventriloquist of much talent and considerable reputation, had devoted "his time, energy, and property to the introduction of his system of the international exchange of books, and, incidentally, of any products of nature or human skill which might increase knowledge in science and art." According to Josiah P. Quincy, who knew Vattemare well, the purpose of the plan was "to give the intellectual treasures of the civilized world the same dissemination and equalization which commerce [had] already given to its material ones."[33] In Boston, as elsewhere in the United States, Vattemare found no great public libraries which might receive the books that he wished to send into the country, and the promotion of public libraries, or depositories, was a corollary of his system of international exchanges.[34] He therefore proposed in Boston that the several local libraries, controlled by private associations, be united into one public institution. The suggestion met with an enthusiastic response, and the meeting at the Mercantile Library did not adjourn until a resolution that promised full support for "the great project" had been unanimously adopted. A committee to plan further meetings to encourage public action was authorized, and an expression of gratitude was extended to "those liberal shareholders of the Boston Athenaeum, and other libraries in this City, who have generously signified their willingness to relinquish their shares for the public good."[35] Concerning Vattemare's ideas, Josiah Quincy, Sr., had previously written to his son: "In short I see but few obstacles, and a great advantage in the scheme proposed, and I am not for rejecting it, on the consideration that it did not originate with us. I hope some meeting may be had and an attempt made. We can never hope to succeed in anything, if we begin

33. Josiah P. Quincy, "The Character and Services of Alexandre Vattemare," *Massachusetts Historical Society, Proceedings*, XXI (1884), 260–72.

34. Elizabeth M. Richards, *Alexandre Vattemare and His System of International Exchanges* (Columbia University Master's essay, 1934, p. 90; abstract published in the *Bulletin of the Medical Library Association*, XXXII [1944], 413–48). See also Gertrude Barnes Fiertz, "Charley McCarthy's Grandfather," *New England Quarterly*, XI (1938), 698–708.

35. The complete text of the resolution is reproduced in Horace G. Wadlin, *The Public Library of the City of Boston, a History* (Boston: The Library, 1911), pp. 2–5.

with a preconception that it is unattainable."[36] Though one should recognize that Vattemare's enthusiasm for public library promotion was a by-product of his passion for the international exchange of books, especially government reports, the important part which his system played in public library encouragement must not be discounted.

A second meeting was held on the seventh of May following, and in these two public gatherings was embodied the first general expression of the desire for a public library in Boston. Again of Vattemare's efforts in behalf of such an institution Quincy wrote:

> The idea of establishing a free library in this City seemed to pervade him to his fingers' ends. He followed it up with a vehemence which might well startle the guardians of the sluggish proprietors. He pursued the Mayor with visits and by correspondence; he wrought upon that functionary to make a conditional offer of $5,000. towards providing books for the Library, and to see that a petition was sent to the Legislature for permission to levy taxes for its support.[37]

In spite of the Frenchman's enthusiasm and energetic efforts the Boston Public Library might not have been realized had it not been for the tireless labor of Ticknor, Everett, the Quincys, and their group. Probably Vattemare did little directly for the establishment of the library, but indirectly he did much, for not only did he encourage a nuclear collection of books, he stimulated interest in enlarging the collection by reciprocal action. As Justin Winsor has said, "In the agitation that Vattemare incited we must look for the earliest movements which can be linked connectedly with the fruition now enjoyed."[38]

More than a decade separated the first visit to Boston of this eccentric ventriloquist and apostle of culture from the realization of his dream of a public library for the city of Boston—years during which it required the combined influence of many civic leaders to overcome the inertia of popular apathy. Long periods of indifference were followed by brief outbursts of renewed activity. After a particularly trying session with the Joint Standing Committee on the Library, Josiah Quincy, Jr., then mayor of Boston, wrote in his journal:

36. Josiah Quincy, Sr., to Josiah Quincy, Jr., Cambridge, April 14, 1841, in the Boston Public Library; reprinted in *More Books*, II (1927), 267–68.

37. Quincy, *op. cit.*, pp. 268–69.

38. Quoted by Wadlin, *op. cit.*, p. 18.

Wednesday, Dec. 15[?], 1847. Committee on Public Library. I wished to report an order binding the City to provide a room and conveniences whenever the books contributed amounted in value to thirty thousand dollars, but the majority over-ruled me, and would only declare that it would be expedient so to do. This apparently trifling difference may defeat the whole project.[39]

A gift of books was received from the city of Paris, and in October, 1847, the Boston city council authorized the mayor to acknowledge the donation.[40] The same order also created a committee "to consider the expediency of commencing the formation of a public library under the control and auspices of the City."[41] Influenced by the recommendations of this committee and encouraged by Mayor Quincy, the council, on January 24, 1848, authorized an application to the state legislature for power to establish and maintain a public library. In response to this request there was passed an enabling act that was signed by the governor, March 18, 1848.

CITY OF BOSTON
AUTHORIZATION TO ESTABLISH A PUBLIC LIBRARY

Be it enacted by the Senate and House of Representatives, in General Court assembled, and by the authority of the same, as follows:

SECTION 1. The City of Boston is hereby authorized to establish and maintain a public library, for the use of the inhabitants of the said city; and the city council of the said city may, from time to time, make such rules and regulations, for the care and maintenance thereof, as they may deem proper; provided, however, that no appropriation for the said library shall exceed the sum of five thousand dollars in any one year.

SECTION. 2. This act shall be null and void unless it shall be accepted by the city council of the said city of Boston, within sixty days of its passage.[42]

The passage of this statute was the first official recognition by a state governing body of the principle of municipal library support. But neither the act nor its acceptance was a guaranty of the library's realization. As late as 1851 Mayor Bigelow thought it desirable to remind the city council that financial support for the proposed public library had never been approved: "I commend

39. MS journal in the Boston Public Library. The day of the month is not clear.

40. The gift consisted of about fifty volumes, and the mayor was instructed to solicit, receive, and transmit any volumes deemed suitable as a return gift (Wadlin, *op. cit.*, pp. 5–7).

41. *Ibid.*, pp. 8–10.

42. *Massachusetts Acts and Resolves, January 1848–April 1848*, pp. 636–37. The act was accepted by the city council on April 3.

the subject to your favorable consideration, and trust that an appropriation will be made, worthy of a project that has an auspicious bearing, prospectively, upon the moral and intellectual character of the people of Boston."[43] A year later Mayor Seaver made the public library the subject of a special message:

> I deem it expedient, at this early period of the year, to call the attention of the City Council to the present condition of the Public Library. It has now been four years since the Legislature of the Commonwealth passed an act authorizing the City of Boston to establish and maintain a Public Library. . . . There should be, it seems to me, no unnecessary delay in placing the Library on such a foundation as will entitle it to, and secure for it, the fullest confidence of the community.[44]

To this end the mayor offered three suggestions: the appointment of a librarian, the acquisition of ample quarters in a central portion of the city, and the creation of a board of trustees composed of five or six interested citizens to be selected from the community to act with the council's Joint Standing Committee on the Library.[45] The recommendation that a board of trustees be selected was adopted May 3, 1852, and its members were elected on May 24.[46] It was this committee that sponsored the Ticknor report of July 6, 1852,[47] and the preliminary draft of the ordinance for the administration of the library, which was adopted on October 14.[48] The trustees expected that the library could be in operation

43. John P. Bigelow, *Inaugural Address to the Aldermen and Common Council, January 6, 1851* (City Document No. 1 [Boston: J. H. Eastburn, 1851]), p. 11.

44. Benjamin Seaver, *Message of the Mayor on the Subject of a Public Library*, in *Common Council [February 19, 1852]* (City Document No. 10 [Boston: No publisher, 1852]), pp. 3–4.

45. *Ibid.*, p. 6.

46. Citizens-at-large, elected: Edward Everett, George Ticknor, John P. Bigelow, Nathaniel B. Shurtleff, and Thomas G. Appleton. With these were to serve the following, who constituted the Joint Standing Committee on the Library: Mayor Seaver, Aldermen Sampson Reed and Lyman Perry; from the Common Council, James Lawrence, Edward S. Erving, James B. Allen, George W. Warren, and George Wilson.

47. Boston Public Library, *Report of the Trustees . . . July 1852* (City Document No. 37 [Boston: J. H. Eastburn, 1852]).

48. This was the first ordinance to give definite form to the library organization. It empowered the trustees to select one of their number as president and to make rules and regulations for their own government and for the administration of the library. To the trustees was given general care and control of the library, together with authority to spend the money appropriated, subject to any limitations that might be imposed by the council. It was required that the trustees report annually

within a year, but it was not until the spring of 1854 that the library rooms in the Adams schoolhouse in Mason Street were made available to the public.[49]

The years of delay in establishing the Boston Public Library as an operating institution are not to be taken as symptomatic of opposition to the idea. The record reveals no antagonism from any quarter. Even the failure in 1848 and again in 1853 to merge the Athenaeum and the proposed public library is not indicative of resentment against the latter. When George Livermore, supported by the effective pamphleteering of Josiah Quincy, Sr.,[50] waved his proxies in the faces of Ticknor and his little band of renegade proprietors and thereby defeated a motion to unite the two collections,[51] neither he nor his followers were denying the

---

to the council concerning the condition of the library, the number of books added during the year, and the receipts and expenditures. The ordinance also provided for the annual election of a librarian by the concurrent vote of the two branches of the city council, his compensation to be fixed by the council. The librarian, who was also to serve as secretary to the board, was to have immediate care and custody of the library, subject to the rules made by the trustees. The trustees were required to appoint annually a committee of five citizens-at-large, together with a trustee as chairman, to examine the library and make report on its condition to the trustees. Finally, the ordinance provided for the formal acknowledgment of gifts (Wadlin, op. cit., pp. 39–40). On May 13, 1852, the council had chosen Edward Capen as librarian, and he was re-elected in accordance with the ordinance on October 17.

49. The reading-room was opened on March 20, and the circulation department began operation on May 2 (ibid., p. 46). This, of course, does not mean that the library did not actually exist until that time. As a matter of fact the library received a considerable quantity of books and money from individual donors beginning when Vattemare first sponsored the gift of books from the city of Paris. On January 1, 1852, the Joint Standing Committee on the Library reported to the council that the library then possessed "scarcely less than 4,000 volumes" (quoted in ibid., p. 27). This total included the books purchased with the $1,000 appropriated by the council upon the recommendation of Mayor Bigelow. Wadlin discusses the more important gifts in his first chapter.

50. Note by Eliza Susan Quincy, dated April 27, 1872, in the Boston Public Library. See also letter from George Livermore to Josiah Quincy, Sr., March 18, 1853, in Boston Public Library ([George Ticknor], Union of the Boston Athenaeum and the Boston Public Library [Boston: Dutton & Wentworth, 1853], 14 pp.), signed: "An Old Proprietor of the Athenaeum"; Josiah Quincy, An Appeal in Behalf of the Boston Athenaeum, Address to the Proprietors (Boston: John Wilson, 1853), 15 pp.; Boston Daily Adviser, March 14, 17, 18, 19, 22, 26, 28, 1853; Boston Daily Courier, March 28, 1853; Boston Evening Transcript, March 29, 1853.

51. An account of this historic meeting is given in Boston Athenaeum, The Athenaeum Centenary: Influence and History of the Boston Athenaeum, from 1807 to 1907 . . .

right of the city to create a library for the public use. Livermore was merely defending the traditions of the Athenaeum and seeking to preserve its quiet reading-rooms from the jostle of the populace. Such frustrations as this were no great hazard to the future of the public library; the greatest barrier to its success was that slow uncertainty of progress, inertia, and evasion of decisive action so frequently characteristic of co-operative undertakings. Boston was youthful, venturesome, and vigorous of spirit, yet also staid and conservative, already respectful of tradition. The early history of its public library is largely a story of the internal struggle engendered by this paradox.

The adherents to the proposal for a public library were favored by contemporary events. The entire cultural milieu of mid-nineteenth-century Boston was basically sympathetic to such a scheme. The intellectual awakening that characterized the New England of that period consisted of a variety of forces that created a desire for a wider distribution of books and other reading matter than had been possible under the limitations of the privately supported subscription institution. American literature was achieving a new level of maturity, and reading was becoming popular to an unprecedented degree. The volume of book production had been increased both by growth in publishing establishments at home and by increased importation from abroad. New York, Philadelphia, and Boston were intense rivals in economic and social life; and the receipt in 1848 by the city of New York of $400,000 from John Jacob Astor for the establishment and maintenance of a public library that would "be accessible at all reasonable hours [and] times for general use, free of all expense to persons resorting thereto,"[52] was the sharpest of spurs to Bostonian civic pride. "Boston ought not long to be far behind

---

(Boston: The Athenaeum, 1907), pp. 46–48. Attempts to unite the Athenaeum and the Public Library are considered in Wadlin, *op. cit.*, pp. 11–14, and in Josiah Quincy, *The History of the Boston Athenaeum* . . . (Cambridge, Mass.: Metcalf & Co., 1851), p. 204.

52. Harry Miller Lydenberg, *The History of the New York Public Library* (New York: New York Public Library, 1923), p. 6. It is interesting that Astor's original plan to give the library (1838) was first made known to the New York press through the pages of the *Boston Daily Advertiser* (*ibid.*, pp. 3–4). The Astor Library was a reference library and received no public support.

her sister City of New York, in the establishment of a Public Library," Mayor Seaver warned the council in 1852, "and while we can scarcely hope to rival her princely Astor, it cannot be doubted that we have many citizens who would be ready to bestow upon it large sums of money."[53] This increasing importance of books to a maturing culture, in conjunction with the rise to social influence of the common people, fostered by private philanthropy and encouraged by the example of free tax-supported public schools makes abundantly clear just how propitious the time was for the beginning of a popular library movement.

The historical importance of the Boston Public Library transcends its existence as the first public library in one of the largest American cities. The founders of the library had indeed to venture into untried paths of municipal administration—trails which would soon be beaten by the feet of many followers. "Linked together as we are by political and business relations the character and intelligence of the people in every city between Massachusetts and Oregon is of vast importance to the citizens of Boston. If a free public library is established here our example will be imitated."[54] Thus, in 1847, wrote the first joint committee on the library of the Boston city council, for its authors knew that, while they had no precedent to follow, what they did would soon be a guide to others.

The enabling act of 1848 and the general Massachusetts law of 1851 were of no aid in determining the governmental form of this new addition to Boston's municipal responsibilities; neither specified the governmental machinery needed for effective operation. Joeckel has pointed out that the city government of Boston was itself diffuse and decentralized, function having been added to function as the need arose, without regard to any basic plan.[55] From the days of Josiah Quincy the elder, Boston had preserved the tradition of a "strong mayor," so that there would have been good reason for establishing the library under the direct control of a single administrative officer.[56] Peterborough had, twenty

---

53. Seaver, *op. cit.*, p. 4.   54. Quoted by Wadlin, *op. cit.*, p. 9.
55. Joeckel, *op. cit.*, pp. 19–21.
56. At this time Boston was governed by a large and unwieldy bicameral council under which functioned thirty-three committees, each performing a particular

years before, adopted the principle of the board of trustees for the management of its municipal library, but there is no evidence that this precedent had any influence in Boston. More significant is the fact that many of the promoters of the Boston library were also proprietors of the Athenaeum, with the result that they naturally turned to that institution as an administrative model. Basically it was the administrative form of the social library, of which examples were everywhere present, that was the pattern for both the Peterborough and Boston libraries. An ordinance passed October 14, 1852, provided that the "general care and control" of the Boston Public Library should be vested in a Board of Trustees comprising one alderman, one member of the Common Council, and five citizens chosen annually by the concurrent vote of the combined city council. By the terms of this ordinance the trustees were given the specific power to control all expenditure of library funds, make rules and regulations for the use of the library, appoint subordinate officers and fix their respective compensations. The city council retained for itself the important right to the annual appointment of the librarian and the determination of his salary.[57]

Largely because the original board was dominated by such strong personalities as Ticknor and Everett, the ordinance engendered a long struggle between the city council and the board over the complete autonomy of the latter. In this the trustees were eventually victorious, so that Boston, because of her importance in American municipal life, by the power of example alone did much to commit American librarianship to the board plan of administrative management.

The influence in public librarianship of Boston's first board

---

governmental service. There were five appointed boards and one, the school committee, elected.

57. *An Ordinance in Relation to the Public Library, October 14–18, 1852. Concurred. Benjamin Seaver, Mayor* (City Document No. 57 [Boston: Municipal Register, 1853]), pp. 80–81. Not for many years did the librarian have any real administrative authority; he was no more than a custodian; the trustees made every decision of importance. The principle which assigned to the trustees broad policy-making powers and reserved to the librarian authority over administration did not come until librarianship, under such vigorous leadership as that of C. C. Jewett and Justin Winsor, began to stand upon its own professional feet.

was marked. Not only did the followers of Ticknor and Everett contribute to the public library its administrative pattern, they also wrote into the record the first comprehensive statement of the functions and objectives of the American public library. At its first meeting, May 31, 1852, the board instructed a committee, consisting of Everett, Ticknor, Reed, and Shurtleff, to prepare a report that would "take into consideration the objects to be obtained by the establishment of a public library, and the best mode of effecting them."[58] This report (see Appen. V), which was submitted on July 6 and was largely written by Ticknor (see annotation on copy of *Report*, Appen. V), is the first real credo of the public library.[59] Modified by experience only in minor detail, it still stands as the best single statement of the relation of the library to the social order. What was said then has been repeated many times since, but seldom with equal clarity and precision. In the words of Ticknor and Everett, Boston was expressing clearly the totality of public library motivations prior to 1850.

The Beginnings of State Legislation

While the events that led to the establishment of the Boston Public Library were taking place, similarly important activities were afoot in the state capitols of New Hampshire and Massachusetts. That Salisbury, Connecticut, Lexington, Massachusetts, and other towns[60] had by local municipal initiative appro-

58. Minutes of the Board, Boston Public Library.

59. Boston Public Library, *Report, July 1852*.

60. In 1837 the town of Arlington, Mass., voted $30 annually for the support of the West Cambridge Juvenile Library, provided that the books were to be made available freely to all families in the town. The collection had been established in 1835 by the legacy of $100 from the estate of Ebenezer Learned, M.D., of Hopkinton, N.H., and was placed under the management of the "Selectmen, Ministers of the Gospel, and the Physicians of West Cambridge." In 1860 the annual town appropriation was raised to $100 (Charles S. Parker, *Town of Arlington, Past & Present* [Arlington: C. S. Parker, 1907], pp. 266–67; Samuel A. Drake, *History of Middlesex County* [Boston: Estes & Lauriat, 1880], I, 215–17; and Massachusetts Free Public Library Commission, *Free Public Libraries in Massachusetts: Ninth Annual Report, 1899* (Boston: Wright & Potter, 1899).

In 1835 the Fall River (Mass.) Athenaeum was established, and on April 3, 1837, the town voted to appropriate $800 from the town's share of the U.S. Deposit Fund for the purchase of 160 shares in the Athenaeum, the shares to be placed at the disposal of the town school committee, which would have the authority to assign them to deserving scholars. Thus, Fall River is an early example of municipal aid to

priated public funds for library promotion without benefit of
state legislative authority seems to have worried no one. The
modern concept of the supremacy of the state over local government developed gradually in New England, where it may have
been retarded by the importance of town government. The town

---

a social library. As far as the writer knows, this was the only New England town to
contribute to library support from the U.S. Deposit Fund, but since its share of the
fund was $10,102, even Fall River was contributing only a very small part of the
money thus received to library support (Alanson Borden, *Our Country and Its People*
[Boston: Boston History Co., 1899], p. 532; Henry M. Fenner, *History of Fall River*
[New York: F. T. Smiley, 1906], p. 62; Massachusetts Free Public Library Commission, *op. cit.*; and Rhees, *op. cit.*).

February 19, 1844, the Lowell, Mass., city council appointed a joint special committee to consider the establishment of a city school library. On May 20 an ordinance
was passed carrying out the recommendations of the committee and appropriating
$2,000 for a city library, to which was added $1,215 received from the state for the
establishment of school-district libraries. The library was governed by a board of
seven: mayor, president of the Common Council, and five citizens chosen by the
council. Note that this was the same kind of governing board chosen by Boston
almost a decade later. February 11, 1845, the library was opened to the public. However, until 1883, when it was made really free, a charge of $0.50 per year was re-
quired of all users (Henry A. Miles, *Lowell* [Lowell: Powers & Bagley, 1845], pp.
201–2; Charles Cowley, *A History of Lowell* [Boston: Lee & Shepherd, 1868], p. 127;
D. H. Hurd [ed.], *History of Middlesex County* [Philadelphia: J. W. Lewis, 1890], II,
233–36; Charles C. Jewett, *Notices of Public Libraries in the United States of America*
[Washington: Printed for the House of Representatives, 1851]; and Rhees, *op. cit.*).

The U.S. Bureau of Education, *1876 Report* (p. 447), and Justin Winsor in his
Memorial History of Boston (Boston: James R. Osgood & Co., 1881) state that in 1846
the town of Orange, Mass., appropriated $100 for a town library and thus began
public support that has been continued to the present time. A catalog of the library
was, however, published in 1869, upon the final page of which appeared a historical
account stating that the institution was established in 1859 by the gift of $100 from
David Goddard. The offer, which was subsequently accepted, was made upon the
condition that the town would raise an additional $200 for the same purpose. Two
hundred and eighty-six volumes were purchased, and the library was opened
December 14, 1859.

No one seems to know just when this library was begun, though the present
writer prefers to accept the latter date since the account given in the 1869 catalog
was prepared less than ten years after the events narrated took place. The author
of the historical sketch published in 1933 generally accepts an earlier date but,
strangely, seems not to have been aware of the 1869 catalog, since he states that
"there are no records of the library previous to 1873" (*Catalogue of the Free Public
Library of Orange, Mass. 1869* [Athol Depot: Edward F. Jones, 1869], 44 pp.; and
History of the Orange Public Library, Orange, Mass. [Orange: Orange Enterprise and
Journal, 1933], 16 pp.). Massachusetts Free Public Library Commission, *op. cit.*,
accepts the 1859 date.

meeting did not hesitate to take action upon almost any problem, national, state, or local, that might be placed before it, and New Englanders generally seem to have felt that local government was competent to deal with any aspect of social welfare. Under a doctrine of the state's pre-eminence, it is doubtful whether a New England town could legally perform any function without specific legislative authority from the state, but from the Colonial period the New England towns had not been reluctant to assume such authority as they might need. "The spirit of local self-government was at its maximum in these New England towns," writes Griffith, "and those that imitated them; and they furnished in colonial times and after, the very centre of the idea of the prescriptive rights of a locality over against legislation by the state."[61] Not until the middle of the nineteenth century did these previously ill-defined relationships between the state and the towns begin to be crystallized in precise terms.

All the six New England states had freely granted private corporations the right to establish book collections and manage them for the best interests of all concerned. In 1837 Massachusetts, under the educational leadership of Horace Mann and following the example of New York two years before,[62] had enacted legislation permitting school districts to raise and expend funds for the purchase of libraries selected by the school committee.[63] This legislation was copied by Connecticut in 1839 and by Rhode

61. Ernest S. Griffith, *History of American City Government: the Colonial Period* (New York: Oxford University Press, 1938), p. 337. See also John F. Sly, *Town Government in Massachusetts, 1620–1930* (Cambridge: Harvard University Press, 1930), pp. 100–104.

62. New York, under the influence of Governor DeWitt Clinton, was the first state to pass school-district library legislation (1835) (*Laws of the State of New York, 1835*, chap. 80). For a discussion of the school-district library laws and their results see Joeckel, *op. cit.*, pp. 8–14, and U.S. Bureau of Education, *op. cit.*, pp. 38–59.

63. Massachusetts, *Acts*, 1837, chap. 147, signed April 12, 1837. The original act provided that the school districts might raise and appropriate $30 the first year and $10 each year thereafter for this purpose. Faced by indifferent success of the plan, proponents of the measure sponsored the enactment of legislation in 1842 providing that $15 of state funds would be appropriated to each district for library purposes, provided that the district would contribute a like amount. In 1843 the same legislative grant was made to towns not divided into school districts. At the middle of the century Jewett estimated seven hundred such libraries in Massachusetts. The school-district library law was repealed in 1850 (Jewett, *op. cit.*, p. 190).

Island in 1840, as well as by certain states outside New England.[64] In Rhode Island, largely because of the vigorous leadership of Henry Barnard, these school-district libraries evinced some measure of success, having been established in all but four towns in the state by 1849 and averaging nearly six hundred volumes in size.[65] Though these libraries generally "dragged out a moribund existence,"[66] the laws creating them did define a system of library service—a service that was established by state law, supported by public funds, and mainly free to the public at large. As Joeckel has pointed out:

Of the three essentials for an efficient library—books, staff, and building—the school-district system provided only books, and those inadequately. Nevertheless, it did much to establish certain principles which form the basis of our present public library system. For one thing, it provided for taxation for free library service and also for state aid to libraries, both important milestones in library history. Even more significant, perhaps, it recognized the library as an educational agency, an extension of the system of public education beyond the formal instruction offered by the schools; in other words, it was a movement toward what we now call "adult education."[67]

Joeckel might have added that in at least one instance, that of Lowell, Massachusetts, a school-district library law was directly responsible for the establishment of a public library. On February 19, 1844, the council of Lowell appointed a committee to consider the establishment of a school library under the authority of the Massachusetts law. On May 20 of the same year an ordinance was passed creating the Lowell City School Library and authorizing the withdrawal of $1,215 from the state school-library fund for its initiation. This collection, first opened on February 11, 1845, though not free to the public until 1883, did become the Lowell Public Library.[68]

64. Michigan, 1837; Iowa, 1840; Indiana, 1841; Ohio, 1847–48; and Wisconsin, 1848. All followed the same general pattern, and all were permissive, not mandatory. U.S. Bureau of Education, op. cit., pp. 38–59).

65. They were open to all residents of the town but were not entirely free since one cent per week was charged for the use of each volume (Jewett, op. cit., pp. 62–63).

66. Joeckel, op. cit., p. 10.

67. Ibid., p. 12; George W. Cole, Early Library Development in New York State, 1800–1900 (New York: New York Public Library, 1927), pp. 11–12.

68. Until 1883 a fee of fifty cents per year was required of each patron (Jewett, op. cit.; Rhees, op. cit.; Massachusetts Free Public Library Commission, op. cit.; D. Hamilton Hurd, History of Middlesex County . . . [Philadelphia: Lewis, 1890], II, 233–36).

The New Hampshire Law

Probably most of the preliminary experimentation in public library promotion was known to the members of the New Hampshire state legislature when, during the first week of July, 1849, they set themselves to the task of considering "An Act Providing for the Establishment of Public Libraries," which later became the well-known law of 1849. As residents of the state they would doubtless have learned, either from personal experience or from the reports of their colleagues, of the successful town library at Peterborough. Furthermore, on the very evening before the New Hampshire act was first introduced into the legislature, Vattemare, who had been encouraging the formation of a public library in Boston, had addressed the New Hampshire statesmen on the subject of international exchanges.[69] This address, according to the published version,[70] made no direct reference to the formation of town libraries; so it cannot be established that there was any basic relationship between Vattemare's remarks and the New Hampshire law. But between the years 1839 and 1841, and again from the spring of 1847 to the autumn of 1849, Vattemare had been "stumping" the state capitals in the promotion of his system of exchanges. Everywhere he had been warmly received, and his second visit was even more successful than his first. As a result of his efforts thousands of books, maps, medals, statues, and engravings had been sent from France to the United States. In Washington his plans were unanimously approved by both branches of the Congress, and in February, 1840, that body passed a resolution giving authority to the Librarian of Congress to exchange such duplicates as might be in the Library. It was also decided that fifty additional copies of each volume of docu-

69. "On Motion by Mr. Lee—*Resolved*, that M. Vattemare, agent for this state for effecting national exchanges of public documents, be invited to address the members of the Legislature on Thursday evening next at half-past seven o'clock, in the Representatives' Hall" (*Journal of the House*, Wednesday, June 27, 1849, p. 187).

70. Alexandre Vattemare, *International Exchanges, an Address Delivered before the Legislature of New Hampshire, June 28, 1849, with Introductory Remarks by Thomas P. Treadwell, Secretary of State* . . . (Concord: Published by order of the Legislature, Butterfield & Hill, 1849).

ments should be printed for exchange in foreign countries.[71] The states entered Vattemare's system in rapid succession. Maine was the first to appoint him its literary agent, and a dozen others followed. That he was received with equal welcome by New Hampshire is apparent from the record.[72] This general enthusiasm probably encouraged the passage of the library law, even though it was not directly responsible for the legislation.

The incidents surrounding the passage of the New Hampshire public library law were quite commonplace. On Friday, June 29, 1849, "Mr. Eastman, of Hampstead, under a suspension of the rules and by-laws, introduced a bill entitled 'An Act Providing for the Establishment of Public Libraries,' which was read a first and second time, [and] ordered by the legislature referred to the Committee on Education."[73]

Josiah C. Eastman, who was responsible for the introduction of the bill, was the great-grandson of the first governor of New Hampshire and a practicing physician in Hampstead, which was situated only about thirty miles east of Peterborough—a fact that may be significant. Later he became state senator and president of the New Hampshire Medical Society, and his life, while lacking outstanding achievement, was typical of New England town leadership. A director of the Nashua and Rochester railroad, he was esteemed by his contemporaries as a "substantial citizen" and a member of one of the "best" families. It was individuals such as he who were doing more than any community group to promote the social libraries and to encourage public library development.[74]

71. Zoltan Haraszti, "Alexandre Vattemare," *More Books*, II (1927), 257–66; Richards, *op. cit.*, *passim*.

72. *Journal of the House* (New Hampshire), 1849, pp. 227, 229, 282–83, 323, 357, 362, 372; *Journal of the Senate* (New Hampshire), 1849, pp. 160, 163, 190–91.

73. *Journal of the House*, Friday, June 29, 1849, pp. 228–29.

74. Eastman was born at London, N.H., April 22, 1811, and graduated from Dartmouth in 1837. He was thirty-eight years old when he introduced the New Hampshire law. At first a teacher in the district school and later a student in medicine, he went to Hampstead as a practicing physician in 1839. A representative to the legislature from 1847 to 1850, he was a state senator from 1853 to 1854, and later held minor political offices. He died November 27, 1897. It is significant that his whole life was associated closely with the state of New Hampshire and that by career he was a professional man. Obviously a person of some financial standing, he also belonged to that section of the community which had the greatest need for books (Harriette C. Noyes, *A Memorial to the Town of Hampstead, New Hampshire* . . . [Boston: George B. Reed, 1899], I, 341–43).

Apparently the Committee on Education accepted the bill in the form in which Representative Eastman had introduced it, since five days later, on the following Wednesday, "Mr. Lovejoy, for the same Committee [i.e., the Committee on Education], to whom was referred a bill entitled 'an Act providing for the establishment of public libraries,' reported the same without amendment, [and it was] ordered that it be read a third time tomorrow afternoon at three o'clock."[75] The bill, the last of a long list, was read for the third time according to schedule[76] and was referred to the Senate on the following day.[77] It was immediately sent to the Senate Committee on Education, after its required first and second readings.[78] "Mr. Preston" of the Education Committee, by leave, reported the bill without amendment, whereupon, under a suspension of the rules, it was read a third time, passed, and notice of passage sent to the House.[79] On the following day the respective Committees on Engrossed Bills of the House and Senate, each having reported that the bill had been "Carefully examined and found correctly engrossed,"[80] the Senate was duly informed that the bill had been signed by the Speaker of the House of Representatives.[81]

The striking fact about the entire procedure attendant upon the passage of this act was the rapidity and casualness with which it was effected. If any preliminary groundwork had been required, it was completed prior to the hearings of the Committee on Education. The act was literally jammed through in the closing hours of the session, without any apparent realization on the part of the legislators that their action was at all significant.

The act itself typified the character of the proceedings that created it; short, lacking in specific detail, granting to the municipalities broad general powers, it contained but four essential sections.[82] It provided, first, that towns might lawfully appropriate

75. *Journal of the House*, Wednesday, July 4, 1849, p. 283.
76. *Ibid.*, Thursday, July 5, 1849, p. 318.
77. *Journal of the Senate*, Friday, July 6, 1849, pp. 159–60.
78. *Ibid.*, p. 161.
79. *Ibid.*, p. 172.
80. *Journal of the House*, Saturday, July 7, 1849, p. 371; *Journal of the Senate*, Saturday, July 7, 1849, p. 193.
81. *Journal of the Senate*, Saturday, July 7, 1849, pp. 194–95.
82. See text of law, Table 19. A fifth section was added which merely provided that the act should take effect immediately upon its passage.

funds for the establishment, housing, and maintenance of libraries; second, that such institutions so established under the act should "be opened to the free use of every inhabitant of the town or city"; third, that the town might receive, hold, and dispose of any gifts or bequests that might be made to the library; and, fourth, that libraries established under the act should be entitled to receive "annually a copy of the laws, journals, and all other works published by authority of the State." This final stipulation may have resulted from the influence of Vattemare and his plans for the exchange of public documents. Any regulation concerning the amount of money a town might appropriate from public funds or receive from private benefactions was conspicuously absent, a particularly striking omission since state permissive legislation for the corporation libraries was usually quite precise on this point.

The record does not indicate that the law had marked influence in the immediate encouragement of public library formation. In March, 1850, the town of Concord voted to appoint a committee to consider the organization of a library under the terms of the act, but, though the committee reported favorably and made specific recommendations, no such institution was formally established until August 25, 1855.[83] At about the same time, i.e., 1850, a "public library" was formed at Sanbornton Bridge[84] and at Groton, the latter having been stimulated by gifts from Abbott Lawrence,[85] though it is not certain that either owes its origin to the provisions of this law. More directly influenced by the legislative action were the town libraries of Exeter (1852)[86] and Manchester (1854),[87] both of which were the consequence of municipal action encouraged by sanction of the state.[88]

83. Concord Historical Commission, *History of Concord, N.H.* (Concord: Rumford Press, 1903), I, 444 ff.

84. Jewett, *op. cit.*

85. Rhees, *op. cit.*

86. The Exeter town library was established by vote of the town (*ibid.*).

87. The Manchester Public Library resulted from a contract between the town and the trustees of the Athenaeum (D. H. Hurd, *History of Hillsborough County, N.H.* [Philadelphia: Lewis, 1885], pp. 64–65).

88. During this time, however, the establishment of social libraries was continuing, so that it can scarcely be said that the New Hampshire law was immediately responsible for a shift from the social to the public library form: East Andover Social

The Wayland Gift and the Massachusetts Law of 1851

Permissive legislation in Massachusetts followed close upon that in New Hampshire, though it was not a result of the example set by the latter state. Rather it grew directly from the need of a municipality for the authority that such an act could give.

For the origin of the Massachusetts law approved by the governor May 24, 1851, it is necessary to shift attention momentarily to Providence, Rhode Island, where, at the commencement exercises of Brown University, in 1847, Francis Wayland, president of the institution,[89] informally signified to Judge Edward Mellen his desire to present to the town of Wayland, Massachusetts, the sum of $500 for the promotion of a town library, a donation which, so he hoped, not only would benefit the inhabitants of that small New England community but would encourage similar towns to follow its example. With this proposal the judge from Wayland was in complete accord, though, with the university president's approval, he suggested that the gift be made contingent upon the subscription of an equal sum by the inhabitants of the town. Through the efforts of Mr. Mellen a total of $534 was quickly raised, and this, together with the gift from President Wayland, was held by the judge in anticipation of municipal action. Accordingly, at a town meeting, November 8, 1847, "at the suggestion of Edward Mellen, Esq., a committee was chosen to

Library, 1849; Ladies' Sewing Society Library, Kensington, 1849; Franklin Library Association, Lyndenborough, 1851; Second Town Library (subscription), Windham, 1851; Fitzwilliam Library Association, 1851; Nashua Athenaeum, 1851; Orford Union Library, 1851; Mercantile Library Association, Portsmouth, 1852; Y.M.C.A. Library, Portsmouth, 1852; Ladies' Library Association, Warren, 1853; Shaker Village Community Library, 1854 (precise form unknown, but probably subscription library); Village Library (subscription), Union, 1854; and Tilden Library, West Lebanon, 1854.

89. Francis Wayland (1796–1865) was president of Brown University from 1827 to 1855. Born in New York City, he became known as one of the leading educators of his generation. A proponent of advanced educational theory, his reorganization of Brown in 1850 greatly contributed to the growth and increased usefulness of the school. In addition to writing numerous texts and books on education, he took an active part in the promotion of universal education, was the author of the plan for the Rhode Island free public schools (1828), and proposed a national university as the most desirable use for the Smithsonian bequest (1838). His interest in the movement for public libraries reveals another close link between that institution and the educational system.

confer with him on the subject of a room for a library consisting of the following persons:—James S. Draper, Hervey Reeves, Henry Coggin, Samuel M. Thomas, William Heard, 2d., and John N. Sherman."[90]

At a town meeting held March 6, 1848, Judge Mellen announced that the gift, contingent upon the raising "by subscription or otherwise" of an equal amount, had been received and that the gift had been exceeded in amount by that raised from subscription. Accordingly, the judge then held a sum of over one thousand dollars for a town library. Upon the request of the citizens present he revealed the donor as Francis Wayland. The town voted to accept the money, together with an expression of gratitude to Dr. Wayland, and the record adds:

ARTICLE 13, To see if the Town will provide a suitable room or building, in which said Library may be kept, or do or act in any way relating thereto.

Voted, To refer the subject matter of this article to a committee consisting of the following gentlemen, viz:—Edward Mellen, James S. Draper, Walter Reeves, Henry Coggin, Samuel M. Thomas, Abel Gleason, John N. Sherman, John B. Wight, John W. Allen, Edmund H. Sears. They to report at the April meeting.

Voted, That the committee last named, take the whole subject relating to the Library under consideration and report at April meeting a code of By-Laws or Regulations, the expense of rooms &c.

Voted, That Mr. Mellen retain the money in his hands till April.[91]

It was during the deliberations of this committee that the problem arose over the authority of the town to contribute from municipal funds for the support of a library.[92] The committee reported at the town meeting of April 3, but, because of general uncertainty as to the status of the town in relation to library support, the recommendation was advanced that the appropriation for the erection of a library building be made as "a separate item" and that "it be optional with the individual tax payers, either to pay or not to pay their respective assessments for said item."[93] The

90. *Town Records,* Wayland, Mass.

91. *Ibid.* The committee was essentially an enlargement of the committee appointed on November 8, 1847.

92. There was no question, of course, over the right of the town to hold the money acquired through gift and private subscription.

93. *Town Records,* Wayland, April 3, 1848.

library was established in August, 1850, and Mr. James Sumner Draper, town clerk and surveyor, was appointed librarian. From the beginning the costs of operating the library, including the modest salary of the librarian, were met from public funds, even though the right of the town to do so, in the absence of state permissive legislation, was open to question.[94]

The importance of Wayland in the history of state public library legislation largely results from the work of its liberal minister, Rev. John Burt Wight, who not only was an active member of the town library committee but in 1851 was the representative from the Wayland district to the Massachusetts state legislature.[95] The story of Representative Wight's promotion of the law of 1851 and of his subsequent activities in behalf of public libraries is a record of devotion to the cause of public enlightenment.

94. A building was erected for the library with public funds, but upon completion it was considered to be unsatisfactory. Accordingly, by June, 1850, a room for the library was prepared in the Town House where it eventually occupied the entire lower floor. The first bill for book purchases was dated June 28, 1850, the first delivery of books being made to the library on August 7; and the first catalog was published on September 12, 1850. "Any resident of the Town over the age of fourteen, may have access to the Library, and may take therefrom one volume at a time, provided no family has more than three volumes at a time" (*Library Regulations*, Article 5; Jared M. Heard, *Origins of the Free Public Library System of Massachusetts* [Clinton: Office of the Saturday Courant, 1860], 15 pp.; Alfred Wayland Cutting, *Old-Time Wayland* [Boston: Thomas Todd, 1926], pp. 13–14).

95. The Rev. John Wight came to Wayland in 1815 as pastor of the First Parish Church, where he began as an orthodox Trinitarian, but his pastorate climaxed a growing spirit of liberalism within the church—new influences with which he became increasingly sympathetic. For many years he was chairman of the town School Committee, and in 1856, when the office of superintendent of public schools was created to facilitate the unification of the town school program, Rev. Wight was appointed the first superintendent. Something of a bibliophile and collector of moderately rare imprints, he was an ardent disciple of the belief that books should be free to all and not limited to the use of a few. When he came to Wayland, he found there the East Sudbury Social Library, but because its books were restricted to the membership he assembled a collection of books through subscription, gift, and loan which became known as the East Sudbury Charitable Library. The books, which eventually numbered some three hundred volumes, were first kept at his home and afterward at the church and were available to all who might wish to use them (Alfred Wayland Cutting, *An Historical Address Delivered in the First Parish Church, Wayland, Mass., Sunday, June 25, 1911, on the Occasion of the Dedication of a Mural Tablet to the Memory of Four Former Pastors of the Church* . . . [Boston: George H. Ellis, 1911], pp. 26–28; Cutting, *Old-Time Wayland*, pp. 5, 19, 21).

Though a proposal to the state legislature for permissive library legislation was made by a group of Wayland citizens in 1850, no effective action was forthcoming until 1851 when on Thursday, February 13, "on motion by Mr. Wight of Wayland," the House of Representatives of the Massachusetts General Court

ordered that the Committee on the Judiciary be instructed to inquire whether any, and if any what legislative action is requisite and expedient to enable the towns and cities in this Commonwealth to receive, hold, and appropriate any donations or bequests which may be made to them, for the formation or increase of town or city libraries designed for the use and benefit of all the inhabitants within their respective limits, to authorize them to make such provision, to designate and appoint such officers, and to prescribe such regulations as they may deem requisite to the suitable selection, the safe keeping, the good functioning, the free distribution, and seasonable return of the books; and to empower them to receive from time to time such sums as shall be necessary to defray the *incidental* expenses, and also to receive annually, if they shall see fit, a sum not exceeding blank cents on a hundred dollars of the last valuation for the annual purchase of additional books for said libraries; to the *intent* that if the people so please they may be made perpetual and increasing sources of useful knowledge, and mental, moral, and religious advancement to every family and person within the respective limits throughout all generations.

And that said committee have power to report by bill or otherwise.[96]

The Hon. Caleb Cushing, chairman of the House Judiciary Committee, expressed to Representative Wight his complete sympathy with public library objectives and proposed that Wight himself prepare the appropriate bill.[97] Accordingly, on Wednesday, April 2, the journal of the House reports: "Mr. Wight of Wayland presented a bill concerning the establishment of public libraries which was referred to the Committee on the Judiciary and ordered to be printed."[98] On the following Saturday, April 5, "Mr. Cushing for the Committee on the Judiciary reported on an order from the House concerning town libraries, and a bill on the same subject, that said Committee be discharged from further consideration thereof, and the same be referred to the Committee on Education."[99] Mr. Cushing's report was accepted, the library bill was referred to the Committee on Education, and at

96. Massachusetts General Court, *Records* (House), 1851, p. 237.

97. Heard, *op. cit.*, pp. 9–11.

98. *Journal of the House*, 1851, p. 480.

99. *Ibid.*, p. 500.

An act providing for the establishment of public libraries.

SECTION 1. Be it enacted by the Senate and House of Representatives in General Court convened, that any town in this State, at any legal meeting notified and holden for the purpose, and the city council of any city in this State, may raise and appropriate money to procure books, maps, charts, periodicals, and other publications, for the establishment and perpetual maintenance within the limits of such town or city of a public library, for the purchase of such land and the erection of such buildings as may be necessary for the suitable accommodation thereof, and for the compensation of such officers or agents as may be necessarily employed in the establishment and management of such library.

SEC. 2. Every public library established under the provisions of this act, shall be opened to the free use of every inhabitant of the town or city where the same exists, for the general diffusion of intelligence among all classes of the community, subject to such rules and regulations for the well ordering and careful preservation thereof as may be established and ordained by such town or city.

SEC. 3. Any town or city may receive, hold and possess, or sell and dispose of, all such gifts, donations, devices, bequests and legacies as may be made to such town or city, for the purpose of establishing, increasing or improving any such public library, and may apply the proceeds, interests, rents, and profits accruing therefrom, in such manner as will best promote the prosperity and utility of such library.

SEC. 4. Every town or city in which a public library shall be established under the provisions of this act, shall be entitled to receive annually a copy of the laws, journals, and all other works published by authority of the State, for the use of such library; and the Secretary of State is hereby authorized and required to furnish the same from year to year to such town or city.

SEC. 5. This act shall take effect from and after its passage.

APPROVED, July 7, 1849

TABLE 19

COMPARISON OF LIBRARY LEGISLATION, NEW HAMPSHIRE
AND MASSACHUSETTS

Proposed Massachusetts Law
(*House Document No. 124*)

To authorize, encourage, and ensure the formation, increase and perpetuation of Public Libraries, in the several cities and towns of this Commonwealth for the use and benefit of all their respective inhabitants.

WHEREAS, A universal diffusion of knowledge among the people must be highly conducive to the preservation of their freedom, a greater equalization of their social advantages, their industrial success, and their physical, intellectual and moral advancement and elevation; and

WHEREAS, It is requisite to such a diffusion of knowledge, that while sufficient means of a good early education shall be furnished to all the children in the Common Schools, ample and increasing sources of useful and interesting information should be provided for the whole people in the subsequent and much more capable and valuable periods of life; and

WHEREAS, There is no way in which this can be done so effectually, conveniently and economically as by the formation, increase and perpetuation of Public Libraries, in the several cities and towns of this Commonwealth, for the use and benefit of all their respective inhabitants:—

Be it enacted by the Senate and House of Representatives, in General Court assembled, and by the authority of the same, as follows:

SECTION 1. Any city or town of this Commonwealth is hereby authorized to establish and maintain a public library within the same, for the use of the inhabitants thereof, and to provide a suitable room or rooms therefor, under such regulations for the government of said library as may, from time to time, be prescribed by the city council of such city, or the inhabitants of such town.

SEC. 2. No city or town may appropriate, for the foundation and commencement of such library as aforesaid, a sum greater than the amount of one dollar multiplied by the number of its polls in the year in which such appropriation shall be made; and any such city or town may appropriate annually, for the maintenance and augmentation of such library, a sum not greater than the amount of twenty-five cents, multiplied by the number of its polls in the year in which such appropriation shall be made.

SEC. 3. Any city or town may receive in its corporate capacity, and hold and manage, any devise, bequest, or donation, for the establishment, augmentation, or maintenance of a public library within the same.

SEC. 4. Any city or town which shall have established such a library shall be entitled to receive from the school fund, or other proceeds of the public lands not appropriated, twenty per cent. on any sum within the last named limit which it may in any year expend for the augmentation of the same.

An Act to authorize Cities and Towns to establish and maintain Public Libraries.

SECTION 1. Any city or town of this Commonwealth is hereby authorized to establish and maintain a public library within the same, with or without branches, for the use of the inhabitants thereof, and to provide suitable rooms therefor, under such regulations for the government of such library as may, from time to time, be prescribed by the city council of such city, or the inhabitants of such town.

SEC. 2. Any city or town may appropriate for the foundation and commencement of such library, as aforesaid, a sum not exceeding one dollar for each of its ratable polls, in the year next preceding that in which such appropriation shall be made; and may also appropriate, annually, for the maintenance and increase of such library, a sum not exceeding twenty-five cents for each of its ratable polls, in the year next preceding that in which such appropriation shall be made.

SEC. 3. Any city or town may receive, in its corporate capacity, and hold and manage any devise, bequest, or donation, for the establishment, increase, or maintenance of a public library within the same.

APPROVED BY THE GOVERNOR, May 24, 1851

the same time it was sent to the Senate for concurrence.[100] On Tuesday, April 8, the Senate acted: "An order and bill from the House respecting town libraries was referred in concurrence to the Committee on Education."[101] What actually took place during the deliberations of the Committee on Education is unknown. On Thursday, April 17, the committee reported favorably, and the bill was ordered to a second reading.[102] Since two forms of the proposed legislation exist, it is probable that the Committee on Education made certain minor alterations.[103]

In the statute as enacted a two-hundred-word preamble, outlining the advantages and benefits of public libraries, was entirely eliminated. Also the committee appears to have balked on the approval of section 4, which provided that public libraries might receive some financial aid from the School Fund "or other proceeds from the public lands." Minor changes include one interesting addition; the law not only permitted towns to establish public libraries but also provided that such libraries might maintain "branches." This was twenty years before the staff of the Boston Public Library assembled in the Lyman school building of East Boston the collection that is generally regarded as the first public library branch in the United States and eighteen years before the Boston city council passed the necessary legislation permitting the Public Library to create such subsidiary units.[104]

The Committee on Education having reported favorably on this bill, it was, on May 16, ordered to a third reading and on Thursday, May 22, was sent up, along with others, to the Senate

100. *Ibid.*
101. *Journal of the Senate,* 185 , p. 392.
102. *Journal of the House,* 185 , p. 547.
103. *House Document No. 124* is the bill as introduced by Wight, which on April 2 was ordered to be printed. *House Document No. 140* bears the inscription "Reported by the Committee on Education" and is almost identical with the act as finally signed by the governor, May 24, 1851. A comparison of these two forms appears in Table 19.
104. Wadlin, *op. cit.,* pp. 108–9. Actually, of course, there was nothing really new in the branch library concept. In 1816 the Western Library Association, better known as the "Coonskin Library," of Ames, Ohio, established a "branch" some twenty miles distant at Dover. This branch collection was changed every six months (Sarah J. Cutter, "The Coonskin Library," *Ohio Archaeological and Historical Society, Publications,* XXVI [1917], 58–77).

for concurrence.[105] On the following day the Senate reported that it had received the bill from the House and that it had ordered it "engrossed as concurred."[106] On Saturday, May 24, 1851, the bill was passed by a vote which Representative Wight said was "almost unanimous. . . . Every one to whom it was mentioned approved it and welcomed it as a measure of more than ordinary importance. At the passage of the bill . . . several of the prominent members [of the General Court] came forward and strongly expressed their satisfaction and congratulations at its nearly unanimous adoption and manifest certainty of its being enacted."[107] Upon receiving the governor's signature, it became the second state public library law. Though the action in Massachusetts does not display the same haste that had characterized the passage of the New Hampshire law, it is notable that the Massachusetts legislation was the result of deliberations that were by no means lengthy.

The third reading of the bill in the House was accompanied by an address in its support by its chief sponsor, whose remarks were subsequently published in Horace Mann's *Common School Journal*.[108] Mr. Wight's argument in defense of the legislation, though much less extensive than the first reports of the Boston Public Library trustees, ranks with those documents as an important early attempt to formulate and codify public library objectives. After a preliminary statement of the position of the library as a logical extension of the public school system, Wight enumerated four major advantages of that act which he had placed before the Massachusetts legislature: (1) The law was permissive, not mandatory: "It does not *require* the Citizens of Towns to act on the subject, but only gives the necessary authority, whenever the inhabitants shall have become desirous so to do by a suitable con-

105. *Journal of the House*, 1851, p. 736.
106. *Journal of the Senate*, 1851, May 23.
107. *Journal of the House*, 1851, p. 810; John B. Wight, "A Lecture on Public Libraries Delivered in Boston in the Hall of Representatives, 1854, and in Several Other Places" (unpublished MS in possession of Mrs. John B. Wight of Wayland, Mass., and used with her permission).
108. John B. Wight, "Our Common School System," chap. xv, "Public Libraries," *Common School Journal*, XIII (1851), 257–64.

sideration of its utility and importance."[109] (2) It imposed an upper limit on the extent of municipal support: "It guards against any lavish and unnecessary expenditures which might otherwise be incurred in a time of excitement."[110] (3) By specifically authorizing the acceptance and use of bequests and donations, the law not only obviated the necessity of special legislation for that purpose but by suggestion encouraged men of wealth to make such gifts for library formation. (4) Wight foresaw the possibility of state aid from the education fund, and made provision for it in *his* draft of the bill.

The major portion of Wight's apologia was an examination of the anticipated social benefits that would derive from the establishment of public libraries formed in response to the enactment of the law. Wight saw the legislation he had espoused as something much greater than an instrument created to give legal sanction to the Wayland Public Library and others like it. It was the law itself that would give impetus to the slowly emerging movement for public libraries throughout the towns of the Commonwealth. "It will, unquestionably," he said, "lead to the establishment of good public libraries in many instances, by making them an object of general attention, by enabling intelligent and public spirited individuals to avail themselves of the cooperation of all their fellow citizens in their efforts."[111]

The major advantages of this anticipated growth in public libraries were four in number. First, as the speaker had already indicated, such libraries were to become a necessary and important supplement to the public school system. "With good public libraries, every one will have it in his power to supply the deficiencies of his early acquisitions, and every one will be able to make whatever knowledge he had acquired available in facilitat-

109. *Ibid.*, p. 259. Italics his.

110. *Ibid.*

111. *Ibid.* About eighteen months later, in a printed circular letter distributed by Wight to promote public library establishment, he again made it clear that the real purpose of the law was to advance the formation of public libraries: "The design of the measure was not merely to prevent the necessity of special legislation in particular instances, but also and chiefly to suggest, recommend, and facilitate the formation of a good, permanent, increasing Library in every city and town of the Commonwealth, for the use and benefit of all its inhabitants."

ing his further progress."[112] Second, libraries would have an intensely utilitarian value in their capacity to supply the people with important practical information.[113] Third, intellectual and moral advance would be a consequence of public library establishment.

> How much more ignorance would thus be removed, how much vice reformed, how much slumbering talent awakened, how much awakened talent aided and made efficient, how much done to make many in a high degree intelligent, well informed, useful and respectable citizens, and to correct, improve, and elevate the general character of the whole community, in five, in ten, in twenty, in fifty, in a hundred years.[114]

Fourth, the libraries so established would generate many minor benefits. They would serve as depositories for the care and preservation of important public documents as well as the accumulation of "rare and curious books." They would encourage creative writing by providing a medium for the general dissemination of the printed word. They would be a focal point for contemporary reform, and, finally, they would increase the abilities and efficiency of all other mediums for public instruction.

That such advantages would accrue from public libraries Representative Wight was certain. In his own town of Wayland, where, some two years before, such an institution had been founded, marked improvement in the moral and intellectual tone of the community was already apparent:

> On Saturday afternoon ladies, and young ladies, and girls, frequent it, and have a good time of friendly greetings and pleasant intercourse. In the evening men, and young men and boys may be found there, spending an hour or two in a rational and useful manner, under the quiet influence and suggestive association of the place. All carry away with them instructive and interesting books adapted to their peculiar capacities, tastes, and wants, and furnishing them with innocent and improving occupation in their leisure hours. . . . Every Father and Mother who understands the subject, must feel, that in such a library their children will have advantages for acquiring much of that mental culture and general information, which is the principal and most valuable result of an extensive and liberal education.[115]

Such were the advantages and demonstrated benefits of a municipally owned library, but the speaker did not surrender the

112. *Ibid.*, p. 260.   114. *Ibid.*, p. 261.
113. *Ibid.*   115. *Ibid.*, p. 263.

floor without a concluding appeal to the economic realism of his audience. Apart from the social and cultural advantages, the support of a public library would reward its community with a full return on the invested capital, interest at a rate that would satisfy the most avaricious speculator. "And to meet an objection which may arise in some few minds, before the subject is generally well understood, will not the increased value of their real estate, in consequence of having such a library, exceed a hundred fold all that they have expended in its establishment, or may yet expend in its augmentation?"[116]

The passage of the act in substantially the form in which it had been introduced gave to its chief sponsor the opportunity for library promotion that he had been seeking. "I had not heard of Rev. Mr. Wight's labors in the cause," wrote Francis Wayland to Edward Mellen, at the very time that the act was before the General Court,[117] but the many towns of Massachusetts were soon to learn of Mr. Wight's ambitious scheme. On January 1, 1853, the Wayland minister prepared a circular letter of which some four thousand printed copies were distributed, "postage collect,"[118] urging the formation of public libraries throughout the Commonwealth. In this document the bulk of Wight's argument is an abbreviated recapitulation of that presented before the General Court. But he did inform the public that such libraries "were now forming or are about to be formed" in Wayland, Concord, Southboro, Boston, Worcester, New Bedford, Danvers, and Northampton.

116. *Ibid.*

117. Unpublished letter from Francis Wayland of Providence, R.I., to Judge Edward Mellen, of Wayland, Mass., March 25, 1851, in Wayland Public Library. In this same letter President Wayland wrote of these early efforts at library promotion: "I thank you abundantly for the interest which you and your fellow-citizens have taken in this effort. I was going to say *little* effort, but it is now by no means little if by example it should be permitted to spread and cover the soil of New England so that every man amongst us should have an abundant supply of intellectual food."

118. "It is hoped that the great number of this circular, 4,000, distributed throughout the Commonwealth, and the public importance of the subject, will be a sufficient apology for omitting the prepayment of postage" (Wight, circular letter, p. 3).

The record of library establishment during the years immediately following the enactment of the Massachusetts law goes far to justify Wight's optimistic belief that the new act would become an effective agent of promotion. Between June, 1851, and December, 1854, at least ten such institutions were created by as many cities and towns in the state:

New Bedford Free Public Library, 1851
Beverley Public Library, 1851
Winchendon Town Library, 1851
Fay Library, Southborough, 1852
Lenox Public Library, 1853
Newburyport Public Library, 1854
Framingham Town Public Library, 1854
Groton Public Library, 1854
Woburn Public Library, 1854
West Springfield Town Library, 1854

The middle of the nineteenth century was indeed a turning-point in the history of the public library movement in the United States. The enactment of the New Hampshire and Massachusetts laws was tacit acknowledgment of the essential failure of the social library form as an adequate instrument for public book distribution. "It will probably be, as it has already been," wrote Mr. Wight in 1854, "that in some instances the public spirited proprietors of social or associational libraries will be desirous to increase their resources and extend their usefulness by offering them to the town or city as the foundation of a public library to be much enlarged and annually augmented and freely opened to all the people."[119] The death warrant of the social library as the dominant institutional type was clearly legible between the lines of the Boston Public Library charter. For years the forces that were to converge to form the American public library had been steadily gathering strength for this inevitable step. There were not many among the New England populace who were aware that the old order was about to surrender to the new, but it *was* apparent to an obscure minister in a small Massachusetts community:

119. Wight, "A Lecture . . . ," *op. cit.*

Nor is the establishment of public libraries premature. The people are prepared for their introduction by the proprietary and common-school libraries which have preceded them, and by the increasing desire for information which is spreading through all classes; and will approve them, and provide for them, and welcome them everywhere, as soon as they shall be led to consider and understand their nature and importance. The universal establishment of such libraries in this Commonwealth—and may I not say in the New England states, in the United States, and throughout the civilized world—is a question only of time.[120]

This was to be the future story of the public library, and John Wight of Wayland himself had written into the statutes of the Commonwealth one of the opening chapters.

120. Wight, circular letter, pp. 2–3.

CHAPTER VII

CAUSAL FACTORS IN PUBLIC LIBRARY DEVELOPMENT

COMPLEX social agencies do not arise in response to a single influence; the dogma of simple causation is an easy and ever threatening fallacy. It cannot be said that the public library began on a specific date, at a certain town, as the result of a particular cause. A multiplicity of forces, accumulating over a long period of time, converged to shape this new library form. Some were obviously more important than others, but to evaluate each in precise quantitative terms is impossible. Nevertheless, some generalizations concerning the elements that contributed to the emergence of the public library are possible, and these, together with an indication of the relative importance of each, will be presented in this concluding chapter.

Economic Ability

Among the many social conditions that made the public library possible the one basic element was economic potential. Without financial resources superior to the demands of mere subsistence, no community could assemble and maintain a library. Tax support for libraries presupposes a source from which revenue may be derived. The American public library was evolved and supported by community action; and, because it was dependent upon democratic processes, its advance was slow and its acceptance forced to wait upon general recognition of libraries as at least desirable, if not essential, adjuncts of a culturally sophisticated society. Yet no library was possible in the absence of an available reservoir of wealth. In the advance of tax support for libraries desire and ability were equally important and interdependent; either without the other was incapable of action.

Economic ability contributed to the advance of the library in two major ways: (*a*) the accumulation of private fortunes by philanthropic individuals and (*b*) a rising level of community wealth; and these produced the two aberrant forms of the evolutionary process by which the modern public library arose. These forms are represented by libraries established and supported by (*a*) wealthy philanthropists and (*b*) groups of individuals of more modest means. The former exhibits three variations depending upon the conditions of gift, inasmuch as libraries were inaugurated by an initial gift of expendable money, by an endowment of which the income only was available, and by a combination of expendable gift and endowment.

Private philanthropy antedated tax support by many years because it was simple, direct, and dependent only upon the accumulation of wealth by a generous individual. Philanthropy is a normal process whereby economic inequalities are voluntarily leveled off by individuals acting on their own initiative or in response to public opinion. Public libraries in America may rightly be said to have begun with the bequest of Captain Keayne, and they have been heavily indebted to the generosity of individuals ever since. The first tax-supported libraries drew much of their strength from the donations of wealthy men. Wayland's public library and even the Massachusetts law itself were direct results of a gift from the president of Brown University. The original success of the Boston Public Library can scarcely be attributed to any single influence, but it is certain that the benevolence of Joshua Bates gave to that institution an early stability.

So meager were the first contributions from the town treasuries that the sponsors of early public libraries anticipated that such slender resources would be amplified by private gifts. Edward Everett wrote into the preliminary report of the Boston Public Library trustees his conviction that a large municipal appropriation "was entirely out of the question" and even that there were "advantages in a more gradual course of measures," adding that with only "moderate and frugal expenditure on the part of the City . . . the Trustees believe that all else may be left to the public spirit and liberality of individuals."[1] John B. Wight said of the

1. Boston Public Library, *Report of the Trustees . . . July 1852* (City Document No. 37 [Boston: J. H. Eastburn, 1852]), pp. 221–22. Cf. Appen. V.

Massachusetts library law that it "precludes any large expenditures for library purposes by any city or town in its corporate capacity. It was thought best to leave room for the exercise of private liberality and public spirit in aid of their establishment and augmentation."[2] Likewise, the directors of the Athenaeum of Portland, Maine, when considering the possibility of initiating a public library in their community, remarked in 1855:

> With reference to a free public library, no example is known to us, of any such institution, in this country, established by any municipal corporation or otherwise, which has not had its origin in some large private benefaction, made for the purpose by one or more individuals. . . .
>
> The private generosity, which may be wished for to make this undertaking practicable, has not yet appeared. It may not be unreasonable to *hope*, that coming time will reveal the benefactor, who shall make an effectual contribution to the general intellectual improvement of our city, after the resplendent examples, that have illustrated the annals of some other places; but that chapter in the history of Portland, which shall record such a bounty, is as yet unwritten.[3]

With the dependence of New England upon commerce and industry, there developed an economy in which the general income level was relatively low and wealth tended to concentrate in the hands of the few. The public could not afford the costs of adequate library support. Aid through taxation and its resultant spreading of the financial burden over the entire community was, even in its earlier forms, an advance beyond the voluntary association represented by the social library. But only the wealthy were able to give the movement the aid it required.

The dominant characteristic of that benevolence upon which the public libraries of New England were so heavily dependent was the psychology of the generous native son. The individual histories of New England town libraries tell again and again the story of those who, recalling the hardships of youth, returned to their native communities a portion of the rewards gained during a lifetime of economic venturing. The successful Boston publisher Caleb Bingham gave to Salisbury, Connecticut, the library which later became the first collection to receive financial aid from pub-

---

2. John B. Wight, "A Lecture on Public Libraries Delivered in Boston in the Hall of Representatives, 1854, and in Several Other Places" (unpublished MS).

3. Portland Athenaeum, *Report of the Directors Submitted at the Annual Meeting of the Proprietors, November 8, 1855*, p. 5; copy in Maine Historical Society.

lic funds.[4] From London, George Peabody, merchant, financier, and philanthropist, established in South Danvers the Peabody Institute, "in acknowledgment of the payment of that debt to the generation which preceded me in my native town . . . and to aid in its prompt future discharge."[5] Joshua Bates was not a native of Boston, but he had been born at Weymouth in the Bay region and his business life was so closely associated with the capital of Massachusetts that when he received from Mayor Seaver the report of the trustees on the proposed Public Library for Boston, his response was immediate and generous. On October 1, 1852, he wrote to T. W. Ward:

> My own experience as a poor boy convinced me of the great advantage of such a library. Having no money to spend, and no place to go to, not being able to pay for a fire in my own room, I could not pay for books, and the best way I could pass my evenings was to sit in Hastings, Etheridge, & Bliss' Bookstore, and read what they kindly permitted me to.[6]

Said John Wight in urging the promotion of libraries under the provision of the Massachusetts law:

> It may be justly expected that in the future . . . as has already occurred, intelligent and far seeing individuals who have risen to affluence in our large cities, or in foreign countries, will be disposed to remember in this regard the place of their birth . . . in the welfare of which they cannot but feel a peculiar interest, by laying the foundation of an institution which will be a rich and increasing source of useful knowledge and mental cultivation open to all the inhabitants throughout all generations.[7]

Of course, not all the benefactions for New England libraries were the contributions of those who from the security of a profitable career remembered the privations of youth, but the philanthropy that contributed so much to the encouragement of public libraries in that region was strongly centripetal, drawing toward

4. Charlotte B. Norton (comp.), *History of the Scoville Memorial Library* (Salisbury: Lakeview Journal Press, 1941), pp. 8–10.

5. Massachusetts Free Public Library Commission, *Free Public Libraries in Massachusetts: Ninth Annual Report* (Boston: Wright & Potter, 1899), p. 93. This was, of course, not the only benefaction of George Peabody. He gave a Peabody Institute to Danvers and to Baltimore, as well as the museums of archeology and ethnology to Harvard and of natural history to Yale, and there were numerous other gifts of lesser magnitude.

6. Quoted by Horace G. Wadlin, *The Public Library of the City of Boston: A History* (Boston: Boston Public Library, 1911), p. 42.

7. Wight MS.

its vortex the wealth produced beyond its immediate boundaries. Abbott Lawrence, William Wood, Kirk Boot, William Maclure, and many others who lived in places remote from the recipients of their generosity contributed to the growth of libraries in New England towns which they themselves may never have seen.[8]

The growth of industrialization and of the factory system, with its resultant concentration of capital in the hands of a small proportion of the population, was the real factor behind the expansion of philanthropy. As industry began to return to ownership the rewards of investment and as money accumulated at an unprecedented rate, the individual sought a proper object for his munificence. It was generally acknowledged that a library was a wholesome community influence, and its encouragement could be regarded with the highest approbation. The endowment of a library did not demand extravagant wealth; by comparison to colleges, universities, or art galleries, its requirements were extremely modest. Hence the library could, and did, attract the generosity of men of moderate means—men who, like Francis Wayland or Josiah Quincy, Jr., were able to contribute in a relatively small way toward the support of collections which they sincerely believed to be essential to the encouragement of an indigenous culture.[9]

8. William Maclure, who established the Maclure Library at Pittsford, Vt., was moved to do so through the efforts of Thomas Palmer, but Maclure himself had no connection with the town (records in Maclure Library). See, further, the supplementary list of donors of library buildings in the Massachusetts Free Public Library Commission, *op. cit.*, pp. 457–59.

9. There is perhaps no finer example of this spirit than that of Quincy's gift to the incipient Boston Public Library. In his journal for Tuesday, October 12, 1847, he wrote: "I have determined to endeavor to found a city Library and Museum, and for that purpose to give Five Thousand Dollars on condition that the City double the donation. I have been very prosperous and feel as though it were my duty to improve this opportunity of starting an institution which may, if it 'takes' with my fellow citizens be of great and lasting benefit and honor to the Public."

On the following day, Wednesday, October 13: "Conversed with my wife concerning the Vattemare donation. She entirely approves of everything that is liberal and noble. She is indeed the virtuous woman whose price is above rubies."

The next day, Thursday, October 14, he journeyed to Quincy, where he dined with the family and "walked over the place with my father. Consulted them about the donation, and they all of course approve." Returning to Boston that evening, "... sent in my ... offer of Five Thousand dollars for a Public Library. I, of course,

The libraries which derived support from numbers of small gifts rather than from a single large donation approached the democratic ideal of general community participation. But the great weakness of philanthropy as a medium of library promotion lay in its independence of public desire. It was not a direct expression of popular need. In a sense it was forced upon society; and while it may have been accepted and even fostered by the recipients, it was in its origins a thing apart. In 1785 the inhabitants of Franklin, Massachusetts, wishing a bell for their meeting-house, communicated the fact to the American minister to the Court of France in whose honor the town had been named. From Passy, Franklin responded with a gift of a library, "sense being preferable to sound," which, though received by the community with appropriate expressions of gratitude, remained for half a century in the hayloft of a barn.[10] Similarly, John Quincy Adams' handsome gift of three thousand volumes, taken from his own rich collection, to the town of Quincy was but slightly esteemed by the recipient municipality; and though provision was made for its preservation, the residents of the community derived little benefit from it.[11]

In an effort to avoid just such misplaced generosity and to broaden the democratic base of the institutions they hoped to found, it became a general practice among donors to require of a community that by voluntary contributions or other means it match the proffered gift.[12] But even at its best, philanthropy, be-

---

for the present shall conceal my name as it might be looked upon as an electioneering movement."

On January 17 of the following year he wrote: ". . . no one seems to suspect that I am the donor of the Five Thousand dollars, for its [the public library's] commencement. If I can start this during my administration it will be second only to the introduction of water" (MS journals of Josiah Quincy in the Boston Public Library).

10. Franklin's original letter is reprinted in Massachusetts Free Public Library Commission, *op. cit.*, p. 131; see also Mortimer Blake, *History of the Town of Franklin* (Franklin: Published by the town, 1879), pp. 69–72.

11. George Whitney, *Some Account of the Early History and Present State of the Town of Quincy* . . . (Boston: Christian Register Office, 1827), p. 44.

12. One of the best examples of this was the offer of Amasa Manton of Rhode Island, who proposed to give $150 for the purchase of new books to any new public library society which would double his donation. In this way he encouraged the

cause it lacked the spontaneity of unified collective action, created an institutional superstructure that existed because it had been built upon rather than grown from the life of the town. As a sustaining force in the expansion of the library the importance of private donation is not to be minimized. Many times it saved institutions which would have perished because of the poverty of the communities they endeavored to serve. Moreover, it bridged the gap between the period of the voluntary association and the emergence of tax support by keeping alive social library collections which later were absorbed into the governments of their towns.

Nevertheless, philanthropy, for all the material benefits it conferred, was a contributory rather than a causal factor in public library development. It was not the expression of group action. As an embodiment of the donor's wish to further the welfare of society it was personal and individual, an instrument rather than a cause of public library promotion. But it was not the only medium by which the economic ability of the region contributed to the enthusiasm for public libraries. When the economic structure of New England became more stable and wealth began to accumulate, other social phenomena appeared which stimulated the desire for greater library resources that would be freely available to all who needed them.

Scholarship, Historical Research, and the Urge for Conservation

"What is the nest that hatches scholars but a library?" asked Oliver Wendell Holmes,[13] and this one question epitomizes what was probably the greatest single force in the expansion of the public library. In the decades that preceded the middle of the nineteenth century, scholarship, especially as it found expression in historical inquiry and research, was definitely increasing. With the development of settled conditions and the increase of wealth in New England, there appeared a class of professional and ama-

---

formation of a number of quasi-public library societies in Rhode Island (see Charles Carroll, *Rhode Island: Three Centuries of Democracy* [New York: Lewis History Pub. Co., 1932], II, 1073).

13. Quoted in *Athenaeum Items*, February, 1938, p. 1.

teur scholars who desperately needed libraries, and the accumulation of private wealth richly served the historian. Prescott, Motley, and Parkman were all men of considerable means. George Ticknor, whose *History of Spanish Literature* cost as much to produce as a public building, owned a great house at the head of Park Street, which dominated the Common from Beacon Hill, and there, in its largest and finest room, he kept the most extensive private library in Boston. It was Ticknor who, as a trustee of the Boston Athenaeum, proposed to unite all the libraries of the city with that institution and make the whole freely available to the entire population. On February 2, 1826, he wrote to Daniel Webster:

We are making quite a movement about libraries, lecture-rooms, Athenaeum, etc. I have a project, which may or may not succeed; but I hope it will. The project is, to unite into one establishment, viz. the Athenaeum, all the public libraries in town; such as the Arch Library, the Medical Library, the new Scientific Library, and so on, and then let the whole circulate, Athenaeum and all. In this way there will be an end of buying duplicates, paying double rents, double librarians, etc.; the whole money raised will go to books, and all the books will be made useful. To this great establishment I would attach all the lectures wanted, whether fashionable, popular, scientific,—for the merchants or their employees; and have the whole made a Capitol of the knowledge of the town, with its uses, which I would open to the public, according to the admirable direction in the Charter of the University of Göttingen, *quam commodissime, quamque latissime.* Mr. Prescott, Judge Jackson, Dr. Bowditch, and a few young men are much in earnest about it.[14]

Having assumed leadership in the movement for establishing the Boston Public Library, Ticknor collected lists of essential books from every interested scholar he could find, planned with C. C. Jewett the accession policies of the new library, and toured Europe purchasing large quantities of books in London, Paris, and Rome.

The growing consciousness of the inadequacy of American libraries was given dramatic expression by Fisher Ames. At the close of a strenuous political career, plagued by rapidly failing health, and furious over a rising Jeffersonian democracy, Ames, with characteristic eagerness to discredit everything American to the eternal glorification of the British, insisted that in all our uni-

14. George Ticknor, *Life, Letters, and Journals* (Boston: Houghton Mifflin, 1909), I, 371.

versities combined there was not a sufficient supply of books to
furnish the essential materials for such a work as Gibbon's.

> Nor will it be charged as a mark of our stupidity . . . that we have produced
> nothing in history. Our own is not yet worthy of a Livy; and to write that of any
> foreign nation where could an American author collect his materials and
> authorities? Few persons reflect, that all our universities would not suffice to
> supply them for such a work as Gibbon's.[15]

The accusation was doubtless just, and it was eagerly snatched by
many a mid-nineteenth-century proponent of public library development and bandied about until it became little more than an
empty cliché.[16] Finally John Quincy Adams set about collecting
at his own expense the titles necessary for the verification of Gibbon's citations.[17] Throughout New England there arose a great
outcry from the academicians for more adequate library resources. The *American Almanac* spoke with feeling of the embar-
rassment felt by every American scholar who, confronted by the
most meager of library facilities, attempts to pursue "one point
of science or literature through all or a considerable portion of
what has been written on it."[18] In 1850 George Livermore exceeded the charge of Fisher Ames by asserting that the scholar of
his generation did not have access to sufficient material to write
the history of the *New England Primer*, and C. C. Jewett, with
scarcely less restraint, maintained that not one American library
could meet the wants of a student in any department of knowledge. In this general opinion Prescott concurred, holding that
the American historian was forced to create a personal library if
he wished to write extensively on historical themes; and Bancroft, who was relatively poor, found himself obliged, in the
preparation of his earlier works, to spend as much as the salary
of the president of the United States.

In spite of general dissatisfaction over the poverty of materials,
the historians were active. In this sudden outburst of enthusiasm

15. Fisher Ames, *Works*, ed. Seth Ames (Boston: Little, Brown, 1854), II, 440.

16. Quoted by an anonymous author in the *North American Review*, XLV (1837),
137, it was used by Judge Story in an address before the Phi Beta Kappa society at
Cambridge. It was again quoted in the *North American Review*, LXXI (1850), 186.

17. *Ibid.*, LXXI (1850), 186. Also A. R. Spofford, "Public Libraries in the
United States," *Journal of Social Science*, II (1870), 113.

18. *American Almanac and Repository of Useful Knowledge* (Boston: Charles Bowen,
1836), pp. 81–82; also 1834, pp. 148–49.

for historical investigation American writers reflected interests that were awakening in England and on the Continent. The aftermath of the Napoleonic Wars brought an aroused nationalism which revitalized historical research. Under the leadership of Niebuhr new standards of critical scholarship in historical writing, both in the search for materials and their objective examination, were established. Macaulay, Grote, and Carlyle in England, Theirs and Guizot in France, and Niebuhr and Von Ranke in Germany were making history popular as never before. American scholars who had traveled in Europe were stirred by the work of these men, and they began to study not only the history of other peoples but also that of their own nation. In increasing numbers young New Englanders with literary tastes were drawn into historical research, as decades before they had been called into the ministry. To the quiet reading-rooms of the Athenaeum came the stalwarts of the *North American Review:* Ticknor, Palfrey, Sparks, Everett, and even Hannah Adams, the first woman permitted to use the collections—locked in while the librarian was at lunch because he was too polite to put her out.

Events had prepared the New England mind for concentration on history. Old bitternesses and conflicts engendered by the Revolution were forgotten in the nationalism that was sweeping the country. Old men who as youths had fought together in '76 foregathered to relive the battles of Lexington and Concord. Inspired by Webster's orations, the public thronged to the shrine of Plymouth Rock and read again Mather's *Magnalia Christi* and other half-forgotten chronicles of our national heritage.

To the end of encouraging historical research, scholars throughout the New England area united in voluntary associations to promote mutual understanding and to encourage and facilitate the assembly of basic source materials. In 1791 Jeremy Belknap, John Pintard, and Ebenezer Hazard laid the foundation of the Massachusetts Historical Society and its long line of distinguished publications. In 1812 Isaiah Thomas gave his private library to form the American Antiquarian Society and eight years later built with his own money Antiquarian Hall at Worcester where, being in a small town, it would be safer from the fires of large cities and, being inland, less exposed to the ravages of war. In 1821 there was established at Salem, Massachusetts, the Essex Historical Society, which later became the Essex Institute; and the year following both Rhode Island and Maine founded historical societies, the former issuing, appropriately enough, Roger Williams' treatise on the Indian languages in America. New Hampshire, eager to celebrate in 1823 the two-hundredth anniversary of her first Colonial settlement, incorporated her historical society with thirty-one charter members. In Connecticut a state historical society was initiated in 1825, but it did not become active until 1839, when its charter was revived. In 1838 Vermont established at Montpelier the Historical and Antiquarian Society of that state. All over the country, in the middle states and the South as well as in New England, the reading of history was popular as never before; a veritable flood of local histories rolled from the presses, and Parson Weems's *Life of Washington* went through some seventy editions. A generation later James Parton concluded his three-volume biography of Andrew Jackson with the credo of the age:

> And to comprehend the state of things in which we find ourselves, it is necessary, first of all, to show every step of the progress by which the present state of things has been reached. It is necessary that the writings of Washington, Adams, Hamilton, and Jefferson should no longer remain in the public libraries with the leaves uncut. It is necessary, in a word, that the educated intelligence of the United States should begin to understand that there is nothing in recent European history half so worthy of study as the history of the United States since the adoption of the present constitution.[19]

In the wake of this enthusiasm for the past came a natural urge to preserve for future generations the more fragile records of the growing nation. Gales and Seaton began their monumental *American State Papers,* and Congress contracted with Peter Force and Matthew St. Clair Clarke for the publication of the "American Archives Series," originally suggested a half-century earlier

19. James Parton, *Life of Andrew Jackson* (New York: Mason, 1860), III, 701. John F. Sly, by counting the entries in Jeremiah Colburn's *Bibliography of the Local History of Massachusetts,* finds that twenty-one local histories were published prior to 1830, a total which excludes fragments, "discourses," "sketches," and the transactions of learned societies. Approximately half of these titles were less than one hundred pages in length. Eighteen towns were represented. For the years between 1830 and 1845 thirty comparable histories, representing forty-three towns and villages, were recorded. Between 1845 and 1855 twenty-one new titles were added, of which fifteen were over two hundred and fifty pages in length (John F. Sly, *Town Government in Massachusetts, 1620–1930* [Cambridge: Harvard University Press, 1930], p. 107 n.).

by Ebenezer Hazard. At the beginning of the century the national Congress, largely through the efforts of Elbridge Gerry, Samuel Latham Mitchill, and John Randolph of Roanoke,[20] had laid the foundation for a great book collection, and though this Library of Congress was to suffer somewhat more than its share of adverse fortune, by the middle of the century it gave promise of ranking among the best of American book collections.[21]

In 1812 Joseph Stevens Buckminster wrote into a preface intended for the first printed catalog of the Boston Athenaeum a plea for the formation of a "complete Bibliotheca Americana," toward which some progress had then already been made,[22] and fifteen years later a similar ideal was proposed for the state of New Hampshire by the trustees of the Portsmouth Athenaeum.[23]

20. John Randolph was the author of the phrase, "a good library is a statesman's workshop"; and though he owned a large personal collection, he is supposed to have told Nathan Sargent that he would not have in his possession an American book, not even an American Bible (William D. Johnston, *History of the Library of Congress* [Washington, D.C.: Government Printing Office, 1904], I, 24).

21. Jewett (*ca.* 1850) credits the Library of Congress with fifty thousand volumes, though it then still ranked below Harvard with eighty-four thousand volumes and the Philadelphia Library Company with sixty thousand. It was approximately equal in size to the collections of the Boston Athenaeum and Yale University.

22. A circular addressed to American authors asking, on behalf of the Athenaeum, for their works and signed by George Livermore, E. A. Crowninshield, and Charles E. Norton [1849] (in Boston Athenaeum), says in part: "The Class [of books] which demands and has received the most anxious care of the Trustees is that which comprises works which relate to America, and in the completion of which we have made some rapid advances. We beg leave, therefore, to call the attention of the public to this subject, and to solicit the donation of any tracts published here or in England, which throw light on our early annals; of works of any kind printed in America, or written by American authors; and, in fine, of anything, even to a single leaf, relating to our literary, civil, religious, natural, or moral History, and to aid us in forming a complete Bibliotheca Americana.

"If the time should ever come, which we fondly expect, when a suitable structure shall be raised in this town, in which to deposit the crowded treasures of this literary institution, we shall then have approached nearer to the accomplishment of a darling object, the formation of a complete American Library."

23. "The deficiency in the department of American history and statisticks, ought especially to be supplied; and to this end unwearied and individual efforts ought to be made, both by the Corporation and its members individually, until it be supplied. Every publick American library ought certainly to be complete in American history; and in the state of New Hampshire there ought to be at least one library to which every citizen in the State may be able to go with the certainty of being able to find there any needed information in relation to the history of his own country" (Portsmouth Athenaeum, *Annual Report, January 1827*, p. 5; in Portsmouth Athenaeum).

As early as 1836 an anonymous writer in the *American Almanac* was urging the creation of a series of regional libraries "under the patronage and direction of the government" that were to be "judiciously placed at the principal centers of population and intelligence."[24]

By 1811 Massachusetts had enacted legislation providing for the exchange of her official state documents for those of other states, thus laying a cornerstone for the future state library, which was established in 1826. Priority in state library establishment belongs to New Hampshire, where in 1818 an act was passed authorizing the secretary of state "to collect and arrange all books belonging to the State," and in 1823 a resolution was adopted appropriating one hundred dollars annually for the increase of the collection.[25]

Much of the passion for the historic became an empty antiquarianism that soon degenerated into mere collecting for its own sake with little or no regard to the value of the materials thus assembled. Libraries eagerly brought together "cabinets of specimens," and historical societies assembled with reckless abandon museums of curios and memorabilia that would have been better forgotten. But at its best this activity did salvage much of value to the historian, and it did help to build up a solid body of source materials upon which might be erected a substantial scholarship. It was through the efforts of such men as William Smith Shaw that later generations have inherited libraries as important as the Boston Athenaeum. Not without reason was he known by his contemporaries as "Athenaeum Shaw":

That dog of a Shaw [said Judge William Tudor] goes everywhere. He knows everybody. Everybody knows him. If he sees a book, pamphlet, or *manuscript*— Oh! Sir! the Athenaeum must have this. Well, *have it he will*, and *have it he must*, and *have it he does*, for he seldom goes out of a house without having something under his arm; and his large pockets, made on purpose, are crammed. Now, he never refuses anything whatever. With him a book is a book, a pamphlet a pamphlet, a manuscript a manuscript.[26]

24. *American Almanac and Repository of Useful Knowledge* (1836), p. 82.

25. The Vermont state library was established November 17, 1825; that of Maine in 1836; Connecticut in 1854; and Rhode Island in 1868 (state law library).

26. Quoted by C. K. Bolton, *The Boston Athenaeum, 1807–1927, a Sketch* (Boston: The Athenaeum, 1927), p. 2.

This urge to preservation, when in conjunction with the demand of the historian for collections adequate to his research needs, could not fail to influence the course of the public library and contribute to the movement for library establishment a most powerful impetus. Ticknor, despite his predilection for maximum accessibility, wrote into the first report of the Boston Public Library trustees (see Appen. V) his conviction that there was a basic core of books which should not be permitted to circulate— books which because of their rarity and costliness it was the first duty of the library to provide but which it was the obligation of the library also to protect.[27] Though Ticknor was not reluctant to acknowledge that one of the important functions of the public library was to preserve for posterity the bibliographical treasures of the present, it was Everett who was the high priest of preservation. Writing in 1850 to Mayor Bigelow to offer his collection of public documents to the city of Boston as a nucleus for the proposed library, he asserted:

Perceiving that a commencement is likely to be made toward the establishment of a public library, I will thank you to inform the city government that this collection is at their service, whenever it will suit their convenience to receive it. I have for nearly thirty years devoted a good deal of time and labor and considerable expense to its formation. It amounts at present to about one thousand volumes. From the foundation of the government up to the year 1825, when I first went to Congress, it contains nearly everything material. While I was in Congress I took great pains to preserve and bind up everything published by either house; and from that time to the year 1840, when I went abroad, the collection is tolerably complete. It is my intention to add to it, as far as they can be procured, the documents since published, and I omit no opportunity of supplying the deficiencies in other parts of the series.[28]

Similarly, John B. Wight, in urging upon the Massachusetts General Court the need for state-wide public library legislation, argued: "Such libraries . . . will furnish suitable and accessible depositories for the preservation of important public documents, and the collection of rare and curious books. They will encourage those who are preeminently capable of teaching and improving others to produce works of great utility and interest."[29]

27. Boston Public Library, *Report . . . July 1852*, p. 16.
28. Quoted by Wadlin, *op. cit.*, p. 20.
29. John B. Wight, "Public Libraries," *Common School Journal*, XIII (1851), 261.

Local Pride

The conservational function of the library appeared very early, and the urge toward book preservation has always been a great driving force, but in New England of the 1840's its appeal was especially strong. Everywhere during these years the young Republic evinced the pride of youth that looked with satisfaction upon the past. Perhaps in no other region was this attitude more intensely expressed than in New England. With the statesmen of Virginia, the hardy Yankees had taken the lead in the Revolution. Twice Britain had been defeated, and on both occasions New England had played a noteworthy part. Confronted by the threat of economic domination from the expanding West and the growing industrialism in the middle states, New England was more than ever forced to reflect upon the glory of a former day. Pride in the cultural heritage, the accomplishments of its authors, the development of education, the number of its libraries—all were natural responses to a latent apprehension that henceforth other sections of the nation would dominate American economic life. Even the champions of New England cultural supremacy were haunted by ominous forebodings. An Astor fortune had given to New York the money necessary for a public library, and Boston was truly alarmed. Already men were beginning to express the fear that unless something of a like character were done in Boston, science and literary culture in that city would follow trade and capital to its metropolitan rival. "That Boston must have a great public library," wrote Everett to Ticknor, "or yield to New York in letters as well as in commerce, will, I think, be made quite apparent in a few years."[30] Six weeks earlier he had written to Mayor Bigelow in similar vein:

> The City of Boston expends annually, I believe, a larger sum for Schools and School Houses, in proportion to its population than any city in Europe. Nothing

30. Everett to Ticknor, July 26, 1851, in Ticknor, *op. cit.*, II, 303. It is interesting that Ticknor took up the cry of alarm two years later when, in urging the union of the Athenaeum with the Boston Public Library he wrote, almost in Everett's precise words: "Unless a *real* public library can be instituted in Boston, we may justly expect, in the quarter of a century, to fall as much behind New York, with its Astor Library, in the means of intellectual culture, as we do already in the advantages for commercial success ([George Ticknor], *Union of the Boston Athenaeum and the Boston Public Library* [Boston: Dutton & Wentworth, 1853], p. 7).

like the same sum is appropriated by the City of London for these purposes. . . . Is it not then a reproach to our City, that,—as far as the means of carrying on the great work of instruction beyond the limits of School Education are concerned,—no public provision exists in favor of those unable to indulge in what is now the expensive luxury of a large library?[31]

The theme was a familiar one in the argument of those who were most seriously concerned with the establishment of the public library. The editor of the *Boston Daily Courier* wrote in his paper for March 26, 1853:

It is gratifying to observe that the rapid and unremitting growth of this metropolis in population, wealth, all the activities of outward life, and all the materials of physical greatness and strength, is accompanied by an augmenting and sharpened attention to those matters which concern the intellect and morals of the community. What, indeed, is the value of all this wealth—accumulated by the industry, enterprise, and ingenuity of the people of New England, drawn out from our own bosom, gathered from the four corners of the globe, and concentrated in her ancient capital—if we cannot number among its uses that of aiding the intelligence, developing the intellect, and improving the morals of those within its reach?

The interest which is now manifested by the citizens of Boston in the subject of a public library, is one of the encouraging signs of the times, and evidence that the people of this city will not allow it to be outstripped by any other in a care for the nobler objects of human pursuit.[32]

Boston was not alone in her eagerness to achieve national distinction as a guardian of the cultural heritage and as a patron of libraries. In 1836 a meeting was called to consider the union of the Providence Library and the Providence Athenaeum into a public library for the community as a whole. In supporting the movement an anonymous writer in the *Journal* expressed his conviction that so pre-eminent a municipality would not neglect so important an agency for public enlightenment:

I . . . trust my fellow citizens in great numbers will join me. I look, then, to the reputation of our beautiful city. I look to the intelligence of its population. I look to the increasing knowledge, refinement, virtue, and love of virtue, of the rising generation, and of the generations to come. All these are deeply involved in the success of the proposed enterprise. What can more worthily appeal to patronage, to any liberal and enlightened community? In this busy, flourishing, and wealthy city, there is not, to our shame, be it recorded, a single building which belongs to our citizens, aside from our school-houses, yet dedicated to

31. Letter from Everett to Bigelow, June 7, 1851, quoted by Wadlin, *op. cit.*, pp. 24–25.

32. *Boston Daily Courier*, March 26, 1853.

the great interests of learning and science. Many towns in New England, quite behind us in population and wealth, have largely surpassed us in the encouragement of such undertakings. Such an institution as is contemplated it is high time we had.[33]

An appeal to local pride interwoven with the ever effective plea for the necessity of outdistancing one's neighbors gave to the argument a vitality that on more than one occasion strongly influenced popular sentiment in favor of creating a library which in later years, when initial enthusiasm had waned under the pressure of economic restriction, suffered inadequate support. It is difficult to envisage an agency more characteristic of this period than the emerging public library. America, proud of her economic growth but confronted by the ancient tradition of European culture, sought eagerly to demonstrate her awareness of the necessity for preserving her own national heritage. America might anticipate a time when she would become a great power in the economic world, yet in the development of a cultural tradition there would always be the handicap of those centuries when she was an unbroken forest inhabited by only savages and beasts. America could build factories, railroads, and all the other physical properties of a growing industrialism; so, too, she could erect libraries, within the walls of which to assemble the cultural monuments of the entire world, and thus in a measure find compensation for the shortcomings of her national immaturity. Such reasoning was particularly appealing to New England, where the existence of a relatively long Colonial history and the threat of declining economic leadership forced the people to seek in cultural achievement the satisfaction of desire for regional prestige.

The Social Importance of Universal Public Education

Second only to the desire for conservation and local pride was the growth in New England of an awareness of the need for universal educational opportunity. However influential the conservational motive was, its basic appeal was to the scholar, the man of letters, and the leader in political and civil life. It did not arouse the enthusiasm of a large portion of the people. But the public

33. Letter from "F" in the *Providence Journal*, January 25, 1836.

library, if it was to enlist the support of the voters in its campaign for municipal funds, had of necessity to appeal to the popular mind. In this the public library was favored by a spirit that was developing in New England, as elsewhere in America. There was a widespread conviction that universal literacy was necessary, and there was much enthusiasm for education for its own sake. Many believed in the possibility of self-education and the practical value of vocational and technical studies. Finally, there was a prevalent assumption that reading promotes morality. From these convictions there emerged a popular awareness of the importance of the public library to the people, and as the people began to express themselves more freely in political activity, the public library became a necessity.

Jackson's election to the presidency proved the reality of that boundless optimism that characterized the expanding frontier, a seemingly inexhaustible energy that lashed backward over the Atlantic Coast. Even in conservative New England was felt the sudden impact of this robust enthusiasm in the discovery of romance, culture, altruism, self-reliance, and a sense of one's own individuality. Everywhere the spirit of youth was dominant. With the rise of Jackson, the presidency began to seem attainable to every American boy. Democracy became popular to a degree that had never been achieved before, and in its defense Bancroft wrote "history that voted for Jackson on every page." Humanitarian movements developed with all the enthusiasm that attaches to the untried. Social experiments, such as Brook Farm and New Harmony, evinced this same spirit of youthful buoyance and confidence. In New England the trend was a local manifestation of a world movement that swept over Europe in a great wave of humanitarianism, benevolence, and desire for improvement. There it was terminated by the revolutions of 1848; in America it was halted by the cataclysm of the Civil War. But even under the shadow of that conflict popular faith in man's innate competence of social judgment persisted until from Tennessee, Andrew Johnson flung out his challenging credo:

I believe man can be elevated; man can become more and more endowed with divinity; and as he does he becomes more god-like in his character and capable of governing himself. Let us go on elevating our people, perfecting our institutions, until democracy shall reach such a point of perfection that we can acclaim with truth that the voice of the people is the voice of God.[34]

This affirmation of faith in the perfectibility of man was the very lifeblood of the incipient public library; for, if every man possessed within himself the power to develop a wisdom adequate to the needs of judicious self-government, any agency directed toward the improvement of that intellectual power must necessarily become the recipient of public support. Wrote Edward Everett to Mayor Bigelow:

The first principles of popular government require that the means of education should, as far as possible, be equally within the reach of the whole population. . . . The sons of the wealthy alone have access to well-stored libraries; while those whose means do not allow them to purchase books are too often deprived of them at the moment when they would be most useful.[35]

The theme of democratic necessity was recurrent in the arguments of those who sought to further public library establishment. Its implication was written by Everett into the trustees' report of 1852. It was advanced by Mayor Seaver when he urged upon the Common Council the need for action in support of a public library in Boston. It was repeated by John B. Wight when he persuaded the Massachusetts General Court to enact the law of 1851.

But the argument carried with it a power which many of its most ardent advocates did not foresee, a force which threatened the supremacy of even the conservational motive and which was to reshape the dominant pattern of the public library that was to come. Only Ticknor envisaged the real significance of the democratization of the public library and what it would mean in terms of function. With Everett he shared the honor of having done most to encourage the founding of the Boston Public Library. They were the most powerful members of its first board of trustees, and together they prepared the first report. Each accepted the axiom that the public library, if it were to be an agent

34. Andrew Johnson, *Speeches*, ed. Frank Moore (Boston: Little, Brown, 1866), p. 56.

35. Quoted by Mayor Benjamin Seaver in his *Message of the Mayor on the Subject of a Public Library, in Common Council [February 19, 1852]* (City Document No. 10 [Boston: No publisher, 1852]), pp. 4–5.

of democracy, must be for all the people, but it was Ticknor rather than Everett who could translate this concept into functional terms. In the mind of Everett conservation was still dominant; and though his objective was a collection that would be open to all classes of the population, such a library would remain primarily a storehouse from which the treasures were not to be removed.

On July 14, 1851, Ticknor wrote to Everett encouraging him in his promotion of the undertaking and suggesting that it be

a library which, in its *main* department and purpose, should differ from all free libraries yet attempted; . . . one in which any popular books, tending to moral and intellectual improvement, should be furnished in such numbers of copies that many persons, if they desired it could be reading the same book at the same time; in short, that not only the best books of all sorts, but the pleasant literature of the day, should be made accessible to the whole people at the only time when they care for it, i.e. when it is fresh and new. I would, therefore, continue to buy additional copies of any book of this class, almost as long as they should continue to be asked for, and thus, by following the popular taste—unless it should demand something injurious—create a real appetite for healthy general reading.[36]

In his reply Everett confessed that the "extensive circulation of new and popular works" was a feature of a public library which he had "not hitherto much contemplated," and, though he admitted that the suggestion was deserving of consideration, he professed a predisposition toward intramural book use.[37] Though Everett was not in agreement with Ticknor's opinion, he acquiesced in the proposal because he believed that it should have a fair chance to prove its true worth, and accordingly he acceded to the incorporation of the principle in the trustees' report.[38] The

36. Ticknor, *Life*, II, 301–2.

37. *Ibid.*, p. 303.

38. See Boston Public Library, *Report . . . July 1852*, pp. 9–21. These pages were entirely the work of Ticknor; the remaining portions, at the beginning and the end, were by Everett (annotated copy in Boston Public Library). See also Ticknor, *Life*, II, 305. Ticknor did not hold that *all* library books should circulate freely, in fact he divided the library collections into four major groups: (1) books that should not be circulated because of their cost or rarity; (2) books for which there was a relatively slight demand which, though free to circulate, were not to be necessarily duplicated; (3) books that were to be duplicated as much as the demand seemed to justify; and (4) periodicals, exclusive of newspapers, which were to be circulated on rare occasions when justified by some special need. It was his contention that these categories be completely fluid.

plan was adopted, and from the beginning book purchase proceeded on the assumption that certain types of materials for which there was an anticipated demand were to be acquired in duplicate.[39] The circulation of popular literature is not inherent in the definition of the public library, but it came to be an important function upon which public support was predicated, and its positive affirmation at the time that the Boston Public Library was founded represents a significant recognition by municipal authority that the supplying of books for popular consumption is a proper public responsibility.

The most significant influence of this expanding belief in the importance of the common people was expressed in the advance of popular education and the support which educators gave to library promotion. During the decade of the 1830's elementary education underwent momentous change. The advent of this educational renaissance brought legislative reforms that began the transfer of the school from the custody of voluntary and charitable associations to newly established state systems of education. The New England mind had long accepted the dual principle that the community had an obligation to educate its children by tax-supported schools; and such opportunities having been provided, the children must be compelled to take advantage of them.[40] Nowhere was this urge to mass education more powerful than in Boston, and, in 1840, Prescott could write of the city that its population had all become "cultivated up to the eyes."[41] The

39. Boston Public Library, *Report . . . 1854*, p. 5, states: "A considerable number of the new books added to the library the present year are duplicate sets of popular new publications, which have been purchased in pursuance to the principle on which the circulation department is founded. . . . It is expected that for a certain class of books this demand will be temporary, and that in due time . . . all but a single copy, or very few copies, may be dispensed with.

40. The first Massachusetts laws relating to education, passed in 1642 and 1647, asserted that it was the duty of the state to compel the education of every child. By the terms of these acts the power was given to the selectmen to enforce its provisions, and parents neglecting the education of their children were subject to fine. Though the law made education compulsory, there was no provision for schools or teachers, and the children were taught either by their parents or by private tutors (*Records of the Governor and Company of the Massachusetts Bay in New England*, ed. Nathaniel B. Shurtleff [Boston: William White, 1853], II, 6, 9, 203).

41. "We are all becoming cultivated up to the eyes . . . *tiers état* and all. A daughter of an old servant of ours, whose father is an Irish bogtrotter that works on

region was a veritable seedbed for education throughout much of the Middle West, but even in New England as late as 1840 a relatively small proportion of the school population was being educated "at public charge" since the condition of the public schools of that day encouraged all who could to send their children to private institutions.[42]

The first to lay bare the defects of the Massachusetts schools was James G. Carter, whose *Letters on the Free Schools of New England* (1826) resulted in the laws of 1826, 1834, and 1837, establishing, respectively, the town school committees, the state school fund, and the first real state board of education. Carter planted the seeds of reform that Horace Mann reaped with such spectacular success, but it was the latter who gave to the Massachusetts public schools the effective leadership they so sorely needed and who influenced educational development far beyond that state. At the same time, Henry Barnard, at first in Connecticut and later in Rhode Island, was promoting similar, though somewhat less dramatic, reforms and establishing himself, largely through his extensive writings, as the outstanding scholar of the great public school awakening. In the extension of schooling to a great number of people, by material improvement in the physical environment, through the advancement of instruction and preparation of teachers, and by giving to their followers a rational social responsibility, both Mann and Barnard saved public education at a critical time from a disastrous school system.

The relations between this educational renaissance and the movement for tax-supported public libraries were far reaching and numerous. There were at least four factors involved: (*a*) a growing awareness of the ordinary man and his importance to the group, (*b*) the conviction that universal literacy is essential to an enlightened people, (*c*) a belief in the practical value of technical studies, and (*d*) an enthusiasm for education for its own

the roads, told me yesterday, 'she had nearly completed her English education, and was very well in her French, and should only give one quarter more to her music and drawing' " (William H. Prescott, *Correspondence*, 1840, quoted by Van Wyck Brooks, *The Flowering of New England* [New York: Dutton, 1937]), p. 172 n.

42. U.S. Census Office, *7th Census, 1850: Statistical View of the United States . . . , Being a Compendium of the Seventh Census . . . , 1850* (Washington, D.C.: A. O. P. Nicholson, 1854), pp. 150–51.

sake. Structurally the school and the public library were akin because each represented a substitution of the principle of public support for dependence upon private resources. Largely through the efforts of Mann the public school emerged victorious from a previously losing struggle against the competition of the private school, just as the public library was to supersede the social library. Though the principle of public responsibility for primary education had long been acknowledged by New Englanders and some measure of progress had been made in that direction, it was Carter, Mann, and Barnard who really translated the concept into effective reality at precisely the same time that the need for public libraries was beginning to find expression. Public library development was of necessity forced to wait upon educational reform for the simple reason that an adequate library patronage presupposes an educated, or at least literate, public. Finally the proponents of public education were themselves champions of the public library as a logical extension of the elementary-school system.

"After the rising generation have acquired habits of intelligent reading in our schools, *what shall they read?*" wrote Horace Mann in his third annual report as secretary of the Massachusetts Board of Education, "for, with no books to read, the power of reading will be useless."[43] To answer the question, he surveyed the several counties of the state, requesting statistics on the number of social libraries and lyceums, with the book holdings of each.[44] The results revealed that the social libraries of the state contained an aggregate of one hundred and eighty thousand volumes, and these were available to but one-seventh of the population.[45] Knowing that the average home of the period was stocked with only "the Scriptures, and a few school books . . . [which were] protected by law, even in the hands of an insolvent," in addition to some "of a most miscellaneous character . . . which had found their way thither rather by chance than by design,"[46] and being quite aware that even the social libraries possessed mainly

43. Horace Mann, *Life and Works* (Boston: Lee & Shepherd, 1891), III, 8–9; reprints most of his third annual report, for the year 1839; full report appears in *Common School Journal*, II (1840), 113–53.

44. *Common School Journal*, II (1840), 123–35, 137–39.

45. *Ibid.*, pp. 125–26.   46. *Ibid.*, pp. 120–21.

books "of the historical class" as well as "novels, and all that class of books which is comprehended under the familiar designation of 'fictions,' 'light reading,' 'trashy works,' 'ephemeral' or 'bubble literature,' "[47] Mann urged more extensive support for the ill-conceived and abortive school-district libraries.[48] He clearly perceived the weaknesses inherent in the social library form as a medium of general book distribution, while in the school-district library he recognized the essential elements that might develop into the basis for public library support. "Had I the power, I would scatter libraries over the whole land, as the sower sows his wheat-field."[49] That was his aim, and while these school-district libraries did not yield the full return that he anticipated, he did plant in the minds of many a conviction of the need for some form of public library support.

Like Mann, Henry Barnard conceived the library as essential to the cultural life of the people:

A library of good books, selected in reference to the intellectual wants of the old and the young should be provided in every village . . . [he wrote in his report on the condition and improvement of the Public Schools of Rhode Island, in 1845]. All that the school . . . all that the ablest lecture . . . can do towards unfolding the many branches of knowledge and filling the mind with various information, is but little compared with the thoughtful perusal of good books, from evening to evening, extending through a series of years.[50]

Barnard thought it was, therefore, the responsibility of the community to provide such libraries, equipped with

reading rooms, furnished with the periodical publications of the day, with maps and books of reference, and if possible with portfolios of engravings and pictorial embellishments. . . . To these rooms . . . all classes should have access, and especially should the more wealthy and intelligent resort there, if for no other reason than to bear testimony of their presence and participation.[51]

Barnard also shared Mann's faith in the ability of the school-district libraries to assume the broader responsibility of public library service.

The school-house is the appropriate depository of the district library, and a library of well selected books, open to the teacher, children, and adults general-

47. *Ibid.*, pp. 127–28.   48. *Ibid.*, pp. 151–53.
49. Quoted by Paul Bixler, "Horace Mann—Mustard Seed," *American Scholar*, VII (1938–39), 32.
50. Quoted in John S. Brubacher (ed.), *Henry Barnard on Education* (New York: McGraw-Hill, 1931), p. 53.   51. *Ibid.*, pp. 55–56.

ly of the district, for reference and reading, gives completeness to the permanent means of school and self-education. . . . Without such books the instruction of the school-room does not become practically useful, and the art of
printing is not made available to the poor as well as to the rich. . . . The establishment of a library in every school-house, will bring the mighty instrument of
good books to act more directly and more broadly on the entire population of
the state, than it has ever yet done, for it will open the fountain of knowledge
without money, and without price, to the humble and the elevated, the poor
and the rich.[52]

But he was quite conscious, too, of the social library as an agent of
public book distribution, and to encourage its formation he published in his 1848 report as commissioner of the public schools of
Rhode Island a detailed account of the Pawcatuck Library Association, together with its constitution and bylaws, and a complete
catalog of its holdings.[53] The problem of book selection crystallized for Barnard and Mann alike the entire concept of the function of these "public" libraries. To each the library was more
than an instrument for deepening the cultural stream, it was intensely practical and utilitarian.

The farmer, mechanic, manufacturer, and in fine, all the inhabitants of a
district, of both sexes, and in every condition and employment of life, should
have books which will shed light and dignity on their several vocations, help
them better to understand the history and condition of the world and the country in which they live, their own nature, and their relations and duties to
society, themselves, and their Creator.[54]

Thus wrote Barnard in 1842, and the catalog of the Pawcatuck
library which he so warmly praised displayed a wide variety of
subjects, including books for the artisan and craftsman as well
as the usual assortment of titles in history, travel, literature, and
fiction. Mann's choice was equally catholic and eclectic. He, too,
emphasized the utilitarian as essential to the selection of books
for the district libraries, and though he was wont to warn against
a too great indulgence in the reading of ephemeral books, he

52. From the Appendix to his fourth annual report as secretary to the Board of
Commissioners of Common Schools in Connecticut, reproduced in Brubacher, *op.
cit.*, pp. 248–50.

53. Henry Barnard, *Report and Documents Relating to the Public Schools of Rhode
Island, 1848* (Providence, 1849), pp. 424–548.

54. Brubacher, *op. cit.*, pp. 249–50.

freely acknowledged that "reading, merely for amusement, has its fit occasions and legitimate office."[55]

A realization of the essential unity of the public school and the public library was not confined to the mind of the professional educator. Laymen throughout New England saw the agencies as interdependent and supplementary. Even to the politician the two were intimately associated; for whenever library legislation was introduced, it was regarded as the proper province of the committee on education, and the library was considered as a logical and appropriate supplement to the work of the public school. As has been shown, the inhabitants of Peterborough who construed the phrase "other purposes of education" as encompassing the library voted to allocate a portion of their share of the New Hampshire State Literary Fund to the establishment of a town library. "It has seemed to me for many years," wrote Ticknor to Everett in 1851, "that such a free public library, if adapted to the wants of our people, would be the crowning glory of our public schools,"[56] and the phrase, repeated by him in the trustees' report of 1852,[57] soon became the rallying cry of all who were concerned with the welfare of the library. A similar point of view had been advanced by Everett himself, when, in 1850 and again in 1851, he expressed to Mayor Bigelow the opinion which in 1852 Mayor Seaver presented to the Boston Common Council.

Such a library would put the finishing hand to that system of public education that lies at the basis of the prosperity of Boston. . . . I cannot but think that a Public Library well supplied with books in the various departments of art and science, and open at all times for consultation and study to the citizens at large, is absolutely needed to make our admirable system of Public Education complete; and to continue in some good degree through life that happy quality of intellectual privileges, which now exists in our schools, but terminates with them.[58]

55. *Common School Journal*, II (1840), 128 ff.
56. Ticknor, *Life*, II, 301.
57. Boston Public Library, *Report . . . July 1852*, p. 21. Much of the report deals with the relation of the public library to the public school.
58. Two letters from Everett to Mayor Bigelow, dated August 7, 1850, and June 7, 1851; quoted by Wadlin, *op. cit.*, pp. 21 and 25–26; quoted by Mayor Benjamin Seaver, *op. cit.*, p. 4.

There was never any uncertainty about the division of function between the school and the library, for lines of responsibility were clear and distinct. The school was primary and compulsory, the library supplemental and voluntary. The school was pointed at the education of the child, and, though the library might also serve to expand the reading resources of the young, its major objective was to promote the education of the adolescent and the adult. From its inception the public library was conceived as being primarily an agency of self-education. This attitude has been admirably summarized by Ticknor in his letter to Everett: "But I think it important that it [i.e., the public library in general and the proposed Boston Public Library in particular] should be adapted to our peculiar character; that is, it should come in at the end of our system of free instruction, and be fitted to continue and increase the effects of that system by the self-culture that results from reading."[59]

Self-education and the Lyceum Movement

Faith in the capacity of the ordinary man for self-education and reliance upon personal initiative in extending the opportunities for "cultural development" were not excessively optimistic. Dependence upon voluntary group action for effecting many community undertakings was characteristic of the period. The college graduate of that day was thoroughly familiar with the literary society as an important and almost universal device for extending academic experience. Beyond the college walls these associations had a counterpart in the lyceums and institutes that suddenly became prominent between 1830 and 1850.

From Milbury, Massachusetts, in 1826 Josiah Holbrook set forth his scheme for a "Society for Mutual Education," which later became known as the American Lyceum. Holbrook conceived this new agency as a great national organization that would foster in every town and village the formation of societies designed to enhance the education of the child and encourage continued learning by the adult. Aided by the enthusiastic support of such men as Henry Barnard, Edward Everett, and Daniel Webster and favored by contemporary zeal for the improvement

59. Ticknor, *Life*, II, 301.

of the common man, the organization spread rapidly. Crowded audiences listened to Emerson, Dickens, Thackeray, or Garrison; and to rapt listeners Wendell Phillips was said to have delivered his discourse on "The Lost Arts" two thousand times. In 1831 a National Lyceum was formed by delegates from Massachusetts, Maine, and New York. From this parent-organization, state and county subsidiaries extended through the country from New England to the far reaches of the frontier. The national body died in 1839, but its local branches persisted much longer; and when interest generally declined prior to the Civil War, the agency was reborn in the Chautauqua movement, which reached its height in the first decades of the twentieth century.

The lecture platform soon became the focal point of the lyceum, though the original intention of the founders was to use any device for advancing knowledge that might properly be employed by the participants. Debates were common, and the collection of minerals and fossils was encouraged. Interest in the preservation of materials for the study of local history was aroused, and, because the larger program of the lyceum was based upon continuous study and reading of the members, library establishment was fostered. The lyceum, like the school, was book centered.

In 1830 the Lyceum of Middlesex County, Massachusetts, appointed a committee to prepare a model constitution for the guidance of lyceum groups in the surrounding towns. This committee urged the possession of a library as a "primary object with all lyceums"; suggested the purchase of books in biography, travel, and voyages as aids in the development of a taste in reading; and recommended the acquisition of scientific works and encyclopedias as soon as financial circumstances permitted.[60] The Massachusetts State Lyceum boasted in 1832 that, in consequence of its encouragement of popular reading, new libraries had been established and neglected ones revived;[61] and the Connecticut State Lyceum, meeting in special session in 1839, voted favorably on a resolution to encourage the establishment of library collec-

60. "Middlesex County Lyceum," *American Journal and Annals of Education and Instruction*, I (new ser., 1830), 454.
61. "Massachusetts Lyceum," *ibid.*, II (1832), 121.

tions, suitable to the needs of the older children and adults, in every school district of the state.[62] At a convention held in Boston to consider the benefits accruing from lyceums, the delegates remarked on the instability of the "public libraries," fully nine-tenths of which had either perished or fallen into complete decay, a fact which implied that some more direct and immediate stimulus was needed to encourage the public generally to read.

> It is believed that at least nine-tenths of the public libraries which have been established in New England since its first settlement, have been sold at public auction, distributed among their proprietors, or fallen into neglect or disuse. Nor have those truly benevolent and patriotic institutions, mechanics' and apprentices' libraries, excited that extensive and lasting thirst for reading and information, which might naturally be hoped.[63]

They expected the lyceum to supply this stimulus, and Josiah Holbrook wrote that the "demands immediately and uniformly created for books by the meetings and exercises of Lyceums" had called "into use neglected Libraries and given occasion for establishing new ones."[64] Such statements, however, were largely groundless, for the lyceum movement seems to have contributed little aid to the library. The delegates to the Boston lyceum convention of 1828 were correct in believing that something more than the mere presence of books was required to induce the general public to read. But, supported mainly by the modest admission fees to its public meetings,[65] the lyceum itself was too lacking in stability to contribute much of its slender resources to library encouragement. Yet the movement has significance as an indication of the culture that encouraged the public library. Through the influence of the lyceum the city and the town were brought into closer contact. Everywhere people were being exposed to similar cultural stimuli. Both the library and the lyceum were parts of the general faith in man's ability for self-improvement.

62. "Connecticut State Lyceum," *Connecticut Common School Journal*, II (1839), 83–84.

63. "American Lyceum," *American Journal of Education*, III (1828), 719.

64. [Josiah Holbrook], *The American Lyceum, or Society for the Improvement of Schools and Diffusion of Useful Knowledge* (Boston: T. R. Marvin, 1829), p. 5.

65. The average price received by Emerson for an evening lecture was $10.00 and traveling expenses. On one occasion, when he received the maximum of $50.00, he expressed grave doubt as to the morality of accepting such excessive remuneration. A season ticket for a course of ten to fifteen lectures usually cost about $2.00.

The Vocational Influence

A belief in the necessity of education was further encouraged by a growing demand for vocational training. The rise of industrialization, the rapid growth of a population congested in cities, the increase of the working classes through immigration of new national stocks, and the decline of the earlier apprentice system, all contributed to the need for new social agencies that would satisfy the human urge for the improvement of the individual's economic status. The factory system, the introduction of power machinery, and the extensive utilization of water-power and later of steam, which must be used close to the place of origin, brought together in highly congested areas men, women, and children who were engaged in similar pursuits, who had common economic and social problems, and who quite naturally turned to the formation of voluntary associations for improvement of their working lives. These impulses on the part of the workers were expressed in four major lines of endeavor: (a) the organization of trade-unions and their amalgamation in a national federation, (b) the encouragement of co-operative activities, (c) the formation of workingmen's political parties, and (d) the establishment of newspapers, journals, institutes, associations, and libraries for the education and advancement of the worker. Such early movements suffered heavily in the panic of 1837 and, after the passage of the Homestead Act, lost much of their appeal when an abundance of free land in the West made it relatively easy for the employee to pass to the position of the employer. Nevertheless, a very definite impression had been made on the course of American institutions, and much social legislation had accumulated as a consequence of this early striving.

Concern with the problems confronting the workers did not leave the library untouched. To some extent labor leadership participated in the movement for library establishment, as it had shared in support of public schools. In the case of the library the vocational interests of the workers made its greatest contribution in the form of mechanics' and mercantile libraries that appeared during the first half of the nineteenth century and in the factory book collections in a few industrial towns. It was a utilitarian urge that prompted the mechanics and apprentices to adapt the social library pattern to their specific needs, just as a century earlier Benjamin Franklin and his small group of artisans and other "citizens in the middle and lower walks of life" had met together and pooled their book resources, knowing that their progress would come more rapidly through the mutual interchange of thought and experience.

Basically the mechanics' and apprentices' libraries were an adaptation of the social library form, and they grew directly from the workers' institutes first established in England at the close of the eighteenth century.[66] These institutes spread over England until by 1850 there were some seven hundred such associations there. The main object of these groups was the intellectual development of the artisan, and science was the principal subject considered; though, as time went on, literature, history, and the arts were included. The programs centered about lectures and discussions; more than half of the institutes had libraries, and many also developed elementary scientific laboratories.

At approximately the same time that this movement was gaining headway in England it was also becoming prevalent in America. In 1823 Timothy Claxton of the Mechanics' Institute of London came to Methuen, Massachusetts, where a cotton-mill and a machine shop were in operation. There he revived the defunct Methuen Social Society for Reading and General Inquiry, which had been founded about 1819, and aided in the establishment of a library for the use of the members. In 1826 Claxton moved to Boston where he promoted the Boston Mechanics' Institute. Though the institute was undoubtedly of English origin, Claxton did not introduce it to America. A Mechanics' Library was in operation in Bristol, Connecticut, in 1818,[67] and in 1820

66. The workers' institutes apparently developed from the lectures in natural philosophy given by Dr. John Anderson in Glasgow in 1760. Similar illustrated talks and scientific demonstrations, designed primarily for the laboring man, were continued in the same city by George Birkbeck in 1799. It was during this period that Birmingham became a center for organizations established to better the lot of the worker, and there was founded in 1795 the first Artisans' Library, which was followed in 1823 by the Mechanics' and Apprentices' Library of Liverpool (Clarence R. Aurner, "Mechanics' Institutes," *Iowa Journal of History*, XIX [1921], 389 ff.).

67. Trumbull MSS in Yale University Library; E. Peck, *A History of Bristol, Connecticut* (Hartford: Lewis Street Bookshop, 1932), pp. 245–47.

there was established in Boston the Mechanics' Apprentices' Library, the first such library to be formed through the philanthropy of William Wood. Also founded at an early date were the Mechanics' Library of Portland, Maine; the Mechanics' Social Library Society of Nantucket, Massachusetts; and the library of the Salem Charitable Mechanics' Association, the books of which finally found their way into the Essex Institute.

The general development of the mechanics' and apprentices' associations and their affiliated book collections was encouraged by professional educators, particularly Henry Barnard and Horace Mann. Of the Boston Mechanics' Institution the editors of the *American Journal of Education* wrote in part: "It is with much pleasure that we contemplate the prospect afforded by this and similar institutions in our own country; their benefits are perhaps more direct and substantial, and their sphere of usefulness is necessarily much wider, than those connected with any other department of scientific instruction."[68] Such philanthropists as William Wood frequently contributed substantial sums to establish and support these organizations, of which many were created for the protection and support of widows and orphans of mechanics, and, since the argument for the library as a bulwark against the corruption of youthful morals was always potent, the libraries were encouraged by those actively engaged in the prevailing humanitarianism. Basically, the concept sprang from the growth of the industrial system and consequent breakdown of the master-apprentice relationship. Abbott Lawrence strongly felt the absence of adequate training in the industrial arts when he gave fifty thousand dollars for the establishment of a scientific school at Harvard. He recognized that education in law, medicine, theology, and the humanities had been monopolizing the attention of educators when he wrote to Samuel Eliot:

But where can we send those who intend to devote themselves to the practical applications of science? How educate our engineers, our miners, machinists, and mechanics? Our country abounds in men of action. Hard hands are ready to work upon our hard materials; and where shall sagacious heads be taught to direct those hands?[69]

68. II (1827), 273.
69. Letter to Samuel A. Eliot, treasurer of Harvard University, June 7, 1847, in Hamilton A. Hill, *Memoir of Abbott Lawrence* (Boston: Privately printed, 1883), p. 109.

These institutes would, in a measure at least, meet this want in the educational system, for their object, as George B. Emerson remarked at the opening of the Boston Mechanics' Institution, was to give to persons, whose time is chiefly occupied with business or labor, knowledge of a kind to be directly useful to them in their daily pursuits. . . . The principles of science have hitherto been accessible to those only who were pursuing a course of study preparatory to what are called the liberal professions. The poor and the occupied, if destined to the active pursuits of life, have been almost necessarily debarred from them. By Mechanics Institutions they are offered to all, to the busy, the poor, and the uninformed.[70]

In this plan the lecture was to supplant the personal teaching of a master, but the lecture alone was insufficient if the apprentice was to derive the greatest possible benefit. A library was essential as a supplement to the lecture platform, for the listener, "to derive the greatest advantage from his lecture . . . , must also read."[71]

In general the social philosophy of the mercantile libraries was quite different from that of the mechanics' institutions, though the line of demarcation was not always sharp and there were occasional blendings of the forms. Fundamentally the mercantile libraries were designed to meet the reading needs of the young merchants' clerks and were established by the youthful merchants who were beginning their professional careers. The movement appears to have had its inception in Boston, where, on March 11, 1820, the Boston Mercantile Library was established by a group of young clerks whose initiation fee was the gift of one book on "biography, history, voyages, travels, or work relative to mercantile subjects."[72] Unlike the apprentices' institutions, the mer-

70. George B. Emerson, "Mechanics' Institutions," *American Journal of Education*, II (1827), 273, 278.

71. *Ibid.*, p. 275. An excellent example of the extent to which these libraries reflected the utilitarian needs of their supporting members and the degree to which their book collections emphasized science and the practical arts is to be found in *Catalogue of the Library of the Massachusetts Charitable Mechanics' Association, 1853* (Boston: Danvell & Moore, 1853), in Massachusetts Historical Society.

72. This plan was later abolished because the books thus received were generally worthless. Subscriptions were $2.00 annually. There were some two hundred and twenty members the first year, but the organization had a long and difficult fight for survival. It was helped by frequent gifts from Abbott Lawrence. In 1877 its books were added to the collections of the Boston Public Library.

cantile libraries began as libraries and later assumed additional educational functions—lecture courses, museums, or exhibitions.[73] But the two were similar in the advantage they received from the increasing complexity of the occupations each represented. Because of the expanding horizons of applied science, the mechanics and apprentices felt the need for educational mediums that would increase their familiarity with scientific advance. Likewise, the young merchants were keenly affected by the growing intricacy of the commercial structure, the advent of new governmental regulations, the complications of foreign exchange, and the shifting patterns of production and consumption and their impact on market conditions. In addition to its strict professional utility, the mercantile library reflected certain cultural interests. Literature and history, especially the history of the mercantile profession, were conspicuously represented in the book collection since it was generally conceded that no knowledge was foreign to the merchant.[74]

73. On June 24, 1846, Elliot C. Cowdin of the Boston Mercantile Library Association wrote to James Fenimore Cooper inviting him to lecture before the association, stating that the usual attendance at such lectures was between twenty-five hundred and three thousand (see Dorothy Waples, "An Unpublished Letter from James Fenimore Cooper to Elliot C. Cowdin," *New England Quarterly*, III [1930], 126).

74. The Massachusetts Historical Society has many printed addresses delivered before the Mercantile Library Association of Boston. These, when taken together constitute a good general statement of the purposes of the mercantile library as conceived by their early promoters: George W. Tyler, *Address Delivered before the Mercantile Library Association of Boston on the Evening of Their Sixteenth Anniversary, March 11, 1836* (Boston: Hitchcock, 1836), 32 pp.; Robert C. Winthrop, *An Address Delivered before the Boston Mercantile Library Association on the Occasion of Their Twenty-fifth Anniversary, October 15, 1845* (Boston: Marvin & Co., 1845); Edward Everett, *An Address before the Mercantile Library Association* (Boston: W. D. Ticknor, 1838); George Lunt, *Anniversary Poem Delivered before the Mercantile Library Association of Boston, October 3, 1843* (Boston: W. D. Ticknor, 1843); James T. Fields, *Anniversary Poem Delivered before the Mercantile Library Association of Boston, September 13, 1838* (Boston: W. D. Ticknor, 1838); Philip Hone, *An Address Delivered before the Mercantile Library Association, at the Odeon in Boston, October 5, 1843* (Boston: W. D. Ticknor, 1843), 44 pp.; Alfred Norton, *An Address Delivered before the Mercantile Library Association, January 19, 1836* (Boston: N. Southard, 1836), 23 pp.

In general the speakers all emphasize the same basic points: (1) The merchants of the rising generation will be trained through the use of library books. (2) The library will improve the morals of the profession by keeping the young clerks out of

The artisans and merchants were not alone in their response to the need for books. Amid the whirring spindles and in the lint-filled air of the cotton-mills at Lowell, Lawrence, and Peterborough countless girls, newly imported from the rural areas, eager for the adventure of a strange city life, and earning money for the first time, were enthusiastically subscribing to joint-stock pianos for their boarding-houses, studying German, reading the British reviews, and filling the pages of their own literary journal, the *Lowell Offering*, with romantic stories and poetry. Today much of the sentiment with which Harriet Farley and her associates built up the circulation of the *Offering* sounds like courageous whistling to keep up hopes and aspirations that all too frequently were the prey of monotonous toil and heartbreaking loneliness; but some of the girls, at least those in the Merrimack mills, did evince an interest in literature, support subscription libraries, and make plans for a book collection and reading-room of their own.[75] How

places of ill-repute. (3) Culture is attainable by the merchant class, and the industrious use of the library will encourage this cultural growth. The one outstanding characteristic of all these addresses is their quality of unlimited optimism.

Ditzion has drawn some interesting parallels between the apprentices libraries and those of the merchants' clerks and, though he has ridden the proletarian theme too hard, has in general given the best consideration of the subject that has yet appeared (Sidney Ditzion, "Mechanics and Mercantile Libraries," *Library Quarterly*, X, No. 2 [April, 1940], 192–219).

75. The editorials in the *Lowell Offering* reveal that the magazine was under frequent and heavy attack from those who considered it a colossal hoax perpetrated by the management of the mills to discredit any criticism of their labor policies. This controversy—for the case was neither proved nor disproved—must be borne in mind in relation to any quotation from the *Offering*. Certainly there was a tendency to "play up" the cultural aspects of the mill-girls' lives. In reviewing Dickens' *American Notes* for the *Offering*, Harriet Farley challenged his statement that "nearly all" of the girls subscribe to circulating libraries, but though *"nearly all* do not thus subscribe . . . very many are supporters of other libraries" (*Lowell Offering*, III [1843], 96). See also her editorial "Books and Reading," which gives a good presentation of the reading of the mill girls (*ibid.*, pp. 143–44).

"The Improvement Society will meet on Monday evening, March 11th., [1844] at Mrs. Barnes'; and we wish all . . . who are interested in the establishment of a Reading Room to join us on that evening. Mr. Clark, the Superintendent of the Merrimack Corporation, to which we have always belonged, offers his female operatives the use of an excellent room for the purpose, provided they will, by subscription, furnish fuel and lights" (*ibid.*, Vol. IV [1844], inside back cover). This request that the girls furnish fuel and light was not insignificant since at that time they were earning $1.75 a week "clear of board" (*Lowell Offering*, V [August, 1845], 190).

many such libraries were established on the initiative of the workers is not known, but it is likely that at least some of them were imposed upon the operatives by a management which was perhaps eager to foster its reputation for benevolence. Such were the libraries established in the 1830's at the Union and Phoenix Cotton Mills of Peterborough, New Hampshire,[76] and the Manufacturers and Village Library of Great Falls, New Hampshire, of which the last was sponsored by the Great Falls Manufacturing Company and for the use of which "females" in the employ of the company were required to pay fifty cents per year, though only the subscribers paying a dollar had any voice in the management of the collection. The library of the Pacific Mills of Lawrence, Massachusetts, was assembled in 1854, largely through the efforts of Abbott Lawrence and with the consultation and advice of Henry Barnard.[77] For its support the workers were taxed $0.01 per week, though their wages for the same period varied from $6.75 for men to $1.82 for children, from which "one third of the average" was deducted for board and room at the residence buildings.[78] At Northfield, Vermont, the Vermont Central Railroad offered the income from a $1,000 bond to initiate a library

76. Albert Smith, *History of the Town of Peterborough* . . . (Boston: George Ellis, 1876), pp. 213–14.

77. *Catalogue of the Pacific Mills Library, Lawrence, Mass., Opened August 21, 1854* (Boston: Darnell & Moore, 1855); copy in Boston Public Library.

78. "To secure the permanence and increase of the library, the contribution of one cent per week to its funds is made a condition of employment in the Mills" (*ibid.*, p. 3).
The Pacific Mills began operation at the end of the year 1853, though no cloth was marketed until the spring of 1854. So the library was begun less than a year after the mill was opened. In 1867 the mill employed thirty-six hundred people, thus giving the book collection an annual fund of slightly more than $1,800. The mill management made much of the library as an important part of their employee welfare program. At the Paris Exposition of 1867 they boasted that the "Library is managed by the employees, they choosing their own officers for the control of affairs and the selection of books." But the company was careful to see that this did not get out of hand, for it was required that the president of the library association and chairman of the Library Committee be a resident manager of the mill (*Statement of the Pacific Mills Presented to the Special Jury of the Paris Exposition of 1867* [Lawrence: G. S. Merrill, 1868], in Massachusetts Historical Society). The catalog of 1855 lists an unusually broad range of subjects, though proportions are, in general, comparable to those of contemporary social libraries, except that juvenile literature is strong, theology only slightly represented, while history, biography, travel, and the practical arts are most emphasized. Clearly the base collection shows the influence of Henry Barnard.

for its employees, but this library was a joint-stock association in which shares sold at $3.00 each.[79] Such factory collections differed sharply from the "vocational" libraries formed by the artisans and merchants. Recreational reading and self-improvement were the major objectives of the former, but probably, as in the case of the library of the Great Falls Manufacturing Company, "fiction" was "most read." The sudden desire for "culture" that animated the mill girls of Lowell was but a passing fancy—the hard realities of factory toil remained. Twelve long hours of tending the spindles were not usually climaxed by an evening of intellectual pursuit.

The vocational libraries did not live long except in those cases where they were fortunate enough to receive large gifts or to become general social libraries. A decline in initial enthusiasm on the part of readers and a general disillusionment when reading failed to produce marked increase in either skills or income were the intangible factors in the deterioration of these libraries. To-day the Young Men's Institute Library of New Haven, Connecticut, typifies complete transformation and rejection of primary function. No longer dedicated to the principle of "mutual assistance in the attainment of useful knowledge," its efforts are now directed toward supplying promptly the current best-sellers to those willing to pay for the privilege, and in its effort to survive it has diverted a measure of popular support from the public library of its own city. Similarly, in an attempt to save the Middlesex Mechanics' Association from an untimely death the membership subordinated its original objectives until the institution was so changed that Coburn could write of it in his three-volume history of Lowell:

It used to be a source of boyish wonder, in the seventies and eighties, just what the Middlesex Mechanics' Association and its excellent library in Dutton Street, had to do with mechanical affairs. In conspicuous positions hung several rather awe-inspiring full-length portraits. These were obviously not portraits of mechanics. . . . The library was of a general sort, and the well-informed librarian was not one to whom one would turn for information about gears, shafting, or high-speed steels. . . . Most of those who used the library seemed not to be of the mechanic sort, but rather to be people who preferred its quiet exclusiveness to the democracy of the public library. The Mechanics' Associa-

79. Lewis C. Aldrich, *History of Franklin and Grand Isle Counties, Vermont* . . . (Syracuse: D. Mason, 1891), pp. 390–91.

tion of 1885 . . . appeared to be one . . . in which an overalled mechanic would be particularly ill at ease . . . in fact the library was something of a Lowell analogue of the Boston Athenaeum.[80]

But if the working classes of the nineteenth century achieved only a temporary success in founding libraries planned to meet their needs, the importance of the vocational motive in public library encouragement is not thereby discredited; for, as the wage-earning portion of the population steadily increased and it became correspondingly more difficult for the uneducated individual to compete successfully with his highly trained fellows, there developed an increasing pressure for any agency that would raise the apprentice out of the ranks of the day laborer and into the middle class.

Public Libraries will supply the whole people with ample sources for important practical information. . . . Where they are provided every farmer will have access to the best books on agriculture, every mechanic to the best books on the arts, every merchant . . . to the best exposition of the laws of trade and the sources of wealth. Would not this be a great advantage? Is it not important to practical men? Would it not much promote their success, to become acquainted with what is already known on the subjects which occupy their attention? And is it not undeserving of remark, that, even in the most simple and uniform operations of labor, it has been found that . . . more is accomplished, and the work better done, by intelligent and well-informed individuals?[81]

These were the rhetorical questions with which Representative Wight challenged the Massachusetts General Court: and in a day when America was prosperous as it had never been before, when both industry and labor were expanding, and when education was regarded by all as the panacea for every social ill, no one could answer in the negative. The argument was convincing.

Other Causal Factors

In addition to the influences already considered, there were certain other factors which contributed to the growth of public libraries in New England. Primary among these lesser influences were religion, morality, and the church, for, though the proportion of theological works in New England library book collections generally declined after the establishment of the Republic, the

80. Frederick W. Coburn, *History of Lowell and Its People* (New York: Lewis Historical Publishing Co., 1920), I, 263–64.

81. John B. Wight, "Public Libraries," *Common School Journal*, XIII (1851), 260.

importance of organized religion in public library promotion continued. New England religion was bookish, and its intellectual heritage reveals the extent to which the philosophical content of the discipline drew from many sources.[82] The belief was widely held that reading was a "good" thing in itself and that the act of reading tended to elevate the reader, and this faith in the printed word as an instrument for the building of character was often expressed by the proprietors of corporation libraries. The "promotion of Virtue, Education, and Learning, and . . . the discouragement of Vice and Immorality" was the dual purpose of the Social Library of Salisbury, Connecticut.[83] The members of the Young Men's Institute of Hartford, Connecticut, found themselves unable to estimate "the amount of good accomplished by [its] 25,-000 volumes, which have gone forth to exert their silent unobtrusive influence throughout this community." Nor could they ascertain "in how many have the inclinations of vice been diminished; how many leisure hours, which would otherwise have been wasted in idleness, or a thousand-fold worse than wasted, in the pursuit and enjoyment of pleasures which end only in sorrow, have been delightfully employed in the acquisition of useful knowledge."[84] "To excite a fondness for books, to afford the most rational and profitable amusement, to prevent idleness and immorality, and to promote the diffusion of useful knowledge, piety, and virtue" was the objective of the social library of Castine, Maine.[85] Inevitably, those who were campaigning for the creation of public libraries adopted this argument. In addressing the Boston city council on the need for a public library, Mayor Bigelow spoke of it as having an important bearing on the moral as well as the intellectual character of the city.[86] Similarly, Joshua Bates, in setting forth the motives which prompted his gift to Boston,

82. From the citations of Perry Miller's *New England Mind* (New York: Macmillan, 1939) alone, it would be possible to construct a catalog of books which in both quantity and quality would be impressive.

83. Constitution of the library, 1771, in the Scoville Memorial Library.

84. Young Men's Institute, Hartford, *Fourth Annual Report, 1842*, p. 7. Henry Barnard II was the first president of this Institute.

85. Reproduced in U.S. Bureau of Education, "Public Libraries in the United States," *1876 Report* (Washington, D.C.: Government Printing Office, 1876), p. 446.

86. Wadlin, *op. cit.*, p. 26.

expressed the opinion that, though at first the library would attract only the "worthy young men," later it would "draw others from vice to tread in the same paths, and . . . the moral effect will keep pace with mental improvement."[87] "The promotion of virtue," "the reform of vice," "the increase of morality"—with such phrases Representative Wight liberally sprinkled his address before the General Court in support of the Massachusetts law of 1851; for public libraries would "be favorable to all the moral reforms of the day, by leading to more domestic habits of life, by diminishing the circulation of low and immoral publications, and by producing higher and more worthy views of the capabilities of human nature."[88]Small wonder that Francis Wayland looked with such revulsion upon the practice of the Providence Athenaeum in buying "books of at least doubtful character, frivolous, and not innocent . . . because the young people desired them," and "would as soon give a child arsenic because he liked it."[89]

Finally, one must not forget that the parish and church libraries contributed in some measure to the demand for public libraries. Ubiquitous little Sunday-school libraries dotted the intellectual terrain almost as thickly and conspicuously as the Colonial churches accented the New England landscape.[90] That min-

87. Letter from Joshua Bates to T. W. Ward, October 1, 1852, quoted by Wadlin, *op. cit.*, p. 42. In November of the same year he also wrote to Ward: "My experience convinces me that there are a large number of young men who make a decent appearance, but living in boarding houses or with poor parents, cannot afford to have fire in their rooms. Such persons in past times having no place of resort have often loitered about the streets in the evenings and got into bad company, which would have been avoided, had such a library as is now proposed been in existence. The moral and intellectual improvement such a library would produce is incalculable" (*ibid.*, pp. 45–46).

88. Wight, "Public Libraries," *op. cit.*, p. 261. In the hands of the professional librarians at the turn of the twentieth century it became an even more potent argument for improving the condition of public libraries. Also see Sidney Ditzion, "Social, Reform, Education, and the Library, 1850 to 1900," *Library Quarterly*, IX (1939) 156–84.

89. MS letter to Judge Mellen, March 25, 1851, Wayland Public Library.

90. The significance of these Sunday-school libraries has been too much neglected. Of them Jewett wrote: "The aggregate number of books which they contain i s very large. These books, though mostly juvenile readers, are always of a moral or religious tendency, and they have vast influence in forming the intellectual as well as the moral character of the people" (Charles C. Jewett, *Notices of Public Libraries*

isters gave to Peterborough, New Hampshire, our first public library and to Massachusetts the law of 1851 was hardly accidental. The position of pre-eminence attained by Puritan intellectualism in the American cultural heritage is clear, and the early public libraries, as shaped by their coeval culture, could scarcely have escaped the influence of the church.

In a sense all the foregoing causal factors in public library establishment may be reduced to a common denominator—personal benefit. As one might expect, the public library received its strongest support from those groups in the community who were in a position to gain from the benefits it offered. Primarily, it was the professional classes—the teachers, scholars, ministers, lawyers, doctors, and especially the historians—who were in the greatest want of adequate book resources, so it was they who assumed leadership in the new movement. They were the most vocal because their needs were the greatest and their training and experience facilitated public expression. Following the example of the learned professions, the young tradesmen and mechanics supported the public library as a potential aid in the mastery of their crafts. Even the publishers and booksellers, who might have been expected to oppose free libraries as possible competitors, encouraged the movement by offering generous discounts to buyers for libraries. As early as the concluding decades of the eighteenth century the practice of competing for the patronage of social library officials was common. The school-district libraries offered an excellent opportunity for actual exploitation. Publishers openly confessed to having reaped a substantial harvest from the sale of hastily assembled sets of standard authors for school library use. "Harper's School District Library" was one such series is-

---

in the United States of America [Washington, D.C.: Printed for the House of Representatives, 1851], Appendix). In addition to their significance as an indication of religious influence, these Sunday-school libraries represented a humanitarian impulse. It should be remembered that in the beginning the Sunday school was a means for educating the poor.

In structure these libraries were akin to the social libraries generally. Their shares sold usually at very low prices. Though individually they were weak, collectively they did contribute to the movement for school libraries and children's collections in later public libraries (see Frank K. Walter, "A Poor but Respectable Relation—the Sunday School Library," *Library Quarterly*, XII [1942], 731–39).

sued in response to the school-district library laws of New England and New York, and bookmen throughout the region became actively concerned in the passage of legislation providing for the establishment of libraries in the public schools. Soon publisher participation in local politics became so prevalent and subject to so many abuses that the state of New York found it necessary to pass, in 1856, a law forbidding school commissioners to act as the agents of publishers in the awarding of contracts for book purchase.[91] Fear that similar exploitation would be introduced into the management of town libraries was expressed at the 1853 convention of librarians. Edward Everett Hale, though he approved the enthusiasm of the assembled librarians for the formulation of a plan which would promote the establishment of well-selected public libraries throughout the towns and villages of the country, called attention to the danger that the formulation of recommended lists of books for such libraries would serve only to promote publishers' monopolistic practices.

By the middle of the nineteenth century the activities of professional librarians in encouraging library establishment was not conspicuous, but some halting steps in that direction were taken in 1853 when an assembly of eighty-two librarians met in New York City for the purpose of forming a permanent library association that would bring to a focus the professional problems that confronted the practitioners of the craft. These meetings, which were sponsored by Charles C. Jewett, librarian of the Smithsonian Institution; Charles E. Norton, publisher and bookseller; Seth Hastings Grant, librarian of the New York Mercantile Library; Reuben A. Guild, librarian of Brown University; and Daniel Coit Gilman, then just graduated from Yale, promised much for the encouragement of professional solidarity. But initial enthusiasm sputtered out in forensic appeals for a great national library for reference and research to be subsidized by the Smithsonian gift, Jewett's own grandiose and impracticable scheme for a union catalog of stereotype plates of all American libraries to be deposited at the Smithsonian Institution, and innumerable resolutions providing for library promotion. The group, confronted by the dispersion of its leaders, the financial crisis of 1857, and,

91. New York State, *Laws,* 1856, chap. 179, sec. 8.

four years later, the Civil War, never reconvened, and it was not until the Centennial Exposition of 1876 brought to public notice the library development throughout the country that the profession achieved a real unity. The convention of 1853 accomplished little that was either positive or constructive, yet it revealed a latent professional consciousness that was indicative of future trends.[92]

The factors which contributed to public library development should not be dismissed without re-emphasizing the European influence, for many of the ideas which prepared the way for a public library system were not native to America. From England and perhaps from the Continent the idea of the book club had been imported by migrants who came to the Atlantic coast early in the eighteenth century. A colonial environment altered somewhat the outward form of the agency, and the new social conditions initiated a process of natural adaptation, but these did not obliterate the transatlantic influence. The social, and circulating libraries, lyceums, and museums all resulted from the importation and diffusion of institutional forms.[93] The experiences of New England scholars who sought in European universities of the nineteenth century a training beyond that available at Cambridge or New Haven encouraged library formation in this country. Jared Sparks was inspired by the patronage of the British Museum and hoped that the Athenaeum would achieve equal

92. The Proceedings of the 1853 convention are reported fully in *Norton's Literary Register*, III (1854), 62 ff. Reuben A. Guild discusses the reasons why the organization failed to survive in the *Library Journal*, XXVII (1902), c.120–c.121. The history of the conference has been informally written by George B. Utley, "The Librarians' Conference of 1853" (unpublished MS), 120 pp.

93. The Boston Athenaeum, for example, was directly influenced by the Athenaeum at Liverpool. When the early success of the *Monthly Anthology* encouraged exchanges with the editors of English reviews, its youthful publishers began to feel the need for a supporting reference library and reading-room. "One of our members," wrote Robert Gardiner, "having received an account of the Athenaeum recently established in Liverpool, read it to the [Anthology] Club. We were all at once impressed with the great advantage there would be in having such an institution in Boston; we determined at once that it should be established with the same name" (Robert Hallowell Gardiner, *Early Recollections of Robert Hallowell Gardiner, 1782–1864* [Hallowell, Me.: R. H. & W. I. Gardiner, 1936], p. 96).

popularity;[94] and George Warren, member of the first board of trustees of the Boston Public Library, submitted materials relating to the Free Library of Manchester, England, for the guidance of his colleagues.[95] Through the efforts of Vattemare and his plans for the international exchange of official publications, France, too, was contributing in a substantial way to the formation of public libraries in her sister-republic.

These European influences upon the American public library were twofold. Directly they contributed to the promotion of the agency by the actual transfer of organizational patterns. The book clubs, the social libraries, and the circulating collections were all either derived from European models or brought to this country by enterprising merchants who sought to exploit the reading interests of the American public, just as they had capitalized on the desires of readers in their native lands. Indirectly, by the example of its own great collections and their organization, Europe suggested to the American mind the significance of the library in the integration of an emerging culture. At Peterborough, Wayland, and Boston, where the initial steps were taken that resulted in the foundation of a public library system as it is known today, the action was characteristically American, but the antecedents of that movement were largely derived from European sources.

Historical scholarship and the urge to preservation, the power of national and local pride, the growing belief in the importance of universal education, the increasing concern with vocational problems, and the contribution of religion—these, aided by economic ability and encouraged by the example of Europe, were the causal factors in the formation of libraries that would be free to all the people. Underlying these was the influence of the people themselves—countless individuals in innumerable towns who had faith in the public library and believed implicitly in its social

94. "In the reading-rooms are daily congregated more than a hundred readers and transcribers, of all nations and tongues, plodding scholars, literary ladies, and grave old gentlemen with mysterious looks. When shall we see the like in the Athenaeum?" (quoted by Brooks, *op. cit.*, p. 121).

95. "Proceedings of the Trustees, February 14, 1853," I, 8 (MS in Boston Public Library).

value. The library movement did not generate "great" leadership. It attracted the support of men who were distinguished in public life—Everett, Ticknor, the Quincys, Mann, Barnard—and it profited much from their efforts. But these men are remembered less because of what they did for the public library than for their achievements in other fields. Community leadership was necessary to give the library movement the impetus and direction it required, but it was essentially a small-town leadership—a leadership that was largely unknown outside its native environs. Today Caleb Bingham, Abiel Abbot, Josiah Eastman, and John B. Wight are almost forgotten, yet it was the cumulative influence of such men that contributed most to the support the library needed. Librarians will continue to honor the names of Winsor, Jewett, Dana, and Brett, as indeed they properly should, but in doing so they should not forget that "the growing good of the . . . [library] is partly dependent on unhistoric acts; and that things are not so ill . . . as they might have been is half owing to the number who lived faithfully a hidden life, and rest in unvisited tombs."

CONCLUSION

LESS than a decade after the Pilgrims landed at Plymouth Rock, John Endicott's pioneer settlement at Salem received a collection of books that evidently was intended for community use. Two and a quarter centuries later the citizens of Boston, inspired by the enthusiasm of their municipal leaders, voluntarily appropriated from the city treasury enough money to inaugurate a free library that was to become a cornerstone of the American public library system. Between these events extend more than two hundred years during which the public library pattern, under the influence of continuing economic and social change, was slowly taking shape.

Within the compact New England region, sharply circumscribed by the natural barriers of mountain range and sea, there developed a population that in age, nationality, culture, and social ideals was unusually homogeneous. The people were young, vigorous, and eager for the excitement of living.[1] Concerning religion, politics, morals, and education, New Englanders generally thought in similar terms. Confronted by the expansion of the rest of the country, the region was more and more forced into a sectional solidarity that even the later extremes of economic status and the social cleavages engendered by the factory system did not destroy. A continuing process of urbanization brought economic power and cultural influence to the maximum point of concentration. The intensification of human relationships that results from town and city life encouraged the substitution of complex patterns of group action for the simpler and more primitive forms.

Between the years 1629 and 1855 the region underwent a complete economic transformation. An early pioneer agriculture, be-

1. In Massachusetts in 1850, 42 per cent of the population was under twenty years of age, and 64 per cent was under thirty (U.S. Census Office, *7th Census, 1850: Statistical View of the United States . . . , Being a Compendium of the Seventh Census* [Washington, D.C.: A. O. P. Nicholson, 1854], p. 51).

245

cause of the rapidity with which the soil was depleted, was supplanted by commerce, trade, and, later, manufacturing.[2] Culturally the change was no less complete. An initial dependence upon Europe was superseded, at first, by awkward attempts to create a native literature but, afterward, by the full and mature expression of Emerson, Hawthorne, and their contemporaries. When primary human needs were satisfied and economic conditions made possible the attainment of cultural advantages, men began to seek those activities which would extend experience beyond the tedium of daily toil and give to life a new depth and meaning. In this search for cultural expression the desire for books was conspicuous. But even as late as 1850 the supply of books was not so great that the wants of certain users, especially the scholars, were easily satisfied; so group ownership was the only feasible solution to the problem of scarcity.

In the beginning, town book collections generally resulted from the gifts of individuals because that was the simplest and most direct method. There were occasional purchases of selected titles by town authorities, but such instances were rare. Even at their best these early town libraries were small, scattered, and capricious in the manner of their establishment and maintenance.

As the need for books became more keenly felt, it grew increasingly clear that only by the union of individuals into voluntary associations could a reasonably adequate supply of books be attained. This pattern of group action had long been familiar. Everywhere men had united in informal societies or formalized corporations to achieve, with increased efficiency and effectiveness, tasks which men as individuals could not perform. Whether the objective was to clear the forest, build a railroad, erect a cotton-mill, educate the youth, assemble a "cabinet of curiosities," or establish a library, men found strength in unity of action.

2. When Abbott Lawrence endowed a scientific school at Harvard, he wrote to Samuel A. Eliot on June 7, 1847: "We have, perhaps, stronger motives in New England than in any other part of our country to encourage scientific pursuits, from the fact that we must hereafter look for our main support to the pursuit of commerce, manufacture, and the mechanic arts; to which it becomes our duty, in my humble judgment, to make all the appliances of science within our power. We inherit, and are forced to cultivate, a sterile soil; and what nature had denied should be, as far as possible, supplied by art" (Hamilton A. Hill, *Memoir of Abbott Lawrence* [Boston: Privately printed, 1883], p. 110).

So the social libraries that were abundant throughout New England at the end of the eighteenth century flourished and for a time seemed successfully to meet prevailing needs.

But most of the social libraries did not achieve the promise or justify the anticipation of their founders. The social library soon became an anachronism born of the demands of a previous century but no longer in harmony with an age that attributed such importance to public concern for the education and welfare of the whole people. So, by 1855, the public generally lost interest in the social library, which had passed the zenith of its development, and, though individual institutions continued to prosper, the case against it as a library form was unmistakably clear. A more effective substitute was found, and 'that substitute was the modern public library, free to all readers of the town, supported from public funds, and an integral part of local government.

From this increasing pressure for the collectivization of library facilities the public library emerged. It was born of the desires, needs, and experiences of the people. Derived from European origins, shaped by two centuries of trial and error, conditioned by the economic and social life by which it was surrounded and of which it was a part, the public library was created because it was essential to the fullest expression of human life. The objectives of its founders were specific and very real. They wished to promote equality of educational opportunity, to advance scientific investigation, to save the youth from the evils of an ill-spent leisure, and to promote the vocational advance of the workers. In short, they were, as Ralph Beals has pointed out, interested in normative ends—in the improvement of men and women and through them of society.[3] The hardships of the frontier had fostered a democracy that was nourished by subsequent generations—generations to whom the rigors of pioneer existence were remote indeed. In the preservation of that democracy the library was to play its part. Mann, Barnard, and their followers held that an intelligent and educated electorate is essential to a democracy, and in the great system of public education which they foresaw the public library was to be a true "people's university."

3. Ralph A. Beals, "Public Libraries and the War," *American Library Association Bulletin*, XXXVI (1942), 478.

Judged by every standard and measured by every criterion, the public library is revealed as a social agency dependent upon the objectives of society. It *followed*—it did not create—social change. It was an outward and visible manifestation of the spirit and ideals of the people. Borne on the rising tide of modern democracy, it evolved as society itself developed, though at a somewhat slower pace. As society attained greater complexity, as industry developed and increased in diversity, as populations crowded into congested city areas, as labor and economic life, largely because of the impact of the machine, became more and more specialized, the functions of the library reflected a corresponding intricacy and growing importance.

So the aims, methods, and ideals of the library were modified as life itself underwent profound social changes. The library, in common with all social agencies, moved through alternate periods of fluidity and convention but always responded, in greater or less degree, to its environment.

There was a lag between social stimulus and library response, yet there also existed a reciprocity of relationship between the library and society. Each reacted upon the other. Because the public library contributed to the fullest expression of democracy, it supported that form of social organization. The relationship was constantly evolving.

If future generations can learn anything from an examination of library history, it is that the objectives of the public library are directly dependent upon the objectives of society itself. The true frame of reference for the library is to be found in its coeval culture. No librarian can see clearly the ends which he should seek when his country is confused about the direction in which it is moving. When a people are certain of the goals toward which they strive, the functions of the public library can be precisely defined.

APPENDIX I

ARTICLES OF THE BOOK–COMPANY OF DURHAM
OCTOBER 30, 1733 (CONNECTICUT)[1]

Forasmuch as the Subscribers hereof being desirous to improve our leisure hours in enriching our minds with useful and profitable knowledge by reading, do find ourselves unable so to do for the want of suitable and proper books. Therefore that we may be the better able to furnish ourselves with a suitable and proper collection of books, for the above said end, we do each of us unite together and agree to be copartners in Company together by the name of *The Book-Company of Durham*, united to buy books, and we do agree and covenant with each other, and it is hereby covenanted and agreed upon by each of us the subscribers hereof, that we ourselves and successors, will be for the Future a Society or Company copartners united for said end, viz. to buy books, and we will each of us so often as we shall agree by our major vote bear our equal parts in advancing any sum, or sums of money at any time as a common stock to be laid out for such books as shall be agreed upon by the major vote of the Company to enlarge our Library, and in pursuance of said design, we have each of us put into one stock the sum of twenty shillings, which is already laid out according to our Direction, in purchasing Books, which Books shall be kept as a common stock Library for the use of said company, by some meet person, whom we shall choose, each member having an equal right in said Library, and to use the same under such regulations, as we shall agree upon. And

1. We agree that each member of the company may have one Book at once out of the Library with liberty to use the same, if he please, the space of one month, from the time he takes such book out of the Library, but shall at or before the expiration of said term, after he takes such book out return the same, or forfeit as a fine to said company the sum of two shillings, for any such neglect. N.B. This is not to be understood so, but that any member has liberty to return his Book at any time, within the month, and may then take another. Only he shall return any book so taken out within a month from the time he took such book out or forefeit as above. And further the members of said Company may exchange books if they please one with another. Only everyone shall be obliged to see the Book he took out returned within said term, or forfeit in like manner.

2. We agree that Mr. Elihu Chauncey be our Library-Keeper until another be chosen, having made choice of him by our major vote to that end, who shall

---

1. Original in possession of Mrs. Howard B. Field of Durham, Conn., and transcribed here with her permission.

deal out the Books to the Members of said company as above, and receive them again, and make entry of such books he delivers, to whom, the time when he delivers, and also when they are returned, and shall make and keep true entries of all the agreements of said Company at their meetings from time to time, so long as he shall continue to be our Library-Keeper.

3. We agree that if any member of this company shall suffer any book belonging to said Library to be damnified by tearing, blotting, or any way damnify them, more than the well or careful using of them, shall be thought to do, any such person shall make good, all such damage to said company by paying to them so much as they shall judge such damage to be.

4. We agree that no member shall have liberty to sell his right in said Library without first making the offer of it to said company: and upon their refusing to buy it, only to some person of this town, and to but one: Any member shall have liberty to quit the said company, if he will give his right in the Library to said Company.

5. We agree further that we will have at least annually one general meeting to consult further respecting the premises; and have made choice of Ebenezer Garnsey, Hurt Strong and Mr. Joseph Sanford to appoint time and place, for the holding of such meetings and also to give notice thereof to the members of said company to attend the same accordingly once a year, and oftener, if they see need thereof. And that, which is concluded and agreed upon, respecting said affair by the major part of the subscribers, met according to such warning, shall be binding to the rest of the Company.

6. We agree also, that if any member of the company shall presume to lend any book belonging to said Library to any person, who is not one of the company, he shall forfeit as a fine, the sum of ten shillings to be paid to said company, as often as he shall be found guilty of so doing.

And in Testimony that we have each of us covenanted and agreed together as above, and that we will each of us faithfully observe and perform the above covenant in every part and article thereof according to the true intent and meaning of it, and also of all such articles and agreements, as we shall make hereafter respecting the premises at any of our meetings regularly warned, by our major vote, we have respectively set our hands, this 30th day of October Anno Domini 1733, in the Seventh Year of the Reign of our Sovereign Lord George the Second and King.

APPENDIX II

COVENANT OF THE PHILOGRAMMATICAN SOCIETY OF LEBANON, CONNECTICUT, 1739[1]

THIS COVENANT MADE THIS FOURTH DAY OF JANUARY ANNO DOMINI 1738/9.—Between The Reverend Eleazor Williams of Mansfield, The Reverend Joseph Meacham of Coventry, The Rev. Thomas Clap of Windham, The Rev. Jacob Elliot, The Rev. Eleazor Wheelock, Ebenezer West, Esq., Messers Ebenezor Gray, Joseph Fowler, Gersham Clark, John Williams, William Metcalfe, and Jonathan Trumble (all of Lebanon) In The County of Windham, and Colony of Connecticutt in New England.

On the one part, and The Rev. Solomon Williams of said Lebanon on the other part, Wittneseth That we The above named, The Rev. Messers Eleazer Williams, Joseph Meacham, Thomas Clapp, Jacob Elliot, Eleazor Wheelock, Ebenezer West, Esq., Messers Ebenezor Gray, Joseph Fowler, Gersham Clark, John Williams, William Metcalfe, Jonathan Trumble—do covenant and Agree to and with the said Rev. Solomon Williams, his heirs, Executors, and Administrators in manner and form following, viz. We Do Each and Every of us Severally Oblige ourselves, our Heirs, Executors, and Administrators To pay or Cause to be paid unto the said Sol. Williams, his Heirs or Order The Full and Just Sum of Fifty Pounds Current money; That is, Twentyfive pounds at or before The first day of September next Ensuing, and Twentyfive pounds at or before The first day of September which will be in The Year of Our Lord 1740—All and Every of Which Fifty Pounds by Each and Every of us Agreed and covenanted to be paid; we Do hereby Covenant and Agree Shall be by Said Rev. Sol. Williams his heirs and Executors and Administrators Used and Improved to Purchase and Buy a Library of Such Useful and Profitable Books as The Covenanters by Their Major Vote Taken and Given in Manner hereafter to be Expressed, Shall be Agreed and Concluded upon; to be Holden and Kept in the first Society in Lebanon aforesaid as a Common Library to and Among the Covenantors for Their Use and Improvement Under Such Restrictions, Regulations, and Directions as hereafter in this Instrument, shall be Expressed, or in Due Manner and form Shall be Agreed, Voted, and Concluded on by the Proprietors and Covenanters aforesaid—

Whereupon The Said Rev. Solomon Williams doth for himself, his Heirs, Executors and Administrators: Covenant and Agree To and With The Above

1. From the original in the James Terry papers in the American Antiquarian Society.

Named Rev. Messers Eleazer Williams, Joseph Meacham, Thomas Clapp, Jacob Elliot, Eleazer Wheelock, Ebenezer West, Esq.; Messers Ebenezer Gray, Joseph Fowler, Gersham Clark, John Williams, William Metcalfe, and Jonathan Trumble—

Their Heirs, Executors, Administrators, and Assigns, That he, The Said Rev. Sol. Williams his heirs, Executors and Administrators Shall well and Truly pay or Cause to be paid Towards The Use Aforesaid out of his own Proper Estate the full and Just Sum of Fifty Pounds Money, to be paid toward The Use aforesaid in manner and form As of The Several Fifty Pounds aforesaid, That is Twentyfive pounds at Or Before the first day of September Next, and Twentyfive pounds at Or before the first day of September which will be in the Year of our Lord 1740—And Then further Secondly—

The Rev. Solomon Williams aforesaid doth hereby Bind and Oblige himself, his heirs etc., to Purchase and deliver into the hands of The Covenanters aforesaid A Collection of Such Books and Such Sorts of Books as Shall be Agreed and Concluded To be bought by The Vote of The major Part of the Covenanters made as hereafter expressed which Shall Amount in the whole to the whole of The Several Sums Covenanted to be paid by the Covenanter on The first part To The Said Rev. Sol. Williams, together with the Fifty Pounds Covenanted and Agreed by him The Said Rev. Sol. Williams To Be Added To the Same Total Amount, at The Cheapest Rate they can reasonably be Purchased at in New England To be delivered at or before the first day of September Next, the One half of Them, and The Other of Them at or before the First day of September Anno Dom 1740—(Dangers of Transportation only Excepted and Incident Charges allowed.)

WHEREUPON it is now Further Covenanted, Agreed and Determined to, by, and among all and every of The Covenanters aforesaid, both on ye one and other part mentioned in manner and form following—viz.—first, That The Said Collection of Books made and Purchased as aforesaid Shall be put into One Comon *Library* and Shall be Held and Kept within the Limits of The first Society in *Lebanon* aforesaid, for the Comon Use, Benefit, and Advantage of the Covenanters aforesaid, and Those of Their Heirs and Assigns as by The Votes and Rules Agreed On by the Major Part of The Proprietors thereof, Shall be Allowed to Take and Hold Interest Therein—

Secondly, That The Said Library Shall be Called and known by the Name of The Philogrammatican Library, and that the Proprietors and Owners thereof, in Relation thereto, shall be Called and known by the Name of The Company of The Philogrammatican Library—

Thirdly,—That the Rev. Sol. Williams Shall be the Keeper of The Said *Library* until The proprietors of the Same Shall by their Vote Regularly Given order Otherwise, and so by their choice appoint another person, Proprietor of the *Library* and inhabitant in the First *Society in Lebanon*, to be The Keeper Thereof—Who Shall for Time being Keep Clean and in good Order The Said Library, and Shall Deliver out and Receive in the Books Thereto belonging According to The Orders, Directions, and Instructions to him given from The

Proprietors those of by Their Vote made known In Due form, as hereinafter
shall be Expressed: and So That a *Library Keeper* Shall from time to time be
Chosen and Appointed, out of The Proprietors thereof, Inhabitants in the first
Society in Lebanon, and Shall be under the Conduct and Direction of The
Said Proprietors—

Fourthly: That Immediately upon The Executing this Covenant The
Covenanters, and So from Time to time the Proprietors of The Said *Library*
do form themselves into a Company known by The name aforesaid, who Shall
from Time to Time meet together to make Such Votes, Conclusions, and
Orders Concerning Such matters, business, and Things Relating to The Regulation, Ordering, and Disposition of The Said *Library* for the Use and Advantage
of the Proprietors and Owners thereof, agreeable to the True Intents and meaning of This Covenant: and That The Said Company may from Time to Time
be Regularly Warned To Meet and Assemble Together, it is Agreed—

Fifthly, That some Person, Either of the Covenanters or Proprietors of Ye
Library Shall be from Time to time Chosen and Appointed to warn the Said
Company to meet together at Such Place as Shall be Agreed upon by The Com-
pany, and That he Shall Use Such Method and give Such Timely Notice to
The Company of aforesaid As They Shall from Time to Time agree upon; and
That upon Application made to The Said Person appointed To warn the Meet-
ings, by any Three or more of Said Company, Desiring that a Meeting of Said
Company may be warned, he Shall Then Forthwith Warn a Meeting of Said
Company According To The Time and Place and Method Agreed Upon—.
And That a true Record may be kept and Entries made of the Votes and Doings
of The Said Company, It is Agreed—

Sixthly, That a Book Shall be made and Kept by Some person thereto ap-
pointed; and That from time to time two persons shall be Appointed truly to
Enter all The Votes, Proceedings, and Orders of the Covenanters and Pro-
prietors of Said Library, in The Said Book for That End provided, and Shall
Subscribe their Names Thereunto, which shall become Evidence that Those
Records or Entries made were The acts and Doings of The said Company.

Seventhly, No Acts Shall be Esteemed good and Valid without it be made
and done by the Major Vote of the Covenanters or Proprietors Present at the
Meeting, to be Computed by their Interests, and Further, No Act Shall be
made or done, and be binding to the Company unless there Shall be at Least
two thirds of the Covenanters or Proprietors Present at the meeting—And That
Each Owner and Proprietor in Said Library may be Able to Shew his Interest
in Said Library, and The Votes and Doings of The Proprietors thereof it is
Agreed—

Eighthly, That Three Covenants of Like Tenour and Date of These Presents
Shall be Duely Executed by Each of us, and Our Compliance with One of
Them Shall be a Discharge of Them all, Which Covenants so executed shall be
Lodged, one of them in the Hands of The *Library Keeper* for the time being,
and the other two In The Hands of two other proprietors Regularly Chosen to
keep Them: and That a True Copy of Them Shall be Transcribed In The

Forepart of The Book wherein The Votes and Doings of Said Company are Recorded, We Shall be Attested and Signed by Two Persons Evidencing That The Same is a True Copy thereof; And That it Shall be the Duty of Every of Those persons to Allow True Copies of This Covenant To be Taken, and Two Persons Subscribing Their Names Thereunto as Evidence That Same is a True Copy thereof, Shall be Allowed to be Done by Each of Those Persons to Whose Keeping The Same is Committed: And Further The Keeper of The Book in which The Doings and Votes of The Said Company are Kept and Inscribed, Shall Suffer and Allow True Copies of all The Votes and Proceedings Therein Entered to be Taken and subscribed by any two Sufficient witnesses That The Doings of The Said Company may Thereby be well Evidenced and That Additions may be made to Said *Library*, and Other members provided thereto—it is Agreed

Ninthly, That Other Covenanters with The Present Covenanters may be Admitted and Received To make Additions to Said *Library*, by The Major Vote of The Company, Who Shall be under The Like Restrictions, Regulations, and Directions as The Present Proprietors are Agreeable to The Present Covenant, And The Acts and Future Doings of The Said Covenantors and Proprietors thereof—IN WITNESS whereof, Both Parties, and Each Member of Both Parties, have Subscribed Their Hands and Seals to Three Covenants of Like Tenour and Even date with these Presents, One of Which Being Accomplished, The Rest Shall be Discharged...

Signed, Sealed and D.D.	ELEAZER WILLIAMS [L.S.]
In Presence of us	JOSEPH MEACHAM "
EBENEZER WEST	SOLOMON WILLIAMS "
ELEAZER GILLETT	JACOB ELLIOT "
	THOMAS CLAP "
	ELEAZER WHEELOCK "
	JOSEPH WHEELOCK "
	EBEN GRAY "
	JOSEPH FOWLER "
	GERSHOM CLARK "
	JOHN WILLIAMS "
	JONATHAN TRUMBLE "

[NOTE.—Metcalfe apparently did not sign the covenant.]

Lebanon March 29th 1739—Whereas The Society of The Philogramatican Library Aforesaid Have This Day Voted to Receive and Admitt The Rev. Benj. Throope of Norwich and Sam. Huntington of Lebanon to be Members of This Society, on The Same Conditions, Restrictions, Regulations, and Directions as The Present Proprietors are, Agreable to Their Covenant Imediately foregoing, Persons being. . . .

Now Therefore We The Said Benj. Throope and Sam. Huntington Do Covenant and Agree To Pay Each One The Fifty Pounds Money To The Said Rev. Sol. Williams for The Advancement and Additions to The Said Library to be paid In Manner and Form as by The Rest of Covenanters, and In all Things To be under The Same Restrictions, Regulations, and Directions as The Rest of the Society and Proprietors of The Said Library Are by their Covenants aforesaid Both for Giving and Receiving—

In Witness whereof I have Hereunto Sett Our Hands, and Seals—

Signed, Sealed and D.D.

In presence of us

THOS. FITCH
GIDEON HUNT

BENJAMIN THROOPE
SAMUEL HUNTINGTON

PLATES

PLATE I

BOSTON TOWN HOUSE (FROM BENTON, "STORY OF THE OLD BOSTON TOWN HOUSE")

PLATE II

A CATALOGUE OF BOOKS,

Which belong to the Library of *Saybrook, Lime, and Guilford.*

ASHLEY's Sermons, 8 vo.
Amelia, 4 vol. 8 vo.
Allyn's Synopsis, 2 vol. 8 vo.
Bailey's Dictionary, 5 vol. fol.
Burnet's abridgment of the reformation, fol.
Burnet on the 39 articles, fol.
Blair's Sermons, 2 vol. 8 vo.
Benson's Sermons, 3 vo.
Burnet's Letters, 8 vo.
Boyle's Lectures, 4 vol. 8 vo.
Beach's Reply, 8 vo.
Burnet's History of his own times, fol.
Beattie on truth, 8 vo.
Beveridge on religion, 8 vo.
Baxter on the reformation, 8 vo.
Beneyftreet's Sermons, 3 vol. 8 vo.
Bonnet's Letters, 8 vo.   [ty, 8vo.
Benson on the reasonableness of christiani-
Baxter's call to unconverted, 8 vo.
Benson's Tracts, 8 vo.
Bohun's Pleadings, fol.
Butler's Sermons, 8 vo.
Baron and Feme, fol.
X Bates on the harmony of redemption, 8vo.
Bidford's Chronology, fol.
X Benson's Paraphrase, 3 vol.   4 to.
Barrage on the Jews, fol.
Bradley on gardening, 8 vo.
Bennet's form of prayer, 8 vo.
Blackwell's sacred Classicks, 2 vol 8 vo.
X Butler's Analogy, 8 vo.
X Censor, 8 vo.
Chauncey's Sermons, 8 vo.
Chauncey on Justification, 8 vo.
Clarke's Sermons, 9 vol. 8 vo.
———Paraphrase, 3 vol. 4 to.
Clarke on the attributes, 8 vo.
———on Scripture Doctrine of the Tri-
nity, 8 vo.
Chambers Dictionary, 2 vol. fol.
X Commentary of John Calvin, fol.
X Camden's Britannia, fol.
Calvin's Institutes, fol.
Chauncey on Episcopacy, 8 vo.
Carpzaw's Defence, 8 vo.
Coleman's Sacramental Discourses, 8 vo.
Clap's Remarks, 8 vo.
Clergyman's Vade mecum, 8 vo.
Cook's Second Voyage, 8 vo.
Certainty of a future state, 8 vo.
Charles the 12th, an history, 8 vo.
Cale stated between the Churches, 8 vo.
Charles Grandison, 7 vol. 8 vo.
Corsica, an history, 8 vo.
Doddridge's rise and progress, 8 vo.
X ———Paraphrase, 3 vol. 4 to.
———a Pamphlet,
———Sermons, 2 vol. 8 vo.
———Sermon to Young Men, 8 vo.
De La Bruyre's Works, 8 vo.
Danvers abridgment, 2 vol. fol.
———on Law, 8 vo.
Dalstean Country Justice, fol.
Divine analogy, 8 vo.
Devotion's Sermons, 8 vo.
Drelincourt on Death, 8 vo.
X Don Quixote, 8 vo.
X Ditton on the Resurrection, 8 vo.
Ellis on husbandry, 8 vol. 8 vo.
Evan's lectures, to young people, 8 vo.
———Sermons, 2 vol. 8 vo.
X Essays, moral and philosophical, 8 vo.
X Ethiopia, an history, 4to.
X Evelyn's Sylvia, fol.
Echard's Ecclesiastical history, 2 vol. 8 vo.
Enquiry into the Constitution of the
church, 8 vo.   [12 mo.
Fordyce's Sermons to young women, 2 vol.
Flavel's works 2 vol. fol.
Fisher's remarks, 8 vo.

X French prophets, 8vo.
X Freeholder, 8 vo.
Family Instructor, 8 vo.
Flavel's token for mourners,
Gibson's pastoral letters, 8 vo.
Gay's Fables, 8 vol.
Gentlemen Instructed, 8 vo.
Geography, by Wells, 3 vol. 8 vo.
———by Varenius, 3 vol. 8 vo.
———of our Saviour, by Wells, 8 vo.
Harvie's Sermons, 8 vo.
Hottentots, history of 8 vo.
Hurrion's Sermons on christ crucified,
2 vol. 8 vo.
History a new method of studying of 8 vo.
Henry Exposition, 3 vol. fol.
Howe on blessedness of the righteous, 8 vo.
Hoadley's Sermons, 8 vo.
Hoadley on Sacrament, 8 vo.
X Humphrey's nature displayed, 3 vol. 8 vo.
X Husbandry, an history 8 vo.
Harris's funeral Sermons, 8 vo.
Hooker on Ecclesiastical Polity, fol.
History of the Popes 5 vol. 4 to.
Homer the life of, 8 vo.
The humble attempt, 8 vo.
The humble discourse, 8 vo.
Human prudence, 8 vo.
Harris on the Messiah, 8 vo.
X Jenkin on the reasonableness of Christiani-
ty, 2 vol. 8 vo.
Indian Nations, history, 2 vol. 8 vo.
Johnson against Popery, 4 to.
Jacobs' Law Dictionary, fol.
Idolators Corruptions 2 vol 8 vo.
X Joseph the prime minister, 8 vo.
X Kale's primitive Christianity, 8 vo.
Kettlewell on obedience, 8 vo.
———on Death, 8 vo.
Lewis 14, history of 8 vol. 12 mo.
Law's Serious Call to a devout Life, 8 vo.
Lowman on Revelation, 4 to.
Lowth's Commentary, fol.
Lock on Education, 8 vo.
Lardiner, 8 vo.
Lardiner's Credibility of the Gospel histo-
ry 1st. part, 7 vol. 8 vo.
Lardiner's Credibility of the Gospel history
2d. part, 2 vol. 8 vo.
Law and Evidence, 8 vo.
Ludlow's Memoirs, 3 vol. 8 vo.
Ledyard's Voyage, 8 vo.
Lucas on happiness, 8 vo.
———on perfection, 8 vo.
Leigh's critica sacra, 8 vo.
Law of consideration, by Horneck, 8 vo.
Leland's view of Deistical writers, 8 vo.
Moss's Sermons, vol. 8 vo.
Miscellaneous pamphlets,
Mascow on the Germans, 4 to.
X Milton's Memoirs
Memoirs of Quillane, 8 vo.
Minute Philosopher, vol. 8 vo.
Molloy's treatise of commerce, 8 vo.
Morocco, the revolutions of, 8 vo.
Malebranche's search after truth, fol.
Norton's method Evangelist, 8 vo.
Nelson's judgment, 3 vol. fol.
Newton's Philosophy, 4 to.
Necessity of Communion, 8 vo.
Nye on the Trinity, 8 vo.
Owen on the Hebrews, fol.
Observations, Moral, and political, 8 vo.
Prideaux connections, 4 vol. 8 vo.
Parker's demonstration, 8 vo.
Patrick's Mensa Mystica, 8 vo.
X Portugal, history of, 8 vo.
Pemberton's Sermons, 8 vo.
Poole's annotations, 3 vol. fol.
Puffendorfe's Nations, fol.
Prince's Chronology, 8 vo.

X Parable of Pilgrims, 4 to.
Present state Great-Britain, 8 vo.
Pierson on the Creed, fol.
X Pascal's thoughts on Religion, 8 vo.
Rollin's ancient history, 10 vol. 12 mo.
X Revelation examined with candor, 8 vo.
X Rapin's history of England, 5 vol. fol.
Rollin's Belles Lettres, 3 vol. 8 vo.
Miss Rowe's Letters 2 vol. 8 vo.
———Letters, Moral and Entertain-
ing, 8 vo.
Revolution, Politicks, 8vo.
X Rasby's Memoirs, 8 vo.
Richard's Vindication, 2 vol. 8 vo.
Rule of Methodology 8 vo.
Sherlock's Sermons, 7 vol. 8 vo.
Sharp's Sermons, 6 vol. 8 vo.
Shuckford's Connections, 3 vol. 8 vo.
Sherlock on Death, 8 vo.
Spanish Settlements, 8 vo.
Salter Hall Sermons, against Popery, 2
vol. 8 vo.
X Sians history of fol.
Sleiden, on the reformation, fol.
Scott on the Christian Life, fol.
Stackhouse body Divinity, fol.
X Spon's history of Geneva, 4 to.
Sherlock on divine Providence, 8 vo.
Schaverell's Trial, 8 vo.
Smollet's history of England, 7 vol. 8 vol.
———continuation of the history of
England, 3 vol. 8 vo.
Stoddard's safety of appearing in the righ-
teousness of Christ, 8 vo.
Shindler's Hebrew, Lexicon, fol.
Telemachus 2 vol. 8 vo.
Tillotson's Sermons, 14 vol. 8 vo.
Trapp on Trinity, 8 vo.
Trial of Church forsakers, 8 vo.
X Tull's husbandry 8 vo,
X Taste of the town, 8 vo.
X Tartary, an history, 3 vol. 8 vo.
X Travels of several learned Missioners, 8 vo
Universal Library, 2 vol. 8 vo.
Voyages and Travels, 7 vol. 8 vo.
Vindication of old Testament, 8 vo.
Wallaston's religion of nature, 4 to.
Watts Logick, 8 vo.
———Supplement, 8 vo.
———Scripture history, 8 vo.
———on various subjects, 8 vo.
———on first principles, 8 vo.
———on Spelling and Writing, 8 vo.
———against Suicide, 8 vo.
X———on astronomy and geography, 8 vo.
———on the Trinity, 8 vo.
———on holiness of time and place, 8 vo.
———his Redeemer and Sanctifier, 8 vo.
———discourses on love of God, 8 vo.
———on the passions, 8 vo.
———on the strength and weakness of hu-
man reason, 8 vo.
———on the affections, 12 mo.
———his Lyrick Poems, 8 vo.
———Sermons 2 vol. 8 vo.
Wright on conversation, 8 vo.
Wake's Sermons 4 vol. 8 vo.
Whitby's Sermons, 8 vo.
X Whole duty of Man, 8 vo.
Wilkin's Sermons 2 vol. 8 vo.
Whitby's Paraphrase, 2 vol. fol.
Wodrav on the Church of Scotland, 2
vol. fol.
X Wilton's Dictionary, fol.
Woodward's call, &c. 8 vo.
Woodward's Fossils, 8 vo.
Whiston's Chronology, 4 to.
Willard's body of Divinity, fol.
Williams on Divine Grace, 8 vo.
Young's Sermons 2 vol. 8 vol.

CATALOG OF THE LIBRARY OF SAYBROOK, LYME, AND GUILFORD, CONN.
(FROM THE COPY IN THE YALE UNIVERSITY LIBRARY)

PLATE III

The Redwood Library, Newport, Rhode Island, Erected 1750. "The Subtle Influence of Use and Respect for General Interests Worked Vigorously in the Mind of the Designer-Carpenter-Builder; There Was a Sense of Fitness, a Grave Power, and an Engaging Serenity in the Structures Erected by Their Hands" (Charles A. Beard) (Photographed by the Author)

PLATE IV

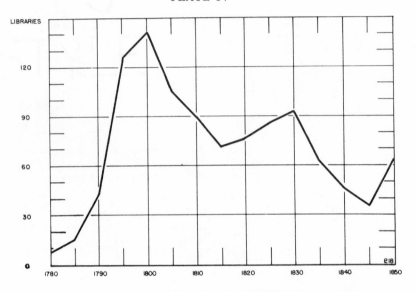

DISTRIBUTION OF LIBRARIES BY DATE OF THEIR ESTABLISHMENT
IN NEW ENGLAND, 1780–1850

PLATE V

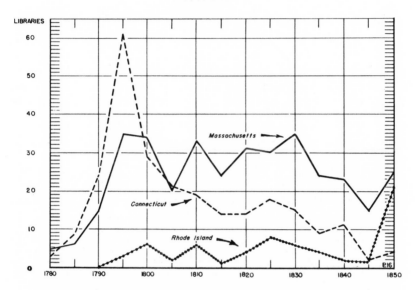

DISTRIBUTION OF LIBRARIES BY DATE OF THEIR ESTABLISHMENT IN MASSA-
CHUSETTS, CONNECTICUT, AND RHODE ISLAND, 1780–1850

PLATE VI

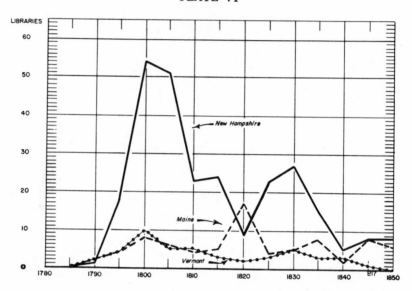

DISTRIBUTION OF LIBRARIES BY DATE OF THEIR ESTABLISHMENT IN NEW
HAMPSHIRE, MAINE, AND VERMONT, 1780–1850

PLATE VII

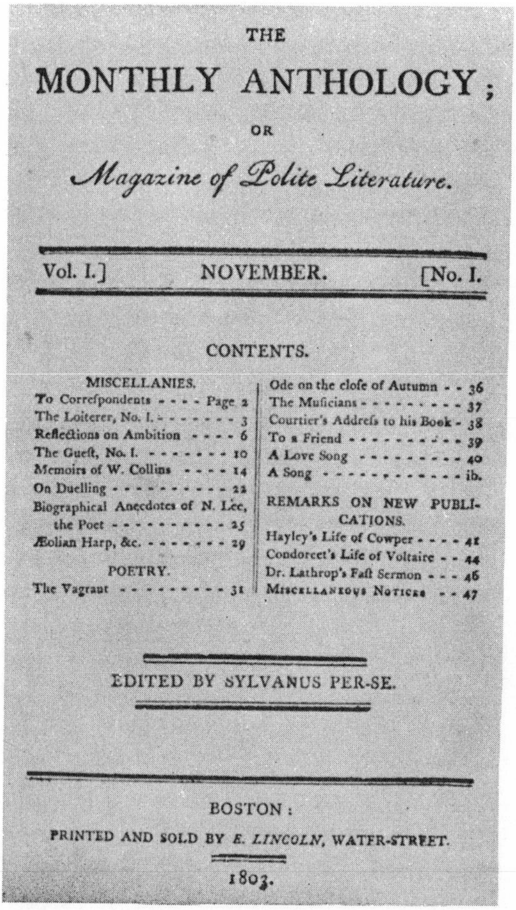

THE

MONTHLY ANTHOLOGY;

OR

Magazine of Polite Literature.

Vol. I.]　　　　NOVEMBER.　　　　[No. I.

CONTENTS.

EDITED BY SYLVANUS PER-SE.

BOSTON:

PRINTED AND SOLD BY *E. LINCOLN,* WATER-STREET.

1803.

TITLE-PAGE OF THE FIRST ISSUE OF THE "MONTHLY ANTHOLOGY," THE
PERIODICAL WHICH RESULTED IN THE ESTABLISHMENT OF THE BOSTON
ATHENAEUM (FROM THE COPY IN THE LIBRARY OF CONGRESS)

PLATE VIII

Thaddeus Mason Harris (from the Collections of the Harvard
University Libraries)

PLATE IX

A

SELECED CATALOGUE

OF SOME OF THE MOST ESTEEMED

PUBLICATIONS

IN THE

ENGLISH LANGUAGE.

Proper to form a

𝔖𝔬𝔠𝔦𝔞𝔩 𝔏𝔦𝔟𝔯𝔞𝔯𝔶 :

With an

INTRODUCTION upon the CHOICE of BOOKS.

BY THADDEUS M. HARRIS, A. M.

Librarian of HARVARD UNIVERSITY, and Author of "THE NAT-
URAL HISTORY of the Bible," and "A Short and Practical SYS-
TEM of PUNCTUATION."

☞ CATALOGUES given GRATIS by the PUBLISHERS.

PRINTED AT BOSTON,

BY I. THOMAS AND E. T. ANDREWS,

FAUST's STATUE, No. 45. Newbury Street.

1793.

TITLE-PAGE OF HARRIS' "SELEC[T]ED CATALOGUE" (FROM
THE COPY IN THE AMERICAN ANTIQUARIAN SOCIETY)

PLATE X

A
CATALOGUE
OF
M E I N's,
CIRCULATING LIBRARY,
CONSISTING

Of above Twelve Hundred VOLUMES, in most
Branches of polite Literature, Arts and Sciences;

V I Z.

HISTORY,	NOVELS,	PLAYS,
VOYAGES,	DIVINITY,	POETRY,
TRAVELS,	PHYSIC,	HUSBANDRY,
LIVES,	SURGERY,	NAVIGATION,
MEMOIRS,	ANATOMY,	GARDENING,
ANTIQUITIES,	ARTS,	MATHEMATICS,
PHILOSOPHY.	SCIENCES,	LAW, &c. &c. &c.

Which are LENT to Read,

At One Pound Eight Shillings, lawful Money, per Year; Eighteen
Shillings per Half-Year; or, Ten and Eight Pence per Quarter;

By J O H N M E I N, Bookseller,
At the LONDON BOOK-STORE,

Second Door above the BRITISH COFFEE-HOUSE,
North-side of KING-STREET, BOSTON.

This COLLECTION will be considerably enlarged from Time to
Time, and the Number of Volumes will be more than doubled
in less than a Twelvemonth, if the Publisher meets with due
Encouragement.

☞ At the above Place the full Value is given for any Library
or Parcel of Books, in any Language or Faculty; and Books
sold or exchanged.

BOSTON: Printed in the Year MDCCLXV.
[PRICE, One Shilling lawful Money.]

TITLE-PAGE OF THE "CATALOGUE OF MEIN'S CIRCULATING LIBRARY
(FROM THE COPY IN THE MASSACHUSETTS HISTORICAL SOCIETY)

PLATE XI

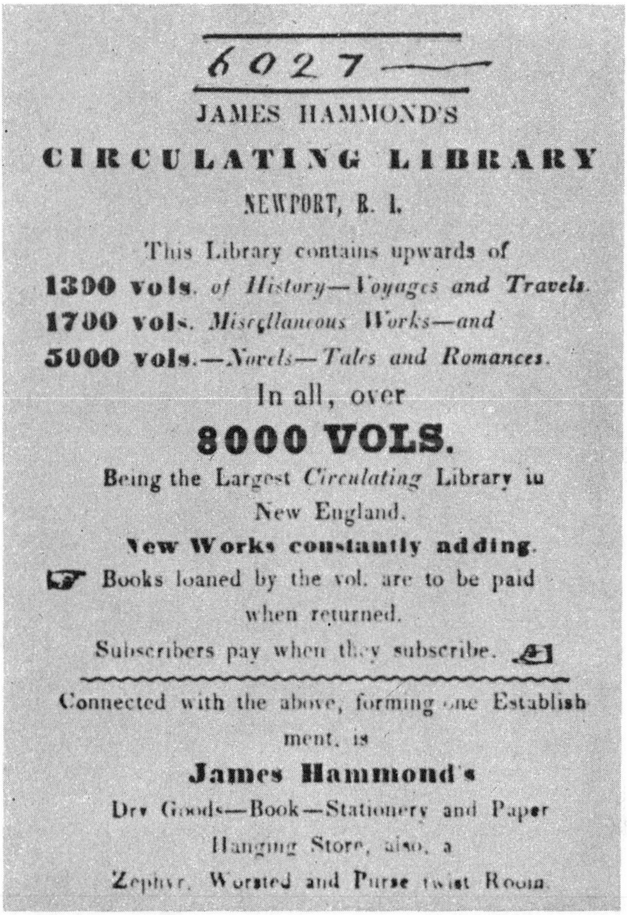

6 0 2 7

JAMES HAMMOND'S

CIRCULATING LIBRARY

NEWPORT, R. I.

This Library contains upwards of

1300 vols. *of History—Voyages and Travels.*
1700 vols. *Miscellaneous Works—and*
5000 vols.*—Novels—Tales and Romances.*

In all, over

8000 VOLS.

Being the Largest *Circulating* Library in
New England.

New Works constantly adding.

☞ Books loaned by the vol. are to be paid
when returned.

Subscribers pay when they subscribe. 🖰

Connected with the above, forming one Establish
ment, is

James Hammond's

Dry Goods—Book—Stationery and Paper
Hanging Store, also, a
Zephyr, Worsted and Purse twist Room.

BOOKPLATE OF HAMMOND'S CIRCULATING LIBRARY (FROM THE
COLLECTIONS OF THE AMERICAN ANTIQUARIAN SOCIETY)

PLATE XII

Town Hall, Salisbury, Connecticut; in the Central Portion Was Enacted the Legislation of April 9, 1810 (Photograph by the Author)

PLATE XIII

Phenix Paper & Cotton

FACTORY LIBRARY.

ARTICLE 1.—Subscribers shall have the privilege of changing their Book once a day, and not oftener; and no book to be kept out any longer than one month.

ART. 2.—Subscribers lending their books, will be charged for them as non-subscribers, separate from their privilege as subscribers.

ART. 3.—Non-subscribers to pay for each Volume as returned; for a duodecimo or smaller volume per week 3 cents; and, after the third week 6 cents: ~~~~~~~~~~~~~~~~~ per week.

ART. 4.—Every Volume not returned within one week, enter on a second, and so on till returned.

ART. 5.—The value of the books to be deposited when required.

ART. 6.—Books lost, written in, torn, leaves turned down, or otherwise damaged, must be replaced or paid for; and if they belong to a set, the whole must be taken, or a reasonable compensation made. This last article applies also to Subscribers.

BOOKPLATES OF THE NEW HAVEN, CONNECTICUT, MECHANIC LIBRARY AND LIBRARY OF THE PHOENIX PAPER AND COTTON MILL OF PETERBOROUGH, NEW HAMPSHIRE (FROM THE COLLECTIONS OF THE AMERICAN ANTIQUARIAN SOCIETY.)

APPENDIX III

THE DISPERSION OF PUBLIC AND QUASI-PUBLIC LIBRARIES THROUGHOUT NEW ENGLAND, 1650–1850

ONE DOT = ONE LIBRARY

0 6 12 18 24 30 36
MILES

Public and Quasi-public Libraries in New England before 1776 (Copyrighted Outline Map Reproduced through the Courtesy of the Hagstrom Map Co.)

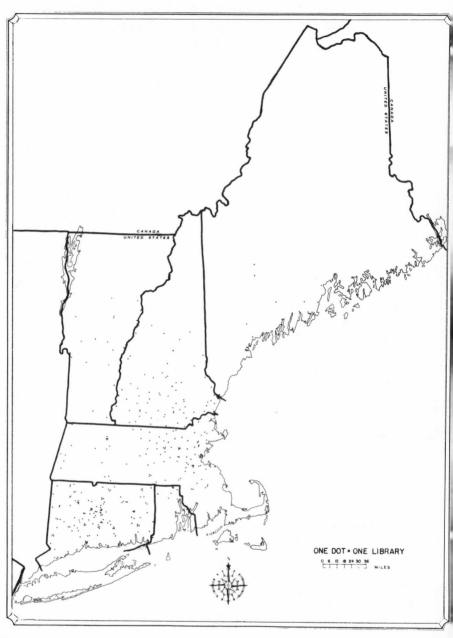

ONE DOT = ONE LIBRARY

PUBLIC AND QUASI-PUBLIC LIBRARIES IN NEW ENGLAND BEFORE 1801 (COPYRIGHTED
OUTLINE MAP REPRODUCED THROUGH THE COURTESY OF THE HAGSTROM MAP CO.)

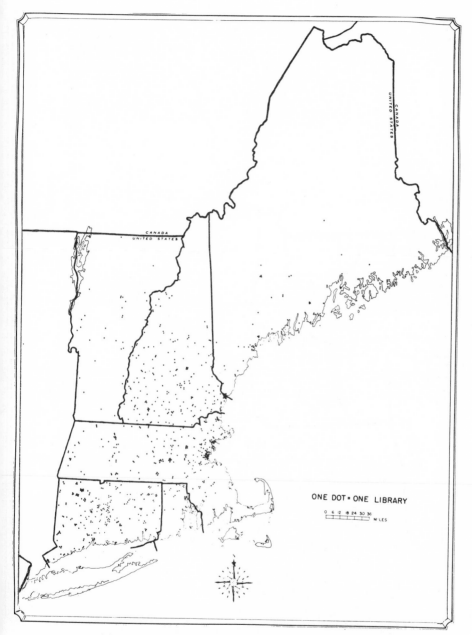

ONE DOT = ONE LIBRARY

0 6 12 18 24 30 36
MILES

Public and Quasi-public Libraries in New England before 1826 (Copyrighted Outline Map Reproduced through the Courtesy of the Hagstrom Map Co.)

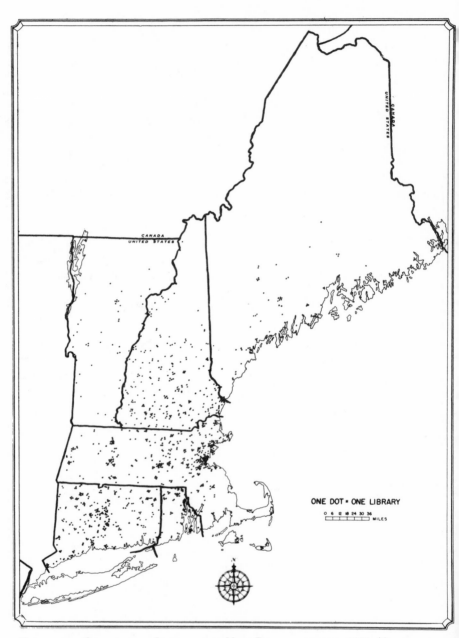

Public and Quasi-public Libraries in New England before 1851 (Copyrighted Outline Map Reproduced through the Courtesy of the Hagstrom Map Co.)

260

APPENDIX IV

CHECK LIST OF CIRCULATING LIBRARY BOOK CATALOGS, NEW ENGLAND, 1765–1860

MEIN, JOHN. *A Catalogue of Mein's Circulating Library, Consisting of above Twelve Hundred Volumes, in Most Branches of Polite Literature, Arts and Sciences.* . . . "Which are lent to read, at one pound, eight shillings, lawful money, per year; eighteen shillings per half year; or ten and eight pence per quarter; by by John Mein at the London Book-store. . . . Boston. Printed in the year 1765." 56 pp. (Massachusetts Historical Society.)

MARTIN, WILLIAM. *Catalogue of Martin's Circulating Library at 45 Main St. Boston.* "Boston. Printed by Edmund Freeman. 1786." 16 pp. (John Carter Brown Library.)

GUILD, BENJAMIN. *Select Catalogue of Benjamin Guild's Circulating Library, Containing Principally Novels, Voyages, Travels, Poetry, Periodical Publications, and Books of Entertainment.* "At the Boston Bookstore, No. 59 Cornhill. Boston. Printed by Edmund Freeman. 1788." 20 pp. (Harvard University Library.)

GUILD, BENJAMIN. *New Select Catalogue of Benjamin Guild's Circulating Library, Containing Principally Novels, Voyages, Travels, Poetry, Periodical Publications, and Books of Entertainment.* "At the Boston Book-store, No. 59 Cornhill. Boston. Printed for Benjamin Guild. 1789." 36 pp. (Massachusetts Historical Society.)

GUILD, BENJAMIN. *Addition to a Catalogue of a Large Assortment of Books Consisting of the Most Celebrated Authors.* . . . "To be lent or sold by Benjamin Guild at the Boston Book-store, No. 59 Cornhill, Boston. 1791." 16 pp. (American Antiquarian Society.)

DABNEY, JOHN. *Catalogue of Books for Sale or Circulation, in Town or Country, by John Dabney.* "At his Book and Stationary Store and Circulating Library in Salem, consisting of the most approved authors in history, lives, memoirs, novels, antiquities, geography, poetry, voyages, travels, divinity, husbandry, navigation, miscellaneous, arts, science, etc. Including many of the latest and most celebrated volumes in Europe and America. . . . Printed by J. Dabney. 1791." 33 pp. (American Antiquarian Society. Essex Institute.)

BLAKE, WILLIAM P. *Catalogue of Books for Sale or Circulation by William P. Blake at the Boston Book-Store, No. 59 Cornhill.* "Consisting of the most approved authors. . . . Boston. Printed for William Blake. . . . 1793." 47 pp. (American Antiquarian Society.)

DABNEY, JOHN. *Additional Catalogue of Books, for Sale or Circulation, in Town or Country, at the Salem Bookstore; Comprising among Other Subjects of Universal Literature and Entertainment.* . . . [List.] "Together with a numerous collection of modern novels and histories. Also an extensive and elegant assortment of books and stationary . . . at Osborne's office, printed for J. Dabney. 1794." 34 pp. (American Antiquarian Society. Essex Institute.)

BLAKE, WILLIAM P., AND BLAKE, LEMUEL. *Catalogue of Books for Sale or Circulation by W. P. & L. Blake, at the Boston Book-Store, No. 1 Cornhill, Consisting of the Most Celebrated Authors. . . .* "Boston. Printed for William P. and Lemuel Blake. 1798." 36 pp. + (remainder missing). Last entry: *Ring; or the History of Lady Jemima Guzman,* a novel. (American Antiquarian Society.)

DABNEY, JOHN. *Catalogue of Books for Sale or Circulation, in Town or Country, by John Dabney, at His Book and Stationary Store and Circulating Library, in Salem. . . .* "Printed for J. Dabney. 1801." 50 pp. (American Antiquarian Society. Essex Institute.)

PELHAM, WILLIAM. *Catalogue of Pelham's Circulating Library, No. 5 School Street. . . .* "Boston. Munroe & Francis. 1804." 62 pp. Advertisement signed by William Blagrove, who had just purchased the Pelham collection. (American Antiquarian Society.)

PIERCE, CHARLES. *Circulating Library and for Sale. . . . Catalogue of Books for Sale and Circulation by Charles Pierce at His Brick Book-Store, in Daniel Street, Portsmouth, New Hampshire. . . .* "Portsmouth, N.H. Printed for Charles Pierce. March, 1806." 105 pp. (American Antiquarian Society.)

HOWE AND DEFOREST. *A Catalogue of Books in Howe and Deforest's Circulating Library, Chapel Street.* "New Haven. From Sidney's Press. 1814." 40 pp. (New Haven Colony Historical Society.)

WHIPPLE, CHARLES. *Catalogue of Books at the Newburyport Circulating Library, Kept at Charles Whipple's Book-Store, No. 4, State Street, Newburyport. . . .* "Newburyport. C. Norris. 1816." 107 pp. (American Antiquarian Society.)

CUSHING AND APPLETON. *Essex Circulating Library: Catalogue of Books for Sale or Circulation by Cushing and Appleton, No. 8, Central Place, Essex-Street, Salem.* "Daily additions of new publications. Books &c., especially procured from London, Philadelphia, New-York, Boston &c., on reasonable terms. Price of the catalogue 12½ cents. Printed by Thomas C. Cushing. 1818." 108 pp. (American Antiquarian Society. Essex Institute.)

CUSHING AND APPLETON. *Essex Circulating Library: Supplementary Catalogue of the Essex Circulating Library, Kept by Cushing and Appleton, No. 8, Central Place.* "For 1820. John D. Cushing, printer." 12 pp. (Essex Institute.)

IVES, JOHN M. *Catalogue of the Essex Circulating Library Kept by John M. Ives at His Book, Stationary, and Music Store, Essex Street, Salem, Containing Upwards of Three Thousand Volumes and Daily Increasing.* "Salem. John D. Cushing & Bro. 1822." 83 pp. (Essex Institute.)

COLEMAN, S. *Catalogue of the Public Library, 1831.* [Portland, Me.: S. Coleman.] 14 pp. Lists 1,073 titles, of which 501 are fiction, 276 history and biography and travel, 128 religious, 80 juvenile, 57 plays and poetry, and 31 annuals. (Maine Historical Society.)

COLEMAN, S. *Catalogue of Coleman's Public Library.* "Portland. [1834.]" 48 pp. (Maine Historical Society.)

COLEMAN AND CHISHOLM. *Catalogue of Coleman and Chisholm's Circulating Library, Kept at Their Bookstore.* . . . "This library comprises a large collection of Light Literature, History, Voyages, Travels, Biographies, &c. &c. Portland. [n.d.]" 25 pp. (Maine Historical Society.)

SMALL, A. E. *Catalogue of the Books Contained in the Saco Circulating Library Kept by A. E. Small.* . . . "Saco, [Me.]. W. J. Condon. 1834." 12 pp. Lists 265 titles, of which 105 are fiction, 70 history and biography, 37 travel, 20 miscellaneous, 13 literature, 11 religion, and 11 science. (Maine Historical Society.)

MAYHEW AND BAKER. *Catalogue of Mayhew and Baker's Juvenile Circulating Library.* "No. 208 Washington St. Boston. Mayhew and Baker. 1860." 16 pp. (Massachusetts Historical Society.)

APPENDIX V

REPORT OF THE TRUSTEES OF THE BOSTON PUBLIC LIBRARY, 1852

(From the annotated copy in the Boston Public Library)

REPORT

OF

THE TRUSTEES

OF THE

PUBLIC LIBRARY

OF THE

CITY OF BOSTON

JULY, 1852.

BOSTON:
1852.
J. H. EASTBURN, CITY PRINTER.

CITY OF BOSTON.

In Board of Mayor and Aldermen, June 30, 1852.

Ordered, That the Trustees of the City Library be requested to report to the City Council upon the objects to be attained by the establishment of a Public Library, and the best mode of effecting them; and that they be authorized to report in print.

Passed. Sent down for concurrence.

BENJAMIN SEAVER, *Mayor.*

In Common Council, July 1, 1852.

Concurred.

HENRY J. GARDNER, *President.*

A true copy. Attest:

S. F. McCLEARY, Jr., *City Clerk.*

REPORT.

The Trustees of the public library, in compliance with the order of the two branches of the City Council, submit the following report on the objects to be attained by the establishment of a public library and the best mode of effecting them :—

Of all human arts that of writing, as it was one of the earliest invented, is also one of the most important. Perhaps it would be safe to pronounce it, without exception the most useful and important. It is the great medium of communication between mind and mind, as respects different individuals, countries, and periods of time. We know from history that only those portions of the human family have made any considerable and permanent progress in civilization, which have possessed and used this great instrument of improvement.

It is principally in the form of books that the art of writing, though useful in many other ways, has exerted its influence on human progress. It is almost exclusively by books that a permanent record has been made of word and deed, of thought and feeling; that history, philosophy and poetry, that literature and science in their full comprehension, have been called into being, by the co-operation of intellects acting in concert with each other, though living in different countries and at different periods, and often using different languages.

Till the middle of the fifteenth century of our era, it was literally the *art of writing* by which these effects were produced. No means of multiplying books was known but the tedious process of transcription. This of course rendered them comparatively scarce and dear, and thus greatly limited their usefulness. It was a chief cause also of the loss of some of the most valuable literary productions. However much this loss may be regretted, we cannot but reflect with wonder and gratitude on the number of invaluable works which have been handed down to us from antiquity, notwithstanding the cost and labor attending their multiplication.

The same cause would necessarily operate to some extent against the formation of public and private libraries. Still however, valuable collections of books were made in all the cultivated states of antiquity, both by governments and individuals. The library formed by the Ptolemies at Alexandria in Egypt was probably the direct means by which the most valuable works of ancient literature have been preserved to us. At a later period, the collections of books in the religious houses contributed efficaciously toward the same end.

The invention of printing in the fifteenth century increased the efficiency of the art of writing, as the chief instrument of improvement, beyond all former example or conception. It became more than ever the great medium of communication and transmission. It immediately began to operate, in a thousand ways and with a power which it would be impossible to overstate, in producing the great intellectual revival of the modern world. One of the most obvious effects of the newly invented art was of course greatly to facilitate the formation of libraries.

An astonishing degree of excellence in the art of printing was reached at once. The typography of the first edition of the whole Bible is nearly equal to that of any subsequent edition. But the farther improvements which have taken place in four hundred years in cutting and casting types and solid pages, in the construction of presses and their movement by water, steam, and other power, in the manufacture of paper, and in the materials and mode of binding, have perhaps done as much to make books cheap and consequently abundant, as the art of printing as originally invented.

It is scarcely necessary to add that these causes have led to a great multiplication of libraries in Europe and America. In nearly all the capitals of Europe large collections of books have been made and supported at the public expense. They form a part of the apparatus of all the higher institutions for education, and latterly of many schools; they are found in most scientific and literary societies; and they are possessed by innumerable individuals in all countries.

In proportion as books have become more abundant, they have become the principal instrument of instruction in places of education. It may be doubted whether their employment for this purpose is not, particularly in this country, carried too far. The organization of modern schools, in which very large numbers of pupils are taught by a small number of instructors, tends to make the use of books, rather than the living voice of the teacher, the main dependence. Still however, this is but an abuse of that which in itself is not only useful but indispensable; and no one can doubt that books will ever continue to be, as they now are, the great vehicle of imparting and acquiring knowledge and carrying on the work of education. As far as instruction is concerned, it will no doubt ever continue to be, as it now is, the work of the

teacher to direct, encourage, and aid the learner in the
use of his books.

In this respect the system of public education in Boston may probably sustain a comparison with any in the
world.   Without asserting that the schools are perfect,
it may truly be said that the general principle and plan
on which they are founded, are as nearly so as the nature
of the case admits.   They compose a great system of
instruction, administered in schools rising in gradation
from the most elementary to those of a highly advanced
character, open to the whole population, and supported
by a most liberal public expenditure.   The schools themselves may admit improvement, and the utmost care
should be taken, that they keep pace with the progress of
improvement in other things; but the system itself, in
the great features just indicated, seems perfect; that is,
in a word, to give a first rate school education, at the
public expense, to the entire rising generation.

But when this object is attained, and it is certainly
one of the highest importance, our system of public instruction stops.   Although the school and even the college and the university are, as all thoughtful persons are
well aware, but the first stages in education, the public
makes no provision for carrying on the great work.   It
imparts, with a noble equality of privilege, a knowledge
of the elements of learning to all its children, but it
affords them no aid in going beyond the elements.   It
awakens a taste for reading, but it furnishes to the public nothing to be read.   It conducts our young men and
women to that point, where they are qualified to acquire
from books the various knowledge in the arts and sciences which books contain; but it does nothing to put
those books within their reach.   As matters now stand,
and speaking with general reference to the mass of the
community, the public makes no provision whatever, by

which the hundreds of young persons annually educated, as far as the elements of learning are concerned, at the public expense, can carry on their education and bring it to practical results by private study.

We do not wish to exaggerate in either part of this statement, although we wish to call attention to the point as one of great importance and not yet, as we think, enough considered. We are far from intimating that school education is not important because it is elementary; it is, on the contrary, of the utmost value. Neither do we say, on the other hand, because there are no libraries which in the strict sense of the word are public, that therefore there is absolutely no way by which persons of limited means can get access to books. There are several libraries of the kind usually called public, belonging however to private corporations; and there are numerous private libraries from which books are liberally loaned to those wishing to borrow them.

It will however be readily conceded that this falls far short of the aid and encouragement which would be afforded to the reading community, (in which we include all persons desirous of obtaining knowledge or an agreeable employment of their time from the perusal of books), by a well supplied public library. If we had no free schools, we should not be a community without education. Large numbers of children would be educated at private schools at the expense of parents able to afford it, and considerable numbers in narrow circumstances would, by the aid of the affluent and liberal, obtain the same advantages. We all feel however that such a state of things would be a poor substitute for our system of public schools, of which it is the best feature that it is a public provision for all; affording equal advantages to poor and rich; furnishing at the public expense an edu-

cation so good, as to make it an object with all classes to
send their children to the public schools.

It needs no argument to prove that, in a republican
government, these are features of the system, quite as valuable as the direct benefit of the instruction which it imparts. But it is plain that the same principles apply to
the farther progress of education, in which each one must
be mainly his own teacher. Why should not this prosperous and liberal city extend some reasonable amount of
aid to the foundation and support of a noble public library, to which the young people of both sexes, when they
leave the schools, can resort for those works which per-
tain to general culture, or which are needful for research
into any branch of useful knowledge? At present, if
the young machinist, engineer, architect, chemist, en-
graver, painter, instrument-maker, musician (or student
of any branch of science or literature,) wishes to consult
a valuable and especially a rare and costly work, he
must buy it, often import it at an expense he can ill afford,
or he must be indebted for its use to the liberality of
private corporations or individuals. The trustees submit,
that all the reasons which exist for furnishing the means
of elementary education, at the public expense, apply in
an equal degree to a reasonable provision to aid and
encourage the acquisition of the knowledge required to
complete a preparation for active life or to perform its
duties.

We are aware that it may be said and truly, that
knowledge acquired under hardships is often more thorough, than that to which the learner is invited without
effort on his part; that the studious young man who
makes sacrifices and resorts to expedients to get books,
values them the more and reads them to greater profit.
This however is equally true of school education and of
every other privilege in life. But the city of Boston

has never deemed this a reason for withholding the most
munificent appropriations for the public education. It
has not forborne to support an expensive system of free
schools, because without such a system a few individuals
would have acquired an education for themselves, under
every possible discouragement and disadvantage, and because knowledge so acquired is usually thorough, well-
digested and available, beyond what is got in an easier
way. The question is not what will be brought about
by a few individuals of indomitable will and an ardent
thirst for improvement, but what is most for the advantage of the mass of the community. In this point of
view we consider that a large public library is of the
utmost importance as the means of completing our system of public education.

There is another point of view in which the subject
may be regarded,—a point of view, we mean, in which a
free public library is not only seen to be demanded by
the wants of the city at this time, but also seen to be
the next natural step to be taken for the intellectual advancement of this whole community and for which this
whole community is peculiarly fitted and prepared.

Libraries were originally intended for only a very
small portion of the community in which they were
established, because few persons could read, and fewer
still desired to make inquiries that involved the consultation of many books. Even for a long time after the
invention of printing, they were anxiously shut up from
general use; and, down to the present day, a large proportion of the best libraries in the world forbid anything
like a free circulation of their books;—many of them
forbidding any circulation at all.

For all this, there were at first, good reasons, and for
some of it good reasons exist still. When only manuscripts were known, those in public libraries were, no

doubt, generally too precious to be trusted from their usual places of deposit; and the most remarkable, if not the most valuable, of all such collections now in existence—the Laurentian in Florence—still retains, and perhaps wisely, its eight or nine thousand manuscripts chained to the desks on which they lie. So too, when printed books first began to take the place of manuscripts, the editions of them were small and their circulation limited. When, therefore, copies of such books now occur, they are often regarded rightfully as hardly less curious and valuable than manuscripts, and as demanding hardly less care in their preservation. And finally, even of books more recently published, some,—like Dictionaries and Cyclopædias,—are not intended for circulation by means of public libraries, and others are too large, too costly, or otherwise too important to be trusted abroad, except in rare cases.

But while there are some classes of books that should be kept within the precincts of a public library, there are others to which as wide a circulation as possible should be given; books which, in fact, are especially intended for it, and the end of whose existence is defeated, just in proportion as they are shut up and restrained from general use. It was, however, long after this class was known, before it became a large one, and still longer before means were found fitted to give to the community a tolerably free use of it. At first it consisted almost exclusively of practical, religious books. Gradually the more popular forms of history, books of travel, and books chiefly or entirely intended for entertainment followed. At last, these books became so numerous, and were in such demand, that the larger public libraries,—most of which had grown more or less out of the religious establishments of the middle ages, and had always regarded with little interest this more popular literature,—could not, it was plain, continue to be looked upon as the only or as the chief resource for those who were unable to buy for themselves the reading they wanted. Other resources and other modes of supply have, therefore, been at different times devised.

The first, as might naturally have been anticipated, was suggested by the personal interest of a sagacious individual. Allan Ramsay, who, after being bred a wig-maker, had become a poet of the people, and set up a small bookseller's shop, was led to eke out an income, too inconsiderable for the wants of his family, by lending his books on hire to those who were not able or not willing to buy them of him. This is the oldest of all the numberless "Circulating Libraries;" and it sprang up naturally in Edinburg, where in proportion to the population, it is believed there were then more readers than there were in any other city in the world. This was in 1725 ; and, twenty years ago, the same establishment was not only in existence—as it probably is still—but it was the largest and best of its class in all Scotland. The example was speedily followed. Such libraries were set up everywhere, or almost everywhere in Christendom, but especially in Germany and in Great Britain, where they are thus far more numerous than they are in any other countries; the most important being now in London, where (for at least one of them) from fifty to two hundred copies of every good new work, are purchased in order to satisfy the demands of its multitudinous subscribers and patrons.

All "Circulating Libraries," technically so called, are however, to be regarded as adventures and speculations for private profit. On this account, they were early felt to be somewhat unsatisfactory in their very nature, and other libraries were contrived that were founded on the more generous principle of a mutual and common interest in those who wished to use the books they contained. This principle had, in fact, been recognized somewhat earlier than the time of Allan Ramsay, but for very limited purposes and not at all for the *circulation* of books. Thus the lawyers of Edinburg, London, and Paris, respectively had already been associated together for the purpose of collecting *consulting* Law Libraries for their own use, and so it is believed, had some other bodies, which had collected consulting libraries for their own exclusive especial purposes. But the first *Social Library* of common or popular books for popular use, in the sense we now give the appellation, was probably that of the "Library Company," as it was called, in Philadelphia, founded at the suggestion of Dr. Franklin in 1731, by the young mechanics of that city, where he was then a young printer. The idea was no doubt a fortunate one; particularly characteristic of Franklin's shrewd good sense, and adapted to the practical wants of our own country. The library of these young men, therefore, succeeded and was imitated in other places. Even before the Revolutionary war, such libraries were established elsewhere in the colonies, and, after its conclusion, many sprang up on all sides. New England, in this way, has come to possess a great number of them, and especially Massachusetts; two-thirds of whose towns are said at this time, to possess "Social Libraries," each owned by a moderate number of proprietors.

That these popular "Social Libraries" have done great good, and that many of them are still doing great good, cannot be reasonably doubted. But many of them,— perhaps the majority in this Commonwealth,—are now languishing. For this, there are two reasons. In the first place, such libraries are accessible only to their proprietors, who are not always the persons most anxious to use them, or, in some cases, but not many, they are accessible to other persons on payment of a small sum for each book borrowed. And, in the second place, they rarely contain more than one copy of a book, so that if it be a new book, or one in much demand, many are obliged to wait too long for their turn to read it; so long that their desire for the book is lost, and their interest in the library diminished. Efforts, therefore, have been for some time making, to remedy these deficiencies, and to render books of different kinds more accessible to all, whether they can pay for them or hire them, or not.

Thus, within thirty years, Sunday School Libraries have been everywhere established; but their influence—great and valuable as it is—does not extend much beyond the youngest portions of society and their particular religious teachers. And, within a shorter period than thirty years, District or Public School Libraries have been scattered all over the great State of New York, and all over New England, in such abundance, that five years ago, (1847) the aggregate number of their books in the State of New York was above a million three hundred thousand volumes, and fast increasing; but neither do these school libraries generally contain more than one copy of any one book, nor is their character often such as to reach and satisfy the mass of adult readers.

Strong intimations, therefore, are already given, that ampler means and means better adapted to our peculiar condition and wants, are demanded, in order to diffuse through our society that knowledge without which we have no right to hope, that the condition of those who are to come after us will be as happy and prosperous as our own. The old roads, so to speak, are admitted to be no longer sufficient. Even the more modern turnpikes do not satisfy our wants. We ask for rail-cars and steam-boats, in which many more persons—even multitudes—may advance together to the great end of life, and go faster, farther and better, by the means thus furnished to them, than they have ever been able to do before.

Nowhere are the intimations of this demand more decisive than in our own city, nor, it is believed, is there any city of equal size in the world, where added means for general popular instruction and self-culture,—if wisely adapted to their great ends,—will be so promptly seized upon or so effectually used, as they will be here. One plain proof of this is, the large number of good libraries we already possess, which are constantly resorted to by those who have the right, and which yet—it is well known,— fail to supply the demand for popular reading. For we have respectable libraries of almost every class, beginning with those of the Athenæum, of the American Academy, of the Historical Society, and of the General Court,—the Social Library of 1792, the Mercantile Library, the Mechanics Apprentices' Library, the Libraries of the Natural History Society, of the Bar, of the Statistical Association, of the Genealogical Society, of the Medical Society, and of other collective and corporate bodies; and coming down to the "Circulating Libraries" strictly so called; the Sunday School Libraries, and the collections of children's books found occasionally in our Primary Schools. Now all these are important and excellent means for the diffusion of knowledge. They are felt to be such, and they are used as such, and the trustees would be especially careful not to diminish the resources, or the influence of any one of them. They are sure that no public library can do it. But it is admitted,—or else another and more general library would not now be urged,—that these valuable libraries do not, either individually or in the aggregate, reach the great want of this city, considered as a body politic bound to train up its members in the knowledge which will best fit them for the positions in life to which they may have been born, or any others to which they may justly aspire through increased intelligence and personal worthiness. For multitudes among us have no right of access to any one of the more considerable and important of these libraries; and, except in rare instances, no library among us seeks to keep more than a single copy of any book on its shelves, so that no one of them, nor indeed, all of them taken together, can do even a tolerable amount of what ought to be done towards satisfying the demands for healthy, nourishing reading made by the great masses of our people, who cannot be expected to purchase such reading for themselves.

And yet there can be no doubt that such reading ought to be furnished to all, as a matter of public policy and duty, on the same principle that we furnish free education, and in fact, as a part, and a most important part, of the education of all. For it has been rightly judged that,—under political, social and religious institutions like ours,—it is of paramount importance that the means of general information should be so diffused that the largest possible number of persons should be induced to read and understand questions going down to the very foundations of social order, which are constantly presenting themselves, and which we, as a people, are constantly required to decide, and do decide, either ignorantly or wisely. That this *can* be done,—that is, that such libraries *can* be collected, and that they will be used to a much wider extent than libraries have ever been used before, and with much more important results, there can be no doubt; and if it can be done *anywhere*, it can be done *here* in Boston; for no population of one hundred and fifty thousand souls, lying so compactly together as to be able, with tolerable convenience, to resort to one library, was ever before so well fitted to become a reading, self-cultivating population, as the population of our own city is at this moment.

To accomplish this object, however,—which has never yet been attempted,—we must use means which have never before been used; otherwise the library we propose to establish, will not be adjusted to its especial purposes. Above all, while the rightful claims of no class,—however highly educated already,—should be overlooked, the first regard should be shown, as in the case of our Free Schools, to the wants of those, who can, in no other way supply themselves with the interesting and healthy reading necessary for their farther education. What precise plan should be adopted for such a library, it is not, perhaps, possible to settle beforehand. It is a new thing, a new step forward in general education; and we must feel our way as we advance. Still, certain points seem to rise up with so much prominence, that without deciding on any formal arrangement, until experience shall show what is practically useful—we may perhaps foresee that such a library as is contemplated would naturally fall into four classes, viz:

I. *Books that cannot be taken out of the Library*, such as Cyclopædias, Dictionaries, important public documents, and books, which, from their rarity or costliness, cannot be easily replaced. Perhaps others should be specifically added to this list, but after all, the Trustees would be sorry to exclude any book whatever so absolutely from circulation that, by permission of the highest authority having control of the library, it could not, in special cases, and with sufficient pledges for its safe and proper return, be taken out. For a book, it should be remembered, is never so much in the way of its duty as it is when it is in hand to be read or consulted.

II. *Books that few persons will wish to read*, and of which, therefore, only one copy will be kept, but which should be permitted to circulate freely, and if this copy should, contrary to expectation, be so often asked for, as to be rarely on the shelves, another copy should then be bought,—or if needful, more than one other copy,—so as to keep one generally at home, especially if it be such a book as is often wanted for use there.

III. *Books that will be often asked for,* (we mean, the more respectable of the popular books of the time,) of which copies should be provided in such numbers, that *many* persons, if they desire it, can be reading the same work at the same moment, and so render the pleasant and healthy literature of the day accessible to the whole people at the only time they care for it,—that is, when it is living, fresh and new. Additional copies, therefore, of any book of this class should continue to be bought almost as long as they are urgently demanded, and thus, by following the popular taste,—unless it should ask for something unhealthy,—we may hope to create a real desire for general reading ; and, by permitting the freest circulation of the books that is consistent with their safety, cultivate this desire among the young, and in the families and at the firesides of the greatest possible number of persons in the city.

An appetite like this, when formed, will, we fully believe, provide wisely and well for its own wants. The popular, current literature of the day can occupy but a small portion of the leisure even of the more laborious parts of our population, provided there should exist among them a love for reading as great, for instance, as the love for public lecturing, or for the public schools ; and when such a taste for books has once been formed by these lighter publications, then the older and more settled works in Biography, in History, and in the graver departments of knowledge will be demanded. That such a taste can be excited by such means, is proved from the course taken in obedience to the dictates of their own interests, by the publishers of the popular literature of

the time during the last twenty or thirty years. The
Harpers and others began chiefly with new novels and
other books of little value. What they printed, however,
was eagerly bought and read, because it was cheap and
agreeable, if nothing else. A habit of reading was thus
formed. Better books were soon demanded, and gradually the general taste has risen in its requisitions, until
now the country abounds with respectable works of all
sorts,—such as compose the three hundred volumes of
the Harpers' School Library and the two hundred of their
Family Library—which are read by great numbers of
our people everywhere, especially in New England and
in the Middle States. This taste, therefore, once excited
will, we are persuaded, go on of itself from year to year,
demanding better and better books, and, can as we believe, by a little judicious help in the selections for a Free
City Library, rather than by any direct control, restraint,
or solicitation, be carried much higher than has been
commonly deemed possible ; preventing at the same time,
a great deal of the mischievous, poor reading now indulged
in, which is bought and *paid* for, by offering good reading, *without pay*, which will be attractive.

Nor would the process by which this result is to be
reached a costly one ; certainly not costly compared with
its benefits. Nearly all the most popular books are,
from the circumstance of their popularity, cheap,—most
of them very cheap,—because large editions of them are
printed that are suited to the wants of those who cannot
afford to buy dear books. It may, indeed, sometimes be
necessary to purchase many copies of one of these books,
and so the first outlay, in some cases, may seem considerable. But such a passion for any given book does not
last long, and, as it subsides, the extra copies may be
sold for something, until only a few are left in the library, or perhaps, only a single one, while the money re-

ceived from the sale of the rest,—which, at a reduced price, would, no doubt often be bought of the Librarian by those who had been most interested in reading them, —will serve to increase the general means for purchasing others of the same sort. The plan, therefore, it is believed, is a practicable one, so far as expense is concerned, and will, we think, be found on trial, much cheaper and much easier of execution than at the first suggestion, it may seem to be.

IV. The last class of books to be kept in such a library, consists, we suppose, of *periodical publications,* probably excluding newspapers, except such as may be given by their proprietors. Like the first class, they should not be taken out at all, or only in rare and peculiar cases, but they should be kept in a Reading Room accessible to everybody; open as many hours of the day as possible, and always in the evening; and in which all the books on the shelves of every part of the Library should be furnished for perusal or for consultation to all who may ask for them, except to such persons as may, from their disorderly conduct or unseemly condition, interfere with the occupations and comfort of others who may be in the room.

In the establishment of such a library, a beginning should be made, we think, without any sharply defined or settled plan, so as to be governed by circumstances as they may arise. The commencement should be made, of preference, in a very unpretending manner; erecting no new building and making no show; but spending such moneys as may be appropriated for the purpose, chiefly on books that are known to be really wanted, rather than on such as will make an imposing, a scientific or a learned collection; trusting, however, most confidently, that such a library, in the long run, will contain all that anybody can reasonably ask of it. For, to begin by making it a really useful library; by awakening a general interest in it as a City Institution, important to the whole people, a part of their education, and an element of their happiness and prosperity, is the surest way to make it at last, a great and rich library for men of science, statesmen and scholars, as well as for the great body of the people, many of whom are always successfully struggling up to honorable distinctions and all of whom should be encouraged and helped to do it. Certainly this has proved to be the case with some of the best libraries yet formed in the United States, and especially with the Philadelphia Library, whose means were at first extremely humble and trifling, compared with those we can command at the outset. Such libraries have in fact enjoyed the public favor, and become large, learned, and scientific collections of books, exactly in proportion as they have been found generally useful.

As to the terms on which access should be had to a City Library, the Trustees can only say, that they would place no restrictions on its use, except such as the nature of individual books, or their safety may demand; regarding it as a great matter to carry as many of them as possible into the home of the young; into poor families; into cheap boarding houses; in short, wherever they will be most likely to affect life and raise personal character and condition. To many classes of persons the doors of such a library may, we conceive, be at once opened wide. All officers of the City Government, therefore, including the police, all clergymen settled among us, all city missionaries, all teachers of our public schools, all members of normal schools, all young persons who may have received medals or other honorary distinctions on leaving our Grammar and higher schools, and, in fact, as many classes, as can safely be entrusted with it *as classes*, might enjoy, on the mere names and personal responsibility of the individuals composing them, the right of taking out freely all books that are permitted to circulate, receiving one volume at a time. To all other persons,—women as well as men—living in the City, the same privilege might be granted on depositing the value of the volume or of the set to which it may belong; believing that the pledge of a single dollar or even less, may thus insure pleasant and profitable reading to any family among us.

In this way the Trustees would endeavor to make 'he Public Library of the City, as far as possible, the crowning glory of our system of City Schools; or in other words, they would make it an institution, fitted to continue and increase the best effects of that system, by opening to all the means of self culture through books, for which these schools have been specially qualifying them.

Such are the views entertained by the Trustees, with reference to the objects to be attained by the foundation of a public library and the mode of effecting them.

It remains to be considered briefly what steps should be adopted toward the accomplishment of such a design.

If it were probable that the City Council would deem it expedient at once to make a large appropriation for the erection of a building and the purchase of an ample library, and that the citizens at large would approve such an expenditure, the Trustees would of course feel great satisfaction in the prompt achievement of an object of such high public utility. But in the present state of the finances of the city, and in reference to an object on which the public mind is not yet enlightened by experience, the Trustees regard any such appropriation and expenditure as entirely out of the question. They conceive even that there are advantages in a more gradual course of measures. They look, therefore, only to the continuance of such moderate and frugal expenditure, on the part of the city, as has been already authorized and commenced, for the purchase of books and the compensation of the librarian; and for the assignment of a room or rooms in some one of the public buildings belonging to the city for the reception of the books already on hand, or which the Trustees have the means of procuring. With aid to this extent on the part of the city, the Trustees believe that all else may be left to the public spirit and liberality of individuals. They are inclined to think that, from time to time, considerable collections of books will be presented to the library by citizens of Boston, who will take pleasure in requiting in this way the advantages which they have received from its public institutions, or who for any other reason are desirous of increasing the means of public improvement. Besides the collections of magnitude and value, which can hardly fail in the lapse of years to be received in this way, it may with equal confidence be expected, that constant accessions will be made to the public library by the donation of single volumes or of small numbers of books, which, however inconsiderable in the single case, become in the course of time, an important source of increase to all public libraries. A free city library, being an object of interest to the entire population, would in this respect have an advantage over institutions which belong to private corporations. Authors and editors belonging to Boston would generally deem it a privilege to place a copy of their works on the shelves of a public library; and the liberal publishers of the city, to whose intelligence and enterprise the cause of literature and science has at all times owed so much, would unquestionably show themselves efficient friends and benefactors.

In fact, we know of no undertaking more likely, when once brought into promising operation, to enlist in its favor the whole strength of that feeling, which, in so eminent a degree, binds the citizens of Boston to the place of their birth or adoption. In particular the Trustees are disposed to think that there is not a parent in easy circumstances who has had a boy or a girl educated at a public school, nor an individual who has himself enjoyed that privilege, who will not regard it at once as a duty and a pleasure to do something, in this way, to render more complete the provision for public education.

In order to put the library into operation with the least possible delay, the Trustees would propose to the city government to appropriate for this purpose the ground floor of the Adams school house in Mason street. They are led to believe that it will not be needed for the use of the Normal School proposed to be established in this building. It may be made, at a small expense, to afford ample accommodation for four or five thousand volumes, with an adjoining room for reading and consulting books, and it will admit of easy enlargement to twice its present dimensions. Such an apartment would enable the Trustees at once to open the library with five thousand volumes, a collection of sufficient magnitude to afford a fair specimen of the benefits of such an establishment to the city.

Should it win the public favor, as the Trustees cannot but anticipate, it will soon reach a size, which will require enlarged premises. These, as we have said, can be easily provided by the extension of the present room on the ground floor; and it will be time enough, when the space at command is filled up, to consider what further provision need be made for the accommodation of the library. Should the expectation of the Trustees be realized, and should it be found to supply an existing defect in our otherwise admirable system of public education, its future condition may be safely left to the judicious liberality of the city government and the public spirit of the community.

BENJAMIN SEAVER,
SAMPSON REED,
LYMAN PERRY,
JAMES LAWRENCE,
EDWARD S. ERVING,
JAMES B. ALLEN,
GEORGE W. WARREN,
GEORGE WILSON,
EDWARD EVERETT,
GEORGE TICKNOR,
JOHN P. BIGELOW,
NATHANIEL B. SHURTLEFF,
THOMAS G. APPLETON.

Boston, July 6, 1852.

BOSTON, July 26, 1852.

At a meeting of the Trustees of the Public Library held on the 6th instant, the foregoing Report was submitted by a Sub-Committee previously appointed for that purpose, consisting of EDWARD EVERETT, GEORGE TICKNOR, SAMPSON REED, and NATHANIEL B. SHURTLEFF, and was unanimously accepted and ordered to be printed.

GEORGE WILSON, *Secretary.*

SELECTED BIBLIOGRAPHY

Major Primary Sources

BARNARD, HENRY. *Public Libraries of Rhode Island: Report and Documents Relating to the Public Schools of Rhode Island, 1848.* Providence: Published by order of the General Assembly, 1849.

BIGELOW, JOHN P. *Inaugural Address to the Alderman and Common Council, January 6, 1851.* Boston: J. H. Eastburn, 1851.

BINGHAM LIBRARY FOR YOUTH, SALISBURY, CONNECTICUT. Manuscript records in the Scoville Memorial Library, Salisbury, Conn.

BOOK-COMPANY OF DURHAM, CONNECTICUT. Manuscript records.

BOSTON. *An Act To Authorize a Public Library, March 23, 1848.* City Document No. 15.

———. *An Ordinance in Relation to the Public Library, October 14, 1852.* City Document No. 57.

BOSTON ATHENAEUM. *Memoir of the Boston Athenaeum, with the Act of Incorporation and Organization of the Institution.* Boston: Munroe & Francis, 1807.

BOSTON PUBLIC LIBRARY, TRUSTEES. *Reports,* 1852–56.

BROOKFIELD PUBLIC LIBRARY. Manuscript records, 1791 (in Vermont Historical Society).

FARMINGTON LIBRARY, FARMINGTON, CONNECTICUT. Manuscript record book, 1785 (in Farmington Village Library).

FRANKLIN LIBRARY COMPANY, NORWICH, CONNECTICUT. *Constitution, Also Subscribers' Names and Catalogue of Books.* Norwich: John Trumbull, 1794.

HARRIS, THADDEUS MASON. *A Selected Catalogue of Some of the Most Esteemed Publications in the English Language Proper To Form a Social Library, with an Introduction upon the Choice of Books.* Boston: I. Thomas & E. T. Andrews, 1793.

HARTFORD LIBRARY COMPANY. *Catalogue of Books, April 1, 1818, and Extracts from the By-laws of Said Company.* Hartford: Hamlen & Newton, 1818.

———. *Catalogue Number Two of Books Added from April 1, 1818 to April 1, 1822.* Hartford: Peter B. Gleason, 1822.

HARTFORD YOUNG MEN'S INSTITUTE. *Catalogue of Books in the Library, 1839.* Hartford: Case, Tiffany & Burnham, 1839.

JUVENILE LIBRARY, PETERBOROUGH, NEW HAMPSHIRE. Manuscript catalog, November 1, 1827 (in Peterborough Town Library).

KEEP, AUSTIN B. Manuscript collection of materials on early American libraries in New York Historical Society.

LIBRARIAN SOCIETY, PITTSFORD, VERMONT. Manuscript record book, 1796 (in Maclure Library, Pittsford).

LIBRARY OF SAYBROOK, LYME, AND GUILFORD, CONNECTICUT. Broadside catalog, *ca.* 1760 (in Yale University Library).

MANN, HORACE. "Report on Libraries, Institutes, and Lyceums in Massachusetts," *Common School Journal*, II (1840), 122–28.

MASSACHUSETTS CHARITABLE MECHANICS' ASSOCIATION LIBRARY. *Catalogue, 1853*. Boston: Darnell & Moore, 1853.

MECHANIC LIBRARY SOCIETY, NEW HAVEN, CONNECTICUT. *Constitution and By-laws, with a Catalogue of Books and List of Proprietors*. New Haven: Abel Monroe, 1793.

MERCANTILE LIBRARY ASSOCIATION, BOSTON. *Thirty-first Annual Report*. Boston: Dutton & Wentworth, 1851.

MILLER, SAMUEL. *A Brief Retrospect of the Eighteenth Century*. 2 vols. New York: T. & J. Swords, 1803.

NEW HAVEN SOCIAL LIBRARY. Manuscript records, 1806 (in New Haven Colony Historical Society).

NEWPORT MECHANICS' AND APPRENTICES' LIBRARY. *Catalogue of Books in the Library*. Newport: James Atkins, 1835.

———. *Catalogue of Books in the Library*. Newport: James Atkins, 1841.

NORTHINGTON PUBLIC LIBRARY. Catalog of books, 1798. Broadside (in Yale University Library).

PACIFIC MILLS LIBRARY, LAWRENCE, MASSACHUSETTS. *Catalogue*. Boston: Darnell & Moore, 1855.

PETERBOROUGH LIBRARY COMPANY, PETERBOROUGH, NEW HAMPSHIRE. Manuscript records (in Peterborough Town Library).

PETERBOROUGH TOWN LIBRARY, PETERBOROUGH, NEW HAMPSHIRE. *Catalogue of Books of the Town Library, 1837*. Keene, N.H.: John Prentiss, 1837.

———. Manuscript records of the library.

PORTLAND ATHENAEUM. *Catalogue of Books in the Library . . . with the By-laws and Regulations of the Institution*. Portland: Shirly & Hyde, 1828.

PROVIDENCE ATHENAEUM. Records of the library.

PROVIDENCE LIBRARY COMPANY, PROVIDENCE, RHODE ISLAND. Manuscript records, 1754 (in Providence Athenaeum).

QUINCY, JOSIAH. *An Appeal on Behalf of the Boston Athenaeum: Address to the Proprietors*. Boston: John Wilson, 1853.

———. "The Character and Services of Alexandre Vattemare," *Proceedings of the Massachusetts Historical Society*, I (1884), 260–72.

———. *History of the Boston Athenaeum, with Biographical Notices of the Founders*. Cambridge, Mass.: Metcalf, 1851.

REDWOOD LIBRARY, NEWPORT, RHODE ISLAND. *Catalogue of the Books Belonging to the Company of the Redwood in Newport, R.I.* Newport: S. Hall, 1764.

———. *The Company of the Redwood Library and Athenaeum: Charter, Amendments, and By-laws*. Newport: Franklin Printing Office, 1937.

Redwood Library and Athenaeum, Addresses Commemorating Its 200th Anniversary, 1747–1947. Newport: The Library, 1947. Pp. 31.

ROXBURY SOCIAL LIBRARY, ROXBURY, MASSACHUSETTS. *Catalogue of Books in the Social Library of Roxbury, January 1, 1832. . . .* Boston: Munroe & Francis, 1832.

SEAVER, BENJAMIN. *Message of the Mayor on the Subject of a Public Library, February 19, 1852.* City Document No. 10. Boston: No publisher, 1852.

SHURTLEFF, NATHANIEL B. *A Decimal System for the Arrangement and Administration of Libraries.* Boston: Privately printed, 1856. Pp. 80.

TERRY, JAMES. Manuscript collections on early American libraries (in American Antiquarian Society).

[TICKNOR, GEORGE.] *Union of the Boston Athenaeum and the Public Library.* Boston: Dutton & Wentworth, 1853.

TRUMBULL, BENJAMIN. Manuscript collections of materials on early Connecticut libraries, 1799–1818 (in Yale University Library).

WIGHT, JOHN B. Manuscript papers in possession of the family, Wayland, Mass.

———. "Public Libraries," *Common School Journal,* XIII (1851), 257–64.

YOUNG MEN'S LIBRARY, DEEP RIVER, CONNECTICUT. Manuscript record book, 1831 (in Connecticut Historical Society).

YOUNG MEN'S LIBRARY ASSOCIATION, NEW LONDON, CONNECTICUT. *Catalogue of the Books, 1841.* New London: Benjamin Bissell, 1841.

Major Secondary Sources

BENTON, JOSIAH. *Story of the Old Boston Town House, 1658–1711.* Boston: Privately printed, 1908.

BERTHOLD, ARTHUR. "American Colonial Printing as Determined by Contemporary Cultural Forces, 1639–1763." Unpublished Master's thesis, Graduate Library School, University of Chicago, 1934.

BOLTON, CHARLES K. *American Library History.* Chicago: American Library Association, 1919.

———. "Circulating Libraries in Boston," *Colonial Society of Massachusetts, Publications,* XI (1906–7), 196–207.

———. *Proprietary and Subscription Libraries.* Chicago: American Library Association, 1917.

———. "Social Libraries in Boston," *Colonial Society of Massachusetts, Publications,* XII (1908–9), 332–38.

BORDEN, ARNOLD K. "Seventeenth-Century American Libraries," *Library Quarterly,* II (1932), 138–47.

———. "The Sociological Beginnings of the Library Movement in America," *ibid.,* I (1931), 278–82.

BOSTON ATHENAEUM. *The Athenaeum Centenary, the Influence and History of the Boston Athenaeum from 1807 to 1907.* Boston: The Athenaeum, 1907.

BRENNAN, J. F. "Peterborough Town Library; the Pioneer Public Library," *Granite Monthly,* XXVIII (1900), 281–91.

CANAVAN, MICHAEL J. "The Old Boston Public Library, 1656–1747," *Colonial Society of Massachusetts, Proceedings,* XII (1908), 116–33.

COLE, GEORGE WATSON. *Early Library Development in New York State.* New York: The Public Library, 1927.

DITZION, SIDNEY. *Arsenals of a Democratic Culture, A Social History of the American*

Public Library Movement in New England and the Middle States from 1850 to 1900. Chicago: American Library Association, 1947.

——. "The District-School Library, 1835–1855," *Library Quarterly*, X (1940), 545–77.

——. "Mechanics' and Mercantile Libraries," *ibid.*, pp. 192–219.

——. "Social Reform, Education, and the Library, 1850–1900," *ibid.*, IX (1939), 156–84.

EDWARDS, EDWARD. "Free Town Libraries in America," in *Free Town Libraries, Their Function, Management, and History in Britain, France, Germany, and America.* London: Trubner, 1869.

——. *Memoirs of Libraries, Including a Handbook of Library Economy.* 2 vols. London: Trubner, 1859.

FOOTE, HENRY. "Remarks on the King's Chapel Library, Boston, Mass.," *Massachusetts Historical Society, Proceedings*, XVIII (1st ser., 1881), 423–30.

GRAY, AUSTIN K. *Benjamin Franklin's Library: A Short Account of the Library Company of Philadelphia.* New York: Macmillan, 1937.

HOULETTE, WILLIAM D. "Parish Libraries and the Work of Rev. Thomas Bray," *Library Quarterly*, IV (1934), 588–609.

JEWETT, CHARLES C. *Notices of Public Libraries in the United States of America.* Washington, D.C.: Printed for the House of Representatives, 1851.

JOECKEL, CARLETON B. *The Government of the American Public Library.* Chicago: University of Chicago Press, 1935.

JOHNSTON, WILLIAM DAWSON. *History of the Library of Congress*, Vol. I: *1800–1864.* Washington, D.C.: Government Printing Office, 1904.

KEEP, AUSTIN B. *History of the New York Society Library, with an Introductory Chapter on Libraries in Colonial New York, 1698–1778.* New York: DeVinne, 1908.

KEYS, THOMAS E. "The Colonial Library and the Development of Sectional Differences in the American Colonies," *Library Quarterly*, VIII (1938), 373–90.

LEWIS, JOHN F. *History of the Apprentices' Library of Philadelphia, the Oldest Free Circulating Library in America.* Philadelphia: No publisher, 1924.

LYDENBERG, HARRY MILLER. *History of the New York Public Library.* New York: The Public Library, 1923.

MASON, GEORGE C. *Annals of the Redwood Library and Athenaeum.* Newport, R.I.: Redwood Library, 1891.

MASSACHUSETTS, PUBLIC LIBRARY COMMISSION. *Ninth Report: Free Public Libraries of Massachusetts, 1899.* Public Document No. 44. Boston: Wright & Potter, 1899.

RHEES, WILLIAM J. *Manual of Public Libraries, Institutions, and Societies in the United States and British Provinces of North America.* Philadelphia: J. B. Lippincott, 1859.

RICHARDS, ELIZABETH M. "Alexandre Vattemare and His System of International Exchanges." Master's thesis, Columbia University, 1934. Abstract published under the same title in *Bulletin of the Medical Library Association*, XXXII (1944), 413–48.

SILLS, R. M., and UPTON, E. S. "The 'Trumbull Manuscript Collection' and Early Connecticut Libraries," in *Papers in Honor of Andrew Keogh*, pp. 325–42. New Haven: Privately printed, 1938.

STEINER, BERNARD. "Rev. Thomas Bray and His American Libraries," *American Historical Review*, II (1896), 59–75.

TAPLEY, HARRIET S. *Salem Imprints, 1768–1825: A History of the First Fifty Years of Printing in Salem, Massachusetts*. Salem: Essex Institute, 1927.

TOLMAN, FRANK L. "Libraries and Lyceums," *History of the State of New York*, Vol. IX. New York: Columbia University Press, 1937.

UNITED STATES BUREAU OF EDUCATION. *Public Libraries in the United States of America, Their History, Condition, and Management*. Washington, D.C.: Government Printing Office, 1876.

WADLIN, HORACE G. *The Public Library of the City of Boston*. Boston: The Public Library, 1911.

WALTER, FRANK K. "A Poor but Respectable Relation—the Sunday School Library," *Library Quarterly*, XII (1942), 731–39.

INDEX

Abbot, Abiel, 166–69

Abington (Conn.) Junior Library, organization of, 106, 116

Abington (Conn.) United Library, formation of, 106 n.

Acts of incorporation, for social libraries, 59–60

Adams, Hannah, 209

Adams, John Quincy, 205, 208

Adult education, 226–28

Agricultural specialization, 9

Agriculture, 7–10, 14

Allen, John W., 190

American Academy of Arts and Sciences, 95

American Antiquarian Society, 70, 87, 209

American Association for the Advancement of Science, 95

American Imprints Inventory, 48

American Library Association, 125

American Lyceum, 226

American Minerva, 92

American Philosophical Society, 14, 95

Ames, Fisher, 86, 88, 89, 207, 208

Ames, Timothy K., 168

Ames (Ohio) Western Library Association, 114, 193 n.

Anthology Reading Room; *see* Boston Athenaeum

Apprentices' libraries, 58, 230–32

Architecture during the Colonial period, 42

Arlington (Vt.) Library Society, book collection of, 108

Arlington (Mass.) West Cambridge Juvenile Library, 181 n.

Art during Colonial period, 45

Astor, John Jacob, 178, 179

Backhouse, William, 16

Baker, T. M., 145 n.

Barlow, Joel, 90

Barnard, Henry, 247; and formation of libraries for the working classes, 231,

235; and formation of social libraries, 224–26; inventoried library resources of Rhode Island in 1848, 146; promoted public schools in Connecticut and Rhode Island, 221–23; promoted school-district libraries, 188

Barnard, John, 22

Bates, Joshua, 171, 201, 203, 238–39

Battelle, Ebenezer, 137

Baxter, Wilson, 144 n.

Bay Colony, 10

Bay Library; *see* Salem Library of Massachusetts Bay Company

Beals, Ralph A., 247

Beard, Charles A., 102, Pl. III

Beers, Henry A., 98

Belfast, Me., circulating library, 147 n.

Belknap, Jeremy, 209

Bentley, William, 142

Berkeley, George, 34, 36, 45

Bermuda, projected college in, 35–36

Berthold, Arthur B., 48

Bigelow, John P., 175–76, 213, 214, 218, 225, 238

Billing, William, 45

Bingham, Caleb, 158, 159, 202

Bingham Library for Youth, Salisbury, Conn.; *see* Salisbury (Conn.) Bingham Library for Youth

Birth rate, 6–7

Blagrove, William, 139

Blake, Lemuel, 138

Blake, William P., 138, 141

Blunt, Edmund, 144 n.

Book auctions, 104 n.

Book clubs in England, 55–56; influence of, on American library development, 56–57

Book collection: of Arlington (Vt.) Library Society, 108; of Boston Athenaeum, 110; of Boston Mercantile Library Association, 109; of Brookfield (Vt.) "Publick Library," 104; of Concord (Mass.) Agricultural Library, 106; of Deep River, Conn., library, 109; of Farmington, Conn.,